PROFESSIONAL SELLING

David L. Kurtz
The Thomas F. Gleed Chair
in Business and Finance
Seattle University

H. Robert Dodge
Dean, School of Business Administration
Youngstown State University

Jay E. Klompmaker
Associate Professor of Business Administration
University of North Carolina

PROFESSIONAL SELLING

Third edition • 1982

BUSINESS PUBLICATIONS, INC. Plano, Texas 75075
Irwin-Dorsey Limited Georgetown, Ontario L7G 4B3

ISBN 0-256-02700-5

Library of Congress Catalog Card No. 81–68467

Printed in the United States of America

1234567890D098765432

To our families

Preface

The third edition of *Professional Selling* is a refinement of the two earlier editions. The authors have tried to retain the content and conceptual format that made it a popular text selection in the sales course. All of the material has been thoroughly updated. In addition, considerable attention has been devoted to furthering *Professional Selling*'s advantage as the most real-world-oriented volume now available. Real people and real situations are featured whenever possible.

Selling is a profession every bit as vital as those of medicine, law, dentistry, and education. Admittedly, it has had a few rough spots along the way, much like the quack cures of an earlier day of medicine. But today selling may be a stronger profession because of the obstacles it has overcome and sometimes still battles. Hence the dominant theme of the text is professionalism in contemporary selling.

The authors' primary objective has been to prepare a text that is directed toward student needs, rather than one advocating a particular philosophy of selling. *Professional Selling* is a comprehensive learning package. Each chapter begins with a list of key points that are developed in depth in the text that follows. At the end of each chapter is a list of 20 review and discussion questions and exercises, plus two case studies. Examples (and even cartoons) are used extensively throughout the text to illustrate important topics. A glossary is provided at the end of the volume. Four appendixes are also included. Appendix D: "The Case of The Suspect Salesman" is new to this edition.

The appendixes are:

    Appendix A: How to Get a Job in Selling
    Appendix B: Selected Readings

Appendix C: The Time-Is-Money Game
Appendix D: The Case of The Suspect Salesman

This third appendix is an exciting game that allows students to compete against each other in trying to reach specific sales goals. The Time-Is-Money Game allows one to practice some of what has been learned in *Professional Selling*. The fourth appendix is a comprehensive case about personal selling.

Professional Selling contains 17 chapters and four appendixes. It is organized into 7 major parts, each beginning with the true story of a successful sales personality. The parts are (1) The Sales Function, (2) Planning and Strategy for Effective Selling, (3) Initiating the Sales Process, (4) Presenting the Sales Message, (5) Securing Sales Today and Tomorrow, (6) Personal Selling as a Career Field, and (7) Additional Dimensions of Selling.

This text is also unique in that it has tried to recognize the important role women are now playing in personal selling. More and more women are electing sales as a professional career field. While *salesman* remains standard terminology, the authors have used the more contemporary *salesperson, seller,* or *sales representative* in this edition (except in cases of quotations, copyrighted material, and so forth). Gender is not important in selling; professionalism is.

Welcome to the exciting world of professional selling!

Acknowledgments

Many people have contributed to the three editions of *Professional Selling*. The authors are most grateful to the people who granted us permission to use their materials in the current and preceding editions. Our editors, typists, production people, and the BPI field staff deserve a special word of thanks for keeping the book on target.

But the real key to writing a book that truly reflects the professionalism of contemporary selling is an excellent group of reviewers and instructors who were willing to share their observations on how to improve the project. The authors are most appreciative of the comments, criticisms, and suggestions provided by the following individuals: Ted Erickson, Normandale Community College; John Mozingo, University of Wisconsin–Stevens Point; Henry W. Nash, Mississippi State University; John B. Southern, Adams State College; Ralph M. Davenport, Jr., University of Dubuque; Jack E. Forrest, Middle Tennessee State University; Jacob Goodman, Bergen Community College; Gary M. Grikscheit, University of Utah; Thomas Grissom, Pima College; Robert E. Harrison, Northeast Louisiana University; Nathan Himelstein, Essex County College; James C. Kerr, Phoenix College;

Jerome M. Kinskey, Sinclair Community College; Z. W. Koby, Mississippi State University; Steven C. Lawlor, Foothill College; Harry Moak, Macomb Community College; and Marion R. Sillah, Tuskegee Institute.

David L. Kurtz
H. Robert Dodge
Jay E. Klompmaker

Contents

Part Three
INITIATING THE SALES PROCESS
A PROFILE OF PROFESSIONAL SELLING, Louis J. Manara, 98

Part Four
PRESENTING THE SALES MESSAGE
A PROFILE OF PROFESSIONAL SELLING: Ralph W. Ketner, 142

Part Five
SECURING SALES TODAY AND TOMORROW
A PROFILE OF PROFESSIONAL SELLING, Eric W. Goldman, 186

The concept of sales resistance. Reasons why prospects raise objections. Types of objections: *Objections to delay action. Product objections. Source objections. Service objections. Price objections. Objections related to the salesperson.* When to handle objections. Methods of handling objections: *Rebuttal. The "Yes, but . . ." approach. Counterquestions. Testimonials. Restating the objection. Positive conversion. Warranties and guarantees.* The price objection. A systematic approach to handling objections.

Closing—a definition. The causes of closing failures: *Fear—the sales killer. Improper attitude. Verbal overkill. Failure to ask for the order.* When to close a sale: *Closing cues. Trial closes.* Final closing techniques: *Assumptive close. Direct approach. Alternative decisions. Summary and affirmative agreement. Balance sheet approach. Emotional close. Critical feature close. Extra inducement close. SRO method. Silence as a closing technique. A word of caution about closing. Another type of closing.* Postsale activities.

Maintaining current sales volume: *Building goodwill. Handling complaints. Processing rush delivery requests. Handling other special requests.* Expanding sales volume: *Expanding sales to current customers. Developing new customers. Reclaiming lost sales.* Increasing selling efficiency: *Expense reports and activity reports. Call reports.*

The self-management concept. Sales calls and expenses. The value of time. Analysis of selling activities. Varying potential of time. Account classification: *"A" accounts. "B" accounts. "C" accounts. Selective selling.* Routing. Reducing travel costs. Handling paper work: *Call reports. Other reports. Customer sales plan. Time management records. Efficiency in paper work.* Self-motivation.

PROFESSIONAL SELLING

A Profile of Professional Selling

Elbert Hubbard

Elbert Hubbard was a classic salesman. In 1894, at the age of 35, he "retired" as a highly successful soap salesman. He later triumphed as a magazine publisher, a marketer of books, furniture, and other products, and as a direct mail specialist. At his death in 1915, he was one of the most popular writers and lecturers.

I believe in myself.

I believe in the goods I sell.

I believe in the firm for whom I work.

I believe in my colleagues and helpers.

I believe in American Business Methods.

I believe in producers, creators, manufacturers, distributors, and in all industrial workers of the world who have a job, and hold it down.

I believe that Truth is an asset.

I believe in good cheer and in good health, and I recognize the fact that the first requisite in success is not to achieve the dollar, but to confer a benefit, and that the reward will come automatically and usually as a matter of course.

I believe in sunshine, fresh air, spinach, applesauce, laughter, buttermilk, babies, bombazine and chiffon, always remembering that the greatest word in the English language is *Sufficiency*.

I believe that when I make a sale, I make a friend.

And I believe that when I part with a man, I must do it in such a way that when he sees me again he will be glad—and so will I.

I believe in the hands that work, in the brains that think, and in the hearts that love.

Amen, and Amen.

Source: Excerpted from *Elbert Hubbard of East Aurora* by Felix Shay. By permission of Wm. H. Wise & Co., Inc., publishers.

Part 1

THE SALES FUNCTION

Nothing of permanent value has come down to us from the past, save by the grace of good salesmanship on the part of somebody.*

> GLENN FRANK
> Former President of
> the University of
> Wisconsin

KEY POINTS

- Personal selling can be defined as an interpersonal persuasive process designed to influence another person's decision.

- The importance of personal selling can be discussed from three viewpoints: (1) economic contribution, (2) competitive importance, and (3) public contribution.

- Selling has gone through four distinct eras: (1) early traders, (2) the selling revolution, (3) American peddlers, and (4) the professional salesperson.

- In the marketing concept, all parts of an organization are oriented toward solving consumer problems and meeting the needs of the marketplace.

- A mark of professionalism in sales is that sales personnel adopt a problem-solving approach to their work. Professionalism also implies that the salesperson will act in an ethical manner.

- Professional selling strategies and techniques can be learned.

- There are three primary reasons why every student should learn something about selling: (1) selling offers numerous employment opportunities, (2) consumers need to know about selling, and (3) personal selling is important in many facets of everyday life.

Chapter

1

AN OVERVIEW OF
PERSONAL SELLING

Martin Shafiroff—a stockbroker with Lehman Brothers in New York—leads the highly competitive field of securities sales. Shafiroff sells some $1.2 million worth of securities daily. Most of his clients are top corporate executives with salaries in excess of $250,000 annually. Shafiroff's annual commissions are nearly $3 million. How does he do it?

Shafiroff says his selling formula consists of product, conviction, cold calls, and contacts. Shafiroff thoroughly researches the securities purchases that he recommends. He looks for investments with basic value that he can appreciate and then communicate to his clients. This extensive preparation allows him to express the conviction that he considers necessary to successful selling.

Cold calls, or initial sales contacts, are also part of Shafiroff's approach. He averages some 60 telephone calls and attempts to find three new customers a day. Shafiroff's customer contacts are often based on referrals. He spends only a minimum amount of time on the introductory portion of the sales presentation. Next, Shafiroff states the reasons why the client should make the investment he recommends. But the bulk of the customer contact is spent answering the customer's questions and soliciting the order. Shafiroff's philosophy is to ask for the order three times during the interview, contrasted to the one try common with most brokers.*[1]

Martin Shafiroff knows his product and his customer, and his sales presentation is thoroughly professional. These are the ingredients for success in the modern sales environment.

SOME BASIC OBSERVATIONS ABOUT PERSONAL SELLING

A good way to begin the study of personal selling is to look at some essential facts about the sales field. Some of these observations are counter to what many college students believe, yet all are true. Consider the statements in the box on the following page.

Selling is a people-oriented activity in which success can be easily and objectively measured. Selling has been the path to success for literally millions of people over the years. Since *people* and *success* are so important in any discussion of personal selling, this textbook features case histories of people who have achieved sales successes. These histories appear at the beginning of each of the book's major parts. Much can be learned from the professionalism exhibited by these individuals.

The difference between success and failure is often very slight.

*Notes to each chapter can be found at the end of the book.

Selling is of vital importance to our economy, our competitive system, and public welfare.

Salespersons are among the best paid personnel in most companies.

Successful sales representatives are among the most secure of all participants in the private enterprise system.

Selling provides meaningful career opportunities for women and minorities.

Personal selling allows you to apply much of what you have learned in college and other educational experiences.

Sales is one of the quickest routes to business success.

Selling is increasingly recognized as a profession.

This book could have featured examples of unsuccessful selling. Successful sales personnel are typically those who learn from their failures rather than being overcome by such events.

Personal selling can be defined as an interpersonal persuasive process designed to influence some person's decision. Sales personnel accomplish this objective in a variety of ways. Vincent Riggio, former president of American Tobacco Company, influences others' decisions by practicing showmanship.[2] As a beginning salesperson, Riggio practiced his delivery before a mirror. When he sold nothing the first day, he returned to the mirror. On the second day he generated 26 new customers. Riggio later set a new sales record for his company. He reached top management, but he still practiced presentations in front of a mirror.

How someone sells depends upon a host of factors, such as what is being sold, the type of customer, and the setting in which the sales interview occurs. Some excellent sales approaches in one sales situation would be wrong in another. Good sales personnel (as distinguished from unsuccessful ones) are able to correctly identify the persuasive message that is proper in a given situation. The cost savings possibilities of a new cutting machine might be demonstrated to a firm that has had cost overruns on recent contracts. Expectant parents might be ideal prospects for a life insurance agent.

Personal selling is dynamic, flexible, and volatile. Our definition of personal selling is an interpersonal persuasive process designed to influence some person's decision. Traditionally, the influence process has been concerned with commercial transactions. In fact, the Amer-

DEFINING PERSONAL SELLING

ican Marketing Association defined selling as the "process of assisting and/or persuading a prospective customer to buy a commodity or a service or to act favorably upon an idea that has commercial significance to the seller."[3]

The definition used in this book is somewhat broader, since a "persuasive process" could also be used by a United Way campaigner, the minister of a local church, a Navy recruiter, a football coach, or a politician. This issue will be developed further in the next chapter.

IMPORTANCE OF SELLING

A. L. Kirkpatrick, an Atlanta-based sales and marketing consultant, has noted one criterion for judging the importance of selling:

> One salesman keeps 19 other workers (production, clerical, inspectors, and so forth) employed, according to recent business statistics. Not long ago these statistics indicated that one salesman kept 17 other workers employed. Even with the growth of computers and the many other technical advances that have been made, we in sales are more important than ever.[4]

Kirkpatrick's comments point out the importance of sales personnel in our economy. The importance of personal selling can be discussed from three viewpoints: (1) economic contribution, (2) competitive importance, and (3) public contribution.

Many of the criticisms advanced against selling stem from ignorance. This is corrected when the critical function of selling in society is understood.

Economic contribution

Selling is a means for improving our standard of living. It generates the revenue upon which the business system depends, as well as provides the consumer with the goods and services necessary for an improved quality of life.

Effective selling is important to the economic growth and development of any society. Countries with high standards of living have advanced marketing and distribution systems. Nearly 200 years ago, Alexander Hamilton recognized selling's economic contribution when he asked Congress to study the way England has spread "her factories and agents [sales personnel] over the four quarters of the globe."[5] Hamilton saw that England's economic growth was a joint product of its emerging manufacturing sector and its expertise in the field of selling.

New and improved consumer products, better industrial technology, and the like are not automatically accepted in the marketplace.

These innovations have to be sold, and through the years, North America has been gifted with many effective salespeople. The early traders who extended civilization to the frontier, the 19th-century sellers who made further expansion of our infant manufacturing sector possible, and the consumer-oriented professional salespeople of today have all made major economic contributions.

Selling can also be a defensive marketing tool. Even economic and industry downturns can be overcome by a good personal sales effort. During a slack sales period, Herbert Dow of Dow Chemical fame personally called on most pharmacies in Detroit and Chicago to promote his Red Seal Bromine Purifier.[6] Consumers today may be reluctant to make purchase decisions because of inflation, and effective selling can be of help in counteracting this trend. Real estate salespeople, for example, use data that assume a given rate of inflation to show why it is unwise to delay a home purchase.

The importance of selling for every business concern is self-evident; unless the firm can sell its product, there is no reason for its continued existence. Good production and engineering facilities, an excellent accounting department, and the best staff personnel available are of no significance if the firm's sales force does not move enough volume.

Competitive importance

**Hirsch USA relies on its
sales strategy to counter an
unfavorable competitive environment**

Leather watch straps account for only 23 percent of the market. Jewelers prefer to sell metal watch bands because of higher markups. Hirsch USA countered this unfavorable competitive environment by offering a high fashion, premium-priced product line. Then, the company recruited a primarily female sales force on the premise that women tend to do better than men at selling fashion items. Hirsch salespersons average $20,000 a year.

The Hirsch sales effort is based around special counter top displays that are serviced twice monthly by the sales force. Hirsch sales representatives select the straps that are to be displayed from among the firm's 4,000-item inventory. The salesperson is responsible for picking the straps that best match the store's clientele. Slow sellers are quickly replaced during the bimonthly servicing visits. The net result of Hirsch's sales strategy has been a three-fold increase in sales volume.

Source: Thayer C. Taylor, "Hirsch Gets Its 10 Precious Minutes," *Sales & Marketing Management*, November 12, 1979, pp. 39–40. © 1979. Used with permission.

Salespeople are the foot soldiers of the marketing effort. They require accurate intelligence reports (marketing research) and a substantial support effort (advertising, dealer promotions, and public relations), but it is the salespeople who have to move the widgets, zonkles, and the like.

Every businessperson knows that new customers are the key to a firm's success. Acquiring new business is usually an impossible goal unless sales personnel are in the field looking for potential new users of their products. A firm can sometimes survive for long periods of time by servicing an existing group of clients; however, such an organization will not prosper or continue to grow. The development of new business is one of selling's most vital objectives.

Public contribution

Selling makes an important contribution to the public in that it is essential to competition. Aggressive marketing helps prevent collusion in the marketplace. It also assists in the achievement of consumer-oriented objectives in such areas as pricing and customer services. A freely competitive business environment is an important consumer safeguard, and selling plays a vital role in assuring it.

The sales force also makes a public contribution by identifying customer needs. A large portion of new product ideas originates with salespeople who discover unfulfilled needs. Salespeople can also spot legitimate needs that are not recognized by industry or the consumer and suggest product development that provides solutions.

Another public contribution is selling's role in the marketing of social causes. We have defined selling as an interpersonal persuasive process designed to influence some person's decision, and selling is as appropriate in a community's United Way campaign as it is in a firm's promotional strategy.

ERAS IN SELLING

Today's jet-age sales representative is only a distant cousin to the salesperson who worked the trade in earlier years. Intercity air travel, rental cars, and credit cards give modern salespeople tremendous range and flexibility in servicing the market. But to fully appreciate modern selling sophistication, it is necessary to know something about the history of personal selling.[7]

Selling has gone through four distinct eras, which can be characterized as the time of: (1) the early traders, (2) the selling revolution, (3) the American peddlers, and (4) the professional salesperson. In each era a distinct type of selling was characteristic; both selling techniques and sales ethics varied from period to period.

The earliest sales personnel, who were usually called *traders,* existed in even the most ancient societies. Numerous historical references can be found to the traders operating in Greek, Roman, and other early cultures. Some of the earliest city-states based the major portion of their economies on trading with other communities.

Traders typically had an ownership interest in the goods they sold. Generally they or their families had produced the products. In most instances, these traders performed other marketing functions, such as transportation and storage, in addition to their selling duties.

For the most part, these early sellers were not held in high regard. Their merchandise was often shoddy, their sales claims exaggerated, and the state-of-selling ethics dismal by today's standards. The early Greek and Roman authors chastised the traders for failing to contribute to society. The general public distrusted most salespeople and usually insisted upon the personal inspection of the goods they bought. *Caveat emptor* (let the buyer beware) was the rule of the marketplace.

This era of personal selling lasted into the Middle Ages. The sales function was mixed with other business tasks, and it was difficult to identify individuals whose primary responsibility was selling.

History books traditionally describe the Industrial Revolution during the mid-1700s in terms of the development of a factory system of manufacturing. Admittedly, industrial output and product quality improved substantially during this period. But expanded production would not have improved the standards of living as it did if an effective sales organization had not developed to move the products from the factory to the consumer. The Industrial Revolution occurred because there was a corresponding "selling revolution." It is unfortunate that so many histories of that era fail to point out the vital role of personal selling.

England's Industrial Revolution started in the textile industry, where sales personnel became known as *bagmen.* Because the bagmen had selling as their sole responsibility, they can be distinguished from the traders of earlier years. They sold from samples, which marked a significant switch from the days when consumers insisted upon personal inspection. This change suggests that much of the traditional criticism of sales ethics was directed more to product quality than it was to deceptive sales practices.

In America, the early sellers were a colorful lot upon which a substantial amount of folklore is based. The *peddlers* of colonial times

The early traders

The selling revolution

The American peddlers

traveled the wilderness of North America to sell their wares to the settlers. Many of these peddlers were new immigrants who viewed their job as one of the few available means of getting a fresh start in a new country.

Later, when a retail sector emerged, *greeters* represented wholesalers and manufacturers to the retailers during their periodic buying trips to major cities. These greeters became standard fixtures in hotel lobbies. When sales representatives began to call on retailers at their stores, they became known as *drummers*. These sellers, who also often sold directly to the consumer, were the basis of much American folklore. Toward the end of the 19th century, members of a field sales force became known as *commercial travelers*—a title that is still used today in some industries. These travelers typically depended upon a memorized sales presentation that was designed to handle all possible customer objections and "assure" a sale. Salespeople during the first half of the 20th century still depended upon some type of memorized presentation.

The professional salesperson

Professional selling developed shortly after World War II. The economy had switched from a *seller's market,* with a relative scarcity of goods, to a *buyer's market,* in which products were plentiful. Prior to this shift, many companies had operated under the philosophy, "If we can supply it, the customer will buy it!" A buyer's market was created when American industry that had been geared up for the war effort switched back to the production of consumer goods. Products had to be marketed, since the consumer had a choice. Selling changed to meet this challenge.

PROFESSIONAL-ISM IN SELLING

Most marketing experts agree that American industry has entered the marketing concept era.[8] In the *marketing concept,* all parts of an organization are oriented toward solving consumer problems and meeting the needs of the marketplace. Sales personnel no longer concentrate solely on increasing sales volume; rather, the prospect's real needs become the basis of the marketing plan. The evidence indicates that most firms have either adopted the marketing concept or are in the process of doing so. Unfortunately, we can still identify examples of firms and industries that ignore the consumer's welfare. If these organizations wish to remain competitive, however, they will have to change quickly in the years ahead.

Companywide acceptance of a consumer orientation requires the sales force to become thoroughly professional in its dealings with

"The salesman said it was the most effective home security system on the market."

Reprinted by permission The Wall Street Journal.

The drive toward professionalism remains an important issue in personal selling.

prospects and customers. A mark of professionalism in sales is that sellers adopt a problem-solving approach to their work. A professional salesperson does not wonder, "What can I sell this individual?" but instead asks, "How can I best solve this person's problem?" John H. Patterson, the founder of the National Cash Register Company, used to instruct his sales force: "Don't talk machines. Don't talk cash registers. Talk the customer's business."[9] Professional sales forces are service-directed. They identify needs and determine how the customer can best satisfy these needs.

Professionalism in selling also implies that the sales representative will always act in an ethical manner, even at personal or the company's expense. The essence of ethical selling conduct is seen in the Code of Ethics adopted by Sales & Marketing Executives International, a leading professional organization in the field of selling (Figure 1–1).

Various trends, such as the wider adoption of the marketing concept and better-informed consumers, indicate that selling will become increasingly professionalized. This fact is an underlying premise of this book. Effective sales personnel today and in the future *must* be professionals!

Figure 1–1
Code of ethics

SMEI shall support and preserve the highest standards of professional conduct in the field of sales and marketing management. Toward this end, its members should reflect this objective in their individual activities at all times under this code:

1. It is the responsibility of SMEI and its entire membership to maintain honesty and integrity in all relationships with customers, and to put first emphasis upon quality of product and service, with accurate representation to the public.
2. *SMEI* recognizes the basic marketing principle that there must be mutuality of benefit and product to the buyer and seller in order to insure true economic progress, and thus to fulfill the inherent responsibility of marketing to advance our country's standards of living.
3. *SMEI* is keenly alert to the need for constant advancement and protection of individual and corporate rights in the entire marketing concept. It is therefore inherent that SMEI shall always crusade to protect the freedoms of choice and competition which are a fundamental part of the free enterprise philosophy.
4. *SMEI* shall always strive for constructive and effective cooperation with governmental agencies in areas of appropriate interest, always with the objective of supporting and maintaining the free enterprise system.
5. *SMEI* shall ever be dedicated to the information and education of the public, in all its segments and age levels, to the true values and advantages of the free enterprise system.

Source: Used by permission of Sales & Marketing Executives International.

REASONS FOR STUDYING PROFESSIONAL SELLING

If one has the interest and basic intelligence necessary for success, the essential concepts of professional selling can be learned just as any other professional skills. The argument that "Good salespeople are born, not made" should be identified with an earlier age in selling. Modern professional sales personnel fully realize the importance of study, practice, and effective sales education.

There are three primary reasons why every student should learn something about selling.

1. Selling offers numerous employment opportunities. About six million people, or 6 percent of the workforce, are engaged in sales work in the United States.[10] Sales occupations are one of the major segments of the labor force, and projections indicate that there will be substantial employment opportunities for qualified applicants in the years ahead. Table 1–1 shows some employment projections for selected sales occupations. College-trained sales personnel have sev-

Table 1–1 Employment projections for selected sales occupations

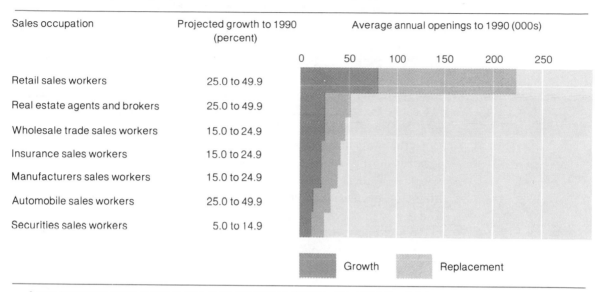

Sales occupation	Projected growth to 1990 (percent)	Average annual openings to 1990 (000s)
Retail sales workers	25.0 to 49.9	
Real estate agents and brokers	25.0 to 49.9	
Wholesale trade sales workers	15.0 to 24.9	
Insurance sales workers	15.0 to 24.9	
Manufacturers sales workers	15.0 to 24.9	
Automobile sales workers	25.0 to 49.9	
Securities sales workers	5.0 to 14.9	

Growth   Replacement

Source: Adapted from Bureau of Labor Statistics, *Occupational Outlook Handbook, 1980–1981 Edition,* (Bulletin 2075), pp. 5, 188–208.

eral advancement paths from entry-level sales positions. These are outlined in Chapter 13.

2. Consumers need to know about selling. As consumers, we all have to deal with various types of salespeople. It is beneficial to know how salespeople operate—their strategies, tactics, and the like. Consumers should be able to identify sales professionalism so they can deal with sales representatives who exhibit this quality.

3. Personal selling is important in other facets of everyday life. The study of personal selling has many related applications, such as interpersonal communications among friends, relatives, and associates. *Effective selling is effective communication.* The basic concepts of professional selling can be used in other daily activities.

Many other reasons for exploring the subject of personal selling could be listed. Selling is an exciting field, but careful study is necessary in order to understand and appreciate its conceptual foundations, principles, and tactics.

SUMMARY

Chapter 1 has presented an overview of the field of personal selling. *Personal selling* can be defined as an interpersonal persuasive process designed to influence some person's decision. Exactly how the salesperson sells depends upon a host of factors, such as what is being sold, the type of customer, and the setting in which the sales interview occurs.

The importance of personal selling can be examined from three viewpoints: (1) economic contribution, (2) competitive importance, and (3) public contribution. Four distinct eras in selling are those of: (1) early traders, (2) the selling revolution, (3) American peddlers, and (4) the professional salesperson.

In the marketing concept, all parts of an organization are oriented toward solving consumer problems and meeting the needs of the marketplace. Adoption of the marketing concept requires sales professionalism. A professional salesperson uses a problem-solving approach and always acts in an ethical manner.

This chapter concludes with a discussion of why students should learn something about selling: (1) selling offers numerous employment opportunities, (2) consumers need to know about selling, and (3) personal selling is important in other facets of everyday life.

REVIEW QUESTIONS/DISCUSSION QUESTIONS/EXERCISES

1. Briefly identify the following:
   a. Traders.
   b. *Caveat emptor.*
   c. Bagmen.
   d. Peddlers.
   e. Drummers.
   f. Commercial travelers.
   g. Seller's market.
   h. Buyer's market.
   i. Personal selling.

2. Some have argued that the classic admonition *caveat emptor* (let the buyer beware) should now be replaced with *caveat vendor* (let the seller beware). Do you agree with this contention? Explain.

3. Contrast the American Marketing Association's definition of selling with that used in this book.

4. Many of the criticisms advanced against selling stem from ignorance. Comment on this statement.

5. Explain the importance of personal selling.

6. Trace the different eras in selling.

7. What is meant by the marketing concept?

8. Do you agree with the view: Good salespeople are born, not made?

9. Discuss the three reasons for studying professional selling.

10. What did you learn from the story of Hirsch's sales strategy?

11. Survey the "Help Wanted" sections of several major newspapers in your area. Prepare a report on the quantity and type of selling jobs that are available.

12. Explain how students can use the basic concepts of professional selling in everyday life.

13. Is the "Code of Ethics" a practical guide to behavior, or is it only an idealized, impractical ethical code? Explain.

14. How would you define *professionalism?* Relate your definition to several occupations with which you are familiar.

15. Write a short report on the marketing concept and how it has influenced personal selling.

16. Identify a sales position that interests you. Prepare a brief report on employment opportunities in this area.

17. Review articles and books about salesmanship in your library. Compare the definitions of *personal selling* found in these sources with the one used in this text. What are the similarities? Differences?

18. Can you identify the firms in your area that have adopted the marketing concept? Which ones do not appear to be consumer oriented?

19. Contact a sales manager at a local firm and ask permission to accompany one of the company's sales representatives for a day. Then prepare a brief report on what you observed.

20. Develop your own *comprehensive* list of reasons why someone should study professional selling. Which of these reasons are most important to you?

CASE 1–1: STIMMICK OFFICE PRODUCTS

Andrea Martin, a sales representative for Stimmick Office Products of Cleveland, had just completed a sales call on Erie Milling Company. As she sat in her car completing the interview report her employer required of each sales call, Martin wondered if she had handled the interview correctly.

Fred Bornick, the purchasing director of Erie, was definitely in the market for some replacement desks for the office staff. Martin sensed that Bornick was very sensitive to the price issue, apparently because of a new cost-cutting directive from management. She also knew that her Woodcraft line was comparable to the desks Bornick was replacing, and with which Erie employees were generally satisfied. But Woodcraft sold at a 20 percent premium over her Fall Harvest line.

Martin decided to propose her cheaper line. Her sales presentation centered around the initial cost savings to Erie, even though she knew of data suggesting that total costs would even out over the lives of the lines (Woodcraft was a less fashionable, but more durable line). Martin reasoned that Bornick's orders were to minimize acquisition costs, and that is what her sales proposal would do.

Questions

1. Do you think Martin handled the interview correctly?
2. What would you have done if you were in Martin's position?
3. Do you think Martin assessed Bornick's position correctly?

CASE 1–2: UPSTATE MUTUAL INSURANCE SOCIETY

On a warm spring day in upstate New York, Stan Borner is coming out of the placement center at the local college when he spots a friend, Mario Farre.

Stan: Hi, Mario. . . . What are you up to?

Mario: About 5′10″!

Stan: Well, I guess I asked for that one! But, I am not as quick as usual . . . since I just got my first bona fide job offer! I guess I was still thinking about what Ellen Van Horne said.

Mario: Who is Ellen Van Horne?

Stan: She is the personnel manager at Upstate Mutual, and she just offered me a position as college sales representative for this area. You ought to start thinking about a job, Mario . . . you know we graduate in just a couple of months.

Mario: So, you are going to be one of these life insurance guys who bother everyone on campus, huh? That's what a college sales representative does, isn't it?

Stan: That's the trouble with you. . . . You always categorize people—or jobs—on the basis of some casual impression. This was my third interview with Upstate, and I have done quite a bit of reading on insurance selling. Do you know that most young people do not have any insurance . . . or what they do have is inadequate?

Mario: So . . .

Stan: That is exactly the point . . . a college sales representative performs a very useful function in society by making students aware of their immediate and future insurance needs. Ms. Van Horne says that a new representative can really help people, while earning excellent commissions. . . .

Mario: Oh, she just sold you a bill of goods. . . . College insurance sales reps are *(expletive deleted)*.

The good-natured argument continues as the friends proceed across campus.

Questions

1. If you were a third party to this discussion, would you agree with Stan or Mario? Why?
2. Do you think sales personnel—particularly insurance sales personnel—perform a useful function in modern society?
3. Evaluate the college insurance sales personnel in your area. How do most students regard these people?

KEY POINTS

- Selling is a universal activity in our society. Everyone engages in selling something at some time.

- A narrow definition of selling sees a salesperson's job as presenting a product or service to a prospect so that a transaction occurs.

- A broadened viewpoint argues that all organizations—private and public, profit and nonprofit—must perform a selling function.

- Sales jobs differ on the basis of various situational factors.

- Sales tasks can be categorized on the basis of: (1) creative/service selling, (2) development/maintenance, and (3) field sales/inside sales.

- A model can also be used to classify sales tasks. In this continuum, (1) service selling is distinguished from creative selling; (2) sales tasks are divided into four categories—support, maintenance, missionary, and development; and (3) sales positions can be identified according to a mix of creative and service skills.

- The primary duties of a sales job include: (1) selling duties, (2) sales-support duties, and (3) nonselling duties.

- The primary responsibilities of a salesperson are to the employer and the customers. For the employer, a salesperson must always try to project the proper image and to sell at a profit. A salesperson must always try to serve and satisfy the wants and needs of the customers.

Chapter 2

THE SELLING SPECTRUM

Dana Corporation's approach to professional selling illustrates the diversity of the tasks that the sales force is required to perform. Dana's Industrial Sales Force of 62 people consists of five different categories of sales personnel, each performing different marketing tasks. The five-fold division is as follows:

> A few generalists in geographically remote areas who sell nearly all Dana products.
>
> "Discipline" sales engineers who sell only one line, such as fluid products.
>
> Single-product salespeople, usually one to a district office, who sell a single, highly technical item. Example: numerical controls that Dana's Summit Div. makes for machine tools.
>
> End-user sales engineers concentrating on processing industries, which in most cases buy through Dana distributors.
>
> Market specialists. In districts where there's a concentration of customers in a particular industry.[1]

The importance of clearly understanding the overall spectrum is highlighted by some recent empirical research. Personnel with clearly defined sales tasks have been found to put greater effort into their jobs since they can observe a linkage between their own efforts and sales results.[2] Other research shows that sales performance is related to how closely the salesperson's characteristics match functional job requirements.[3] Effective personal selling requires that sales jobs be defined correctly, and that the correct people are assigned to the appropriate slots.

DIVERGENT VIEWS ON SELLING

Selling is a universal activity in our society. Indeed, it seems that everyone is involved in selling something at some time. The American Cancer Society sells itself in a fund-raising campaign. The butcher sells Mrs. Onley some steaks for a Saturday evening party, but in turn she sells him three tickets to a drawing at St. Alexis. A Xerox representative calls on the local school system to demonstrate a new copy machine. An attorney-agent sells the services of professional athletes. And so on.

Selling can be said to be the lifeblood of our economic system. As noted in Chapter 1, selling is an interpersonal persuasive process designed to influence some person's decision. Everyone is engaged in selling something at some time. But does this mean that everyone is a salesperson? The answer to this question depends upon how selling is defined.

Traditionally, selling has referred to facilitating the exchange of goods and services. The sales process has varied in style and complexity through the years. The merchants in ancient times who either imported their goods or served as sales agents for a family production unit certainly have little resemblance to today's professional sales representatives as they crisscross the country in a Boeing 747. But in both cases, the role of selling is essentially the same. The primary task is to satisfy consumers' needs for products and services.

A narrow definition of selling

Many marketing experts believe that it is inappropriate to broaden the definition of selling beyond this point. They feel that the sole occupational role of a salesperson is presenting a product or service to a prospect so that a sale occurs. In their view, the person who engages in selling as only a secondary task is not a salesperson.

Others believe that the definition of selling should be expanded to include nonbusiness activities. Proponents of a broader definition of selling say that all organizations—private and public, profit and nonprofit—must perform a sales function. School boards and parent-

A broader definition of selling

"For that matter, *I* haven't seen *you* down at the car showroom lately."

Reprinted by permission The Wall Street Journal.

All organizations—automobile dealerships and churches included—must perform a sales function.

teacher groups sell a school revenue proposal to the public. Political candidates are involved in selling themselves and their ideas. The armed forces maintain an all-volunteer military service by a promotional campaign selling the concept of a military career.

In the broader definition, the salesperson may be involved in situations in which selling is not the primary occupational role. Regardless of the definition, it is important to note that nearly everyone does some selling at some time or other.

TYPES OF SALES JOBS

There is such a great degree of variety in sales jobs that it is nearly impossible to compare them among companies and industries. Sales jobs differ on the basis of various factors, such as:

1. Primary duties and responsibilities.
2. Basic allocation of efforts.
3. Types of customers.
4. Key purchasing influences.
5. Competitive environment.
6. Mix of new and repeat business.
7. Product lines handled.
8. Pricing policies.
9. Level of supervision provided.
10. Compensation plans.
11. Nature and amount of training.
12. Advancement opportunities.
13. Operating philosophy of the company.[4]

It is also important to observe that the salesperson's role or task is not constant. Sales representatives perform a variety of sales tasks within the framework of their normal activity patterns. Nevertheless, it is possible to find ways for describing or classifying sales personnel.

Classifying sales jobs

Various ways for classifying sales tasks have been developed. The most commonly used approaches are: (1) the creative/service classification, (2) the development/maintenance classification, and (3) the field sales/inside sales classification.

Creative/service selling. The most basic classification scheme divides sales tasks into creative or service. *Creative selling* is persuasive selling that attempts to get new business away from competitors and to create demand for a new product. In contrast, *service selling* is low-keyed and oriented toward assisting the customer with the com-

Robert N. McMurry, a leading expert in the field of selling, has suggested an array of seven sales positions based on the creative skill required:

1. Positions where the "salesman's" job is predominantly to deliver the product, e.g., milk, bread, fuel oil.—His selling responsibilities are secondary. Obviously good service and a pleasant manner will enhance customer acceptance and hence lead to more sales. However, few originate many sales.

2. Positions where the salesman is predominantly an inside order-taker, e.g., the haberdashery salesman standing behind the counter.—Most of his customers have already made up their minds to buy. All he does is serve them. He may use suggestive selling and upgrade the merchandise they buy, but his opportunities to do more than that are few.

3. Positions where the salesman is also predominantly an order-taker but works in the field, as the packing house, soap, or spice salesman does.—In his contacts with chain store personnel, he may even actually be discouraged from applying the hard sell. As with delivery salesmen, good service and a pleasant personality may enhance his personal acceptance, but he too does little creative selling.

4. Positions where the salesman is not expected or permitted to take an order but is called on only to build goodwill or to educate the actual or potential user.—Examples here are the distiller's "missionary man" or the medical "detailer" representing an ethical pharmaceutical house.

5. Positions where the major emphasis is placed on technical knowledge, e.g., the engineering salesman who is primarily a consultant to the "client" companies.

6. Positions which demand the creative sale of tangible products like vacuum cleaners, refrigerators, siding, and encyclopedias.—Here the salesman often has a double task: First he must make the prospect dissatisfied with his or her present appliance or situation, then begin to sell his product.

7. Positions requiring the creative sale of intangibles such as insurance, advertising services, or education.—This type of sale is ordinarily more difficult than selling tangibles, of course, because the product is less readily demonstrated and dramatized. (Intangibles are often more difficult for the prospect to comprehend.)

Source: Robert N. McMurry, "The Mystique of Super-Salesmanship," in *Salesmanship and Sales Force Management*, edited by Edward G. Bursk and G. Scott Hutchison (Cambridge, Mass.: Harvard University Press, 1971), p. 64.

pletion of a transaction.[5] Those who engage in service selling can be described as *order receivers*. An order receiver is a salesperson who routinely processes a customer's order, such as a route salesperson or a grocery store checker. The buyer-seller relationship is known. The order receiver provides purchase information (such as price) and, if the prospect elects to buy, completes the mechanics of the transaction.

It should be clear that many salespeople do both creative and service selling during the course of their work. Identifying a particular sales job on the basis of this method depends on the actual mix of sales activity in the position.

Development/maintenance selling.   Another well-known classification scheme is based on development and maintenance activities.[6] *Sales development* is concerned with the creation of new customers. This calls for a persuasive salesperson who is good at prospecting and qualifying, then selling potential prospects. The salesperson engaged in sales development must be persuasive in attempts to solicit new business.

A *maintenance salesperson* is charged with getting sales volume from existing customers. This seller adopts a defensive marketing strategy and attempts to solidify the firm's status with customers that were originally secured by the sales development effort. The maintenance salesperson attempts to build a long-term buyer-seller relationship.

Field sales/inside sales.[7]   A third way to classify salespeople is according to the place in which they sell. *Field sales personnel* perform their primary function at the customer's place of business or residence, while *inside sales personnel* are the customer's contacts within their suppliers' organizations. These are two distinct selling tasks, both vital to the company. Unfortunately, too many firms have permitted (and in some cases even encouraged) rivalry between field and inside salespeople. This is particularly true in larger firms where geographic distance often discourages a feeling of mutual dependency between the two sales forces.

Field salespeople should recognize the important contribution made by inside salespeople, who perform the vital account-servicing functions of expediting orders and providing technical information. Inside sales personnel should complement—not compete with field sales efforts.

Figure 2–1 A continuum of sales tasks

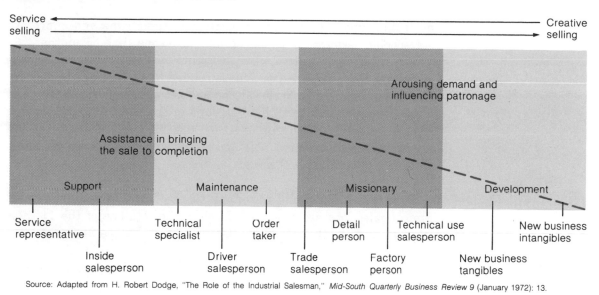

Source: Adapted from H. Robert Dodge, "The Role of the Industrial Salesman," *Mid-South Quarterly Business Review 9* (January 1972): 13.

It is difficult to classify the jobs performed by salespeople. There is even disagreement as to who is and who is not engaged in selling. Three classification schemes have been described, but the problem is that people's jobs do not fit nicely into little compartments. It is more useful to think of sales tasks as falling along a continuum.

The sales task continuum assumes that sales tasks can be arrayed in terms of a varying mix of creative and service activities required by a series of selling situations. In Figure 2–1, sales jobs are arrayed on three levels. First, the basic distinction (shown at the top of the figure) is between service selling and creative selling.

At the next level, sales tasks are arrayed along the development/ maintenance classification, only here the scheme has been altered to include a *support* classification and a *missionary* classification. The support function is primarily involved with providing customer service, such as ontime delivery, repair service, high-quality replacement parts, and accurate information about open orders. The missionary role is to contact indirect customers in an effort to pull the product through the marketing channel. The *detail person* who calls on doctors for a pharmaceutical manufacturer is a good example. The detailer assists drug wholesalers and retail drug outlets by promoting the products to doctors, who then prescribe them to the product's ul-

The sales task continuum[8]

timate consumer—the patient. Salespeople tend to be designated as performing a support, maintenance, missionary, or development role, depending upon the relative allocation of their time and effort. All salespeople perform all of these functions at one time or another.

The third classification level in Figure 2–1 indicates 11 separate sales jobs. Each of these positions is related to a given mix of creative and service skills. The trade salesperson is considered at the midpoint of creative and service skills. Positions to the right of this midpoint require a greater proportion of creative skills, while those to the left are service-skill oriented. All sales positions are viewed as being some mix of creative and service selling.

Some typical sales jobs

To further understand the many types of jobs in selling, several typical sales jobs are described. Each of these is one of the 11 sales jobs listed in the third level of classification in Figure 2–1.

Service representative.   The primary duty of this position is to provide customer service. This service may be replacement parts, repair service, delivery, or product information. Whatever the customer needs in order to use a firm's products satisfactorily may be called service.

Although this is a support function, it can be crucial to maintaining current business and obtaining new business, for service is really an integral part of many products. If customers are dissatisfied with the service, they are also dissatisfied with the product and will go elsewhere for their future needs.

Inside salesperson.   Inside salespeople are the customer's contacts inside the supplier's organization. As such they provide the customer with an ever-ready source of information about the status of current open orders, technical information related to quality control or product specifications, pricing, billing, and other sales order details. Often the inside salesperson develops a close working relationship with customers because of their frequent contacts.

Typically an inside sales position is part of a field salesperson's training program. Many firms use their inside sales force as the primary source of field sales personnel. By doing this, the firm can be sure that its field salespeople are well-versed in the detailed procedures for making order entries, processing shipping papers, and preparing billing documents and technical specifications.

Although inside salespersons are not directly involved in obtaining new business, their role can be instrumental in the buyer's decision to purchase from the firm. Often the level of service provided by a firm's inside sales force is the determining factor in the decision to place an order with one firm or another. Because of this impact on new business, field salespeople are wise to foster sound working relationships with their counterparts in the office.

Technical specialist.   Many people do not think of technical specialists as salespersons. This is because their primary duties are in sales maintenance. Typically technical specialists are responsible for dealing with customer complaints of a technical nature, developing new applications for the firm's products, altering the firm's products so that they will fit a particular customer's needs, and working with customers to see that they purchase the right product for the right job. None of these responsibilities directly involves selling. Yet each plays a major part in maintaining current sales and, in many respects, developing new business.

Much like the inside salesperson, technical specialists often develop close working relationships with customers—particularly with their technical counterparts in customer firms. This relationship can be a major factor in maintaining or gaining customer satisfaction with a firm and its products.

Driver salesperson and order taker.   These functions were described briefly by Robert N. McMurry earlier in this chapter. It is unfortunate how many people working in these jobs view their roles too narrowly. It is important that these personnel develop a professional selling attitude and view their jobs as critical to the firm's long-run success.

Progressive companies like L'eggs Products, Inc., and Abraham and Strauss are recognizing the importance of their driver salespeople and their salesclerks, respectively, by investing large sums of money in their training. Also, they now use these entry-level positions as one of the routes to a management position.

Trade salesperson.   This job involves selling to middlemen who, in turn, resell the products to other firms or individuals. Examples are selling to retailers and wholesalers. Since the product sold by a trade salesperson must be resold at a profit in order for the customer to benefit, the sales task takes on an added dimension. To sell the product, the salesperson must show that the customer's customers will want and be willing to pay for the product. To do this, the trade sales-person must be deeply involved with each customer's sales efforts and inventory policies. He or she must see that each customer is actively promoting the product and maintaining an adequate supply. In addition, the trade salesperson must anticipate changes in customer demand, both in kind and in quantity.

Many new products have failed because the firm's trade sales force was unable to get enough of the product on store shelves for the ultimate consumer to be able to find and buy the product conveniently. Yet many firms assume that somehow their products will get on store shelves under their own power. Smart marketers recognize the critical role played by their trade sales force and provide them with good market information, strong advertising support, and liberal incentives to do their job well.

More and more companies—firms like Procter & Gamble, Clairol, and Richardson-Merrell—are using recent college graduates in these positions. They have found that these jobs are exciting and can lead to broader responsibilities, both within and outside of sales. It is likely that many readers of this textbook will start their careers in trade sales.

Detail person.   Drug and medical equipment sales forces are the best examples of detailing.[9] Their task is to bring basic product information to the attention of physicians in the hope that the physician will specify their product when writing prescriptions. In addition, detailers distribute product samples, educational materials, and other information of interest to physicians. Detailing is discussed further in Chapter 15.

Critics of detailing maintain that the cost of detailing simply adds to the cost of health care. But a study by the Pharmaceutical Manufacturers Association found that "a detailer or a physician's mail are the first sources of information about a new drug for 74 percent of all physicians."[10] And one drug company sales manager commented: "if the time a doctor invested in seeing detailmen wasn't worthwhile, he wouldn't see them. And our people see the doctors."[11]

Technical use salesperson.   Much like the technical specialist described earlier, technical use salespeople provide customers with technical advice, assistance, and information. But they also serve a selling function since they have the responsibility for bringing the sale to a close.

Many technical use salespeople sell products or services that are provided in accordance with the customer's specifications. In these cases the technical use salesperson also acts much like a technical consultant to the customer. Because of their multiple responsibilities, these jobs require people with a high level of technical knowledge combined with special selling skills. Often graduate engineers, scientists, or technical specialists are hired for these positions. In this case, the firm must institute a strong sales training program to augment the technical skills of these people with the selling skills that are critical to their success.

New business tangibles and intangibles. Both of these positions were described earlier in the chapter. Large numbers of sales jobs fall into these two broad job classifications. Everything from the sale of cosmetics door-to-door to the sale of mutual funds can be listed here. In many people's minds, this is really the core of selling!

Test your knowledge

Your instructor probably chose *Professional Selling* as the textbook for your course after considering a wide range of alternatives available in the marketplace. Perhaps your instructor was introduced to *Professional Selling* by one of the field representatives of Business Publications, Inc., the book's publisher. Business Publications, Inc.—BPI for short—is headquartered in Plano, Texas, and maintains a nationwide field sales force to market its product—college textbooks.

The field representatives, or "travelers" as they are sometimes known in the industry, call on hundreds of college instructors in their assigned territories. The BPI representative keeps the firm's mailing list up to date so that instructors teaching a certain course will get examination copies of any new title published in this area. The field representative makes periodic visits to instructor's offices to see that examination copies have been received and to suggest how the book might be used in certain courses. In addition to providing product information, the field representative handles delivery problems, solicits editorial suggestions, looks for new manuscripts that are being developed, and generally acts as a liaison between the publisher and the instructor. Business Publications stresses professionalism in all aspects of the field representative's job.

How would you classify the sales job performed by the field representative of Business Publications, Inc.?

DUTIES OF THE SALES JOB

Even though the sales job varies from one company to the next and from one product to the next, there are certain duties that are common in all sales jobs. The extent of these duties in each job will vary, but they will all be present to some extent in every sales job.

Selling duties

Sales-related duties include prospecting for customers, qualifying prospects, demonstrating the product, writing orders, increasing sales to current customers, and quoting prices. Each of these activities has a direct impact on current and future sales levels. These duties are referred to as the missionary and development functions in the sales continuum in Figure 2–1.

Sales-support duties

While some duties do not have a direct and immediate impact on sales, they still play a major role in maintaining current sales levels and increasing future levels. Some examples of these duties are handling complaints, providing delivery information, assisting in technical problems, and handling special requests. These duties are called the support and maintenance functions in the sales continuum.

How much a particular salesperson becomes involved in these activities will vary. In some cases the salesperson will have little to do with these activities because another person in the firm will have primary responsibility for them. On the other hand, the salesperson may have these duties as a primary responsibility. In either case, the professional salesperson assumes responsibility for these activities because, if these jobs are not done well, sales will be lost and future business will become more and more difficult to get.

Nonselling duties

All professional salespeople must plan and control their activities. To do this they carefully prepare reports, attend sales meetings and conferences, study and learn, monitor competitive actions, and plan their travel. Without careful attention to these "housekeeping" duties, the salesperson's performance can be drastically reduced. The professional salesperson knows this and sees that it does not happen.

RESPONSIBILITIES OF THE SALES JOB

Salespeople have many responsibilities but two areas of responsibility stand out. These are the responsibilities to employers and to customers. Both of these obligations must control every action of the professional salesperson.

In many cases the salesperson is the only contact a customer has with a company. If the salesperson does not act responsibly and project the proper image, the image and performance of the entire firm could suffer. The salesperson must also see that sales are made at a profit. Without profits, the company will not survive.

Serving and satisfying the customer are major responsibilities of the salesperson. In the short run clever salespersons may be able to fool or outwit customers, but in the long run they will lose. Only by sincerely trying to satisfy the particular wants and needs of each customer can a salesperson hope to build the kind of customer relationships upon which all successful sales careers are built.

If a person is not willing and able to assume these difficult and often conflicting responsibilities, he or she is not ready for a career in sales. By the same token, such an individual is not ready to receive the many benefits, both tangible and intangible, that the professional salesperson enjoys. Nothing is more satisfying than knowing that you play a major part in making this awesome economic machine run.

SUMMARY

Chapter 2 has shown that while selling is a universal activity in our society, the definition of a salesperson can vary according to concepts of the role of selling. A narrow definition assumes that selling is involved only with the sales and distribution of goods and services. A broader viewpoint says that all organizations—private and public, profit and nonprofit—must perform a sales function.

Sales tasks differ according to a variety of factors. The most common methods of categorizing sales tasks are: (1) creative/service selling, (2) the development/maintenance classification, and (3) field sales/inside sales.

A simple model was suggested for classifying sales tasks, the sales task continuum. This model or continuum is based on three levels of classification: (1) service selling is distinguished from creative selling; (2) sales tasks are divided into four groups—support, maintenance, missionary, and development; and (3) 11 separate sales positions are identified according to the relative mix of creative and service skills.

The chapter concludes by describing the primary duties and responsibilities common to all sales jobs. The primary duties include: (1) selling duties, (2) sales-support duties, and (3) nonselling duties. The two major areas of responsibility discussed are those of the salespeople to their employer and to their customers.

REVIEW QUESTIONS/DISCUSSION
QUESTIONS/EXERCISES

1. Briefly identify the following:
   a. Creative selling.
   b. Service selling.
   c. Order receivers.
   d. Sales development.
   e. Maintenance salesperson.
   f. Inside salesperson.
   g. Trade salesperson.
   h. Detail person.
   i. Technical use salesperson.
   j. Service representative.

2. Do you agree with the statement: "Selling is a universal activity in our society"? Why or why not?

3. Contrast the narrow and broad definitions of selling. Which viewpoint is closest to your own definition? Why?

4. Prepare a list of examples in which the broadened viewpoint of selling has been applied in your community.

5. Show how each of the 13 factors listed in the chapter can affect the nature of the sales job.

6. Prepare two job descriptions, one for a creative sales position and one for a job in service selling. Compare the descriptions.

7. What kinds of personal characteristics would you look for in a person for a job in sales development? If you were hiring a maintenance sales-person, would you want the person to have different characteristics than the sales development person?

8. When would you use an inside sales force in addition to a field sales force?

9. Critically evaluate the sales tasks continuum model developed in this chapter. Can you make any suggestions for improving this model?

10. Talk with a person you know in selling. Try to determine how much time he or she spends in each of the four functions—support, mainte-nance, missionary, and development.

11. Interview five salespeople and locate each of their jobs on the sales task continuum. Which job do you feel you would most enjoy? Where is it on the continuum? Do you think you would also enjoy other jobs that would fall in about the same place on the continuum?

12. Make a list of 10 to 15 sales positions. Then identify each sales job ac-cording to the various classification schemes outlined in this chapter.

13. Spend several hours in the library studying professional publications in the field of selling. Can you find any other approaches to classifying sales tasks?

14. With the class divided into 11 study groups, each group has the respon-sibility of collecting examples of sales positions that correspond to the third classification level of the sales tasks continuum.

15. Some firms consider a field sales position as a promotion for a successful inside salesperson. Evaluate this policy.

16. Is a salesperson responsible only to his or her employer and customers?

17. Stage a class debate on the following issue: A salesperson's first responsibility is to the customer—the employer comes second.

18. Obtain a job description for a sales job with which you are familiar. Classify all of the duties listed in the job description as either selling, sales-support, or nonselling duties.

19. Interview a salesperson you know. Write a report, based on your interview, describing (a) how much this person enjoys the nonselling duties of the job, and (b) how important these duties are to the job.

20. Read Arthur Miller's play, *Death of a Salesman*. How does this description of the sales job differ from that presented in this book?

CASE 2–1: CHAMBERS MANUFACTURING

Sandra Meyers has just entered a conference room at a Ramada Inn near St. Louis. Her employer—Chambers Manufacturing—rented the room to hold a product introduction session for a new software package to go along with the rest of Chambers data processing line. Meyers has heard that over 100 people were attending the meeting. In fact Chambers had to rent the Ramada facility because of inadequate meeting space in its nearby headquarters.

Meyers, who covered downstate Illinois for Chambers, was immediately spotted by Fred Standish, her counterpart in Iowa. Standish was a company veteran, and he sensed that Meyers had not met many of the people at the table to which both he and Meyers were assigned.

Standish: Let me introduce you to these folks. Sandra, this is Horace Fogarty. He is our government specialist—the guy who helps us deal with all those bureaucrats.

And this is Linda Jacoby, the correspondence coordinator in the national sales office.

And this is Ed Smythe, Ed is the guy who is responsible for making sure all that stuff we sell works once it is on location.

Standish continues to introduce Meyers to people at the table.

Standish: Well, I guess that is everyone. This is going to be a great sales meeting. I understand that tonight's banquet is going to be. . . . . .

But Meyers' thoughts have already drifted away. She wondered: "Why does the company bill this as a sales meeting, these people aren't sales reps like Fred and I."

Questions

1. Do you agree with Meyers?
2. How would you classify each of the Chambers personnel at Meyers' table?

CASE 2–2: VILLA ROMA

Villa Roma is a cocktail lounge in a residential section of Buffalo, New York. The proprietor, Marty Scanneli, has developed a loyal following of residents who spend many of their leisure hours in his establishment. Villa Roma features a cozy, friendly atmosphere, free peanuts, a happy hour, and live entertainment in the evenings.

One of the regular groups that gather at Villa Roma includes Charlie Hoschecki, who works at Mogel and Mogel Men's Store as a salesperson; Fred Constandine, a driver for a local beer distributor; and Cedric Holmes, a barber. The men meet at the lounge after work to have a round or two before going home. One afternoon, the conversation goes along these lines:

Scanneli: Good afternoon, gentlemen. Boy, you look tired, Fred . . . you ought to take a day off once in a while! The usual round?

Constandine: Sure, Marty, that will be fine. And you are right . . . I *am* exhausted. I sure wish I had an easy job like Charlie . . . you know, just standing around in a nice comfortable air-conditioned store all day.

Hoschecki: Wait a minute, Fred . . . things can get pretty hectic down at the store. Sometimes there are so many people in our department that I can't tell who is looking at what! Heck, you know how it can get . . . you're in selling.

Constandine: *I'm* not a salesperson. I drive a truck and make deliveries.

Hoschecki: That makes you a salesperson, doesn't it? For that matter, Cedric here is also a salesperson.

Holmes: Boy, you'd do anything to start an argument, Charlie. How can I be a salesperson when all I do is cut hair?

Scanneli (arriving with the drinks): Well, I see you fellows are at it again. Let me see . . . yesterday, the argument was about how many tournaments some pro golfer would win next year. What is it this time?

Holmes: Well, maybe you can settle this, Marty. As usual, Charlie is making some statements he can't back up with facts. He claims Fred and I are in sales, but we all know that Fred delivers beer and I am a barber. Tell Charlie that he's wrong again!

Questions

1. If you were Scanneli, how would you respond to Holmes?
2. What does Hoschecki mean when he says that Constandine and Holmes are also salespersons?
3. If you agree with Hoschecki's opinion, how would you classify the sales tasks performed by Constandine and Holmes?

A Profile of Professional Selling

Jerry Sanders

To mark the 10th anniversary of Advanced Micro Devices, President Jerry Sanders had a flag run up the company flagpole displaying a bunch of asparagus. Then he plastered the semiconductor maker's corporate walls with asparagus posters and took out full-page, trade-paper ads announcing the dawn of the asparagus age for the Sunnyvale, California company.

Why asparagus? "Asparagus," explains Sanders, "is the perfect symbol for AMD in its next 10 years. If you're just starting in farming, you'd better not plant asparagus: It takes 3 years to get a good crop, and by then you may have run out of money. Growing asparagus is like developing integrated circuits. The more time you can afford for innovative research and development, the greater your profitability. Asparagus means earning power."

AMD is very much the creation of Chicago-born Walter Jeremiah (Jerry) Sanders III. Sanders, 44, came out of the University of Illinois as an electrical engineer. But in the course of working for Motorola he learned an important lesson: The men making the big money on chips weren't the geniuses who created them but the guys selling them. Sanders' priorities being what they were, he switched to sales.

He left Motorola in the early 1960s for Fairchild Camera & Instrument. By age 31 Sanders had become one of Fairchild's youngest marketing managers.

Unlike the founder of Intel, a brilliant engineer, or the founder of National Semiconductor, a master of manufacturing, both of whom left Fairchild around the same time, Sanders had only his salesmanship going for him. So he used it: "If you're 5 feet tall and fat, basketball is not your sport."

But Sanders knew he would have to give his sales force a selling edge. AMD, Sanders told the world, would build its products to something called Military-Standard 883. Simply, that meant AMD tested and inspected parts more carefully than its competition. So AMD was able to keep its average selling price well above the industry average. And since most of its customers were growing rapidly, AMD could ride on their momentum.

Sanders' hard-driving personal style and his love of the grand gesture can hardly be called subtle. He subscribes to the Vince Lombardi school of salesmanship: "We don't tolerate excuses from our sales force," he says. "There is no try, only do."

But he also plays the carrot-as-motivator game, as he did by staging his "American Dream Christmas in May" party for AMD's employees. The grand door prize was $1,000 a month—for 20 years. Sanders himself, with photographers, brought the good news to the home of the winner, a 21-year-old Filipino girl who had been at AMD 14 months.

Source: Adapted from, "Salesman Rampant, on a Field of Chips," *Forbes*, December 8, 1980, pp. 107–8. Reprinted by permission.

Part 2

PLANNING AND STRATEGY FOR EFFECTIVE SELLING

Entertainment is to sales what fertilizer is to agriculture—it increases the yield.*

> **SENATOR RUSSELL LONG**
> *(during former President Carter's ill-fated campaign against the three-martini lunch)*

KEY POINTS

- The most effective way to sell involves understanding and satisfying customer needs.
- Major differences exist in the ways ultimate consumers and industrial users buy. Industrial buyers use fewer personal factors in their decisions, are constrained by purchasing policies, and share buying responsibility with other members of the organization.
- Buying is a process, not a single act. Therefore, purchase decisions take time and vary greatly.
- The steps in the purchase decision process are need identification, information search, alternative selection, and postpurchase evaluation.
- Sales personnel should recognize that consumers buy to satisfy a variety of needs, and a salesperson can play an important role in helping buyers recognize their needs.
- Buyers use many sources in their search for information; one of the most important is the salesperson.
- Alternative selection can be achieved through a variety of approaches: (1) offsetting, (2) dictionary, (3) good enough on all factors, (4) good enough on at least one factor, or (5) some combination.
- Salespeople can increase a buyer's satisfaction if they understand cognitive dissonance.
- The great variety in purchase decisions is due to the differing individual, socioeconomic, and cultural characteristics of buyers.

Chapter
3

UNDERSTANDING
BUYING BEHAVIOR

Joe Gandolfo, an independent insurance agent representing 45 insurance companies, sells more life insurance each year than anyone in the world. In 1975 he sold more than $1 billion, and every year he sells over three fourths of a billion dollars of insurance. Bear in mind, selling $1 million dollars of life insurance is considered quite a feat in lesser human beings. Twice he has earned the prestigious National Sales Master Award.

Joe says that "selling is 98 percent understanding human beings and 2 percent product knowledge."[1] In line with his philosophy of selling, Joe spends a large part of a sales call questioning the prospect about his or her background, personal life, and their financial needs and goals.

IMPORTANCE OF THE CUSTOMER

Marketing's role in the modern organization has been described by Herbert D. Eagle, former president of Sales and Marketing Executives International, as focusing the energies of the organization on its customers. According to this authority, "marketing aims to satisfy the consumer."[2] This basic philosophy of doing business is called the *marketing concept*. Most marketing people agree that it is the best way to sell goods and services in today's environment.

To apply the marketing concept, sales personnel must understand (1) what their customers are like, (2) how they make their purchase decisions, and (3) what factors affect their decisions. Only then can a selling strategy be developed that is responsive to this consumer information. This chapter discusses these three aspects of buyer behavior.

CHARACTERISTICS OF BUYERS

Although it is possible to group buyers in many ways, the differences in buying behavior are greatest when buyers are separated into groups of ultimate consumers and industrial buyers.

In developing their selling strategies, sales personnel must bear in mind three major differences between industrial buyers and ultimate consumers:

1. Industrial buyers normally base their buying decisions on fewer personal factors than ultimate consumers do.
2. Industrial buyers are typically constrained by well-defined buying policies, while ultimate consumers are not.
3. In the industrial situation, the responsibility for buying is usu-

ally spread among several people, instead of one person having total responsibility as in the consumer market.[3]

Industrial buyers normally make their purchase decisions on the basis of factors that are less personal than those used by ultimate consumers. Consumers only have to satisfy themselves and their families when they make a purchase, but industrial buyers' purchase decisions are judged by other people—usually by their superiors, who also decide upon their promotions and raises.

Decision factors

An industrial buyer buys according to written specifications that detail the quality required, the delivery terms, the physical dimensions of the product, and the like. When the product is delivered it may have to pass an extensive testing procedure before the company will accept it and forward payment. If the product fails these tests, it is either rejected and scrapped or returned to the seller. If industrial buyers are to select products that can both meet the specifications and pass the acceptance tests, they must make their selections on the basis of several factors. They must consider the ability of the supplier to provide rapid and timely delivery, the quality of the product, and the ability of the supplier to maintain quality standards throughout the production cycle.

Contrast this purchase behavior with that of ultimate consumers. Their purchase decisions are often influenced by personal factors like style and color. In fact, personal factors are often the most important considerations in consumer purchase decisions, while impersonal factors, such as the chemical content of the product or the ability of the product to pass certain tests, may be virtually useless. Telling the consumer that a particular coffee pot cleaner contains sodium silicate and sodium perborate is senseless; telling the person that it will make coffee taste fresher is useful and important.

The purchase decisions of industrial buyers often must adhere to detailed policies that have been dictated by the management of the organizations for which they are working. Probably the most restrictive organization in this regard is the federal government. A large portion of government contracts is awarded on the basis of *sealed bids*.[4] In this practice, each supplier competing for the business must prepare a price quotation in accordance with detailed specifications and submit it to the buyer in a sealed envelope by a certain date. On that date, the envelopes are opened and the contract is awarded to the supplier with the lowest bid. A purchasing policy that requires

Purchase policies

sealed-bid quotations severely restricts the flexibility of the buyer making the decision.

A less extreme example of a purchasing policy is the common practice whereby management insists that the purchases of a particularly critical component or material be spread among several suppliers. This is done to avoid the major problems that can result from a work stoppage in the supplier's plant if only one supplier provides the entire order. This purchasing policy is known as *multiple-source purchasing*.

In *sole-source purchasing* the entire required amount of a particular component or material is purchased from one supplier. Management uses this policy to foster greater cooperation between the buyer and the seller. The buying firm believes it thus is in a better position to request special services when such needs arise.

Whether a firm uses sole-source purchasing or multiple sourcing is determined by the nature of its particular situation. If multiple sourcing is used, it is either because the firm wants to assure itself of a continuing source of supply or because it wants its suppliers to compete more vigorously.[5]

Ultimate consumers rarely use purchase policies. If they do, the policies are simply rules of thumb. Some people feel that it is best to buy all of their gasoline from one service station so they can get better service when they need it—a form of sole sourcing. Other consumers feel free to change sources whenever they wish; buying gas from other stations when it is difficult for them to buy from their regular vendor. While purchase policies are imposed on the industrial buyer, the ultimate consumer establishes individual policies and can change them at will.

Multiple responsibility

Responsibility for industrial purchase decisions is spread across several departments in an organization. The engineering, manufacturing, laboratory, and marketing departments (as well as the purchasing department) have a major role in the purchase decision. Engineering is responsible for developing specifications and determining each potential supplier's ability to meet them. The laboratory designs and administers the acceptance test procedures, and marketing and manufacturing work together to develop the requested delivery schedules. Salespeople must sell to all these departments, and they must realize the different needs and wants of each of them. Only then can they initiate an effective sales appeal.[6]

Ultimate consumers are largely independent in their purchase decisions. The only others who might have a part in an ultimate consumer's purchase decision are members of the consumer's immediate family. Anyone who has tried to buy a new car for a family with a teenage son or daughter knows that this influence can be substantial. Other than the purchase of a new car, a new house, or something of that magnitude, however, most consumer purchase decisions involve only one or two people. And in those cases in which several people share the responsibility for the decision, all have similar goals and objectives in mind. This is not the case in most industrial purchasing situations. An engineer may want the best possible quality and will consider cost to be the purchasing department's problem.

To some companies, the differences between the buying behaviors of ultimate consumers and industrial buyers are so great that the organization of the firm takes them into account. Figure 3–1 shows the organizational structure of a typical medium-size life and health insurance company. Note that the company has an individual (ultimate consumer) division and a group (industrial buyer) division. By organizing in this way, the company can adapt its health and life insurance policies to the specific needs of the two types of buyers, and it also can allow its sales personnel to specialize. The salespeople in each of the divisions become intimately familiar with the buying behavior of the customers they serve.

The most important characteristic of buying behavior is that purchase decisions are not single acts but a series of acts—a process. The salesperson who tries to learn something about buying behavior by reviewing previous sales experiences overlooks much. It is not enough to review only the outcomes of the decisions; the whole decision process must be studied. Two people may decide to buy the same item, but to understand *why* they did so it is necessary to understand *how* they reached their separate decisions. Similarly, if sales representatives are to be effective in influencing buying decisions, they must understand how these decisions are made. Only by acting during the buyer's decision process can a salesperson hope to influence its outcome; once the decision has been made it is too late.

Before describing each step in the purchase decision process, we will examine two important implications of the fact that it is a process. First, a purchase decision takes time. The amount of time can vary from only a few seconds to several years, but all buying decisions take time. If the time involved is very short, little can be done to influence the buyer during the process; all influences must have had their intended effects before the process begins. On the other

**THE PURCHASE
DECISION
PROCESS**

hand, if the decision process is time-consuming, there is ample opportunity for the salesperson to influence the process. The amount of time available to the salesperson depends upon the buyer's willingness to delay the purchase.

Figure 3–1 Organization chart of a medium-size life and health insurance company

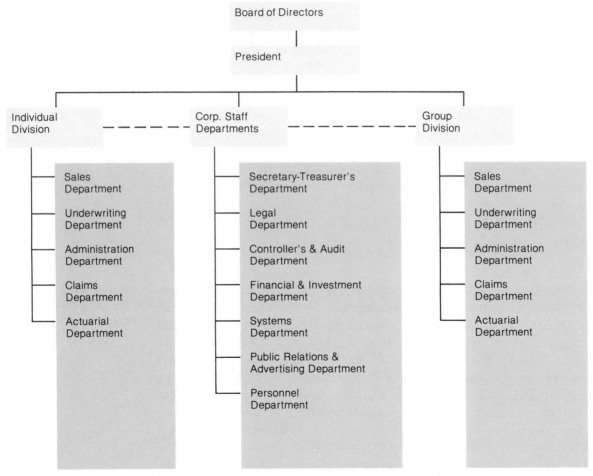

Source: Davis W. Gregg and Vane B. Lucas, eds. *Life and Health Insurance Handbook*, 3d ed. (Homewood, Ill.: Richard D. Irwin, 1973), p. 957. © 1973 by Richard D. Irwin, Inc.

Second, a purchase decision has several steps which can mean a number of things to the salesperson. The buyer may use different information at different steps in the decision process. A new-car buyer usually learns about various cars and the options available on each from advertisements on television and in magazines and newspapers, and from sales brochures, but the final decision is often made on the basis of the price and payment terms negotiated with the seller. In addition, different individuals may have varying degrees of influence at different stages in the decision process. The new-car buyer would probably rely on the opinion of a friend who is interested in cars to learn about the many cars available, but for information about a specific model the purchaser would turn to someone who owns that particular automobile. Also, some stages of the process may be included in some decisions and excluded from others.

The purchase decision process can be divided into the following four stages: (1) need identification, (2) information search, (3) alternative selection, and (4) postpurchase evaluation.

The purchase decision process begins when a person recognizes a need or a want that is unsatisfied. This creates a desire to satisfy the need, and this desire is the motivating force that drives the individual through the various stages of the purchase decision process. Once the process has begun, the various steps proceed until the need is satisfied. But to get the process started, it is necessary to motivate the individual to act, and this can be done only by identifying or appealing to an unsatisfied need or want.

Need identification

"They're much more comfortable than the shoes that are put on with nails!"

Reprinted by permission The Wall Street Journal.

Satisfying customer needs is an important aspect of selling.

Types of needs. Various attempts have been made to categorize human needs. Some classifications include more than 100 different needs; others include only a few. The list developed by the psychologist Abraham H. Maslow is suitable for most marketing situations. Maslow divided all human needs into the following categories: (1) physiological, (2) safety, (3) belongingness, (4) esteem, and (5) self-actualization.[7] Physiological needs are the most basic human needs; they are necessary for a person's survival. Hunger and thirst are examples of these needs. Safety is the need for security and freedom from danger. Belongingness is the need for others to like us, and esteem is the need for others to respect us. The highest-order need in Maslow's list is self-actualization, which is the need for achievement, to find ourselves and to learn how far we can go.

Maslow went further than simply identifying human needs; he also described the order in which these needs are satisfied. Because physiological needs are the most basic, they must be satisfied before other needs can motivate behavior. People who are starving have little interest in satisfying their need for love or esteem—they simply want food. As soon as a lower-order need is satisfied, the next higher-order need motivates behavior. Higher-order needs can motivate behavior only when all lower-order needs have been satisfied. When a person once again becomes hungry or thirsty, attention is directed to satisfying the hunger or thirst.

Maslow also felt that several needs can motivate behavior at the same time. The relative effect of each need on behavior is determined by the extent to which lower-level needs have been satisfied. People with a low level of need satisfaction are motivated largely by their physiological and safety needs. Those whose lower-order needs are satisfied are primarily motivated by their needs for esteem and self-actualization. In both cases, however, all of the human needs are present and have some effect on the person's behavior.

Maslow's theory of need satisfaction has important implications to sellers of consumer and industrial goods alike. W. Noel Eldred, Hewlett-Packard vice president for marketing, illustrates the concept in these terms: "We don't sell hardware. We sell solutions to measurement problems. . . . Selling is the technique of getting people to part with their cash, and is short term and selfish because it focuses on the needs of the seller." He would rather think in terms of "an integrated effort to discover, create, arouse and satisfy customer needs."[8] Sellers of consumer goods also use this approach to selling, especially in marketing household consumer goods, automobiles, and insurance.[9]

Recognizing needs.   Before an unsatisfied need can motivate behavior, it must be recognized. A person may have an unsatisfied need
and not even realize it. Many of us have had times when we were so
engrossed in what we were doing that we failed to realize that it was
time to stop for lunch. In other words, we failed to recognize our unsatisfied need and therefore we were not motivated to satisfy it. Only
when our hunger became so great that it interrupted our thought
pattern were we motivated to satisfy it.

There are two basic ways people become conscious of unsatisfied
needs: (1) they receive new information or (2) they reevaluate their
current situation. In either case, a salesperson can be instrumental
in helping a potential customer recognize an unmet need and find
ways to satisfy it.

Many companies use sales personnel, advertisements, catalogs,
and direct mail to keep their customers aware of what products are
available. Often customers do not know what they need or want because they do not know what they can have. David M. Stander, senior
vice president of Brand, Gruber, Stander and Company, tells a story
that illustrates the point very well:

> . . . several years ago an appliance company wanted some new ideas
> for ranges so they asked nearly 1,000 women, "Ladies, what new range
> features would you like?"
>
> Now, remember, consumers always will give you some kind of an
> answer. That's not the problem. What is usually lacking are responses
> that provide a meaningful insight into their unsatisfied needs. So, when
> the appliance company conducted the interviews, the women obliged
> with all kinds of answers. They said things like, "Make the ovens pret-
> tier"; "Move the dials back so the children won't reach them"; [other
> women with no children said] "Move the dials up front so I don't burn
> myself when I'm reaching over"; and [still others said] "Give me an-
> other burner." But not one woman in the entire sample had the gall to
> say, "Make me an oven that cleans itself!" Yet, when this sample of
> housewives was contacted a second time and exposed to the idea of a
> self-cleaning oven, they all screamed: "That's just what I need!"[10]

Although this story is about new products, the principle is equally
applicable to established products. Customers must be told—and re-
told—about the various products a company has to offer and how
each can satisfy a particular need. The salesperson is probably the
single best source of product information.

Asking customers to reevaluate their current situations is the second way sales personnel can help customers recognize some potentially unsatisfied needs. Any good salesperson knows that when a

woman purchases a new dress, she should be asked whether she needs a variety of accessories to go with it. This is helping the customer to reevaluate her current situation. It is possible that without prompting, the woman may not realize she does not have the proper accessories for the dress, and the sale of a purse or a new pair of shoes could be lost.

Industrial goods sales forces can also use these two approaches to expose unrecognized customer needs. Mack Hanan of *Sales Management* magazine tells the following story about a glass pipe salesperson:

> His customer, a chemical-processing engineer, would neither try nor buy glass pipe. Benefit-selling produced only the response, "But glass breaks." Finally, in desperation, his sales manager counseled him this way:
>
> "Next time you call, don't sell the product. Say only these words: 'I have a way to lower your cost of maintenance and repair by 25% by ending the problems of rust, corrosion, and contamination forever. This will help you improve your pass-along contribution to profit by a minimum of 10%.' "
>
> The salesman asked, "After I've said that, then what?"
>
> "Then leave," his manager said.
>
> "But that's ridiculous," the salesman replied. "If I leave, he'll just get up and come after me, won't he?"
>
> "Why should he do that?" the sales manager asked.
>
> "Well," the salesman said. "Won't he want to know?"[11]

In this case, the salesperson had not been giving the potential buyer the right information. The sales manager was suggesting that the representative give the engineer new information, information that was not only new but would cause a reevaluation of the current situation. The sales manager was suggesting the use of both approaches for exposing an unrecognized need.

Information search

The next step in the purchase decision process is a search for information. All buyers, whether they are industrial buyers or ultimate consumers, have two major sources of information: internal and external.

Internal sources. Internal sources refer to information already known to the buyer. Starting early in childhood, people learn what items to buy, where to buy them, and how much to pay for them. The fact that the average American household has its television set on for more than six hours a day and that almost one fourth of that time is devoted to commercials indicates the vast amount of information that comes from television advertising. When all of the radio commercials, billboards, newspaper and magazine advertisements, and other commercial messages are also considered, it is obvious that advertising alone accounts for a considerable portion of the information available to the typical consumer.

But even this is only a small part of the total information available to the typical buyer. Think how often people talk about their shopping experiences, or how much of each person's day is spent learning—through actual experience—the performance characteristics of automobiles, groceries, utility services, or clothing, for example. Most of this information is stored mentally, even if not consciously. In a very real sense, people are continually shopping. When they find they need, or decide they want, a particular good or service, they already have extensive information on the purchase decision.

Other information related to the purchase decision is stored physically. Most homes have department store catalogs, books, magazines, brochures, and other information sources which have been collected over the years. When information about certain goods or services is needed, these sources provide data about the products and services available.

Industrial purchasers have even more extensive data files at their disposal. Supplier catalogs, purchasing directories, trade journals, company brochures, technical reports, and previous correspondence with suppliers and members of other departments are just a few of the information sources industrial buyers have available to assist them in their purchase decisions. Even with all this information, however, industrial buyers and ultimate consumers alike frequently resort to external sources for further information.

External sources. There are several reasons that buyers often want more information than what is already available to them. Some of the information on hand may be out of date and must be updated before it can be useful. Buyers may feel that an expert's opinion is helpful if their own knowledge of the product or service is limited. Another reason may be that the buyer is required to consult outside sources in the decision. Many industrial purchase decisions must be reviewed by a committee, and the members of that committee frequently provide much input to the decision. Whatever the reason, buyers often seek external information, and they usually have a large number of sources available to them.

Both ultimate consumers and industrial buyers rely on sales personnel for information. A good salesperson can provide a buyer with technical information, product-use experiences, price and financing information, and other data that might be relevant to the buyer's purchase decision. Most often, buyers seek information in addition to that provided by the salesperson because sales personnel have a vested interest—they are trying to sell the product. For this reason, one of the most important characteristics of a good salesperson is credibility; a salesperson must be believable.

If buyers want more information, where do they go? The ultimate consumer can talk with friends and acquaintances, consult a copy of *Consumer Reports,* or browse through stores that carry the wanted item. Industrial buyers act much the same. In addition to talking to suppliers' representatives, industrial buyers study technical reports, talk to other people in the firm, ask for laboratory analyses, and so forth. As industrial buyers or ultimate consumers proceed in their information search, they have extensive information available to assist them in their purchase decisions. While it is true that more information results in better decisions, it is also true that the task of selection becomes more difficult as the amount of information included in the decision increases.

Alternative selection

Once all the information necessary for the decision has been collected, the buyer is ready to select the best alternative. To do this there must be a basis for the selection. Researchers who study decision making feel that there are basically four ways of choosing one alternative from a group of several. These are (1) the offsetting approach, (2) the dictionary approach, (3) the "good-enough-on-all-factors" approach, and (4) the "good-enough-on-at-least-one-factor" approach.

Imagine that four new-car buyers have obtained information on six different cars from six dealers in their area. The information they have obtained is shown in Table 3–1.

Several things should be noted about this table. First, it is assumed that all four buyers agree on some very personal matters, although it is hard to imagine four buyers agreeing on the looks, the interior styling, or the interior roominess of six cars. But for purposes of this illustration, it is assumed that the four buyers can and do agree with the ratings shown in Table 3—1 for each of these decision factors. (The last section of this chapter will show why buyers probably would not agree on such highly subjective evaluations)

Second, all of the decision factors are not rated in the same way.

Table 3–1 Decision matrix for new car selection

Decision factors Make of car	Base price	Looks	Power	Interior styling	Interior roominess	Reputation of dealer	Estimated gas mileage	Warranty
Bond	$7,900	3	4	Pretty	Roomy	Good	27 mpg	12 months, 12,000 miles
Pismo	$7,800	1	2	Pretty	Tight	Good	23 mpg	12 months, 12,000 miles
Rapier	$8,200	2	1	OK	Roomy	Bad	22 mpg	12 months, 12,000 miles
LaBelle	$8,100	1	3	OK	Tight	Good	26 mpg	12 months, 12,000 miles
Volta	$7,700	5	6	Plain	Adequate	Good	33 mpg	12 months, 12,000 miles
Asti	$8,400	4	5	Plain	Adequate	Do not know	33 mpg	12 months, 12,000 miles

Price has an actual value associated with each alternative, but the reputation of the dealer is listed only as good, bad, or do not know. Also, power is ranked in order of preference, with the most powerful car being the one most preferred. Because several rating schemes are used, the selection process is more difficult. Frequently, rating schemes have to be altered to make selection possible.

Third, there are ties on some of the decision factors. Note that the Bond and the Pismo, the Rapier and the LaBelle, and the Volta and the Asti all tie on interior styling. This will also affect the selection process.

Fourth, the warranty is the same for all the cars—12 months or 12,000 miles, whichever comes first. Since all of the alternatives have the same rating on this decision factor, the factor has no effect on the decision process. It could have an effect only if the warranty terms were completely unacceptable to the buyer. In that case the buyer would not buy any of the cars.

Finally, all the decision factors shown in Table 3–1 are features of the cars only. None is a feature of the companies that manufacture the cars, of the dealerships where the cars are sold, or of the salespeople who sell them. Typically, a purchase decision includes factors of this nature also. And the more similar the products, the more important these other decision factors become—particularly the characteristics of the salesperson.

With this information available for a decision, how will the buyer select one car from the six? The decision is dependent upon the alternative-selection approach. Each approach can result in a different selection.

The offsetting approach. The first of the four buyers uses the offsetting approach, in which all factors are considered. Since a $100 difference in price cannot be compared with a 4 mpg difference in gas mileage (as in the case of the Bond and the Pismo), the buyer ranks the cars on all decision factors—not on just some of them. After ranking all of the cars on each decision factor, the buyer's decision matrix looks like the one shown in Table 3–2. Note that all of the factors have been converted to rankings in this table. To select a car, the buyer adds up the rankings for each car and selects the one with the lowest total score. The result is that the buyer selects the Pismo, with a total score of 15.

Table 3–2 Decision matrix for new car selection with ratings converted to rankings

Make of car	Base price	Looks	Power	Interior styling	Interior roominess	Reputation of dealer	Estimated gas mileage	Warranty	Total
Bond	3	3	4	1	1	1	2	1	16
Pismo	2	1	2	1	3	1	4	1	15
Rapier	5	2	1	2	1	3	5	1	20
LaBelle	4	1	3	2	3	1	3	1	18
Volta	1	5	6	3	2	1	1	1	20
Asti	6	3	5	3	2	2	1	1	24

There are two major problems with this approach. First, each factor is given equal importance. A score of 1 on interior roominess is equivalent to a score of 1 on estimated gas mileage. This may be very unrealistic. If gas mileage is more important to the buyer than interior roominess, gas mileage should be weighted more heavily. The buyer would multiply the interior roominess score by 3 if gas mileage were three times as important to the decision as interior roominess.

The second problem with the approach is that differences between ratings on some factors are distorted in the ranking process. When the price factor is ranked, the difference of $100 between the Bond and the Pismo becomes a difference of 1 in the ranking scheme. But the difference of $200 between the Rapier and the Asti also becomes a difference of 1. This is appropriate only if the buyer feels there is no difference between $100 and $200. Hardly likely! This problem is more serious than the first problem mentioned above, but it can be overcome by making the rankings proportional to the buyer's preferences. Then the price ranking would be:

Bond	3
Pismo	2
Rapier	6
LaBelle	5
Volta	1
Asti	8

In this case the proportional ranking scale for the price decision factor does not alter the decision, but in other cases it could.

The offsetting approach derives its name from the fact that a poor score on one decision factor can be offset by a good score on another. The only requirement for an alternative to be selected is that the total score be the smallest. No restrictions are placed on any one decision factor. This is not the case in any of the other three approaches.

The dictionary approach. In using the dictionary approach, the buyer makes the selection on the basis of the most important decision factor. Other decision factors are used only if there is a tie between two or more alternatives on the most important factor. If there is a tie, the buyer uses the second most important factor to make the selection, and so on. This is the same way a word is found in a dictionary. If the first letters are different, it is not necessary to look at the second letters. The second letters are used only if the first letters are the same.

Suppose that the second buyer in our example uses the dictionary approach. The most important factor is price; the buyer simply wants the cheapest car available. Using this criterion, the Volta would be selected because it is the cheapest.

If the buyer considers the $100 difference between the Volta and the Pismo insignificant, there is a tie on the most important factor. The buyer is indifferent between the Volta and the Pismo. Then the buyer must use the second most important factor which, for purposes of this illustration, is estimated gas mileage. Considering this second factor, the Volta would be chosen, because its gas mileage is significantly better than the gas mileage of the Pismo.

A danger with using the dictionary approach is that the selection is made purely on the basis of one factor. The alternative chosen could be very inadequate with respect to other decision factors, but that alternative would still be chosen if it had the highest rating on the most important factor.

The "good-enough-on-all-factors" approach. The "good-enough-on-all-factors" approach considers all the factors, but not in the same way they are considered in the offsetting approach. With the offsetting approach, a very poor score on one factor is offset by a very good score on another. This is not the case with this approach. The good-enough-on-all-factors approach requires that any alternative selected be at least acceptable on all factors. It is not necessary that the alternative even be very good on all factors, only that it meet some minimum level on each one.

Suppose that the third car buyer in the example uses this approach. The consumer has established the following minimum requirements: (1) the car must be base priced no more than $8,000, (2) it must be one of the top four in looks, (3) it must be one of the top four in power, (4) it must have at least an OK interior styling, (5) it must have adequate interior room, (6) it must get at least 23 mpg, and (7) the dealer must be reliable. Table 3–1 shows that the only car that meets all of these criteria is the Bond. The Pismo would meet these specifications except for its tight interior compartment. Volta meets the price constraint but fails on looks, power, and interior styling. If none of the cars had met all of the buyer's minimum requirements, then the buyer would have had to decide whether to lower some of the requirements or not to buy a car at all.

The "good-enough-on-at-least-one-factor" approach. Gathering information can be a costly, time-consuming process. For this reason many buyers cannot afford to assemble as much information as there is in Table 3–1 when making a purchase decision. Instead they choose the "good-enough-on-at-least-one-factor" approach.

Since buyers using this approach do not want to shop any more than necessary, they decide upon the absolute minimum requirements their selections must meet. Once these minimums are established, the buyer shops until an alternative is found that meets the requirements. If more than one factor must be met for the minimum needs, it would still be a variation of the good-enough-on-at-least-one-factor approach.

Imagine that the fourth car buyer sets the following absolute minimum standards for a new car: it can cost no more than $8,000 and it must get at least 23 mpg. This buyer asks about cost and gas mileage when shopping. If the first dealer visited is the Bond dealer, the consumer stops shopping and buys the Bond. If the first dealer visited is the Asti dealer, the buyer goes to a second dealer because the Asti is priced too high. Now if the next dealer visited is the Volta dealer, a Volta is purchased. This example illustrates how the order in which the buyer obtains information helps to determine which of the alternatives is selected. Note that the buyer does not necessarily get the most preferred car using this approach. It is obvious that the Volta is far better than the Bond. It is lower priced and it gets better gas mileage. But this is not important to the buyer, who uses this approach to get the best possible buy with minimal shopping.

The final choice

These examples of the alternative-selection process are extreme. Ultimate consumers and industrial buyers do not actually draw up a grid of information like that shown in Table 3–1. That was done only to illustrate each of the selection approaches. Few buyers calculate which alternative is the proper one based on some mathematical formula. Instead, most buyers use mental processes that resemble those described here but are performed subconsciously. Further, buyers rarely, if ever, use only one of these alternative-selection approaches; most use a combination of approaches in making their purchase decisions. For example, the good-enough-on-all-factors approach could be used to eliminate certain products from consideration, and then the offsetting approach could be used to select one from those remaining.

The salesperson who understands that buyers often collect and evaluate large amounts of information when making a purchase decision realizes that there are two things to be considered in the development of a sales presentation: (1) which characteristics of the product the buyer considers as a factor in the decision, and (2) how the buyer will make the selection.

Assuming that the buyer accepts the product as one of the available alternatives, the salesperson must determine what features of the product, the company, and the salesperson will be considered in the selection decision. Once this has been determined, the salesperson can begin to prepare the sales presentation. It is clear at this point what must be included in the presentation, but it is not clear what relative emphasis to place on each part of the presentation. Knowing which alternative-selection approach the buyer uses will indicate which factors to emphasize.

If the buyer uses the offsetting approach, all the factors should be emphasized according to their relative weights in the decision, with the most important factors receiving the greatest emphasis. If the buyer uses the dictionary approach, only the most important factors deserve emphasis. The same is true if the buyer uses the good-enough-on-at-least-one-factor approach, but if the good-enough-on-all-factors approach is used, it is important to show the buyer that the product exceeds all of the minimum requirements.

It is possible that the reader is wondering whether a salesperson can learn to recognize which factors are included in a decision and how the various factors are treated in the selection of an alternative. The answer is yes! Experience improves the salesperson's ability to identify the factors used in a decision or to identify the selection approach used, but even the inexperienced can do both of these things reasonably well.

Postpurchase evaluation

Once an alternative has been selected from those available, the purchase decision process does not end. The buyer still must decide whether the purchase has been a wise one. The buying decision usually cannot be changed at this point, but in observing the results of a purchase decision the buyer can learn a great deal that will be useful in the next one.

Most buyers have an extensive internal source of information, much of which has been gathered from making earlier purchase decisions and using previously purchased products. The last step in the purchase decision process is really the first step in all subsequent purchase decisions.

While most ultimate consumers make their postpurchase evaluations informally, industrial buyers typically use formal review procedures for this purpose. Suppliers are reviewed on delivery performance, quality, and service. In many firms each supplier is called in one or more times a year and advised of its past performance, as well as what improvements must be made in order to remain a supplier to the firm.

Ultimate consumers do much the same thing, but on a very informal basis. Ask any consumer which grocery store is the most pleasant to shop in, or which is the cleanest, or which has the best prices, and chances are the answer will be on the tip of the tongue. Consumers do not consciously record information about each store; they simply make a mental note of all their shopping experiences.

Cognitive dissonance. The theory of cognitive dissonance is useful in understanding postpurchase behavior.[12] The term *cognitive disso-*

nance refers to the mental state of an individual who feels that his or her attitudes and behavior are inconsistent.

Purchase decisions can create cognitive dissonance in two ways. First, a buyer may feel that the performance of a recently purchased product is not as expected. What was thought to be a wise decision turns out to be a poor one. The person believed himself or herself to be a capable decision maker but the results have not proven this so, and therefore cognitive dissonance is experienced. To eliminate dissonance one can (1) return the product, (2) change expectations for the product's performance, or (3) mentally minimize the importance of the purchase.

A salesperson can play an important role in the reduction of cognitive dissonance. If the seller had made sure that the buyer's expectations were consistent with the product's performance, cognitive dissonance would never have arisen. But even if the salesperson is unable to influence the buyer's expectations before the purchase, there are things that can be done after the purchase to minimize the customer's dissonance. The salesperson can ask the buyer to exchange the product for another that performs more consistently with the buyer's expectations. If this is not possible, the salesperson can try to show that the buyer's expectations are unreasonable and should be made more consistent with the product's performance. The salesperson may also be able to show the buyer how the product's performance can be improved by using it differently or by incorporating accessories to improve its performance.

Cognitive dissonance also arises when a buyer reviews a purchase decision and wonders whether it was the best one. In every purchase decision one alternative is chosen and the others are rejected. The buyer concludes that the alternative selected is the best one, all things considered, but the chosen alternative usually has certain bad features and the rejected ones have several good features. Dissonance occurs when the buyer concentrates on the bad features of the chosen alternative or on the good features of the rejected ones.

The salesperson can play an important role in minimizing this type of dissonance. The best way is to remind the buyer of the product's positive features. There are three other approaches: (1) to minimize the negative aspects of the product, (2) to stress the negative aspects of the rejected products, and (3) to minimize the positive aspects of the rejected products. If a salesperson uses either of the last two approaches, the buyer may feel that the discussion is too one-sided, so the best approach is to stress the positive aspects of the product purchased.

INFLUENCES ON THE PURCHASE DECISION PROCESS

Each purchase decision is peculiar both to the individual making the decision and to the particular decision being made. The process itself differs for each decision. As we have noted, there are at least four different ways to select one alternative from a group of several. The speed of the purchase decision and the relative importance of each factor considered are also subject to the desires and whims of the buyer.

A buyer has a complex set of values, beliefs, attitudes, opinions, needs, goals, wants, and feelings. All of these characteristics, taken together, determine the buyer's predispositions. *Predispositions* are the tendencies of individuals to behave in certain ways in certain situations and to make their behavior consistent over time. Without predispositions, accurate prediction of human behavior (and of buyer behavior) would be impossible. For this reason, it is important for salespeople to understand the sources of predispositions.

A buyer's predispositions are determined by (1) individual characteristics of the buyer, (2) group influences, and (3) cultural influences.

Individual buyer characteristics

Hundreds of individual characteristics affect a buyer's predispositions. Some of the most important influences are cited below.

Demographic characteristics. The word *demographics* comes from the Greek words *dēmos,* meaning people, and *graphōs,* meaning write. Demographics are written descriptions of people, indicating characteristics such as marital status, age, height, weight, sex, residence, and education.

Marketers can learn a great deal about a person's buying behavior solely on the basis of demographics. Almost anyone can predict with a high degree of accuracy what a teenager will do with a sudden windfall of money—probably buy a car, a stereo system, or some new clothes. A young married person will act quite differently (also quite predictably) in the same situation. A good salesperson learns to watch for differences in tastes arising from differences in education, age, or location of residence.

Life-cycle stages. As buyers progress through life, their needs, wants, goals, and attitudes change. Much has been written about the generation gap, an outward sign of these changes.

A person's life can be described as a series of stages or cycles. One life-cycle classification scheme divides households into categories based on the age of the head of the household, marital status, and the presence or absence of children.[13]

It is possible to describe in some detail the purchase tendencies of people as they progress through these stages. For instance, recent studies have shown that single people are a growing segment of American society which tends to be relatively affluent, highly mobile, very self-concerned, oriented to immediate enjoyment rather than long-term concerns, fashion and appearance conscious, and active in leisure pursuits. As a result, singles are very interested in apartment furnishings, automobiles, and toiletries and cosmetics.[14]

Socioeconomic characteristics. Every person can be quite accurately described by membership in a particular social class. Usually people are assigned to a social class on the basis of two factors—their occupations and their income. Individuals with higher incomes are normally members of higher social classes. Certain occupations do not follow this rule; ministers and college professors usually are not highly paid, but they are thought of as members of the high-middle and upper classes. As with demographics and life-cycle stages, a person's social class will influence purchasing behavior.

Group influences

Every consumer belongs to many different groups. Probably the most universal group is the family, but family members also belong to athletic teams, service clubs, social cliques, school classes, business organizations, and labor unions—the list is endless.

Groups affect buying behavior in two ways. First, they provide information. Much of what a buyer learns is gained from group experiences. Second, and more important, groups provide standards of behavior by telling buyers *how* they should act. If a buyer does not act in accordance with accepted modes of group behavior, social pressure is applied to bring comformity.

A salesperson must be conscious of the effects of groups on the behavior of buyers. Earlier in this chapter mention was made of the existence of multiple responsibilities in most industrial purchase situations. Often, the most influential person in an industrial purchase decision is not the purchasing agent but someone in engineering, manufacturing, or the laboratory. To be successful the industrial sales representative has to learn to recognize who is influential and to change sales tactics accordingly. Spending too much time with the wrong people is wasted effort. Industrial salespeople describe situations in which they spend most of their time out in the plant selling, rather than in the purchasing department. This practice is known as *backdoor selling*.

**An aging population—An important demographic
feature of the modern marketplace**

Age is a key demographic variable in the marketplace. A person's likelihood of buying both new and established products is often related to their
age. But earlier rules of thumb may no longer be appropriate. America is
now characterized by an aging population.

The median age for Americans was less than 28 in 1970. By 1981 it
will be 30; and by the year 2000, the median age will be 35. The figure
shows how the age group mix will change in the years ahead.*

The shifting mix of population groups

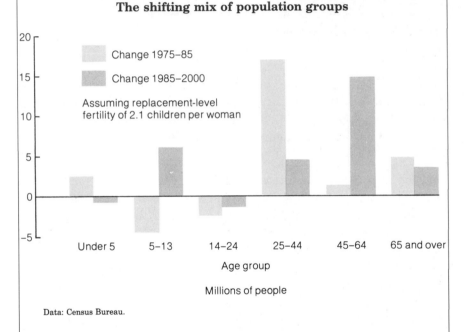

Data: Census Bureau.

It seems certain that these shifts will have a considerable impact on
the markets for certain products and services. Professional salespeople
should be cognizant of such basic structural changes (age distribution is
not the only change occurring in our economy) and be preparing to meet
a different consumer in the future.

*Reprinted from the February 20, 1978 issue of *Business Week* by special permission. Copyright © 1978 by
McGraw-Hill, New York N.Y. All rights reserved.

Culture is the common link among a group of individuals. It represents the ideas, customs, skills, and arts of a given people in a given period. To illustrate what a culture is, think of the differences in the behavior, attitudes, morals, and philosophies of people raised in a Western culture and those in an Eastern or Oriental culture.

Cultural influences

A culture can have a significant impact on the purchasing behavior of its members. To sell a product in another culture may even necessitate a change in product design. For example, it has been found that people in the Netherlands prefer mild cigars, while the French prefer somewhat stronger tobacco.[15]

This chapter has shown that the professional salesperson must know about buyers and how they buy. To satisfy customer wants, a seller must understand customers' needs and how they can be satisfied.

SUMMARY

A distinction must be drawn between the buying behavior of ultimate consumers and that of industrial buyers. The primary differences between the two types of buyers are: (1) industrial buyers use fewer personal decision factors, (2) industrial buyers typically follow detailed policies in their purchases, and (3) industrial purchase decisions are normally made by more than one person.

Buying is a process—a series of acts, not a single act. Because of this, buying decisions can vary greatly with respect to the time involved and the nature of the process itself. The process is divided into four stages: (1) need identification, (2) information search, (3) alternative selection, and (4) postpurchase evaluation.

Buyers purchase to satisfy a variety of needs. A salesperson can play an important role in helping them recognize unsatisfied needs and find ways by which they can be satisfied. The salesperson is one of the major sources of consumer information.

Four different approaches to alternative selection are: (1) the offsetting approach, (2) the dictionary approach, (3) the good-enough-on-all-factors approach, and (4) the good-enough-on-at-least-one-factor approach. Knowing which alternative-selection approach a buyer will take and which decision factors will be used can be of immense importance to the salesperson in the development of the sales presentation.

The last step in the purchasing process, postpurchase evaluation, is the first step in all subsequent purchase decisions. The theory of cognitive dissonance can contribute much to understanding postpurchase evaluation.

The great variety in purchase decisions is a direct result of the different individual, socioeconomic, and cultural characteristics of the people making the decisions.

REVIEW QUESTIONS/DISCUSSION QUESTIONS/EXERCISES

1. Define the following terms:
    a. Sealed bids.   f. Predispositions.
    b. Multiple-source purchasing.   g. Demographics.
    c. Sole-source purchasing.   h. Back-door selling.
    d. Needs.   i. Culture.
    e. Cognitive dissonance.

2. Describe a purchase experience you have had in which the salesperson was sincerely interested in understanding and satisfying your particular needs. Describe an experience where just the opposite was the case. Which salesperson was more effective? Why?

3. Can a single product satisfy more than one of Maslow's needs? Explain.

4. Arrange an interview with an industrial buyer and ask the buyer to describe a recent purchase decision. Try to determine *(a)* which decision factors were considered; *(b)* whether company policies affected the decision; and *(c)* who, besides the buyer, took part in the decision.

5. What is cognitive dissonance? Give an example based on personal experience.

6. How should an automobile salesperson's presentation to an ultimate consumer differ from a presentation to an industrial buyer?

7. What is Maslow's theory of needs? Show how each need can be satisfied by buying something.

8. Select a volunteer, preferably the instructor. The volunteer has to answer truthfully questions the class asks about his or her demographic characteristics, life-cycle, socioeconomic characteristics, and personality. (To protect the volunteer's privacy, some questions may be answered with general descriptive statements.) Using only the answers to these questions, the class should try to determine the type of car he or she drives, where he or she buys clothes, and other things about the person's shopping habits.

9. What questions can a real estate agent ask in order to learn whether a buyer wants a house to satisfy the need for safety or the need for esteem?

10. List five internal and five external sources of information available to an industrial buyer.

11. Examine a recent decision you made to go to a particular movie or restaurant. Describe in detail the entire purchase decision process.

12. Is it unethical for a salesperson to sell a quality wine by appealing to a buyer's need for esteem rather than physiological needs? Is the seller who appeals to the buyer's need for esteem trying to sell the buyer something unnecessary?

13. Should a salesperson ever try to change the way a buyer selects an alternative? Explain.

14. What are the four primary methods of selecting alternatives? Describe each of these methods.

15. Is it possible for a salesperson to create a need in the mind of a buyer? If not, can a salesperson show a buyer that there may be certain needs that the buyer does not recognize?

16. Ask a loan officer at a local bank how he or she decides whether or not to grant a loan application. To what extent does this process resemble the purchase decision process of an industrial buyer?

17. Can much be learned about a buyer's individual characteristics, group influences, or cultural influences without questioning the buyer directly? Illustrate.

18. Under what circumstances would a salesperson prefer buyers who use the dictionary approach to alternative selection to buyers who use the good-enough-on-all-factors approach?

19. Describe the needs you hope to satisfy by reading this book.

20. Select a person to role play a disgruntled customer returning a toaster to a department store. The toaster does not do the things it is supposed to do, and the customer has found one exactly like it in a discount stores costing 10 percent less. Let the rest of the class suggest various ways a salesperson might reduce this customer's cognitive dissonance.

CASE 3–1 THE DYNAFORGE COMPANY

Tom Alves, sales engineer for the Dynaforge Company, has just received a call from Hank Schoof, general manager of the Exacto Corporation plant in Lima, Ohio. Within the next three weeks Schoof wants to negotiate a contract for 40,000 fan blades.

Exacto buys blades from Dynaforge as titanium forgings and then machines, tests, and inspects the blades before shipping them to its customer, Universal Products. Universal Products installs the blades in jet engines. Dynaforge's position as Exacta's sole source of the blade is in jeopardy because Toronto Corporation, a small forge shop in Indiana, has submitted a bid to make the forgings for $39 each. Dynaforge's price is $43.

The largest titanium blade forging Toronto Coporation has ever produced is half the size of this one. Alves estimates that to get the $39 price, Schoof has to agree to pay Toronto Corporation tooling costs of more than $20,000 and to buy over $100,000 in additional equipment to be installed in Toronto's plant. Schoof has never confirmed or denied this, but he did admit that he had some reservations about Toronto's ability to meet the technical specifications and the delivery requirements because of its inexperience with this size blade. All of Toronto's other work for Exacto has been excellent, however.

Universal Products is Exacto's largest and most important customer, and its most important purchase is the fan blade. Exacto cannot afford to lose the blade to competition.

The Dynaforge Company has supplied the fan blade to Exacto for several years, and Schoof is extremely pleased with its performance. Several price reductions due to technological breakthroughs have been passed on to Exacto during this time, and improvements in forging the blade have resulted in economies to Exacto. Schoof has noted this pleasant and rewarding relationship between the two companies on more than one occasion.

Since the fan blade will be produced for several more years, Alves does not want to lose this contract. But he does not want to meet the $39 price if he does not have to because Dynaforge makes very little profit at that price and his performance is measured on profits, not sales. Further, he knows that recent increases in wages and in the price of titanium will necessitate a price increase to about $45 to maintain the existing profit margin.

Because this is the largest blade contract ever negotiated, Alves feels that Schoof might give some of the business to Toronto. In Alves' opinion, Schoof is a gambler and has made riskier decisions than this before.

Alves' decision will be less difficult if the vice president of marketing, Bob Beamer, insists on a specified profit margin, so he calls him. Beamer says that Alves can meet the $39 price if it is necessary to keep the blade business.

Questions

1. What factors should Alves consider before deciding on a strategy for his negotiations with Schoof?

2. If you were Alves, what would you do?

CASE 3–2: COACH JOLLEY ASSESSES HIS RECRUITING STRATEGY

Coach Bill Jolley, head football coach at the University of the Atlantic, was going over the list of graduating seniors. It became readily apparent that he had several positions to fill in the upcoming recruiting season. He decided that he better start laying out his strategy immediately. He picked up his phone and dialed Jack Himebach's number.

Coach Jolley: Jack, would you please come in here? I think we ought to go over our personnel needs, position by position.

Soon Himebach, Coach Jolley's offensive line coach and head recruiter, walked in and took a seat on the couch across from Jolley's desk. Jolley liked Himebach and always enjoyed developing player personnel strategies with him.

Coach Jolley: Jack, as you know graduation hit us hard this year and we have quite a few positions to fill. Fortunately our depth returning from last year will take care of most of these voids. However, there are four positions which I am most worried about—a flanker, a back-up quarterback, a punter, and an outside linebacker.

Himebach: I agree, the kids returning from last year can fill the remaining positions. What kind of young men do you think we ought to look for to fill these four key positions?

Coach Jolley: Let's talk about the flanker first. He should be fast and have a good pair of hands. Other than that he can have just average talent. For the back-up quarterback, it's another story. He must be an all-around athlete; he should have a strong and accurate throwing arm, have good speed, good size, and be smart. If something were to happen to our starting quarterback, this kid would suddenly find himself running the whole offense. For the punter I want just one thing, he has to be able to kick the ball! There is nothing else he has to be able to do. Finally, the outside linebacker. This kid should be quick, have reasonable size, be able to hit hard and know football because we depend on him to read plays. But he doesn't have to be huge; I'd much rather he be quick and smart.

Himebach: Seems like you and I agree on our needs. There's a young man in Raleigh who really fills the bill at outside linebacker. Plus I think he'll accept if we offer him a scholarship.

Coach Jolley: Go get him.

Himebach: OK, no sooner said than done. What about that blue-chipper from Goldsboro for the back-up quarterback?

Coach Jolley: I don't think so. He's not very big and as I recall his time in the 40-yard dash isn't that great.

Himebach: Right on both counts but he's got a great arm and he's one of the most savvy high school players I've ever seen. He's a winner; he makes up for his lack of size and speed.

Coach Jolley: I tend to agree with you. I could always alter the offense a bit to make up for his lack of speed and his size is really only a problem when we play certain teams. Try to find somebody who fits our needs better but don't turn him down; if we don't find somebody better he'll do fine.

Himebach: What about the Jackson kid from Portsmouth for the flanker position?

Coach Jolley: He's certainly quick enough but I'm worried about his hands. The films I've seen of him showed several passes that he dropped which I thought he should have caught. If one of my ends doesn't have good hands, he's useless to me. I don't think Jackson can make this team.

Himebach: Alright, what about the younger brother of Tommy Buscek? You remember him, the kid who caught the winning pass in the East-West All-Star Game?

Coach Jolley: Yeah! Can we get him to sign? I'd love to see him wearing the good old orange and blue!

Himebach: I'll see what I can do; I understand that several other schools are interested in him also. That leaves only the punter. What about the Russ boy who plays for the high school right here in town? He certainly can kick but that's all he can do! In fact it amazes me how someone with so little athletic ability can kick a ball so far and straight.

Coach Jolley: I don't care if he falls down after he kicks it. In fact, I don't care if he lays down after he kicks it! Just so he kicks it high enough and far enough to prevent a runback.

Himebach: Sounds like we've covered all the positions. How about stopping for a beer on the way home?

Questions

1. What different alternative selection approaches are evident in this brief conversation?

2. Why does Coach Jolley use different approaches to select players for the different positions? Does this make sense?

KEY POINTS

- Planning is a projection of a course of action into the future to attain a desired objective.

- An objective is an answer to the question of where or what we want to be at some future date.

- A plan designates the steps necessary in order to achieve an objective and the order in which they are to be taken.

- Planning flows from the top down through the company's organizational structure.

- The key to success in marketing planning is the involvement of sales personnel.

- Two basic decisions are involved in marketing planning—selecting customer targets, and determining the makeup of marketing efforts.

- Primary emphasis for manufacturers of either consumer or industrial goods is on promotion and its sales element.

- The major advantage for selling is a salesperson's uniqueness, whereas for advertising it is low contact cost.

- The roles of personal selling and advertising change, depending upon the market stage.

- Effective promotion depends upon effective communication.

- The communication process is made up of five elements: source, sender, message, receiver, and feedback.

- In personal selling, customers distinguish between the salesperson and the company represented.

- Salespeople are judged by their sales presentations.

- Selectivity and perceived risk on the part of the customer affect the success of communications.

Chapter

4

SELLING'S ROLE IN MARKETING STRATEGY

Mike Curto, group vice president—steel of the United States Steel Corporation, is responsible for the manufacture, distribution, and marketing of this $9 billion giant's primary product. Over 75 percent of U.S. Steel's sales are in steel. Mike has a sales force of 190 salespeople selling about $7 billion of steel each year or over $35 million per salesperson. They serve over 10,000 customers.

One of Mike's major concerns is that his sales force understand all of the facets of this complex corporation. "We're trying to get our people oriented to the total business venture, so that when they make decisions, their broad knowledge of the entire profit picture will help them make the proper decisions," Mike emphasizes.[1]

CORPORATE PLANS AND THE SALES FORCE

Much top-level effort goes into determining objectives or goals for the firm, developing plans to reach these objectives, and setting up ways to measure accomplishment. Often little is done, however, to inform salespeople of sales and marketing plans or to involve them in any way in the planning process. Salespeople look at their jobs in terms of existing contacts with present customers, and many of them have trouble seeing how their selling actions fit into overall company operations.

Sometimes the marketing done by top management makes little impression on the day-to-day performance of the sales force. As one highly placed executive who recognized this predicament said: "What good is all this top-level planning if the salesmen won't change their ways? We plan until we are blue in the face, but it doesn't seem to motivate the fellows on the firing line."[2]

WHAT IS PLANNING?

It has been said that all firms plan, but there are wide differences in how they go about it. At one extreme are firms that make detailed long-range projections. The people who do the planning are specifically assigned this task as part of their jobs. At the other extreme are firms that devote most of their attention to current operations; planning is limited to whatever is required for informal sales projections.

Planning can be defined as the process of determining the necessary steps to be taken to attain a desired future state or condition of business. The desired future state is called an *objective* or *goal*. The steps to be taken in attaining an objective make up a *plan*. The four steps in the decision sequence are (1) setting the objectives, (2) determining the steps to reach those objectives, (3) setting the plan in action, and (4) checking the progress of the plan and reappraising the objectives.

Objectives and goals

The desired state—called an objective by some, a goal by others—is the key element in planning (Figure 4–1). It is the answer to the question of where or what we want to be at some future date. Typical objectives for a firm that have a direct effect on the sales force are specified increases in sales volume, profits, or market share (the firm's percentage of the total sales in a market). Increases in sales volume or market share call for better sales performance, and an increase in profits might call for concentration on the more profitable products. Specification of a minimum order size is another way sales personnel might be affected by the objective of increased profits.

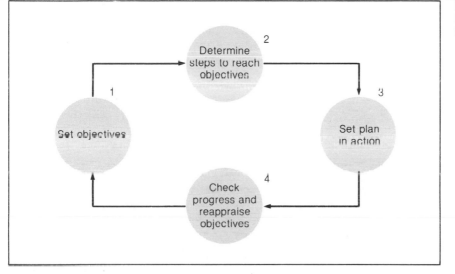

**Figure 4–1
Decision sequence
in planning**

Much less often the objective of management is to keep the company at current levels of business. For instance, an upsurge in bicycle sales has put one of the biggest suppliers of bicycle seats in the position of selling all it can produce. In this case, the job of the salesperson is very difficult, since it involves the allocation of a limited supply of product to customers, both old and new.

There are two good reasons for putting objectives in specific terms. The first is that the salespeople will know exactly what is expected of them; there is very little room for misunderstanding. Second, sales performance can be measured objectively, and salespeople know that what they do will be judged in comparison to these objective measures.

Sales and marketing objectives must also be both challenging and reasonable. Objectives should be set neither too high nor too low. One good way to get reasonable objectives is to involve the sales force actively in the planning process. What management wants should be related to the views and ideas of those who are in daily contact with the marketplace. When salespeople get involved in planning, they become more enthusiastic about meeting the specified goals.

Management plans often have to be compromised with market conditions as reported by salespeople. The more market-oriented a firm is, the greater is the role of the sales force as the "voice of the marketplace." Salespeople are a major source of information in marketing planning.

Implementing a plan

A plan is a course of action that designates the steps necessary to achieve an objective and the order in which they are to be taken. Normally there are at least two ways of reaching an objective. The planner has to decide which path is best for the company.

Assume a firm wants to achieve a certain sales volume for a new product in the first year. Suppose further that there are three alternatives:

1. Use present salespeople.
2. Develop a new selling organization.
3. Use wholesalers.

Each of the choices will have a different effect on the company's salespeople and the job they are to do. The greatest change will come with the first alternative, which means that present salespeople will have to learn about the new product and the new customers for this product. Their territories will be larger with the addition of new customers. They may even have to call on different people in the organization to sell the new product to current customers. A major problem for salespeople will be how to allocate their time between present and new customers.

The second choice is to develop a separate selling organization for the new product. This alternative will have a much smaller effect on the firm's sales force. Some of them may be asked to transfer and will have to be retrained. There may also be a few changes in territorial assignments, and customers may be shifted from one salesperson to another.

The third alternative will not have any effect on salespeople unless management selects a few members of the present sales force to work with the various wholesaler sales personnel. Once this selection is made, the decision maker must set the plan in action, as shown in Figure 4–1.

The final step in the planning sequence is to evaluate how effectively the decision has been carried out. Sales personnel can provide prompt feedback on the progress of marketing plans.

Salespeople should be part of each of the four steps in the planning process. They bring market realism to both objectives and plans. They also are responsible for setting many marketing plans into operation

---

Boeing employs a family strategy

Boeing has learned a lot from its dual disasters—the huge costs of producing the first 747s and the government cancellation of the supersonic transport project. The firm's workforce had to be cut by more than half with the layoffs creating a major economic crisis in Seattle, where Boeing is headquartered.

Boeing is now financially healthy and the workforce has been expanded as the world's airlines are again buying new equipment. Boeing's strategy is to cover a variety of possible market conditions with an unmatched assortment of planes.

Board Chairman and Chief Executive T. A. Wilson puts it this way, "I don't think you necessarily know how a market is going to develop." For instance, Boeing did not expect the continued demand for its medium range 727. But direct flights between destinations intended to bypass routing through congested airports like Chicago have led to new sales of the 727, the only plane of its type. Mr. Wilson comments, "I can't say we projected that and hit it on the head." But he adds, "You have a family of airplanes and try to cover the market."

Boeing's strategy is evident in its new entries, all targeted for the 1980s. The 757, 767, and 777 will all be more fuel efficient, an important feature in the modern marketplace. The 767 and 777, both in the 180–210 seat range, will be positioned somewhere between today's 727s and the wide body aircraft.

Personal selling is also very important at Boeing. The Board Chairman often calls on customers himself. Boeing's top management is actively involved in the sales effort. Eastern Airlines' Frank Borman says: "The people who come here (from Boeing) to sell planes have direct access to Boeing's president and chairman, that's unusual."

and can provide quick feedback on a plan's acceptance and progress. The motivational advantages of involving the sales force in planning should not be overlooked.

TRANSLATING MARKETING PLANS INTO SALES ACTIONS

The flow of planning in a company is from the top down within the framework of the company's organizational structure. Figure 4–2 traces the flow of planning in a business organization.

The first act of planning for management is to define the business it wants the company to be in. This definition or philosophy gives direction to all the efforts made in behalf of the company. It also tells salespeople and other employees what the company is trying to do.[3] Most business definitions are stated in broad terms. The definition for the company in the example includes the line of business (communi-

**Figure 4–2
Company objectives related to objectives for sales personnel**

Definition of business of firm:
To combine research leadership in communications with aggressive marketing

Company — Increase profitability

Net profits/Sales

Marketing — Increase marketing profits

Dollars of marketing profit (gross profit less marketing expenses)

Sales — Increase gross profit | Reduce selling expenses

Dollars of gross profit | Expenses/Sales volume

Sales staff — Increase gross profits — sales territory | Reduce selling expense — sales territory

Dollars of gross profit | Expenses/Sales

Adapted from Ernest C. Miller, *Objectives and Standards of Performance: In Marketing Management,* AMA Research Study #85 (New York: American Management Association, Inc., 1967).

cations research) and how the company will operate in the market-place (aggressively).

Once the business has been defined, the second step in planning is to identify company objectives. These are in areas critical to the success of the company in the long-run. Market standing and profitability are two important areas for salespeople and others in marketing. Another might be product innovation. Figure 4–2 considers only the profitability goal, to be measured in terms of net profits as a percentage of sales.

The planning job now passes to marketing management. Looking at the profitability objective, marketing management must ask: How can marketing help to increase company profits and still remain aggressive? Marketing profit is defined as gross profit less marketing expenses. Gross profit is the difference between the selling price of a product and the cost to produce it.

Now the chain reaction of planning has reached sales. Guided by the goal of increased profits, sales management knows there are two major tasks for the sales force. One is to increase gross profits and the other is to reduce selling expenses.

To reach these two objectives, sales management may adopt a *key-account strategy*. In this strategy sales personnel concentrate their efforts on the major accounts in their territories. Usually a small number of customers account for most of a company's profitable business; these *key accounts* are those customers that are the most profitable to the company. With this strategy, salespeople are asked to stop calling on present customers that are judged to be marginal or unprofitable, thus allowing them to spend more sales time with key accounts. For the company in Figure 4–2, a *marginal customer* might be defined as one whose yearly purchases currently or potentially produce less than a certain amount of gross profit dollars.

Now the planning job falls to the individual salesperson, who must decide how to put the sales strategies into effect in a sales territory. A sales representative for the National Starch and Chemical Corporation analyzes four aspects of the selling situation in developing for the customer a sales plan in line with sales strategies. The salesperson takes a good look at the customer, the customer's needs, the product, and the competition (Figure 4–3).

In another company, Hooker Chemical Corporation, the salesperson formulates what is called a *customer sales plan* (CSP) at the point of sale. In setting up a sales plan for each customer, the salesperson goes through five steps.

1. Development of territorial data on accounts, prospects, and competitors.
2. Determination of planning accounts and sales volume goals for customers and prospects termed major.
3. Development of individual customer sales plan to include sales goal, sales strategy, customer profile, as well as programs and actions.
4. Evaluation of the sales plan to assure a sound investment with a high probability of success.
5. Implementation and measurement by field sales representatives.[4]

In developing a sales plan for each customer, the salesperson is completing the planning job that began with the original definition of the firm's business. Having a sales plan for each customer is nothing more than selling by objectives. The salesperson plans before entering a sales situation rather than reacting to whatever develops in the sales interview. This is not to say that the salesperson who preplans can do without the skills necessary to spot a situation and react quickly. But the chances of selling success are much greater if selling instincts are combined with planning skills.[5]

In developing sales plans for each customer, the salesperson could follow an outline such as the *sales plan* shown in Figure 4–4, which

Figure 4–3
Sales planning in terms of the customer

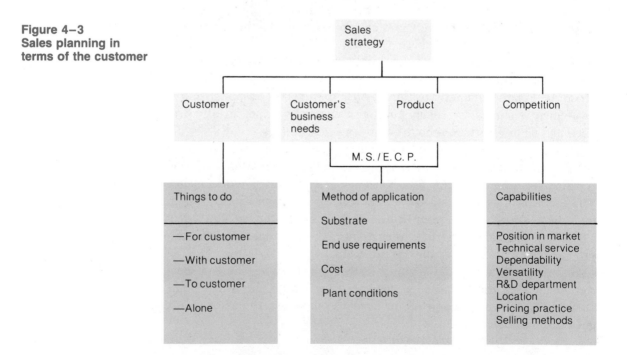

includes key accounts as well as other less profitable accounts. When the salesperson uses profitability to classify customers, the frequency of sales calls made on an account varies in accordance with the account's classification. The salesperson might call on key accounts once a month, or more often if needed; on the next most profitable category of accounts every two or three months; and on the least profitable accounts only three times a year.

---

1. Identify patterns of decision making in purchasing. (Distinguish between decision makers and individuals who merely influence decisions.)
2. Identify present product usage.
3. Identify areas of customer interest.
4. Identify competition.
5. Set up objectives for customer.

**Figure 4–4
Outline of customer
sales plan**

"Have you ever thought of what will happen after you pass away?"

Reprinted by permission The Wall Street Journal.

Developing a sales plan for each sales call is an important dimension of sales planning.

Marketing planners must make two basic decisions. The first concerns selecting the primary customer targets for the firm and the second involves determining the makeup of marketing efforts to be aimed at the selected customer.

**BASIC
MARKETING
PLANNING
DECISIONS**

Selecting customer targets

Many firms realize that attempting to sell to every potential customer is not worthwhile. A more practical approach is to pinpoint a group of customers the firm feels it can best serve and wants to serve.

A firm may be choosing its customers without realizing it. Its product line may appeal to one group of customers more than others. Freight rates may keep the firm from selling outside a certain geographic area, or the location of the firm may make it more convenient for a certain group of customers.

These situations should not be thought of as selecting customer targets, however. Targeting is a conscious and deliberate process of studying the entire market to determine which groups offer the best potential to the company. It is not attempted on a piecemeal basis. Rather, the entire marketing efforts of the company are focused on those consumers selected as targets.

In setting up *customer targets,* the following questions are helpful:

1. What is the strength of the customer's need or desire for the product?
2. How successful have we been in influencing the customer with different sales appeals?
3. What distribution and media channels can be used to reach the customer?
4. How physically accessible is the customer to both the seller and resellers of the product?[6]

The best source of information for the first two questions, which concern present customers, is the salesperson. Marketing research will have to supply the answers for potential customers.

The customer targets picked will be those for which the chances of success are the greatest. The exact number of customer targets depends upon their sales volume in relation to the total sales volume the company feels is necessary for successful operation. In the toy industry, Fisher Price traditionally concentrated on just one customer target, the preschool market. Mattel, on the other hand, sold to a fairly large number of customer targets.

The selection of company targets allows the company to focus its marketing efforts where they can do the most good. When the salesperson can concentrate on one or just a few customer targets, knowledge of customer needs and wants is easier to obtain. This knowledge is essential in the sales process, allowing for improved sales presentations and a resulting increase in sales.

The second basic decision in marketing planning is to determine the makeup of marketing efforts. Management may want a different *marketing mix* for each customer target or the same mix for all.

To get a better understanding of the marketing mix, hypothetical examples of three marketing programs and what might be expected in terms of sales results are shown in Table 4–1. The products for all three competing companies are large kitchen appliances such as ovens, ranges, dishwashers, and refrigerators.

Company A, the most successful of the three competitors, has a complete marketing program. Particular attention is centered on promotion, with one sales representative to demonstrate models at the regional distribution center and another to call on builders. Company B is an example of a company that has not attempted to combine the basic marketing variables. Instead, this company clings to the belief that product quality automatically leads to sales, Company B has not developed a marketing mix, and the result is little demand for their appliances.

Like Company B, Company C seems to be reaching for the same target customer with primary emphasis on the product variable. Company C, however, has paid greater attention to the other market ing variables, and this has fostered a rapid growth in sales. Further emphasis on promotion to stimulate demand and more dealers to handle the appliances could make Company C even more competitive with Company A

The makeup of marketing efforts

Most firms recognize the importance of promotion in their marketing strategy. But they vary in the way they allocate promotion efforts. Table 4–2 indicates that sales management and personal selling are considered most important by the majority of firms, although there are some differences among producers for the various markets.

Industrial goods manufacturers rely principally on sales in their promotional strategies, with little attention to advertising. Research shows sales to be about five times more important than advertising in promoting industrial products. This typical reliance on sales to stimulate industrial demand is disputed by Richard Dempster, vice president—marketing for Black & Decker Manufacturing Co. He believes the sales force does only a limited amount of demand creation for industrial tools and equipment. In his experience, "it was . . . advertising, pricing, or promotion which really created the increased demand—not salesman's activity." The roles he sees for sales personnel are communication of technical information to customers and

The promotion mix

Table 4–1 Example of market reaction to three marketing programs for kitchen appliances

	Company A	*Company B*	*Company C*
Product	Average to fairly good quality. Emphasis on features to increase product convenience. Manufacturer operates repair service.	Very good quality. Emphasis on performance. No authorized repair service.	Superior quality. Emphasis on easy repair. No authorized repair service.
Price	Moderate to high.	Moderate to high.	High.
Promotion	Extensive advertising, both national and local. Large supply of sales aids, demonstration models, and manufacturer's sales personnel available to show and demonstrate models at regional distribution center. Manufacturer's sales representative calls on builders.	Limited national advertising. No local advertising. Only one catalog available in area at repair parts distributor. No demonstration model or manufacturer's sales personnel in area.	Limited national and local advertising. Limited number of sales aids and demonstration models. Distributor has sales personnel available to demonstrate models.
Distribution	Large number of dealers.	No full-time dealers.	Several dealers.
Market reaction	Overwhelming share of area sales.	Almost no sales in area.	Small market share, but fastest growth in area sales.

Element of promotion	Type of industry		
	Industrial goods	Consumer durables	Consumer nondurables
Sales management and personal selling	69.2	47.6	38.1
Broadcast media advertising	0.9 ⎱ 13.4	10.7 ⎱ 26.8	20.9 ⎱ 35.7
Printed media advertising	12.5 ⎰	16.1 ⎰	14.8 ⎰
Special promotional activities	9.6	15.5	15.5
Branding and promotional packaging	4.5	9.5	9.8
Other	3.3	0.6	0.9
Total	100.0	100.0	100.0

Table 4–2
Perceived importance of the elements of promotion (allocation averages based on 100 points)

Source: Adapted from Jon G. Udell, "The Perceived Importance of the Elements of Strategy," *Journal of Marketing* 31 (January 1968): 37, published by the American Marketing Association.

maintenance of good customer relations—in other words, keeping the customer happy.[7]

Advertising does more of the promotional job for manufacturers of consumer products. Indeed, many producers of consumer nondurables believe that advertising is almost as important as sales. Other forms of promotional activity (other than sales and advertising) also take on greater relative importance for consumer goods manufacturers. These other forms, which can be called *sales promotion*, are designed to supplement and strengthen sales and advertising efforts.

Sales promotion varies from samples, coupons, money-refund offers, premiums, contests, and trading stamps to retailer and wholesaler allowances. Also included would be sales force incentives such as sales contests, end-of-year bonuses, and sales meetings. In general, sales promotion works best when closely coordinated with the other promotion tools. "In one study, point-of-purchase displays related to current TV commercials were found to produce 15 percent more sales than similar displays not related to such advertising. In another, a heavy sampling approach along with TV advertising proved more successful than either TV alone or TV with coupons in introducing a product."[8]

Personal selling and advertising

Before making the key decisions regarding the uses of personal selling and advertising, the promotional strategist needs to know two things (1) the characteristics of personal selling and advertising and (2) the basics of marketing communications.

There is an obvious difference between personal selling and advertising as methods of promotion (Table 4–3). Personal selling is a personal, for the most part face-to-face, means of communication. Advertising, on the other hand, is impersonal. Salespeople have the flexibility to adjust to customer reactions, which advertising cannot have. A real estate agent, for example, can find out the type of house a customer is interested in and show only that type of house. The agent does not waste time showing houses that have no interest to the customer, and the sales presentation can be adjusted to relate to a particular customer's interests. The parents may want a large kitchen with modern appliances and a family room with a fireplace. Children may want their own recreation room for parties.

**Table 4–3
General characteristics of personal selling and advertising as promotional methods**

Personal selling	*Advertising*
1. Personal, face to face	1. Impersonal
2. Flexible	2. Inflexible
3. Individual approach	2. General approach
4. Slow market penetration	4. Quick market penetration
5. Costly presentation, usually to target customers	5. Economical presentation, not necessarily to target customers
6. Two-way communication	6. One-way communication
7. Possibility of rebuilding interest	7. One shot at developing interest
8. Ideas tailored to customer	8. Limited number of general ideas
9. Customer carried through reasoning process	9. Suggestions offered
10. No limit on stimuli	10. Limited number of stimuli
11. Much more control over purchasing decison	11. Little control over purchasing decision

Closely allied to flexibility is the individual nature of personal selling as contrasted to the more generalized approach of advertising. Usually a salesperson will focus on one customer or a small group of them, whereas advertising is directed toward broad groups of customers.

Advertising does have the advantage of being a faster and more economical means of contacting customers. A commercial shown on television may reach an audience at a cost of $2 to $10 for every 1,000 viewers, compared to a single sales call, which can cost many times more. Rarely will the sales call be to other than a target customer, however. The same cannot always be said for advertising.

The flexibility and individuality of personal selling make it possible to tailor sales presentations to individual customers. Employing a full range of stimuli, the salesperson can carry a customer through a reasoning process and rebuild interest if it tends to weaken. Advertising is unable to provide this type of unique appeal to the promotion function and is limited in what methods it can use, so there is little wonder that this medium is unable to control the purchasing decision.[9]

Industrial and consumer markets. The differing characteristics of the two methods of promotion discussed above, personal selling and advertising, make it fairly easy to see why personal selling predominates in the promotion of industrial products and advertising gets most of the promotion dollar for consumer products. In industrial marketing, products are typically of a technical nature, and buying motives for the most part are rational. The salesperson has all the advantages in such a market situation, including the capacity to make the sales presentation unique by tailoring ideas to the individual customer and the ability to carry the customer through a reasoning process. The relatively small size and geographic concentration of many industrial markets make it possible to utilize the advantages of personal selling at a reasonable cost. Another offsetting factor may be the large number of dollars involved in an industrial sale.

The greater reliance on advertising in the promotion of consumer products is also understandable. Consumer markets tend to be large and widely scattered. The marketer of consumer products gets more for the promotion dollar with advertising and is not as likely to be concerned with loss of control over the individual purchasing decision.

Market stages. Another way to consider personal selling and advertising is to look at their roles in three market stages (Figure 4–5). These stages are given below.

> *Pretransactional.* Advertising is assigned the dominant promotional role. In readying the market for the salesperson, advertising is given such specific objectives as (1) product promotion; (2) image development; and (3) production of leads for the sales force. The task of the salesperson is to reinforce advertising efforts in the cultivation of the market. This requires an awareness of the firm's advertising efforts. Particularly important is the prompt follow-up of leads produced by advertising.
>
> *Transactional.* It is common for sales personnel to handle this phase alone. The basic job in what most of us think of as personal sell-

ing is to get the order or desired customer response. The job many companies give advertising in this phase is the development of a constant flow of customers.

Posttransactional.   The emphasis here shifts back to advertising because a lot of what has to be done in this stage can be done economically by advertising. Market contact is substantially lower in cost using advertising. The salesperson's job is to follow through to be sure the customer gets the maximum satisfaction from the purchase. Even if the salesperson does not do the work personally, it is his or her responsibility to see that it is done to the customer's satisfaction.[10]

**Figure 4–5
Relative importance
of personal selling
and advertising**

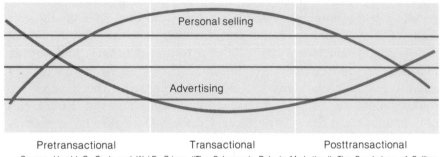

Pretransactional   Transactional   Posttransactional

Source: Harold C. Cash and W.J.E. Crissy, "The Salesman's Role in Marketing," *The Psychology of Selling* 12(1965):68. Personnel Development Associates, P.O. Box 3005 Roosevelt Field Station. Garden City, NY 11530.

**Marketing
communications**

Effective promotion is based on effective marketing communication. Both the planner of promotional strategy and the staff member directly involved in promotion activities, such as the salesperson or advertising copywriter, need an understanding of the basics of marketing communication.

There are countless ways of picturing the communication process. About the simplest way is to think in terms of five basic elements arranged in the order shown in Figure 4–6. For the marketer, *source* will mean the company, whereas the *sender* is any of the three methods of promotion—personal selling, advertising, or sales promotion.

**Figure 4–6
The communication
process**

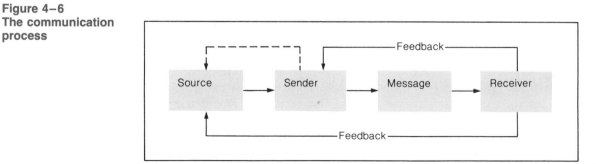

Source.   Unlike the other methods of promotion, the customer target (receiver) draws a distinction between the salesperson as the sender and the company (source) he or she represents. This can affect the performance of the salesperson; some companies have a better reputation or more favorable image than others do.

Generally, the better the reputation of a company selling industrial goods, the greater the chances are that the salesperson will get a favorable first hearing for a new product and then will get early adoption of that product. (See Figure 4–7). The risk a customer is asked to take in making a purchase decision about a new product weakens the effect of the company image.[11] Apparently industrial purchases are influenced by company reputation, but not to the extent that it has any weight in the making of risky purchase decisions.

The positive or negative effect of company reputation does not remain constant over a period of time. Impressions the customer has of company image are forgotten much faster than what the salesperson has to say in the presentation. In actual industrial selling situations, it was discovered that a company's favorable image diminishes with time if it is not bolstered by callbacks and advertisements. Further, the stronger the negative reaction toward the company at the time of the first sales call, the greater the chances of a change later.[12]

Sender.   The communication role of the sender or specific advertising medium is somewhat different from that of the sales force in personal selling situations. Advertising picks its own audience through such devices as editorial content or programming and timing. A magazine on boating will more than likely be read only by those interested in this subject.

Direct mail is the most selective medium in that the source can send it only to those it wants to receive it, such as dairy producers with a particular breed of cattle in certain geographic areas. Television is much more generalized. A sports program will attract more men than women as viewers. Whether this audience is composed of customers or potential customers for the advertised products is much less certain.

With advertising, it is entirely possible that the medium will be more favorably received by customers than the company is. Thus it is possible for a company to gain in prestige because it advertises in a particular publication; the sender's reputation can rub off on the source. This does not seem to be the case in personal selling.

Salespeople typically are given lower image rankings than the companies they represent. This could partly be due to a general lack

Figure 4–7

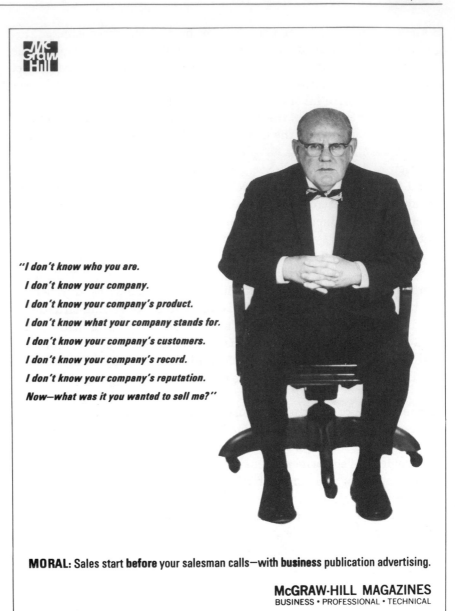

"*I don't know who you are.*

I don't know your company.

I don't know your company's product.

I don't know what your company stands for.

I don't know your company's customers.

I don't know your company's record.

I don't know your company's reputation.

Now—what was it you wanted to sell me?"

MORAL: Sales start **before** your salesman calls—with **business** publication advertising.

McGRAW-HILL MAGAZINES
BUSINESS · PROFESSIONAL · TECHNICAL

Reprinted by permission of McGraw-Hill, Inc.

of job prestige for sales as an occupation. In industrial selling, the trustworthiness of the salesperson is directly related to the quality of the sales presentation.[13] What the salesperson has to say about the product can work to offset any negative effects resulting from company reputation.

Message.   In both personal selling and advertising, the effectiveness of the message depends upon how well product features are translated into customer satisfaction. The message must clearly show how the product is the best way to satisfy the customer's needs or wants. Of course, messages must be based on a thorough understanding of the needs or wants of the customer target.

One way of visualizing the sales presentation is to think of it as a series of questions to be asked of the customer. Customer feedback in the form of answers and other reactions permits the salesperson to make on-the-spot adjustments in the sales presentation. Because the aim is customer satisfaction rather than the sale of a specific-product, the two-way communication possible in personal selling gives it a big advantage over advertising as a form of promotion.

Much of the advantage of two-way communication is lost when the salesperson is more interested in selling a product than in satisfying the customer. In this case customer feedback has no obvious effect on the content of the sales message, and the message is no different than it would be if the method of promotion were advertising. Personal selling could be said to have lost its uniqueness of presentation.

Receiver.   If promotion is to achieve its goals, the receiver (customer) must be properly identified as a purchaser or purchasing influence. This means that the salesperson needs to be talking to the right people on an individual basis or in groups, and advertisements must be placed where they will be viewed by these people. The right people are those who are actively involved in some role in the purchasing decision process.

Selectivity.   Advertising and sales personnel agree that selectivity as practiced by customers screens out many of their efforts in communications. First there is *selectivity of exposure*. Only certain sources are looked to for product information. A dentist, for example, might not think to ask a representative from the local dental supply house about remodeling the office.

Selectivity in perception is a second form. Customers pay little attention to messages about products that are not needed at the time they receive the message. A wintertime sales call or advertisement about air conditioning is not likely to be effective. Finally, customers are *selective in retention* of a message. Effective promotion strategies include repetition to help offset the possibility that the customer will not remember the message. The problem of selective retention is tackled by running a theme or central idea through a series of advertisements that make up a campaign. The salesperson's presentations can achieve about the same effect by consistently emphasizing company reputation for service, engineering or research leadership, reliability, availability, or the importance placed on the customer.

Regardless of what form selectivity takes, it acts to disrupt communications between the source and the receiver. The salesperson thinks of it as not getting across to the customer. Advertising managers wonder if anyone sees, let alone reads or heeds, their advertisements. The answer to the problem of selectivity is not a simple one. It must be recognized that selectivity cannot be eliminated; it helps customers solve problems associated with the purchases they make to satisfy their needs or wants. Selectivity of one sort or the other must be anticipated in planning promotional strategies. One way to do this is to set up what might be called a *selectivity profile* for each customer target, which describes its reaction to the firm and its products in relation to the selectivity factors of exposure, perception, and retention. Table 4–4 gives an example for a marketer of pharmaceutical products whose customer targets include general practitioners and a particular type of specialist.

Table 4–4
Selectivity profiles for customer targets of a pharmaceutical company

Selectivity factor	General practitioners	Specialists
Exposure	Think of only three or four of the larger and more established firms. Our company not normally included.	Do not think a sales representative can tell them anything about drugs.
Perception	Interests limited to products that may help current patients.	Only interested in new products discussed in journals.
Retention	Remember names of salespersons (three or four). Our company sales representative not included.	Remember product types but not brand names.

Perceived risk. The risk a customer perceives in the purchasing decision can also affect communications. One study of industrial selling found that:

1. The effect of a company's good reputation decreases as the decision called for increases in riskiness (such as a further hearing for a new product or a new product adoption).
2. The greater the riskiness of the decision, the more favorably a purchasing agent is influenced by the sales presentation.
3. The greater the riskiness of the decision, the more likely technical personnel are to rely on their own judgments rather than on the sales presentation.
4. The purchasing agent or technical person in a high-risk situation has more confidence in his negative reaction than his positive reaction.
5. The purchasing agent or technical person in a high-risk situation will likely stick with his initial decision if it was negative, but show some self-doubt and make a change if it was positive. In other words, once sold the customer may become unsold.[14]

The degree of risk is the amount at stake in the purchase decision. Usually this is viewed in economic terms.[15] Product adoption is risky because it might result in a loss of money if the wrong decision is made. A low-risk decision such as granting a further hearing for a new product entails only a loss of time and perhaps a loss of status within the organization. The latter is a psychological loss and is similar to that experienced by a person, picking out furniture for a home, who knows his or her taste in decorating will be indicated by the purchases.

Customers reduce risk by first attempting to reduce uncertainty, and if this fails, by trying to lower the amount at stake. Reducing the amount at stake usually means foregoing the purchase entirely. In seeking to reduce uncertainty, the customer will follow either of two ways, but not both: (1) seek out more information or (2) rely on past experience.[16] The sales presentation is a logical source for those seeking information to reduce uncertainty. Customers who fall back on past experiences limit themselves to what has been successful for them in the past.[17] This often means strong loyalties to a brand, company, or even a sales representative.

This chapter has viewed the marketing planning process from the standpoint of the salesperson. The importance of involving salespeo-   **SUMMARY** ple in improving marketing plans and gaining their acceptance of these plans has been stressed.

Planning is defined as the process of determining the necessary steps to be taken in order to attain a desired future state or condition of business. The steps to be taken in reaching these objectives or goals make up a plan.

The flow of planning is from the top down. The starting point is a definition of the business and the objectives for the company, which are translated into marketing objectives. The planning job for the sales force is deciding how to implement the sales strategies to reach assigned sales objectives. To do this job a salesperson has to relate the particular sales strategy to his or her customers: the customers' needs, the product, and the competition. The ideal salesperson develops a sales plan for every customer.

Planners of marketing make two basic decisions. The first is determining who are to be the prime customer targets for the firm and the second is selecting the mix of marketing efforts aimed at the selected customer targets. While sales efforts have the greatest relative importance in promotion strategy, there are marked differences among producers for various markets. The heaviest emphasis on sales efforts is by industrial goods producers, while producers of consumer nondurables give sales efforts considerably less emphasis.

Personal selling and advertising have general characteristics that can make one more appropriate than the other in selling certain types of products or serving various markets. In deciding which to use in a given situation, the critical factors weighed by the promotion strategist are often the salesperson's ability to fit the company's products uniquely to the market, versus advertising's low contact cost. Another way of looking at the two methods of promotion is in terms of their roles in three successive market stages. Advertising has the dominant promotion role in the pretransactional stage. The emphasis shifts to personal selling in the transactional phase, which the salesperson usually can handle alone. In the posttransactional stage there is another shift in which advertising assumes a slightly more important role than personal selling.

Effective promotion depends upon effective communication. The communication process can be thought of as having five basic elements. These include the source or company, the sender or method of promotion, the message, the receiver or customer, and feedback. A company and a salesperson have separate identities to the customer. The effect of company reputation is strongest initially and weakens after a period of time.

Sales personnel are considered less trustworthy than the companies they represent. For salespeople, trustworthiness is related to their sales presentations. What the salesperson has to say can offset the negative effects of company reputation. To be effective, the sales presentation must show clearly how the product's benefits are the best way to satisfy the customer's needs or wants.

Selectivity as practiced by customers can block out communications. It can be anticipated in promotional strategy through the use of such aids as the selectivity profile. The amount of risk the customer believes he or she is being asked to take in making a purchase decision can also interfere with communications. In an attempt to reduce risk and its accompanying uncertainty, the customer may try to find out more about the product or rely upon past experience.

REVIEW QUESTIONS/DISCUSSION QUESTIONS/EXERCISES

1. Briefly identify the following:
   - a. Marketing mix.
   - b. Promotion mix.
   - c. Key-account strategy.
   - d. Marketing communications.
   - e. Customer target.
   - f. Sales plan.

2. List the reasons why objectives should be as specific as possible.

3. Discuss how reasonableness in objectives can be obtained.

4. Market conditions can affect the timing of a plan. Comment on this statement.

5. Using a company objective of increased profitability, trace the evolution of marketing plans through the marketing and sales levels down to the salesperson. Assume the company makes storm windows and the customer target is building supply operations open to the general public.

6. Why should selecting a customer target come before determining the marketing mix?

7. A lot of companies select customer targets without really intending to do so. Explain this statement.

8. Are there any general guidelines a salesperson would need to know in communicating with a customer?

9. Comment on the following statement: You don't need a good product, just good salespeople and advertising.

10. Why do you think the customer makes a distinction between a company and its sales representative?

11. Pick a product, say an automobile, appliance, or major item of clothing, and make up a selectivity profile for yourself.

12. Describe the communication process and define each of its elements.

13. In buying consumer products for which the same brand is available from several sources, do you feel the customer distinguishes between the store and the salesperson? Explain your answer.

14. Contrast the purchasing agent and the technical person in their reactions to risk in an industrial purchasing decision.

15. How would you personally reduce risk for the following products?

  a. Fur coat.   d. Slide projector.

  b. Expensive watch.   e. Vacation home.

  c. New house.

16. For a very complicated consumer product (possibly a heating or cooling system), discuss the advantages of personal selling as a promotion method.

17. Can you think of any situation in which advertising would play a greater role than personal selling in the transactional phase? Explain.

18. Why should a salesperson not rely too heavily on his or her company's good reputation?

19. Why is selectivity practiced by customers?

20. Discuss how a customer becomes unsold.

CASE 4–1: STANDISH GOLF EQUIPMENT COMPANY

The Standish Golf Equipment Company has been a well-known and respected manufacturer of golf equipment for over 50 years. The equipment is sold only through pro shops located on golf courses; about 70 percent of the sales are to shops on private courses. All of the items in the line—clubs, balls, bags—are priced higher than the top of the line for most other manufacturers.

The sales force consists of five sales representatives who are paid a 10 percent commission on all sales, plus expenses. Earnings usually run from $30,000 to $42,000 a year. Each salesperson maintains an inventory of equipment, ordering from the company plant in Pinehurst, North Carolina, when necessary.

Six months ago the Standish Golf Equipment Company was acquired by Worldwide Sports, Inc. Worldwide not only produces and sells all types of sports equipment, but it owns sport and recreational facilities such as golf courses, ski resorts, and camp sites, as well as sporting goods stores. At the time of the merger, Jeff Burey was made marketing manager of Standish, now a division of Worldwide Sports, Inc.

Burey calls a sales meeting at which Barbara Bowers, the division manager, makes the announcement that a contract has been signed with Buddy Mason, the new golf idol and the leading money winner for the last three years on the professional tour. Sets of golf clubs, golf balls, and golf bags bearing his name will be competitively priced and sold through all types of retailers. A line of golf clothing will also be marketed under his name.

To kick off the marketing campaign, extensive advertising is being planned. The first nine months of the year, commercials will be aired on all golf tournament telecasts, and advertisements will appear in magazines such as *Sports Illustrated, Golf,* and *Golf Digest.* In addition, Mason will make an extensive personal appearance tour.

When Burey asks if there are any questions, the first representative to be recognized is John Hyde, who has been with Standish for nearly 25 years. He tells Burey that pro shops rarely handle the same lines as sporting goods stores. Burey answers that times are changing, and even if the pro shops will not go along at first, they will do so later because this new line cannot miss. Burey also points out that several million dollars are going to be spent on advertising, and pro shops will want to get in on a presold item.

Peter Thompson, another sales representative, asks if management expects the sales force to call on retailers in their areas, in addition to pro shops. Burey replies affirmatively, saying that in the beginning, salespersons will have to all but ignore their regular customers and concentrate on those stores that will be selling the Buddy Mason lines. There are plenty of other questions from the other salespeople, most of them directed toward the fact that the new management does not know the market for golf equipment.

Questions

1. What difficulties does the addition of this new product line hold for the sales force?
2. Can any of these difficulties be solved by the addition of more sales personnel? Explain your answer.
3. Do you think that the sales force will actually shift its efforts from pro shops to retail stores?
4. What suggestions can you give Burey to help him in selecting customer targets?

CASE 4–2: NUMERICAL MACHINE TOOL COMPANY

Numerical Machine Tool Company was one of the country's largest producers of numerically controlled machine tools. Customers were located across the entire United States although foreign sales were minimal. Most of Numerical's customers were machining companies who did contract machining for other industrial firms. Another large segment of Numerical's market was made up of manufacturing enterprises who bought numerically controlled machine tools for use in their own manufacturing operations.

Numerical's marketing activities were the responsibility of Tom Parsons, a 53-year-old man who had come up through Numerical's sales force. Tom knew the business inside out; he knew all of the major officers in all of the major accounts. He knew many of the top executives of Numerical's competitors. "Parsons," as one competitor put it, "is one of the top people in this business. He grew up in the industry and helped make it what it is today. Everyone respects Tom's knowledge and integrity."

Late one Friday afternoon, Tom was looking over a report he had just received from accounting. In it he saw that the marketing expenses item in his marketing budget had gone over budget for the third month in a row. He felt something had to be done. Items included in this line were price lists, trade shows, catalogs, trade press advertising, and technical bulletins.

Tom was bothered by this problem for two reasons. First, he never had really seen why so much money had to be spent on these items. They seemed to him to be luxuries; the real meat of his marketing effort—he had always felt—was his experienced, talented sales force. Why so much money had to be spent on these other items, he would never understand. Second, even when he agreed to the budget for these items, he always felt a certain sense of uneasiness over his inability to make the expenditures more productive. He intuitively sensed what had to be done to make the sales force efficient and productive. But the marketing expenses budget was something with which he always had difficulty.

Tom picked up his phone and asked Dick Levin, his administrative assistant who had direct responsibility for the marketing expenses budget, to come into his office to discuss the matter.

Tom: Hi, Dick. Sit down; I want to check the marketing expenses budget with you. We went over budget again. Something's got to be done.

Dick: You're not going to suggest we drop these expenses altogether again are you? I thought we had agreed to burn that bridge behind us.

Tom: No, I'm not suggesting we do that. But I do want a report from you justifying each of these expenditures. Why does a company with our reputation and product quality have to spend over 3 percent of sales on advertising? What do we need exhibits at trade shows for? Explain the purpose of technical bulletins, price lists, catalogs, and so forth. Couldn't we handle a lot of this with letters instead of expensive four-color literature?

Dick: OK, that seems reasonable. Is there anything else you want the report to cover?

Tom: Yes, even more importantly, I want you to show how these items can create a synergy between them and the sales effort. You know how you're always telling me that these expenses more than pay for themselves in terms of reduced selling expenses. Give me several examples of this in your report. Also, show how some of these items work together. That is, show how a synergy is created between, say, catalogs and trade press advertising such that the cost of each is less than if we were to run either without the other. Does that make sense?

Dick: Sure, I'll have the report prepared in a month. Soon enough?

Tom: No! I need this at the latest in two weeks. With all that you know about this matter, it should be easy. I'll see you tomorrow morning at the first tee.

Questions

1. Can you understand why Tom Parsons feels as he does?
2. If you were Dick Levin, what would you say in your report?

A Profile of Professional Selling

Louis J. Manara

Louis J. Manara is a superb salesperson as indicated by his winning the Golden Oval, the highest sales award for American Cyanamid Company, three times in his nine years on the road. When Manara began selling chemicals for Cyanamid in 1971, the job was relatively straightforward. His job was to cover every possible customer in an assigned territory. He was told little about his division's goals, and nothing about the profitability of the various products.

When Manara started selling, the basic idea in industrial sales was to nurture close relationships with the purchasing agent. If the purchasing agent proved difficult the salesperson would try to "backdoor" by going direct to end-users of the product. Prospecting was accomplished by "smokestacking" or dropping in on potential customers whose factory smokestacks were spotted while driving around the sales territory.

Today Manara's sales job is drastically different. He now needs to know about a customer's needs, competitive actions, and financial packaging. In addition Manara must mediate disputes between customers and the credit department, handle customer complaints, and keep abreast of changes in both governmental regulations and world chemical markets.

In a recent year, Manara personally sold almost $10 million worth of chemicals employed for dyemaking and pigment production. He did so despite missing three months recovering from major heart surgery. He exhibits few of the traits normally associated with successful salespeople. Polite and patient with customers he refrains from gregariousness and backslapping.

The need for marketing intelligence has caused Manara to plan his working day with care. Although he still tries to visit his 140 customers, he spends much more time conducting business by phone. When he is with customers, he spends a lot of time gathering information. "My bosses need to know whether there is enough demand out there for a product to warrant manufacturing it."

In describing the more professional and better informed purchasing agent he says, "It's all business. You make your appointment, get in, and get out. It's a matter of quality, price, delivery, schedules, and service. Even working for a famous, well-established company provides very little advantage nowadays."

Used with permission from Hugh D. Menzies, "The New Life of a Salesman," *Fortune*, August 11, 1980, pp. 173–80.

Part

3

INITIATING THE SALES PROCESS

The three greatest essentials to achieve anything worthwhile are, first, hard work; second, stick-to-itiveness; third, common sense.*

THOMAS A. EDISON

KEY POINTS

- A sales lead is someone or some organization possibly in need of the salesperson's product or service.
- A prospect is a sales lead the salesperson has identified as needing or desiring the product or service.
- Prospects are qualified if they have the ability and authority to complete the transaction.
- Without an adequate pool of prospects, the salesperson will eventually fail.
- Sources of prospects include: (1) customers, (2) inquiries, (3) company sources, (4) cold canvassing, (5) friends and social acquaintances, (6) organizations, (7) spotters, (8) sellers of related products, (9) direct-mail prospect lists, (10) public information, (11) other prospects, (12) conventions, meetings, and demonstrations.
- Failure to qualify a prospect can result in a considerable loss of selling time and selling efficiency.
- The three essential steps in qualifying a prospect are: (1) delineate the factors on which a prospect should be qualified, (2) determine whether the prospect possesses these qualifications, and (3) decide whether or not to approach the prospect.
- Once a salesperson has qualified a prospect, it is important to maintain a record about that prospect: problems, operating methods, and buying characteristics.

Chapter

5

PROSPECTING AND QUALIFYING

Ennis Business Forms, Inc., once sent out an army of miniature robots to sales leads in an attempt to identify prospects for their products. "The collapsible, foot-high robots, with eyes made out of coffee pot lids, were sent in light-weight attaché cases complete with tape-recorded sales messages, brochures, printing samples, and request cards to be sent back to Ennis."[1] If the sales lead responded to an Ennis robot (other than fainting, which might be expected), he was regarded as a prospect, and a "human" sales representative followed up with a telephone call.

Several other firms have adopted a similar selling strategy. The All Steel Pipe and Tube Company of St. Louis has a team of $500, 18-inch-tall robots (all of whom are named "Ace") which deliver a seven-minute recorded sales pitch.[2] In fact, "Ace" has been closing one out of every four sales calls to key customers. It is doubtful that robots will ever replace their human counterparts, since, as one commentator has noted:

> Ace isn't going to supplant the human salesman as raconteur and transmission line for spicy stories. About the time he reached the one about the farmer's daughter the Post Office would nail him for sending dirty stories through the mail and throw him in the—well, wherever they keep bad robots.[3]

SALES LEADS AND PROSPECTS

These two examples illustrate the attention that is given in one form or another to generating sales leads, the first step in the task of prospecting and qualifying. A sales lead is some person or organization that might need or desire the salesperson's product. Sales leads come from many sources—present customers, advertising, marketing research, inside salespeople, and the like. Many of these sales leads will amount to nothing because the persons involved will have no need or desire for the product in question. A purchasing agent, for example, may inquire about a product simply for informational purposes. Indeed, in many companies it is policy to maintain a library of product information.

A *prospect* is a sales lead that the salesperson has identified as

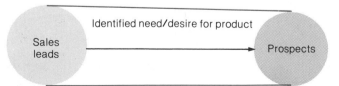

needing or desiring the product or service. The identification of this need converts a sales lead into a prospect.

Prospects, then, are potential customers as measured by their need or apparent desire for the item. Once a sales lead has been identified as a prospect, the next step is to *qualify the prospect* as to ability and authority to purchase the good or service.

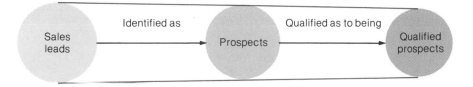

By qualifying a prospect, the salesperson assesses the prospect's ability to buy the product being offered. A successful executive who happens to be 6'8" and 290 pounds may strongly desire an Italian sports car, and will have the income to do so, but it is doubtful that the executive would be happy with such a purchase. A junior executive may aspire to live in exclusive Treadway Acres, but the $250,000 plus price tag rules this person out as a qualified prospect.

Once the salesperson has secured a qualified prospect, the sales process begins. Seven basic steps constitute the normal selling sequence: (1) prospecting and qualifying, (2) preapproach and approach, (3) presentation, (4) demonstration, (5) handling objections, (6) closing, and (7) building future sales. (These are the topics of later chapters.) The sales process, it is hoped, will convert the qualified prospect into a customer. Then, through an effective sales follow-up procedure, a customer who is satisfied with a purchase will lead to repeat sales. This conversion can be shown as follows:

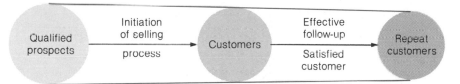

Figure 5–1 presents the complete sequence from sales lead to prospect to qualified prospect to customer to repeat customer. It is important to note that the initial and basic step in obtaining customers is the prospecting and qualifying efforts of the sales force. This step in the sales process is the subject of this chapter.

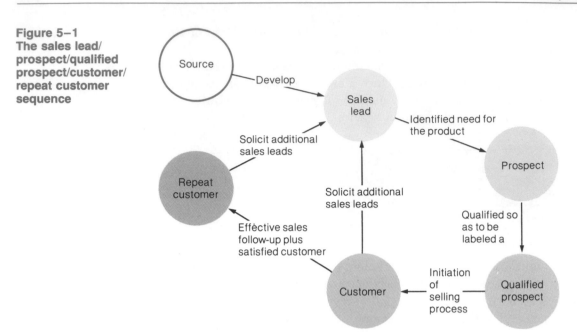

Figure 5–1
The sales lead/
prospect/qualified
prospect/customer/
repeat customer
sequence

THE
IMPORTANCE
OF
PROSPECTING

The importance to the salesperson of prospecting as the first step in converting leads into sales has been recognized by the Ford Marketing Institute, the dealer-training arm of the Ford Motor Company:

> Prospecting is the basis for any successful sales effort and it's important . . . that . . . salesmen not only know how to do it but why it's important to them. When they do, they want to prospect and the result is a better utilization of their time.
>
> With competition for retail automobile sales getting sharper every day, you can't afford to have . . . salesmen standing around that showroom waiting (and hoping) for someone to walk in. If they aren't prospecting, you'd better believe your competition is.[4]

A systematic, well-planned prospecting effort allows a salesperson to get the jump on the competition. In many cases, it is the factor that separates high performers from low performers.

Without an adequate pool of prospects, the salesperson eventually fails. Consider the case of Walt, a recent college graduate, who enters the insurance sales field and in his first year wins several awards from the company and realizes double the earnings of classmates. Yet a couple of years later, his friends find him at another job far removed from the field of insurance. They wonder "What happened to Walt?

Why did he give up selling insurance? I thought he was doing extremely well."

It is quite likely that Walt failed because he ran out of prospects. He began his career with an established pool of prospects: his immediate family, other relatives, friends, and classmates. This select group of prospects did provide him with a good start in selling. Walt's downfall began when he failed to add to his starting pool of prospects with new contacts. When this select group of prospects stopped buying, Walt stopped selling! The New York Life Insurance Company has recognized the importance of prospecting: "As long as prospecting keeps pumping a supply of names, a man continues in the life insurance business."[5]

Prospecting is important to the overall sales effort because existing customers must be replaced periodically. Most estimates of annual customer turnover fall in the 10 to 25 percent range, depending on the source consulted. This means that a significant portion of the firm's customers cease to buy its products every year. Consumers may switch brands, move, decide to shop elsewhere, die, or eliminate certain purchases they have made previously. Industrial customers may change vendors, switch to an alternative product, go bankrupt, or close down the purchasing office in a salesperson's territory.

In addition to maintaining a current number of customers, most companies will want to expand sales through new customers. This places even greater importance on prospecting.

Sources of new prospects are both abundant and varied. Prospects exist in territories currently covered by sales personnel as well as those geographical areas outside present territories. A Los Angeles-based metals distributor, Ducommun, Inc., located prospects by crossing its customer lists with Dun & Bradstreet computer tapes broken down by the standard industrial classification code. Ducommun's senior vice president, Charles K. Preston, noted that "We found we had been missing out on quite a bit of territory. Salesmen have a tendency to go back to the same old folks over and over."[6]

Another firm—Allied Chemical's Fiber Division—uses an outside agency, Field Coordinators, Inc., to conduct cold sales calls for carpeting. Field Coordinators, in turn, employs women to work part time in their local areas. This part-time prospecting force makes industrial sales presentations to architects and interior designers and then turns over "strong leads" (or prospects) to Allied's mill sales represen-

SECURING SALES LEADS AND PROSPECTS

tatives. This approach means that Allied has an ongoing field force that specializes in prospecting for potential customers, allowing carpet mill sales representatives—who average $35,000 to $40,000 per year—to concentrate on closing sales from qualified prospects.[7]

No list of sources of potential prospects is ever complete. The sources are numerous and diverse; some can be exhausted, others may continue to be fruitful for years. An effective salesperson must be knowledgeable concerning all the possible sources of prospects for a product. A good salesperson will be flexible and make use of several sources of prospects.

Prospect sources include (1) customers, (2) inquiries, (3) company sources, (4) cold canvassing, (5) friends, social contacts, and acquaintances, (6) organizational contacts, (7) spotters, (8) sellers of related products, (9) direct-mail and prospect lists (10) public information, (11) other prospects, and (12) conventions, meetings, and demonstrations. These sources are discussed below.

Customers

Customers who are satisfied with their purchases are probably the best single source of additional sales leads. Satisfied customers will usually agree to suggest friends, relatives, neighbors, or associates as prospects. When customers are pleased with a purchase, the usual tendency will be to talk about it to their friends and associates.

The chain of prospects method described above is one way of soliciting sales leads from customers. An even more productive practice is the *referral method,* in which the customer is asked to introduce and recommend the salesperson to other prospects. Personal and telephoned introductions such as the following are extremely effective:

> Hello Ralph . . . I am going to send a representative from Allied Aluminum Products over to see you this afternoon. I think he might have just the item you are looking for.

> Marsha, I'd like you to meet Angie Forsheen from Designs Unlimited. She is the person who solved our decorating problems over at the Briarbush store.

> Leonard, I have a fellow sitting in my office who I think has an insurance plan your association will want to consider. We just signed up with him today.

In other cases, satisfied customers may write brief letters of introduction for salespeople who request them to do so. Short notes of introduction written on the backs of business cards are a traditional practice. The following is an example of such a note:

> Hi, Hal! This will serve to introduce Hewitt Fawson of Consolidated

Insurance. Judy and I recently bought a homeowner's policy from him, and we've been pleased with Consolidated's efficiency and friendly personnel. I'll look forward to seeing you next Tuesday.

Joe

Referrals are of considerable help to the salesperson. They minimize the time spent on prospecting and qualifying, as well as improving the likelihood that the sales presentation will be viewed favorably.

Inquiries

Companies routinely receive direct inquiries about their products or services. Some inquiries are solicited through direct mail or advertisements in magazines and newspapers. Others can come in as a result of nonselling contacts with potential customers by company personnel, publicity releases about a firm's product, community involvement programs, or a luncheon speech by a corporate executive.

Inquiries may come direct from potential customers, but more than likely from responses to advertising. A Reader Service Card such as shown in Figure 5–2 is a convenient way to obtain information on products and as such is used extensively in industrial selling. It will be noted that qualifying information in regard to purchasing authority, job function, and company is also requested from those persons doing the inquiring.

There are two ways of qualifying inquiries. One way is to forward the inquiries to the salesperson serving the particular territory where the inquirer is located. That salesperson can then complete the qualifying process. Another and perhaps preferred way is to do the qualifying at the home office and send to salespeople only those who are qualified prospects.

Company sources

Salespeople can often obtain sales leads from other people within their own company. The service department may be able to pass on word of someone who is about ready to buy a new product. Marketing staff personnel may have contacts who are prospects. Sales managers will usually refer leads to salespeople, and sellers of other product lines in the organization may also prove helpful.

The two most obvious internal sources are the inside salespeople and the marketing research department. Inside salespeople are in continuous contact with customers as well as individuals who might call the firm in regard to a product. Marketing research departments can provide valuable information by defining general customer types who will have a need for the product in question, and the number and size to be found in each geographic area.

**Figure 5–2
Reader service card**

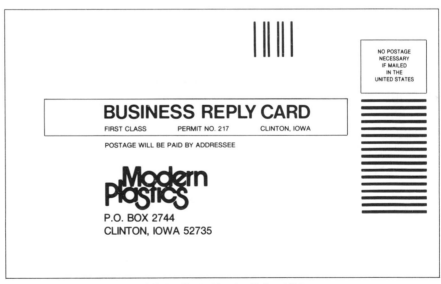

Source: Reprinted by permission of *Modern Plastics* Magazine, McGraw-Hill, Inc.

Internal sources can sometimes be prolific providers of quality sales leads. A good salesperson should do everything possible to nurture and cultivate productive internal sources of prospect information. For instance, a daily visit to the firm's service department can pay substantial dividends.

Cold canvassing

Cold canvassing is the time-honored sales tradition of securing prospects through unsolicited contacts by the sales force. This is accomplished either through personal, face-to-face contact or by telephone canvassing. Direct-to-home marketers, such as Avon Products, have been extremely successful with this approach.

Cold canvassing is based on the idea that the salesperson will cover every person or firm in a given area. Sellers of industrial equipment may "blanket" an area in an effort to uncover sales leads. They will call on purchasing agents in every plant looking for potential customers. Obviously, cold canvassing increases the costs of prospecting, since it is often difficult to obtain good sales leads through unsolicited visits or calls. However, cold canvassing does allow the salesperson to completely cover a given sector of the market and may uncover a previously untapped market segment. Cold canvassing can also be used to fill in "down time" when the salesperson is not actively selling or prospecting through other means.

Beginning salespeople may often be assigned the job of cold canvassing as one of their first duties. When this is the case, an apprentice salesperson will probably secure sales leads, identify them as prospects, and qualify. The results will then be turned over to experienced salespeople for initiation of the selling process.

"I'm sorry, Mr. Baxter isn't seeing any Capricorns today."

Reprinted by permission The Wall Street Journal.

Cold canvassing is a tough aspect of the sales job.

Telephone canvassing is another common technique for obtaining sales leads. The objectives and strategy are similar to those in personal-contact cold canvassing. Unsolicited sales calls have become a major public issue in recent years as some people resist further intrusions on their privacy.

Friends, social contacts, and acquaintances

A rich source of leads is the salesperson's own friends, social contacts, and acquaintances. Because of their close association with the salesperson, they usually are helpful in providing the names of potential prospects. The referral technique is often used to reach sales leads provided by this source.

The *key influence method* is frequently used in connection with this source of prospects. Many people who are influential within their social, work, or professional groups can be solicited for sales leads in a very candid manner. Investment companies, insurance companies, book companies, and direct-to-home sellers of silverware and aluminum ware are examples of users of the influence method of prospecting.[8]

One important note of caution should be sounded. Friends, social contacts, and acquaintances will tend to disappear if they are valued strictly as a source of sales leads. There are limits as to how much a salesperson should impose on any source of leads. An effective prospector should be careful not to cross this barrier.

Organizational contacts

Salespeople join the same civic and professional organizations as their prospects. Many professional associations openly encourage them to do so, because it provides an opportunity for the group's members to keep up to date on the latest products and services available to them. However, it is important for salespeople to draw the line against "excessive commercialism." The salesperson should belong to a professional association of clients because he or she is sincerely interested in the advancement of that profession. If a product can serve a particular segment of the profession, then the sales person has an obligation to demonstrate its usefulness. But a representative does not have the ethical right to use a membership to sell "anything to everybody." Those who do so are usually soon labeled as "hustlers" and effectively excluded from further transactions with the group's members.

Membership in civic organizations is also important. In addition to being a rich source of sales leads, civic organizations allow salespeople to keep attuned to activities and current opinion in the communities in which they work. The value of civic club memberships goes beyond their contributions to the salesperson's prospecting effort. Here too, however, the salesperson must avoid excessive commercialism; the representative should join a civic organization because he or she believes in the goals and objectives of the club—not for business or social reasons alone.

Memberships in civic and professional associations can be an excellent source of sales leads, as long as the salesperson keeps the membership in the proper perspective. Even casual conversations at organization meetings or outings can result in new prospects for the seller's product or service. People recognize you and feel at ease in making a direct product inquiry.

Spotters

Spotters—sometimes referred to as "bird dogs"—are people who make specialized surveys or canvasses to assess the needs of prospects. The field prospecting force of women utilized by Allied Chemical (discussed earlier in this chapter) is an example of the spotter technique. These part-time workers make sales presentations to architects and industrial designers and then turn the names of prospects over to Allied's carpet mill sales representatives.

Spotters allow experienced salespeople to concentrate their specialized selling knowledge on bona fide prospects. This practice can mean considerable economy of the salesperson's working time. Sellers of automobiles, major appliances, home improvements, and house wares often utilize this method of prospecting. Typically, spotters are part time employees who may prospect in conjunction with other daily activities or on a temporary basis.

Sellers of related products

Sellers of related products are another source of prospects. Service station operators and mechanics can provide valuable tips to new-car sellers. A bartender, barber, or waitress is also likely to know who has been discussing the purchase of recreational property, for example. Contractors, real estate agents, and lawyers may be able to suggest leads for various sellers.

In some cases, sellers of related products provide prospect information gratis. In other cases, they receive a fee if the prospect actually buys the item from the salesperson. In one modification of this approach, present customers are asked to provide names of prospects and then are compensated for the information if those prospects buy within a certain time.

Direct-mail and prospect lists

Direct-mail advertisements are sometimes used to develop prospect lists. Vacation home developers use direct mail to invite leads to a dinner and slide presentation about the property or to actually spend a mini-vacation at the site. Stockbrokers and investment counselors send out direct mail invitations to attend an investment seminar. Direct mail has proven to be a very effective method of prospecting for many sellers of industrial goods.

Mailing (or prospect) lists can be obtained from many sources. Some firms develop their own lists; others purchase them from the *list brokers,* which can provide lists of virtually any segment of the population. All sales personnel, however, should also develop their own lists of prospects. Hans G. Moser, field director of Northwestern Mutual Life Insurance Company, has two prospect lists, the first composed of prospects he expects to close within a month and the other comprised of "dream cases" (ranging from $100,000 to over $500,000 in insurance coverage) which may take three months to a year to close. Moser tries to add a new dream case to his list every month and to maintain a working inventory of at least 10 to 12 such cases. This requires him to close a dream case every four to six weeks.[9] Obviously, Moser's approach requires him to devote constant attention to his prospecting effort.

Public information

Many public records are open for inspection by sales personnel. The list of current building permits can provide good leads for building supply houses, exterminators, and furniture stores. Tax rolls can be helpful in developing lists of people in certain financial brackets and thus in selling some types of automobiles and the like.

Clip, clip, clip . . . a new list of prospects in the making

Clipping bureaus, businesses that make a living cutting out newspaper items for clients, can be an invaluable source of prospects for some sellers. For $55–$75 per month and so much a clip, businesses can collect public information on a variety of prospects.

Maynard Fire Apparatus Co. gets clips on fire-truck bids and related stories. A school furniture manufacturer collects stories about new schools and additions. Obituaries are clipped for retailers of gravestones. American Protective Systems buys clips on breakings and enterings in New England. American then has a sales representative call the victim to discuss security systems. American reports that their $50–$70 a month clipping expenditures produce more leads than any other source of prospects and that sales occur in 70 percent of the cases. Clip, clip, clip. . . .

Source: Debbie Simon, "A Triumph to Savor? An Agency Will Snip Your Press Clippings," *The Wall Street Journal,* October 14, 1977, pp. 1, 25. Reprinted by permission of *The Wall Street Journal,* © Dow Jones & Company, Inc. (1977). All Rights Reserved.

Various publications such as magazines, newspapers, and the trade press can provide many sales leads. Insurance sellers look for newspaper accounts of accidents, burglaries, and births. Engagement announcements are followed closely by jewelry and dinnerware sales representatives. A trade press account of a new plant opening in Rochester can be an important lead for many industrial sales representatives in that area.

Telephone calls, direct mail, and personal contacts can be used to determine whether these leads are good prospects for a particular product. Since in these cases the need is already apparent, the salesperson should at least mail or personally present his or her business card. This will help keep the seller's name in front of the prospect while the prospect is contemplating a purchase.

Other prospects

Prospects themselves can often generate other sales leads. Many salespeople make prospecting for sales leads a regular part of each sales interview. Thus they are able to maintain a continuous pool of potential buyers. Simple questions such as the following can be quite effective in obtaining sales leads.

Do you know anyone else who might be interested in this unique set of cookware?

Are there other dentists in your association who currently handle their own accounting records?

Is there anyone else on the block who is considering listing their home?

A technique commonly used to generate additional prospects is the *chain of prospects method,* which can be used in any sales interview situation. The salesperson uses this method to try to get one or more prospects for each prospect to whom he or she talks. The chain is typically used by sellers of insurance, household wares, real estate, and many other types of products. Often the prospect is offered an incentive such as additional merchandise for names of other prospects.

Conventions, meetings, and demonstrations

Many sales leads are obtained from conventions, professional meetings, exhibitions, trade shows, clinics, fairs, and demonstrations. In fact, prospecting is the primary reason for any company to participate in such activities. Publishers display new textbooks at a state teachers' meeting; automobile manufacturers display their new models at a metropolitan auto show; furniture makers have booths at trade shows and marts; the fashion industry displays the latest styles at seasonal showings. Conventions, exhibitions, and demonstrations are excellent methods of finding prospects for new products and aid in identifying previously unexplored markets for established products.

Marketers are constantly seeking new ways to reach prospects. For example, Hoffmann-La Roche, a pharmaceutical company, was the first major firm in the industry to stop exhibiting at the American Medical Association's annual meeting. Hoffmann-La Roche continues to exhibit at specialty meetings such as that of the American Psychiatric Association, where it has a natural market for its tranquilizers, Valium and Librium, which rank first and second in the U.S. ethical drug market. But the bulk of its prospecting effort has been switched to a closed-circuit television setup entitled the Network for Continuing Medical Education (NCME), on which Hoffmann-La Roche sponsors clinical presentations that reach doctors in more than 600 hospitals. Each program is followed by a 60-second commercial message from the pharmaceutical company. Hoffmann-La Roche has found this approach to be extremely helpful in obtaining prospects for its detailers.[10]

Localized clinics given by national manufacturers are another way of obtaining prospects. These clinics may focus on a particular problem area (waste disposal), a type of installation (mezzanine shelving), or some item of equipment (log splitter). Clinics are used extensively where it is not possible or practical to transport the product in question from one customer or prospect to another.

THE IMPORTANCE OF QUALIFYING A PROSPECT

The importance of the next step in the sales process, qualifying a prospect, has been eloquently stated by Edward J. Feeney, vice president of the Systems Performance Division of Emery Air Freight Corporation:

> Most salesmen are sitting in lobbies. They're calling on wrong accounts. They're calling on accounts that give them all the business that they can. They're calling on people that they think can make the buying decision when, in fact, they do not or cannot make much of it at all. They are efficient in talking about what they do—what their company provides—but not in how it fills the customer's need, because they haven't probed to find out what those needs are.[11]

It is obvious that failure to qualify a prospect can result in a considerable loss of the salesperson's time and selling efficiency. A prospect has an identified need for a product, but a qualified prospect is *able* to make such a purchase. Many salespeople launch into a sales presentation as soon as they establish that the prospect has a demonstrated need for the product. This approach may be adequate for low-value consumer goods that nearly everyone is able to purchase. But in most other cases, a prospect should be qualified to determine ability to buy and product suitability.

Salespeople who do not take time to qualify a prospect are less efficient than they otherwise might be. Too often salespeople waste their valuable selling time on unqualified prospects. This means that the salesperson should set up a formalized procedure for qualifying. If the home office or some other agency is going to do the qualifying, the salesperson should make sure he or she understands how the process is implemented.

There are three essential steps in qualifying a prospect:

1. Delineate the factors on which a prospect should be qualified.
2. Determine whether the prospect possesses these qualifications.
3. Decide whether or not to approach the prospect.

HOW TO QUALIFY A PROSPECT

The first step in the qualifying process is to define what factors or characteristics are important to the purchase decision. Age, income, occupation, place of residence, and marital status may be important to many consumer decisions. Credit ratings are considered in nearly all attempts to qualify a prospect. Type of business, input into the buying decision, and the authority to purchase are critical factors in qualifying industrial prospects. Other factors include type of advertising responded to, previous inquiries, and past sales record (see Figure 5–3).

It is not always easy to delineate the relevant characteristics of a qualified buyer. One study of 10 large firms found that sellers usually have significant misconceptions about who initiates purchases, as well as who selects the eventual supplier.[12] A variety of purchasing influences exist at each stage of the purchase decision. A child may initiate the acquisition of a new bicycle, but key buying influences such as parents, grandparents, and other children may alter the final purchase decision.

As the second step in qualifying a prospect, the salesperson must determine whether a particular prospect possesses the relevant qualifications. If the prospect fails this acid test, the salesperson is probably best advised to concentrate efforts in other directions.

Various techniques are used to qualify a particular prospect. In

Figure 5–3
Example of a form used in qualifying prospects

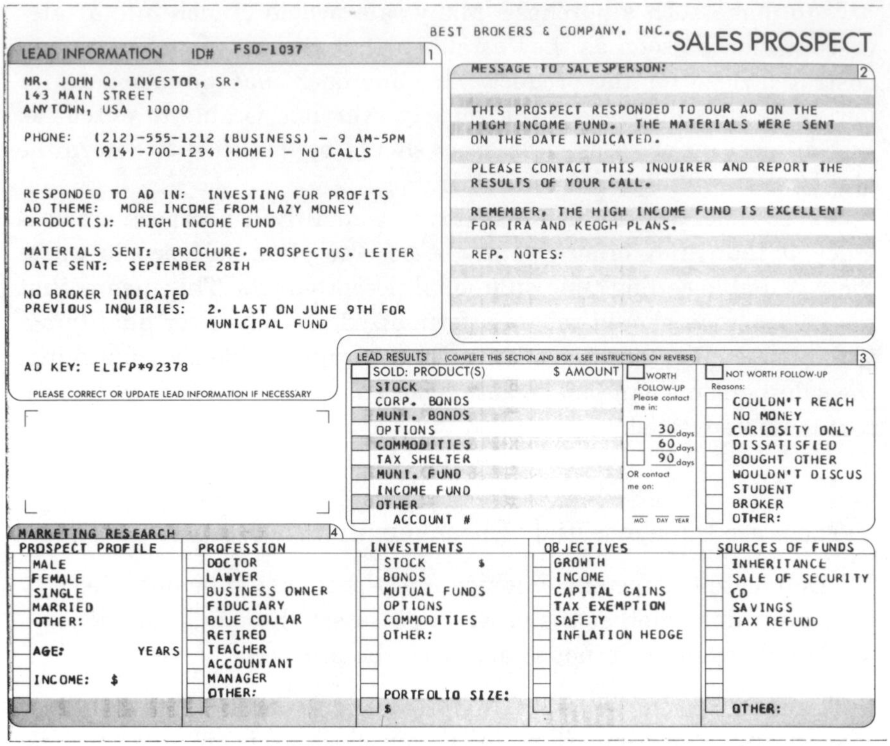

BEST BROKERS & COMPANY, INC. SALES PROSPECT

LEAD INFORMATION ID# FSD-1037 1

MR. JOHN Q. INVESTOR, SR.
143 MAIN STREET
ANYTOWN, USA 10000

PHONE: (212)-555-1212 (BUSINESS) - 9 AM-5PM
(914)-700-1234 (HOME) - NO CALLS

RESPONDED TO AD IN: INVESTING FOR PROFITS
AD THEME: MORE INCOME FROM LAZY MONEY
PRODUCT(S): HIGH INCOME FUND

MATERIALS SENT: BROCHURE, PROSPECTUS, LETTER
DATE SENT: SEPTEMBER 28TH

NO BROKER INDICATED
PREVIOUS INQUIRIES: 2, LAST ON JUNE 9TH FOR MUNICIPAL FUND

AD KEY: ELIFP*92378

PLEASE CORRECT OR UPDATE LEAD INFORMATION IF NECESSARY

MESSAGE TO SALESPERSON: 2

THIS PROSPECT RESPONDED TO OUR AD ON THE HIGH INCOME FUND. THE MATERIALS WERE SENT ON THE DATE INDICATED.

PLEASE CONTACT THIS INQUIRER AND REPORT THE RESULTS OF YOUR CALL.

REMEMBER, THE HIGH INCOME FUND IS EXCELLENT FOR IRA AND KEOGH PLANS.

REP. NOTES:

LEAD RESULTS (COMPLETE THIS SECTION AND BOX 4 SEE INSTRUCTIONS ON REVERSE) 3

SOLD: PRODUCT(S) $ AMOUNT
STOCK
CORP. BONDS
MUNI. BONDS
OPTIONS
COMMODITIES
TAX SHELTER
MUNI. FUND
INCOME FUND
OTHER
ACCOUNT #

WORTH FOLLOW-UP
Please contact me in:
30 days
60 days
90 days
OR contact me on:
MO. DAY YEAR

NOT WORTH FOLLOW-UP
Reasons:
COULDN'T REACH
NO MONEY
CURIOSITY ONLY
DISSATISFIED
BOUGHT OTHER
WOULDN'T DISCUS
STUDENT
BROKER
OTHER:

MARKETING RESEARCH 4

PROSPECT PROFILE	PROFESSION	INVESTMENTS	OBJECTIVES	SOURCES OF FUNDS
MALE	DOCTOR	STOCK $	GROWTH	INHERITANCE
FEMALE	LAWYER	BONDS	INCOME	SALE OF SECURITY
SINGLE	BUSINESS OWNER	MUTUAL FUNDS	CAPITAL GAINS	CD
MARRIED	FIDUCIARY	OPTIONS	TAX EXEMPTION	SAVINGS
OTHER:	BLUE COLLAR	COMMODITIES	SAFETY	TAX REFUND
	RETIRED	OTHER:	INFLATION HEDGE	
AGE: YEARS	TEACHER			
	ACCOUNTANT			
INCOME: $	MANAGER			
	OTHER:	PORTFOLIO SIZE: $		OTHER:

Source: Reprinted by permission LCS Industries.

some sales situations, it is necessary only to qualify the prospect with regard to one variable, such as credit rating. Other sellers use simple checklists to qualify their prospects. An evaluation formula consisting of six factors—age, number of dependents, approximate income, acquaintances, accessibility, and economic status—is used by the New York Life Insurance Company.[13] A prospect is assigned a point rating for each variable, and these are then totaled to provide a total point rating.

Finally, each seller has to decide whether to pursue a particular prospect. This should be a totally rational, economic decision. There are some cases in which a seller is justified in not pursuing a qualified prospect. The key to this decision is whether the prospect would be a *profitable* account. Unfortunately, sales organizations have been traditionally very volume-conscious, even at the expense of profitability. The truth is that some sales are not profitable, either because of an uneconomical order size or the modest margin that is involved. A common occurrence is the *small-order problem,* in which a purchaser buys in such small quantities that it is *currently* unprofitable to supply the account. The seller's eventual decision has to be balanced by an assessment of the likelihood of a larger (and profitable) account in the future, as well as the legal and ethical considerations involved. A complete periodic analysis of all accounts is useful in reaching this decision.

Once a salesperson has qualified a prospect, the seller must maintain a file about the prospect's particular problems, operating methods, and buying characteristics. Such a file allows the salesperson to plan the approach and presentation more effectively. At General Mills a sales manager stresses the importance of this information to the sales representative's daily performance when he tells members of the sales force:

MAINTAINING A FILE ON QUALIFIED PROSPECTS

> The grocery retailer in Harlem or Watts doesn't care about our broad cereal share in the New York and Southern California regions. He wants to know what products and sizes are preferred by the people in his neighborhood. The more you understand about your retailer—his merchandising problems and the merchandising principles and techniques that he applies—the better your chances of selling him.[14]

Some sales personnel just record information on index cards for their own future references. Other firms have set up established procedures for analyzing this important sales data such as a customer sales plan. Syntex Laboratories has established a salesman advisory board for each product division—oral contraceptives, dermatologies, and nutritionals. Syntex in doing this is trying to tap a primary source of marketing intelligence—the field sales force.[15] White Motor Corporation trains its sales personnel to conduct a continuing customer and consumer research program with each call. The information obtained is valuable to several facets of White's operation.[16]

Admittedly, the development of an information file is not the sales force's primary responsibility, but it is certainly a useful adjunct to the accomplishment of its goals. A qualified (or professional) salesperson is one who knows the relevant market information about every prospect.

Chapter 5 has examined the beginning aspects of the sales process—prospecting and qualifying. Prospecting begins when the salesperson uses various sources to develop sales leads, which are businesses or people that might need the particular product or service. A

SUMMARY

sales lead becomes a prospect if the need or desire for the product is established. A prospect is qualified if he or she has the ability and/or authority to complete the transaction. Then, it is hoped that the sales process will convert the qualified prospect into a customer and that effective sales follow-up, combined with customer satisfaction, will result in repeat sales.

The importance of prospecting cannot be overestimated. Without an adequate pool of prospects, the salesperson soon fails. Prospecting is important to the overall sales effort because existing customers have to be replaced periodically, and new prospects are necessary for any sales expansion.

Prospect sources include (1) customers, (2) inquiries, (3) company sources, (4) cold canvassing, (5) friends, social contacts, and acquaintances, (6) organizational contacts, (7) spotters, (8) sellers of related products, (9) direct-mail and prospect lists, (10) public information, (11) other prospects, and (12) conventions, meetings, and demonstrations.

Failure to qualify a prospect can result in a considerable loss of the salesperson's time and selling efficiency. There are three essential steps in qualifying a prospect: (1) delineate the factors on which a prospect should be qualified, (2) determine whether the prospect possesses these qualifications, and (3) decide whether or not to approach the prospect. The salesperson has an obligation to maintain some sort of record on qualified prospects which contains all information relevant to the sales effort.

REVIEW QUESTIONS/DISCUSSION QUESTIONS/EXERCISES

1. Briefly identify the following:
    a. Sales lead.   e. Spotters.
    b. Prospect.   f. List broker.
    c. Qualified prospect.   g. Inquiry
    d. Cold canvassing.

2. Contrast the chain of prospects, referral, and key influence methods of obtaining prospects.

3. Assume that you are a salesperson for the following firms. How would you go about prospecting?
    a. Producer of aluminum siding.
    b. Specialty steel manufacturer.
    c. High-price, quality furniture store.
    d. Lawn care firm.

4. What is your opinion of the prospecting force of robots used by such firms as Ennis Business Forms and All Steel Pipe and Tube Company? Will these robots eventually replace their human counterparts?

5. Have you ever been approached by a seller of insurance, dinnerware, cosmetics, magazines, or the like? Did the salesperson regard you as a sales lead? A prospect? If you were regarded as a prospect, where do you think the seller obtained your name?

6. Visit some local automobile dealers. Can you spot the successful sales personnel? What factors differentiate successful from unsuccessful sales personnel?

7. Without an adequate pool of prospects, sales personnel eventually fail. Discuss this statement.

8. Identify some firms that might benefit from an outside firm specializing in prospecting. Why do you think this would be a useful approach for these firms?

9. Why do some salespeople prefer to canvass via telephone, rather than through personal contacts? Do you think sales leads uncovered by telephone contacts are as useful as those uncovered by personal contacts?

10. Develop an inquiry form that could be used in direct-mail advertising by the following firms:
    a. A well-known chain of family restaurants serving meals in the $5 to $7 range (direct mail promoting the restaurants for banquets and special occasions).
    b. An audio equipment store.
    c. A septic tank service (cleaning and repairing).
    d. A farm implement dealer.
    Assume that this inquiry will be turned over to a sales representative. What types of information would be helpful to the representative?

11. Salespeople should forget prospects who do not qualify at the present time. Comment on this statement.

12. Discuss the steps a salesperson should go through in qualifying a prospect. How can the salesperson's company help?

13. What information should a salesperson collect about qualified prospects for:
    a. A uniformed guard service.
    b. Replacement tires for automobile fleets.
    c. A large book bindery.

14. How would you go about "prospecting" for funding sources in these non-business efforts:
    a. A local Little League program.
    b. United Fund.
    c. Second Chance House (a drug rehabilitation center supported by private funds.)
    d. Catholic Social Services.

15. How would you go about qualifying a prospect for the following items:
    a. The trust services of a bank.
    b. A portable sewing machine.
    c. An African safari costing $3,995.
    d. A complete line of office supplies.
    e. A line of gourmet dog food (to buyers from grocery store chains).

16. Approach an experienced salesperson and ask the individual to describe actual situations where a salesperson has failed because of an inability to prospect. Write this information up in the form of a case (similar to those at the end of each chapter in this book). Test your case with other students or sales personnel.

17. Prepare a bibliography of articles, monographs, pamphlets, and books on prospecting. Duplicate and share this list with friends, salespeople, and other students. It can be the beginning of a very useful personal sales development program.

18. Contact several experienced salespeople in different lines of business. Ask them how they prospect for new customers. Compile their responses in a brief three- to five-page report.

19. Develop a prospecting plan for new business department majors at your college.

20. Many industrial sales representatives are faced with situations in which several people have an input into the buying decision. Suppose you had just completed an interview with a prospect and you believed there were additional people in the company who would influence the purchase decision. How would you raise this subject with the prospect?

CASE 5–1: PROFESSIONAL MEDICAL LIBRARY, INC.

Professional Medical Library, Inc. (PML), is a publisher and seller of reference volumes for the medical profession. The firm, headquartered in Providence, Rhode Island, is 83 years old and is held in high regard by the profession it serves. It has maintained its image as a leading publisher of medical reference books through the use of several advisory boards, one for each medical specialty. Doctors comprising these boards propose new reference volumes in their chosen fields, and then recognized medical educators are commissioned to prepare the books.

Professional Medical Library markets its books via a network of aggressive commission sales agents. PML representatives are classified as employees, but they pay all their own expenses and are remunerated through a schedule of variable commissions. Hospitalization, life insurance, and retirement plans are paid by the company.

Frank Kovich is the PML sales representative serving the Cleveland metropolitan area. Kovich, who has been with the company for nine years, is considered to be in the top 10 percent of the firm's 177 sales agents; his net earnings topped $49,000 last year. Like most PML sales representatives, he maintains an office in his home, employs a part-time secretary, and uses a local answering service to handle his business calls.

Although he is content with his current lifestyle, Kovich thinks that he could substantially enhance his earning power if he were able to find some way to improve his selling productivity. He mentions this idea to an acquaintance, Beth Jennings, a marketing professor at a local college, during a meeting of a club to which both belong. Jennings, who is well known in local marketing circles, responds: "Frank, that is the same problem that has faced every salesperson since time began . . . but I tell you what . . . I have some free time on Friday afternoon, so why don't you stop up at my office and we can go over your situation in detail. Maybe we can come up with a couple of helpful suggestions . . . and best yet, I won't even charge you a consulting fee! You can't beat that offer, can you?"

Kovich accepts Jennings's offer to discuss his concern and at the designated time arrives at the professor's office.

Jennings: Hi Frank . . . good to see you. Have a seat while I get us a cup of coffee.

Kovich: Thanks, Beth.

Jennings (handing Kovich the coffee): Here you are, Frank . . . I always need a cup to keep going near the end of the day.

Kovich: Yes, I know what you mean. . . .Beth, I don't know whether I am wasting your time with a question that is unanswerable, or not. But, here is the situation the way I see it. My company does an excellent job of providing sales leads for its salespeople. Most of these are generated through inquiries resulting from advertisements in professional journals, direct mail, or displays at professional meetings. Actually, my files contain more sales leads than I could ever hope to contact.

My concern really gets down to the fact that I only have time for four or five appointments per day. While my close ratio is very good in comparison to other PML sales personnel, I wish I had some way of screening my sales leads as to the likelihood of their buying our books. This would allow me to concentrate on the best prospects and increase my earnings. So you see, Beth, my problem is not where to find prospects, since I have more than I could ever hope to cover. My problem is how to sort out the best ones.

Jennings: I see . . . well, let's think about your situation for a minute. . . .

Questions

1. How would you go about analyzing Kovich's problem?
2. What should Jennings tell Kovich?
3. Can you think of other types of sales personnel that have similar prospecting and qualifying problems?

CASE 5–2: VALLEY STEEL CORPORATION

Valley Steel Corporation has sold industrial shelving through a nationwide network of distributors for over 40 years. Although not the largest or best known in the industry, Valley Steel Corporation has grown at a rapid rate, particularly in the last five years. This recent growth parallels a decision to advertise extensively in primarily trade publications. The president of the corporation, Keith Diamond, feels the only way to become known if you are relatively small and rely on distributor salespeople is to advertise.

The problem as he sees it is that even though growth has been adequate, sales leads coming from advertising are typically ignored by members of the distributors' sales forces. A study revealed that a typical salesperson will make use of no more than 25 percent of the sales leads supplied him or her. Lori Dewell, a salesperson for one of the largest distributors, is a case in point. She feels that sales leads have very little value in comparison with other forms of prospecting. In her words, "advertising inquiries are a poor substitute for knowing your territory and who is and is not a potential customer for industrial shelving." She goes on to add that a lot of shelving is purchased by her present customers. New customers will contact her.

Questions

1. Since Lori Dewell sells more shelving than anyone else in the country, is the generation of inquiries really important?
2. Should inquiries be forwarded directly to the distributor or should Valley Steel Corporation do the qualifying?
3. Assuming advertising inquiries are valuable, how would you suggest Valley Steel Corporation go about increasing use?

KEY POINTS

- Preparation, combined with the ability to react to the demands of the situation, increases sales effectiveness.
- Preparation is consideration of the *what, who,* and *how* of the sales call or interview.
- The professional salesperson translates product benefits into customer satisfactions.
- Discussion of product benefits and their order of presentation is based on the individual involved.
- Getting the interview and opening the sales presentation are parts of a successful approach.
- Favorable first impressions are a product of what the salesperson says and his or her appearance.
- The amount of product knowledge as opposed to customer knowledge required by the salesperson depends upon the product life cycle.

Chapter

6

PREAPPROACH AND APPROACH

Thomas Gordon Mock, a regional salesperson for Louisiana-Pacific Corp., does not tell his customers jokes or try to overwhelm them with conversation. Instead, he says, he tries to gain his customers' respect. "The best approach is one that sells well over time. I want customers who are loyal and reluctant to change. The salesperson at the industrial level has got to be somebody the customer can depend on."[1]

SOME DEFINITIONS AND GOALS

Once prospects have been identified and qualified, the process of selling begins with the preapproach and approach steps. The *preapproach* is the salesperson's preparation for sales calls on specific customers. The seller prepares in order to know what he or she is talking about and to gain the respect of the customer.[2] The *approach* is opening the sale and setting the stage for the sales presentation. The impression customers get from the opening plays a major part in determining how they will react to the presentation. The customer can create a helpful atmosphere for the sales presentation or one that is decidedly harmful to the remainder of the interview.[3]

The preapproach and approach steps can be looked at differently, depending upon the status of the customer. If the salesperson is making a first call on a qualified prospect, the preapproach and the approach can be thought of as important building blocks in gaining a customer for the company. They are crucial because the salesperson in all likelihood will get only one chance with this particular customer.

If the customer is already an active account, the preapproach and the approach are focused on repurchase. *Repurchase* can involve either maintenance of purchases at their present level or an increase in purchase volume. Increases in purchase volume can be obtained if customers buy more of the items they are already buying or buy other items in the product lines handled by the salesperson's company. Repurchase is also concerned with not losing accounts when customers for some reason cannot get what they want when they want it.

There are a lot of stories about unique approaches that have worked for various salespeople in particular situations. But most salespersons should concentrate on the goals for the preapproach and approach steps:

1. Gain or retain a customer for the firm as opposed to making a sale.
2. Develop a customized approach for each qualified prospect.

By preparing for a sales call the sales representative becomes doubly effective. The individual will be able to react to the particular demands of the situation and at the same time be prepared to talk about specific and appropriate product benefits that may satisfy a customer's needs or wants. Further, preparation helps the salesperson know the prospect's:

1. Position in the decision-making structure.
2. Primary concern (price, service, product quality).
3. Personal interests and hobbies.
4. Receptivity to sales presentations.

PREAPPROACH

Another advantage of preparation is the effect it can have on the salesperson. The representative will have more personal confidence and as a result not be as likely to make mistakes that can cause loss of customer respect. The salesperson will also tend to be more enthusiastic.

The starting point in preparation is the customer sales plan. Reviewing the sales plan, the salesperson will want to consider four aspects of the anticipated selling situation. The first is what will be said, or the content of the sales presentation. Next, the salesperson has to consider the prospect and that person's role in the purchasing decision. This in turn will affect the content of the sales message. Third, the salesperson must consider how to give the presentation, which can be thought of as the selling technique. Finally there is the question of balance between imparting product knowledge and customer knowledge.

In short, preparation for the salesperson is consideration of the *what, who,* and *how* of a forthcoming sales presentation to a specific customer or group of customers. Thoroughness in preparation is a key factor in whether the salesperson will be successful.

Aside from the preliminary remarks used to open the sales interview, all the customer really wants to hear from any salesperson is how that salesperson can satisfy particular needs or wants. Many complaints about industrial sales personnel do not concern the seller's product knowledge, rather they are focused on the inability or failure to translate product benefits into specific customer satisfactions. Buyers are inclined to feel that salespeople do not know what they should about customer problems, processes, or products.

Salespeople must translate product benefits into satisfactions ap-

Contents of the presentation

plicable to a specific customer.[4] One way to do this is to follow a three-step procedure:

1. Select those features of the product that are of interest to the customer.
2. Establish priorities for the selected product features.
3. Develop written statements on how each feature can benefit the customer.

Before this procedure can be followed, however, the salesperson must develop an inventory of product features. This is done by analyzing the features of each product in the line, including not only the physical aspects of the product, such as its durability or ease of repair, but also other features that relate to the company and its sales effort, such as delivery, pricing, and credit. The salesperson with good technical competence and training can be considered another product feature.

This inventory of product features is a guide the salesperson can use to translate product benefits into satisfactions for a specific customer. The first step is to select the features of particular interest to that customer. Reducing the number of features is logical because no customer will be equally interested in all of them. The salesperson has only a limited time to make the presentation, and so must concentrate on what is most important to the customer.

The salesperson who calls on the customer regularly will have a reasonably good idea of the customer's primary interests. Most purchasing agents feel that the frank and open relationships they have with salespeople allow them to volunteer information about the firm's needs and problems, and the buyers in turn can ask for help.[5] Describing this relationship, one purchasing agent was quoted as saying: "We use expensive, complex tubes for radio transmission. A technical salesman can visit the places where these tubes are being used and discuss their performance with the engineers there. Because he may be quite helpful, the engineer may ask me to buy the product."[6] Even if a customer sales plan is not available, the salesperson should not rely on memory alone in selecting product features. Some form of written record about the customer's needs is essential.

When the seller is making the first call on a customer, the job of selecting appropriate product features is much more formidable. Nevertheless, the representative should not let the apparent lack of information about the customer prevent the identification of important product features. The salesperson need not rely entirely on instinct. Several sources of information are available about a new customer:

(1) other customers, (2) published data such as directories, (3) articles about the customer in newspapers or magazines, (4) annual reports, and (5) the customer. The salesperson usually waits until the interview to get information directly from the customer, but an insurance agent in setting up an appointment, for example, might ask a prospective customer his or her age, spouse's age, number of dependents, occupations, and possibly what is sought in the way of insurance. A customer's place of business or residence is another clue that is provided indirectly by the customer.

The second step in translating product benefits into a customer's need satisfaction is the establishment of priorities for presenting the selected product features. This involves analyzing each feature in an effort to determine the relative importance of the customer benefits it can produce. Profit improvement is one benefit that is uppermost in the minds of many business buyers. Above all, the order of priorities should demonstrate that the product is competitively distinct. In opening the sales presentation, the salesperson stresses the product benefit believed to have the highest priority with the customer.

Sales personnel for Gates Aviation, who sell the Learjet, relate the product features of aircraft safety and a power-to-weight ratio (that gives the aircraft speed) to such benefits as cost, size, and climbing ability. The vice president of marketing has been quoted as saying: "These [benefits] are unique differences. To sell, we had to decide what we are. We are the workhorse of the business jet. We are a supplemental aircraft to the larger business jet. We are the middle-management business jet."[7]

The third step is to develop written statements on how each feature can benefit the specific customer. Writing up explanations of benefits helps the salesperson in two ways: (1) it serves as a rehearsal for the sales interview; and (2) it helps the salesperson demonstrate thorough knowledge, which should lead to greater believability and acceptance. For the benefit of profit improvement, for example, the salesperson will want to spell out:

1. The return in dollars and cents the customer can get from the product.
2. The costs, both direct and indirect, the customer should budget for in purchasing the item in question.
3. The yearly contribution to profit improvement estimated for the product through decreasing costs, raising revenues, or both.[8]

The customer

Sales personnel will focus on different benefits, depending upon who they are talking to in the sales interview. In selling the Learjet a distinction is made between the front and back of the airplane; the pilot rides in front, and the corporate executive rides as a passenger in the back. What each wants from an airplane is obviously quite different.[9]

Another very important difference among customers is the extent of their involvement with one or more steps in the buying procedure. Salespeople often find job titles to be misleading. There is little uniformity; people with the same job title can have entirely different types of jobs, depending upon the company. The large number of job titles also limits the use of such as a way to classify customers. It is not uncommon for the various people involved in purchasing a single product to have many different job titles with relatively minor differences in job descriptions.

A more accurate approach is to classify customers by the extent of their involvement at various stages in the buying process. A convenient way to divide up the buying process is in terms of four steps:

1. Identifying the need.
2. Establishing product specifications.
3. Selecting the vendor.
4. Approving the expenditure.

A salesperson calling on a manufacturer could expect to meet with engineering and production personnel to center on need and specifications. The purchasing department, on the other hand, would tend to be more concerned with vendor selection.

A knowledge of the buying process is a necessity for the industrial salesperson, who may see any number of individuals in the course of making a sale. This knowledge may also be helpful in selling consumer goods. In buying clothing, for example, the style-conscious person would be involved with needs and specifications, while the interests of casual dressers would be more likely to be in vendor selection and the actual expenditure.

Degree of product interest is another classification technique that can be used in both industrial and consumer selling. One way is to use four degrees of customer interest in a product:

1. Must have.
2. Should have.
3. Would be helpful to have.
4. Nice to have.[10]

Obviously a salesperson will prepare differently for each degree of customer interest, using one sales presentation for a customer who must have the product and an entirely different one for the lowest level of customer interest (nice to have). Customer interest level will undoubtedly affect the ordering of benefits in the presentation and the question of which selling technique to use with a particular customer.

The selling technique

In preparing for each sales call, the salesperson must determine the approach to take with a particular customer. Success in a sales interview depends as much on selling technique as it does on product knowledge and sales preparation. A salesperson who has done a thorough job of preparing (both content and customer) can select the selling technique that fits the particular customer. As a result, the seller's knowledge will be more evident to the customer and the likelihood of success improved.

There are two common mistakes a salesperson can make in regard to selling technique. One is to assume that there are only two selling techniques: the hard sell and the soft sell. Actually there are varying degrees of aggressiveness, and the hard sell and the soft sell represent only the extremes (Figure 6–1). The *hard sell* is an aggressive selling technique. The salesperson takes on a forceful role, asking for the order repeatedly. The customer is pushed toward a buying decision. Door-to-door and used-car salespeople are normally thought of as hard sellers.

The *soft sell* is designed to develop a satisfactory relationship with the customer over a period of time involving numerous sales calls. Aggressive sales tactics are not used for fear of offending the cus-

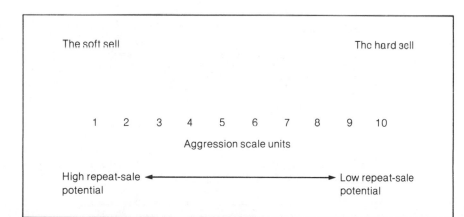

Figure 6–1
The sales aggression spectrum

Source: Reprinted by permission from Barry J. Hersker, "The Ecology of Personal Selling," *Southern Journal of Business* 5 (July 1970): 44.

tomer and disrupting the buyer-seller relationship. The soft sell is low-key selling. The customer never gets the impression of being pushed into doing anything. Salespeople who call on the same customers time and time again tend to rely on the soft sell.

Another common mistake is to adopt one selling technique and use it on all customers. What sellers using this approach are saying in effect is that what worked with one customer should work with all. They forget that customer individuality calls for preparation of each sales call.

The customer's involvement in the buying procedure can affect the level of aggressiveness used by a salesperson. It is possible to be more aggressive with the purchasing agent, who is principally concerned with the decision of vendor selection, than with engineering personnel, who are identifying needs and determining specifications. Aggressiveness can be varied in relation to the degree of customer interest. The less interest the customer has in the product, the more aggressive the salesperson will want to be in the sales presentation.

Also, the degree of aggressiveness can vary in relation to the customer's potential for repeat business. Less aggression is used when many future sales calls are anticipated. The more infrequent the sales call, the more aggressive the salesperson.

"Mr. Gorman is here to see you, sir, and I think he wants to go for your jugular vein."

Reprinted by permission The Wall Street Journal.

Some sellers elect a hard sell technique

The most aggressiveness is demonstrated in a one-call sale, in which the seller knows there is only one chance with the customer in question. For instance, the product may not lend itself to repeat sales to the same customer. When selling large industrial machinery, consumer durables such as a refrigerator or air conditioning unit, and life insurance, the salesperson can expect a very low potential for repeat sales.[11]

PRODUCT KNOWLEDGE VERSUS CUSTOMER KNOWLEDGE

A fourth question in preparation is the balance between product and customer knowledge. Obviously the salesperson needs to know both product and customer. However, as Figure 6–2 shows the salesperson needs to shift the emphasis in sales planning as a product passes through the stages of its life cycle. When the product is new to the market, the salesperson will have to know more about the product than the customer does. The salesperson is the major source of buying knowledge. The longer the product is on the market and becomes what is called a "shelf item," the greater the need for the salesperson to know all he or she can about the customer. The customer will need less and less buying information from the salesperson.

The implications are that even though the salesperson is making a first call, the attention placed on product knowledge as opposed to customer knowledge, or vice versa, is based on the stage of the product life cycle. The reverse of this will also hold true. More emphasis will be needed on product knowledge and correspondingly less on customer knowledge when calling on a regular account with a new product.

APPROACH

The purpose of the approach is twofold: (1) getting the interview with the right person; and (2) opening the sale. If the sales representative cannot get to the right person, the quality of the opening makes little difference. But getting to see the right person is not going to be much help if the salesperson does a poor job of opening the interview.

Getting the interview

Before trying to get an interview, the salesperson should double check to make sure the prospect is the proper person to see to get the sale. Once this is established, any one of several techniques for getting an interview can be used. These include making a cold call, using the telephone, getting an introduction from a third party, or writing a letter.

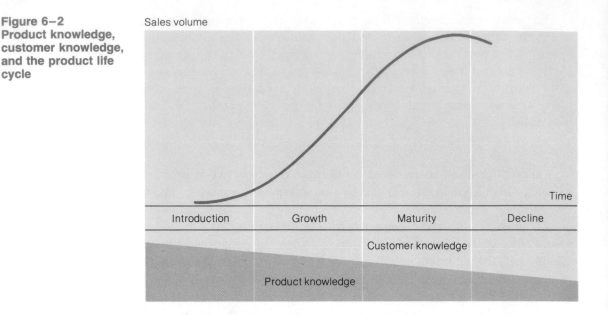

**Figure 6–2
Product knowledge,
customer knowledge,
and the product life
cycle**

Selection of the technique depends upon whether the customer is a new or an existing account and what the customer's preferences are. Obviously, trying to sell to someone neither the salesperson nor the company has had any prior dealings with will require a different technique than calling on a regular customer. There is no one best way to approach all customers.

Cold calls are sales calls made without any prior contact with the customer. The salesperson stops in unannounced and asks to talk to the customer. It is important that the seller's identity and purpose be correctly presented; tricks create the wrong impression and are self-defeating. A big problem in using the cold call is the amount of time the salesperson must spend waiting to see the customer. This will be true even when the customer sets aside certain periods of time for talking to sales personnel.

Use of the telephone to get an appointment is a good way to cut down on waiting time and travel expense. The salesperson must remember, however, that the purpose of the call is to get an appointment, not to make a sale.

An introduction from a third party is effective because it helps to break the ice so that the salesperson is not looked upon as a stranger by the customer. The salesperson needs something tangible by way of introduction from the third party: a business card with a notation, a letter of introduction, or a phone call to the customer.

Using a letter to get an appointment has two possible advantages: getting through to the customer and saving selling time. Many firms use standardized forms that can be typed in such a way that will personalize them. This relieves the salesperson of a disliked task, and there is a good chance that the form letter will do a better preconditioning job than one written by a salesperson. The salesperson's job is selling—not writing letters.

A syrup company found that a letter to bakery owners was able to accomplish something its salespeople said they could not do: Get the owner, plant manager, advertising manager, and purchasing agent of a bakery together to see a film on bakery installations. So successful was the letter in getting appointments that within 60 days after the mailing, the sales force sold almost twice the number of bakery installations it had been able to sell in the preceding 15 years.[12]

Opening the sale

Opening the sale involves creating a favorable first impression that will provide a smooth transition from preparation to delivery of the sales message. First impressions do make a difference in selling. A poor impression may result in the customer not hearing much of what the salesperson has to say in the remainder of the sales presentation.

While sales executives are of the opinion that their salespeople have both the know-how and the motivation to open a sale, they feel the sales force itself can be the biggest stumbling block in opening new sales. In a survey reported in *Sales Management*,[13] sales executives named the following stumbling blocks:

Stumbling block	Percentage of sales executives responding
Complacency among established salesmen	26%
Insufficient homework	25
Poor organization of time	20
Improper, uninformed prospecting	14
Inadequate training	12
Fear among new salesmen	3
Total	100%

In the same survey, sales personnel reported that the types of selling situations that give them the most trouble are reopening a sale, making a cold call, and having only one chance to make a sale. Developing new business among present customers or selling over a period of time give only a few salespeople trouble in opening the sale.

The relative number of sales personnel citing these troublesome openings were as follows:

Troublesome opening	Percentage of sales personnel responding
Reopening the sale	32%
Cold calls	31
One-shot sales	29
Developing new business among existing accounts	4
Long-haul sales	4
Total	100%

The opening of a sale is crucial to any salesperson, but the most difficulty is encountered in meeting customers for the first and perhaps only time and in trying to make repeat customers. The question is: how can the salesperson ensure a favorable first impression?

What the salesperson says in opening the sales presentation should dramatically point out his or her knowledge of the customer. This includes the nonselling preliminary social conversation, as well as the initial attention-getting opener of the actual presentation.[14] The opening must be prepared at the same time as the rest of the presentation. The most dramatic point the salesperson can make is the product benefit felt to have highest priority with the customer, and it follows that the more knowledge a salesperson has of a customer, the better the opening will be. The need for customer knowledge was emphasized by a sales executive from a company marketing packaged grocery products who noted that "It's harder to open a sale today . . . you need more knowledge, more background to sell the customer. There are more items, less shelf space."[15]

Asking the customer to buy the product is a possible opening. The advantage of such a forthright opening is that it gets the customer talking about what is needed or wanted in a product of this type. One marketer noted:

> As to the most reliable sales opening, it depends on the man you are approaching. I've had success with walking in and saying, "Hey, do you want to buy a cash register?" When he comes back with, "No, I don't want to buy one," I then try to get him to tell me why not, and I tell him how much better the new machines are over the one he has.[16]

Above all, the salesperson should not rely on personality to pave the way for the sales presentation. Good openings are based on knowing the product benefits and their order of importance to the customer. This was emphasized by a marketing director of a packaging company, who said, "The more reliable sales opening technique is starting, in a convincing way, to point out benefits for the user over competitive products. The least effective opener would be to expect that your company or your personality will sell anything without proven benefit."[17]

Appearance is another way customers judge salespeople. It is estimated that as many as 8 out of 10 customers can be turned off by poor appearance.[18] A good appearance, on the other hand, builds customer confidence and acceptance.

SUMMARY

The preapproach is the salesperson's preparation for sales calls on specific customers. The approach is opening the sale and setting the stage for the sales presentation. Together they are important in initiating the sales presentation, particularly with new customers.

Preparation supplements the salesperson's ability to react to the particular demands of the selling situation. Starting with the customer sales plan, the salesperson considers what to say, who to say it to, and how to say it.

What the salesperson says should tell the customer how the products presented can satisfy his or her particular needs or wants. A close look at the customer will show which needs to talk about and how involved the particular customer is in the buying process. Involvement can be classified in terms of the steps in the buying procedure or customer interest in the product. The right selling technique makes the salesperson's knowledge evident to the customer. The emphasis on product or customer knowledge is determined by the stage of the product life cycle.

The approach step includes getting the interview and opening the sale. Four of the better-known techniques are (1) cold call, (2) telephone call, (3) introduction from third party, and (4) letter.

In opening the sale, the salesperson is interested in creating a favorable first impression that will allow a smooth transition from preparation to delivery of the sales message. What the salesperson says and his or her appearance make up the first impression.

REVIEW QUESTIONS/DISCUSSION QUESTIONS/EXERCISES

1. Briefly identify the following:
   a. Preapproach.
   b. Approach.
   c. Cold call.
   d. Hard sell.
   e. Soft sell.

2. Describe how the preapproach differs from the approach.

3. Will the question of whether the customer is a new or an existing account make any difference in the preapproach and approach?

4. How can the salesperson become more effective through preparation?

5. List the different customer characteristics with which a salesperson should be concerned.

6. It has been said that preparation gives the salesperson confidence. How would you explain this?

7. Select a product with which you are familiar and identify the primary benefits you would present to a potential buyer.

8. How would you attempt to implement the approach suggested by Thomas Gordon Mock at the beginning of the chapter?

9. Most products have a number of good features. Why should the salesperson limit a presentation to just a few of them?

10. How can the salesperson go about collecting information about a new customer?

11. Suppose you are a buyer in the housewares department of a large department store. A salesperson you have not seen before calls on you with a new line of cooking ware (pots and pans). Should the salesperson stress product knowledge or customer knowledge?

12. In Question 11, how could the salesperson go about collecting information that would show a working knowledge of your department?

13. In Question 11, what are some of the product features that might make one line of cooking ware different from other lines?

14. Select a consumer product that is decidedly more expensive than its competition. Using the product benefit of long-term savings, develop some written statements about the more expensive item.

15. For the following products, identify who in a family would be more interested in each of the four stages of involvement in the buying process:
    a. Family automobile.
    b. Automobile tires.
    c. Life insurance.
    d. Set of dishes.

16. Imagine that you are an insurance salesperson about to call on a homeowner to sell a fire insurance policy. Determine the homeowner's degree of product interest and what selling technique you will use.

17. Is there a simple best way to approach customers?

18. What are the different ways a salesperson can get an introduction from a third party?

19. Sometimes a gift is used to get a sales appointment. In what types of situations do you feel a gift is most suitable?

20. Assume you are a pharmaceutical sales representative. What type of approaches would you use to see physicians?

CASE 6-1: SAFEBUYS, INC.

Jim Schofner has recently started work as a sales representative for Safebuys, Inc., which makes and sells safes for homes and small businesses. Schofner is one of two sales representatives in the Los Angeles area. He concentrates on sales to businesses, while the other salesperson sells to the home market. Before coming to work for Safebuys, Inc., three months ago, Schofner worked four years as a wholesale grocery salesperson.

Schofner feels his best prospects are businesses such as repair shops, barber shops, and beauty salons. They have a need for a safe, but not one that is large and costly. Schofner first selects a general area of the city. He then spends a day locating all the stores he feels have a need for a small safe. Using this list, he starts making sales calls.

Schofner's procedure in a sales call is to talk only to the owner. If the owner is not present, Schofner tries to find out when he or she will be in and returns at that time. In talking to the owner, Schofner begins by showing the small safe he carries with him and saying, "Instead of worrying about the money you leave overnight or making that nightly trip to the bank, install our safe in your store. Anyone who breaks into your store would not be able to find our safe once it is installed. It is so small, I can carry it around without any trouble." What Schofner says after this depends upon the reaction of the store owner.

Schofner has made a large number of sales calls in the three months he has been with Safebuys, Inc. However, he has sold only five safes. Talking over the situation with his sales manager, there seems to be agreement that Schofner is trying to sell to the right prospect and he is using the strongest selling points. The only suggestion of the sales manager is for Schofner to work harder.

Questions

1. What suggestions do you have that would improve Schofner's approach to customers?
2. Do you feel that his preparation is inadequate? If so, how would you go about preparing for the sales calls?
3. What would you say in opening the sale?

CASE 6–2: TEMPERATURE APPLIANCE CORPORATION

For the past 50 years, Temperature Appliance Corporation has been recognized as the quality leader in kitchen appliances. Last month they purchased a company that makes microwave ovens. The ovens are to be marketed under the TEMPCO label and sold through the same distributors that already handle TEMPCO ovens, ranges, refrigerators, and waste disposals.

Susan Herschfield and Allen Thomas, two new sales representatives have been assigned the job of developing a presentation for the new TEMPCO microwave ovens. This presentation is to be made at the next national sales meeting.

Susan and Allen have discussed what should be covered in the presentation and decided that the preparation phase can be skipped because no new customer is involved. What time they have been given will be devoted to supplying other sales reps with product features and the differences between the TEMPCO microwave oven and the competition.

Questions

1. Do you agree with Susan and Allen that preparation (preapproach) is not necessary as part of their presentation? Explain your answer.
2. What should be the mix of product knowledge and customer knowledge?
3. Undoubtedly all the distributors now carry a competitor's line of microwave ovens. What possible benefits to distributors can you see in replacing or adding the TEMPCO product?

A Profile of Professional Selling

Ralph W. Ketner

Look at the track record of the company Ralph W. Ketner runs out of Salisbury, N.C., and guess what business he's in. For the past decade, return on equity has averaged 30 percent and earnings per share have been compounding at a 41 percent annual pace. Oil? Semiconductors? Neither. Groceries. His chain of 108 Food Town stores did $544 million worth of business last year in the Carolinas and Virginia, netting close to 3 percent aftertax. Almost unheard of in an industry where the average is 0.75 percent. In return on total capital, Food Town, at 28 percent, is far and away in first place among the larger supermarket operators.

What's his secret? Ketner will begin by telling you about his "lean and mean" headquarters operation, housed in a crowded one-story building near a railroad siding. Next, Ketner will trot out his executive vice president. He is in charge of the dry-goods warehouse next door that covers 15 acres and every week gobbles up the contents of 250 trucks and 60 railcars. Pennies are watched real close there, from the way paper towels are stacked to the recycling of cardboard (13,925 tons of it last year). Payroll is next, and it's a major factor in the profits of all retailers. At Food Town it runs to 8 percent of sales, a good 4 points below the national average.

The big secret, Ketner finally lets on, isn't any of these things, but ridiculously low prices. He'll talk about beating the pants off his lumbering competitors—national chains like Winn-Dixie and Kroger—and he'll reel off a series of anecdotes to illustrate how. He especially likes the letter from a housewife, irate over a bag boy's rudeness, that closed: "Mr. Ketner, I wish I could afford not to do business with you." There he's finally hinting at the key to his success: salesmanship. His prices aren't that much lower, but he gives customers what they want and makes them think they're getting a good deal.

Ketner has been selling food for most of his 60 years, but he caught the knack of making money at it rather late in life. As a child he hawked ice cream for a nickel an hour and worked after school in his father's grocery store. When the elder Ketner died, during the Depression, Ralph's brother Glenn took over and expanded it into a 25-store chain he sold to Winn-Dixie in 1956. Ralph, at the age of 37, soon decided it was time to strike out on his own. Along with several other Winn-Dixie employees, he scrounged up $75,000 of capital and got another $75,000 by going through the Salisbury City Directory, peddling stock to anyone who would listen. Although he later learned it was probably illegal, he says, grinning, no one's complaining: A $10 share bought then is now 360 shares worth $8,000.

Source: Adapted from, "What's a LFPINC?" *Forbes*, February 16, 1981, pp. 69–70. Reprinted by permission.

Part 4

PRESENTING THE SALES MESSAGE

If you hit a person's logic, you've got'im

JOHNNY BOSWORTH
Automobile Salesperson
Interviewed in Studs
*Terkel's Working.**

KEY POINTS

- Selling success is dependent upon the quality of the sales presentation.
- Empathy allows the salesperson to interact with the customer.
- Formula and stimulus-response selling focus on the ability of the salesperson to trigger buying action.
- Need-satisfaction selling gives the customer a chance to talk about his or her needs or wants.
- Interaction selling is based on the match of salesperson and customer.
- Balanced selling mixes, through interaction, equal parts of customer orientation and control by the salesperson.
- Some structure in the sales presentation is desirable, but standardization conflicts with persuasiveness.
- Customer participation helps tell the salesperson what needs to be known about the customer.
- The credibility of salespeople depends upon their expertness and the validity of their statements.
- Matches of salesperson and customer are strengthened by the salesperson's knowing everything there is to know about the customer.

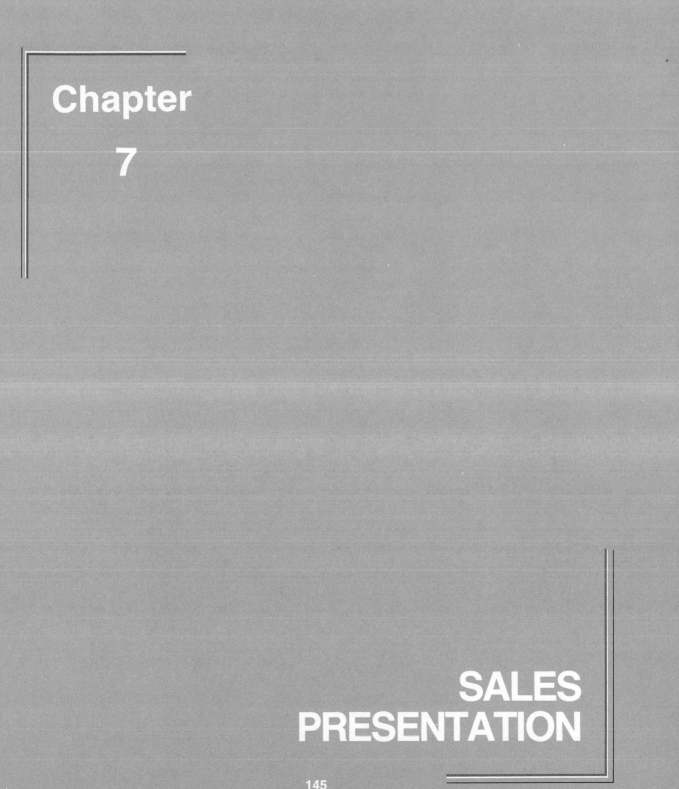

Chapter

7

SALES
PRESENTATION

Sales presentations are anything but cut and dried these days. Take the real estate market at the beginning of the decade. Skyrocketing interest rates required real estate sales personnel to expand their knowledge of home financing techniques beyond conventional mortgages. Contracts, assumptions, and the like became commonplace. Linda Cook, who heads up sales training for Detroit's B.F. Chamberlain Co., and others realized that sales presentations would have to change to reflect the new economic realities. Cook put it this way:

> In this market, we must provide options for our customers. We also emphasize that homes are a better bargain today than they will be in a year. Even though interest rates are expected to decline, appreciation will probably raise home prices by 10 percent.[1]

Few people would argue that one of the most important dimensions of personal selling is the presentation itself. Effective planning and preparation of the sales presentation can have a major impact on improving sales performance.

PREPARING A SALES PRESENTATION

In its broadest sense the sales presentation is professional selling. In a more practical view, however, the *sales presentation* is the message delivered by the salesperson to the customer. While we normally think of the *customer* as one individual, the term can also be applied to a group of individuals, such as a husband and wife or the buying committee of a company.

What makes a sales presentation more effective than an advertisement in a magazine or a commercial on television is the salesperson's ability to tailor it to a particular customer's interests by making use of feedback from the customer. A sales presentation is more than passing on information in a persuasive way to a customer. It is also gathering information about and gaining an understanding of the customer so that needs or wants can be pinpointed. These functions mean that the salesperson is more of a receiver than a sender in the communication process.[2]

How good the sales presentation is will depend on the salesperson's ability to understand the customer's point of view. Without this trait, called *empathy,* the salesperson will find it difficult to establish the relationship so necessary for effective two-way communication. Empathy allows salespeople to maximize their flexibility in responding to customer interests. It has been noted:

> He [a salesman with a good sense of empathy] senses the reactions of the customer and is able to adjust to these reactions. He is not simply bound by a prepared sales tract, but he functions in terms of the real interaction between himself and the customer. Sensing what the customer is feeling, he is able to change pace, double back on this tract, and make creative modifications which might be necessary to home in on the target and close the sale.[3]

APPROACHES TO THE SALES PRESENTATION

The various approaches to selling can be divided into those that are salesperson-oriented and those that are customer-oriented. Two salesperson-oriented approaches involve a formula and the stimulus-response technique, while need satisfaction and interaction are customer-oriented approaches. Balanced selling is a proposed approach combining the advantages of both of these orientations.

Salesperson-oriented approaches

The AIDA formula.   The formula used in selling is usually the *standardized learning approach* (AIDA). The sales presentation is visualized as a buildup process which ends when the customer takes some buying action (Figure 7–1). The four parts to sales presentation, which must be in sequence, are awareness, interest, desire, and action.

In applying the AIDA formula, the salesperson first must create awareness. Once this is done the task is to translate awareness into interest and then to convert interest into desire. Some look on this third step as getting the customer to acknowledge that the product answers some conscious need or want. The salesperson who has de-

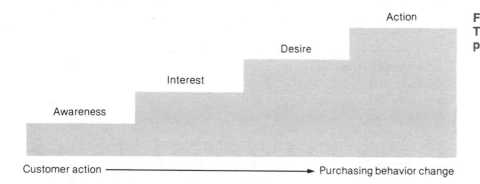

**Figure 7–1
The AIDA learning process in promotion**

"Look up the Guinness record
for being on 'hold'!"

Reprinted by permission The Wall Street Journal.

Gaining customer feedback is often difficult when
making presentations by telephone.

veloped sufficient customer desire for the product can then ask for the
order and get buyer action. Assuming the goals of the previous steps
have been accomplished, the strength of product desire will be enough
to cause the customer to make the purchase.

Presentations in years hence—The salesman

The "communications revolution" will eventually cause a revolution in
the sales presentation. New devices will present the facts, leaving . . .
more time for persuasive selling. Of course, the millions of dollars that
will have to be spent installing hardware at the sending . . . and receiving
. . . ends mean that this change is still many years away.

Nevertheless, such new ideas as Picturephone, facsimile transmission,
video cassettes, and cathode ray terminals already are being used somewhat in selling. All such devices let the salesman make his "presentation"
without being in the prospect's office.

Although technology's contribution to selling will be great, no one expects the salesman to be replaced totally. Staunton Oppenheimer, product
sales manager of Xerox's telecopier group, says, "The salesman is 60 percent of the ball game. Facsimile transmission can be used to 'present' a

Continued

product, but I wouldn't be completely impressed unless I could talk to a salesman." Oppenheimer stresses that the salesman sells himself first, then his product.

It's generally felt that the communications devices will take over the product description phase of the presentation. E. Bryan Carne, director of GTE's electronics technology laboratory, points out that "the salesman is expected to be a walking encyclopedia of his products and company. If a device such as a Picturephone gets the basic descriptive data to the buyer before the salesman's call, the presentation can plunge immediately into the important question-and-answer phase or the critical give-and-take negotiations." Carne also feels that once that encyclopedic load is lifted from the salesman's shoulders, he'll have more time for planning the strategy of his sales presentation.

Future improvements will increase the devices' capabilities in the presentation area. AT&T, for example, discouraged by Picturephone's limited success, is working hard on a second generation model. The company's idea: a machine so designed that it incorporates customer suggestions.

Tom Patrykus, staff member of the Picturephone marketing group, notes that voice-actuated cameras will make group sales presentations more feasible. Three different product specialists could discuss the various features of a product, and the voice of the person talking at any given moment would make the camera focus on him. The new model will also have a higher resolution on its viewing screen to allow products to be shown in finer detail. Also in the works is a facsimile device that would enable the buyer to make a hard copy of whatever caught his interest in the video presentation.

In the videocassette field, GTE's Carne thinks that the disc . . . will be the leader because it is cheaper and more flexible than the videotape in use now. Its 10-minute length is "just about right for a sales spiel," he says. He points out that if the disc is attached to a business magazine ad, "it becomes a presentation when the buyer puts it on his TV player attachment."

Graphic display terminals will also help . . . transmit basic product information to the buyer before a sales presentation. The buyer would use a desk-top keyboard device to interrogate the supplier's computer-based electronic catalogue, extracting information . . . to ask the salesman about later. Or he could use facsimile transmission to send a drawing of suggested product changes that the salesman, after discussing the alterations with his engineers, could use as the basis of his presentation.

In any event, although communications technologies might shift the emphasis the salesman puts on various aspects of his presentation, they will also make him more necessary than ever.

Source: Reprinted with permission from *Sales Management, The Marketing Magazine* © 1973.

Two other steps could be added to this selling formula. One, to be inserted between desire and action, can be called *conviction.* Conviction is intensified desire for the product, particularly in light of the asking price. The job of the salesperson is to convince the customer that the product is worth the asking price.

The other step, which can be called *satisfaction,* is confirmation of the correctness of the purchasing decision after the action has taken place. The salesperson has the job of making sure the customer is getting what is expected from the product. An important part is showing the customer how to use the product.

Those who favor the formula approach feel it gives the salesperson a logical framework for presentation of all possible sales ideas. Highly structured or *canned* presentations (to be discussed later) are often based on a selling formula. Successful utilization of a selling formula depends upon whether the salesperson can lead the customer through the various steps. The question is, can the salesperson lead the customer from awareness to interest, desire, and, finally, buying action?

An obvious objection to the selling formula is that it concentrates on the salesperson's actions, without any regard for customer interests. Another objection is that the selling formula tends to treat all customers alike, which removes the advantage a salesperson has in being able to adjust to individual differences. Further, it has been shown that the effect of communication is not always the same, and a salesperson cannot be sure the customer will respond in the sequence indicated by the standardized learning approach.

Stimulus response.   This approach to selling assumes that certain actions on the part of the salesperson will trigger a response from the customer in the form of buying action. The actions of the salesperson to stimulate the desired response tend to be emotional in content. For example, fear of future uncertainties, such as death or the need for medical care, can be used by an insurance agent to sell a policy. The sales presentation might begin as follows:

> A few days ago I gave Edith Brown a pretty large check. You might know her, she lives just a few blocks on the other side of Main Street. It doesn't replace her husband, who had a heart attack, but there are many bills to pay and she has three children, two of whom will be in college next year.

The stimulus-response approach treats the customer in a rather mechanical way.[4] The salesperson introduces the stimulus, and the customer is supposed to respond in a predicted way. In the above example, the agent brought up the uncertainty of death and the fear of leaving a family unprotected. The salesperson knew that fear is one of the strongest motivators to stimulate people to buy a commodity such as insurance.[5] The anticipated response is for the customer to lessen this fear by purchasing the insurance.

Those who use the stimulus-response approach must realize that different customers may react differently to the same stimulus. The reverse can also be true; different people will have the same response to different stimuli.

The stimulus-response approach can be criticized because it lumps all purchasing behavior into simple, mechanical terms, whereas purchasing behavior is exceedingly complex and there are countless differences between customers.

Need satisfaction.   One of the customer-oriented or need-satisfying approaches that have been developed is commonly referred to as *need satisfaction* (Figure 7–2). In this approach the sales presentation is pictured as having three parts.[6] In the first part, the salesperson queries the customer to determine specific needs, using questions designed to get the customer talking. When the needs of the customer have been identified, the salesperson attempts to get the customer to agree that these are the customer's needs, a step that often involves making the customer conscious of those needs. Finally, the salesperson shows the customer how the product being offered can best solve those needs. By first finding out and then making sure of the customer's needs, the salesperson does not waste time talking about all the features of a product. Instead the salesperson picks out those that

Customer-oriented approaches

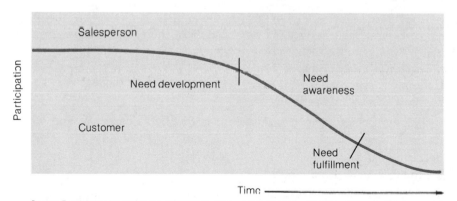

**Figure 7–2
Need-satisfaction approach**

Source: Reproduced by permission of Harold C. Cash and W.J.E. Crissy, "A Point of View for Salesmen," *The Psychology of Selling* 1(1965):15. Personnel Development Associates, P.O. Box 3005 Roosevelt Field Station, Garden City, NY 11530.

will have the greatest impact on the customer. (This process can also be part of the preapproach, as noted in Chapter 6.)

As an example illustrating the need-satisfaction approach to the sales presentation, suppose a new-car salesperson approaches a customer on the showroom floor, and the following conversation takes place:

Salesperson: Do you have any particular car in mind?

Customer: I sure like this four-door model, but I am afraid it's not big enough.

Salesperson: Are you afraid there is not enough seating room?

Customer: No, I want something to use everyday in my work. I am a finish carpenter and have driven a pickup truck, camper, and sedan. Right now I am driving a pickup, but I don't like it.

Salesperson: Why don't you like your truck, may I ask?

Customer: Well it's still a truck. No matter what you add to it, it still handles like a truck. When I had the sedan, I liked to drive it, but it just wasn't big enough for all my tools. I gave the sedan to my wife and she is still driving it. Another thing, pickups and campers invite theft. I have had my pickup broken into several times, while the sedan parked next to it was not touched.

Salesperson: Let me see if I have this right. You need space to store your tools, but you like the luxury and handling of an automobile. Is that right?

Customer: Now I would say you are almost right. I want something nice to drive and, at the same time, something I can use.

Salesperson: Let's go over here and take a look at our best station wagon. Here, let me open the front door. Notice the room. This car also gets good gas mileage.

Customer: Those seats are good-looking.

Salesperson: Come back here; I'll open the tailgate. Notice the well between the seats. There is about 12 cubic feet down there, and the cover can be locked up. In addition there is a small storage compartment over one of the back wheels which can be locked, too.

Customer: You know, this is exactly what I have been looking for. Let me take a look at that sticker price.

The emphasis in need satisfaction is on the salesperson and what he or she does. It is customer-oriented principally because of the early determination of the customer's needs. However, needs are the only customer aspect considered.

Interaction. The interaction approach (Figure 7–3) gives the customer a more active role than any of the others. The basis for success

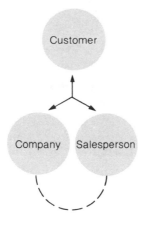

Figure 7–3
Interactions between customer, salesperson, and company

with this approach is the match of the salesperson's and the customer's personalities. It is based on the idea that something in addition to customer's needs will determine the outcome of the sale.[7]

None of the recognized approaches discussed above completely answers the question of how the salesperson can go about making the best sales presentation. The obvious reason is that with each approach there are certain advantages and disadvantages. Salesperson-oriented approaches place too great an emphasis on the salesperson and what he or she does, as opposed to the customer. Yet each of these approaches offers important advice to the salesperson.

Balanced selling

1. The sales presentation is a series of building blocks aimed at favorable buyer action (selling formula).
2. The actions of the salesperson can trigger appropriate responses from the customer (stimulus-response).

The selling formula tells the salesperson that the presentation should be both orderly and persuasive.[8] To achieve the desired organization, the salesperson can follow an outline or devise a structure. From the stimulus-response approach comes the suggestion that the salesperson can trigger responses from the customer. Personal characteristics salespeople should be aware of in making sales presentations include the following:

1. *Words and images.* Above all, the salesman should speak the customer's language. His choice of words should make the sales presentation interesting and unforgettable.
2. *Voice: Tone and sound.* The salesman will want to avoid monot-

ony, mumbling, listlessness, and a pace that is either too fast or too slow.

3. *Eyes*. How a person feels is expressed by his eyes. Therefore, a salesman should maintain eye contact with the customer throughout the sales presentation.

4. *Face*. The salesman will want to smile, not grin, to show warmth and conviction.

5. *Body*. The salesman will want to stand up and avoid any gestures, such as playing with a pencil or pointer, that are distracting.[9]

Borrowing these strong points from the salesperson-oriented approach and combining them with the customer orientation of need satisfaction and interaction, the result can be a new approach called *balanced selling,* a name selected because the approach balances the customer and salesperson orientations. In balanced selling, the sales presentation is seen as mixing, through interaction, equal parts of customer orientation and salesperson control. The stage of the interview determines customer participation.

The salesperson should keep three things in mind in using the balanced selling approach:

1. It is the salesperson's job to fit the company's product line to the needs or wants of the customer, rather than vice versa.

2. It is the salesperson's job to control the sales interview by means of the sales presentation.

3. It is the salesperson's job to present the competitive distinctiveness of the company's products in the sales presentation.

Customer orientation in the sales presentation should not be confused with participation. *Participation,* or active involvement of the customer in the sales presentation, is used as a tool by salespeople to orient themselves to the customer and to achieve the desired interaction. In the beginning stages of the presentation, the salesperson asks enough questions to determine the customer's needs or wants or to see if he or she has the customer's attention and interest. It is a mistake to think that simply getting the customer to talk is customer orientation.

Generally, the customer will participate more in the early stages of the sales presentation than in later ones. One reason for this is that the customer's answers to questions will tend to be longer at first. For example, the salesperson will want the customer to go into considerable detail about problems in order to facilitate the identification of needs. In the later stages of the sales presentation, the customer may only have to give yes or no answers or indicate a preference.

The salesperson's interaction with each customer should be based on a thorough knowledge of that customer. Much of the information about the customer may be available to the salesperson in preparing the sales presentation (the preapproach—see Chapter 6), but the rest will have to be developed during the course of the sales presentation. How much empathy the salesperson has with a customer's point of view will determine in large part how successful he or she is in obtaining specific and timely information about that customer.

CANNED AND VARIABLE SALES PRESENTATIONS

A great deal of controversy and confusion surrounds the question of how much structure there should be in the sales presentation. At one extreme are those who hold that *canned,* or highly structured, sales presentations are best. They feel that canned presentations give them a degree of control over the selling situation that they cannot obtain in any other way. With this approach, the salesperson does not miss any points or make any unethical commitments.

The canned presentation is well organized, and stumbling blocks such as customer objections are anticipated and answered. Salespeople who are new to the job often favor a canned presentation because it gives them confidence. Certainly sales training and supervision are easier when a canned presentation is taught to salespeople.

Other sales personnel feel that the distinctiveness of each selling situation makes canned presentations useless because they are developed for only one type of selling situation or are too generalized. Not only do they take away much of the seller's inherent flexibility, but uniform presentations cannot be used if calls are to be made on the same customer again and again. It is difficult to develop presentations for each item in the product line, and canned presentations usually can be recognized because they sound memorized and lack distinctiveness.

Most sales personnel feel that selling cannot be both standardized *and* persuasive. They do not find canned presentations effective because all customers must be treated alike. Neither do they favor a presentation that has no structure, because some company input is more persuasive than none.[10]

In practice, a sales presentation that uses an outline, checklist, or pattern is usually thought to be best. For this type of sales presentation, the salesperson decides what wording to use in talking to a customer. The framework supplied by the company makes sure nothing is forgotten or overlooked. Next best is the unstructured presentation, in which the salesperson is entirely on his or her own. Canned presentations or those that are dominated by audiovisual aids are not popular because it is felt that such presentations stifle the interaction between the buyer and seller and make it difficult to handle the questions and objections that arise in feedback.[11]

Table 7–1 demonstrates that sales executives rank the organized or slightly structured presentation superior to other forms of presentation in all but the delivery of an accurate, authoritative, and ethical message. Here it is ranked below both the fully automated and semi-automated forms.

Table 7–1 Sales executive rankings of sales presentation effectiveness

Objective	Fully automated	Semi-automated	Memorized	Organized	Unstructured
Conserves the prospect's time	3	2	5	1	4
Tells the complete story	2	3	4	1	5
Delivers an accurate, authoritative, and ethical message	1	2	4	3	5
Persuades the prospect	4	3	5	1	2
Anticipates objections	3	2	5	1	4
Facilitates training of salespeople	3	2	5	1	4
Increases salesperson's self-confidence	4	2	5	1	3
Facilitates supervision of salespeople	3	2	4	1	5

Notes:
   Fully automated: Sound movies, slides, or filmstrips dominate the presentation. The salesperson's participation consists of setting up the projector, answering simple questions, and writing up the order. Many audiovisuals are available.
   Semiautomated: The salesperson reads the presentation from copy printed on flip charts, readoff binders, promotional broadsides, or brochures. The salesperson adds his own comments when necessary.
   Memorized: The salesperson delivers a company-prepared message that he has memorized. Supplementary visual aids may or may not be used.
   Organized: The salesperson is allowed complete flexibility in wording; however, he does follow a company pattern, checklist, or outline. Visual aids are optional.
   Unstructured: The salesperson is on his own to describe the product any way he sees fit. Generally, the presentation varies from prospect to prospect.
   Source: From Marvin A. Jolson, "Should the Sales Presentation Be 'Fresh' or 'Canned'?" *Business Horizons*, October 1973, p. 85. Copyright 1973 by the Foundation for the School of Business at Indiana University. (References to "salesmen" changed to "salespeople" with author's approval.)

GUIDELINES FOR SALES PRESENTATIONS   It has been noted that balanced selling mixes, through interaction, equal parts of customer orientation and control by the salesperson. Interaction, the basic ingredient in the selling situation, is affected by how much and how valuable the customer's participation is, how credible the salesperson appears to the customer, and how effective the salesperson is in the use of selling tactics.

While increasing the amount of customer participation may automatically lead to greater understanding and conviction on the customer's part,[12] the value of customer participation to the salesperson is much more complicated. Customer participation tells the salesperson what he or she needs to know in order to interact with the customer, not only needs or wants but other characteristics, such as personality traits that will affect interaction. Later in the sales interview, customer participation provides reactions that signal the salesperson's progress in making the sale.

Customer participation

The salesperson gets participation from the customer through questions framed to obtain information, particularly early in the sales presentation. Questions designed to determine the customer's needs or wants should allow the customer to think logically about the subject. Later questions should keep the customer on the subject of those needs and wants. While all questions should be focused on getting the appropriate response, some are designed to get the customer talking. Still others are used to provoke customer dissatisfaction with the present state of affairs.

Indirect questions will probably work better than direct ones for the salesperson.[13] *Indirect questions,* which are less structured, allow the most freedom of response, and this is likely to be preferred by the customer. In answering indirect questions the customer is also likely to be volunteering information rather than responding to the demands of the salesperson. Indirect questioning is very useful when the salesperson finds it best to play a subordinate role in the sales interview, as might be the case in selling to professionals such as doctors or dentists.

Salespeople sometimes have trouble developing questions that will get the needed information. As the salesperson shifts from seeking information from the customer to showing how the product will satisfy customer needs or wants, questions can be asked to check the progress being made. Depending upon the customer's reaction, the salesperson may wish to make some sort of adjustment in the sales presentation.

The four-way classification of customer reactions shown in Figure 7–4 can be useful to salespeople. Voluntary reactions should be fairly obvious, but whether the salesperson will be able to pick out and evaluate involuntary reactions will depend to a great extent on how well the salesperson has interacted with the customer. As an example, a salesperson can ask whether a customer sees a product feature as useful and get a simple yes or no. The manner in which the customer responds, as suggested by signs like fidgeting or inattention, can present a difficult evaluation problem.

Figure 7–4
Classification of
customer reactions

	Positive	Negative
Voluntary	Positive voluntary reactions	Negative voluntary reactions
Involuntary	Positive involuntary reactions	Negative involuntary reactions

Source: Based on Harold C. Cash and W.J.E. Crissy, "Tactics for Conducting the Sales Call," *The Psychology of Selling* 5 (1965): 41. Personnel Development Associates, P.O. Box 3005 Roosevelt Field Station, Garden City, NY 11530.

Credibility

If the salesperson appears to be knowledgeable, the customer will usually assume the salesperson is an expert, but the customer may tend to suspect the salesperson's motives despite this expertness. The customer may feel that the salesperson will make incorrect statements just to sell the product.[14] If a salesperson is to be persuasive, therefore, credibility or trustworthiness must be established in the mind of the customer. This seems to be a dual job:

1. Gaining recognition as an expert in the field. (I know what I am talking about.)
2. Projecting the idea that his or her interests as a salesperson and those of the customer are identical. (If I were you, this is the product I would purchase.)

Age, experience, and similar social background are important factors in establishing credibility. Age and experience can indicate the salesperson's expertise to the customer, who feels that "She has been in this business for a long time, and she should know what she is talking about." Door-to-door salespeople experience more success in middle-income neighborhoods because they match those customers more closely on a social basis than they would in either high-income or low-income neighborhoods.

Customer knowledge can help the salesperson achieve interaction and indicate expertise to the customer. One highly visible way to demonstrate competence is for the salesperson to use the same terms the customer does; in other words, salesperson and customer should talk the same language.

Because sales assignments based on matching the salesperson's and customer's characteristics are desirable but impractical, the salesperson must be matched to a variety of customers. The basis for these matches should be what the salesperson and each customer have in common, particularly as regards customer characteristics that will affect the sale. The most important of the customer's characteristics are needs or wants. The success a salesperson has in convincing a customer that they have common interests depends upon:

1. The orientation of the salesperson to the customer.
2. The ability of the salesperson to interact with the customer.

The salesperson must use what he or she knows about a customer to persuade the customer that their interests are the same. The job is much easier if the customer knows the salesperson will be calling again and the buyer-seller relationship will continue over a period of time. In one-time sales, such as that of a new house, the salesperson is more persuasive if after-sale service is emphasized.

In overcoming the customer's idea that salespeople will say anything to get a sale, the salesperson should use knowledge and sales tactics to interact with the customer and convince the customer this is not so.

There are several ways salespeople can increase their effectiveness in making sales presentations. Each salesperson should develop an inventory of sales tactics that fit particular selling situations or that apply regardless of product or customer. Some suggested tactics are discussed below.

Tactics in sales presentations

1. Identify and confirm needs before attempting to supply the customer with product information. A salesperson can get so anxious to show the customer the product that he or she entirely forgets about customer needs. Years ago, a vacuum-cleaner seller, in attempting to show the cleaning power of a product, might have thrown dirt all over a living-room rug, only to discover that the house had no electricity! The customer orientation in balanced selling dictates putting needs before product information.

2. Listen carefully to what the customer says and how it is said. The salesperson should always be a good listener, because this allows the salesperson to interact with customers. The manner in which customers say things and their involuntary reactions are also important. Competitive distinctiveness, whereby salespeople distinguish their products from those of competitors in fitting the customer's needs, is important in translating acknowledged needs into buying action.[15]

3. Give the customer a clear view of product benefits. The customer not only has to accept the salesperson's claim of product benefit, but must also be able to talk about it in his or her own words. Mentioning too many benefits can be as bad as mentioning none at all, because the customer becomes confused.[16]

4. Classify product benefits. This can be in the form of three major groups. The first relates to the customer's organization or household; these benefits could include increased sales, improved operating efficiency, or reduced investment. Second are those benefits that relate to the customer's performance as a buyer, and third are benefits relating to the customer's personal striving, such as job security, status, or feeling of belonging.[17]

5. Get the customer to think of benefits in terms of the supplying company and the salesperson, as well as the physical product. Adding company and sales services to product benefits provides a combination the competition cannot duplicate.[18]

6. Give the product information that is most desirable to the customer first and the least desirable information last. For a customer who is extremely cost-conscious, for example, the best approach would be to talk first about the operational savings in using the product.

7. Use two-sided arguments that present the side favoring the product first. What is presented first to customers will tend to dominate their thinking. There is also a good chance the customers will commit themselves to the first argument before hearing the other one.

8. Draw conclusions whenever possible. Customers who need to be convinced are more likely to change their opinions in favor of salespeople who draw conclusions in their presentations.[19] One way to do this is to review how the product satisfies the customer's needs or wants.

Special selling situations

Interaction is a significant problem when more than two people are involved in the selling situation. In *team selling,* more than one salesperson calls on a customer, and there is limited opportunity to interact individually with the customer. Sales presentations in this situation are usually highly structured and rely on audiovisual aids. A salesperson may or may not play a role in the presentation. The only real opportunities the salesperson has for interaction in team selling come at the end of the presentation and during breaks.

Team presentations may also be made to groups of customers from the same organization or different organizations. In this case the salespeople should pair off with customers at every opportunity. Even though customer feedback does not allow for immediate adjustment in the sales presentation, it will help in planning subsequent presentations. Moreover, pairing-off emphasizes the customer's importance as an individual rather than just a member of a group.

In *group selling,* the salesperson makes a presentation to more than one customer. This is most likely to be used in an industrial situation. Instead of seeing each interested person individually and making sales presentations to every one, the salesperson makes a single presentation to a group of customers. Executives at Fibreboard report tremendous success with a form of group selling. Representatives from various Fibreboard departments—sales, marketing, product development, production, graphics, and machinery management—meet with representatives of similar departments of a prospective customer's company for a two-hour give-and-take session.[20]

Industrial salespeople are not the only ones who must make presentations to a group. Insurance agents, stockbrokers, and real estate agents are just a few examples of salespeople who regularly sell to groups rather than single customers.

The problem for the salesperson in group selling is interaction, whether the group is 2 or 20. The salesperson must not only try to get some interaction with each member of the group, but also must realize that the members of the group are interacting with one another. To help this interaction, the salesperson should classify the members of the group as to their roles in the purchase decision.

How successful the salesperson is in interacting depends upon how well prepared he or she is before starting the presentation. Selling to a group requires a significant amount of planning. The one sales tactic that is of vital importance in this situation is getting the participation of all the members and not letting anyone feel he is being ignored. This tactic is also very difficult. Suppose a salesperson has just finished a sales presentation on a new component part for a lawn mower. The sales manager, who is a member of the buying committee for the Beautiful Lawn Mower Co., asks the first question.

Sales Manager: How can we justify adding more cost to the mower when we are meeting a lot of sales resistance on the basis of our price right now?

Salesperson: What you say is true, but before I answer your question, may I ask the design engineer, production manager, and purchasing agent each a question?

The salesperson then proceeds to ask the design engineer whether the new component would prolong the life of the mower and make servicing easier, the production manager whether the new component would facilitate assembly of the mower, and the purchasing agent whether the component could be ordered in large enough quantities to take advantage of the discount.

What the salesperson in the example is attempting to do is to encourage participation of the other members of the group and to get the other members to answer the question posed by the sales manager and, in effect, to sell themselves. They may recognize that the higher cost of the component may be offset by longer product life and easier servicing, and a better product warranty may increase sales even at a higher price.

SUMMARY
The presentation or message delivered by the salesperson to the customer is a deciding factor in whether the salesperson gets the order. The empathy a salesperson has for the customer's point of view determines how good the presentation will be.

One salesperson-oriented approach to the sales presentation is formula selling. The AIDA formula, for example, visualizes the presentation as a buildup process patterned after the standard learning approach. The stimulus-response approach assumes that actions of the salesperson can trigger responses from the customer ending in buying action. Both of these approaches put the customer in a passive role.

The customer plays a more active role in the need-satisfaction approach, in which the first part of the sales presentation is devoted to identifying customer needs, and the interaction approach, which looks at all customer characteristics that may influence the sale. Balanced selling is an attempt to make use of the principal advantages of each of the four approaches by mixing, through interaction, equal parts of customer orientation and salesperson control. The customer's participation is used to orient the salesperson to the customer and achieve the desired interaction. The basic link between the salesperson and the customer is the customer's needs or wants.

Most sales executives believe that selling cannot be both standardized and persuasive. This argues against canned presentations. Some company input in the sales presentation, however, is better than none at all.

Participation provides the information the salesperson needs to know to interact with the customer and signals progress in making the sale. Indirect questions will probably work better than direct questions in triggering customer participation.

To be persuasive, the salesperson must establish credibility. The salesperson must gain recognition as an expert and project the idea that his or her interests are identical with the customer's. The latter job is easier if the salesperson is able to orient to the customer and achieve a high degree of interaction.

Sales tactics of the salesperson in developing interaction include:

1. Identify and confirm needs first.
2. Listen carefully.
3. Show competitive distinctiveness.
4. Give a clear view of product benefits.
5. Classify product benefits.
6. Get the customer to think of the company and the salesperson, along with the physical product.
7. Give the most desirable product information first.
8. Use two-sided arguments, presenting the favorable side first.
9. Draw conclusions whenever possible.

Interaction is particularly a problem when the salesperson is part of a sales team or sells to a group of customers. When working as part of a sales team, the salesperson should pair off with individual customers at every opportunity. In selling to groups, the salesperson needs to be very well prepared and must make a special effort to get everyone's participation. One sales tactic for securing participation is involving other members of the group in answering a question raised by one member and thus, in effect, getting them to sell themselves.

REVIEW QUESTIONS/DISCUSSION QUESTIONS/EXERCISES

1. Briefly identify the following:
   a. Sales presentation.
   b. AIDA.
   c. Stimulus-response.
   d. Need satisfaction.
   e. Balanced selling.
   f. Canned presentation.
   g. Team selling.
   h. Group selling.

2. Defend the statement: The sales presentation is crucial if the salesperson is to be able to sell.

3. Describe what is meant by empathy on the part of the salesperson. Do you feel a salesperson could acquire empathy through some sort of learning process?

4. Select a product you are fairly familiar with and develop a sales presentation using the AIDA approach.

5. In selling the following products, what would be a good stimulus and the expected response:
   a. Foreign sports car (selling price $21,000).
   b. Super-deluxe washing machine.
   c. Retirement investment program.
   d. Vacation home in Florida ($95,000– $130,000).

6. You sell swimming pools installed in the backyards of homes. Make up a list of questions you will need to ask to determine the needs or wants of customers. Indicate whether the questions are direct or indirect.

7. How can a salesperson tell when he or she is nearing a sale?

8. How does the idea of balanced selling differ from need satisfaction and interaction?

9. One suggested sales tactic is to present the most desirable product information first. What is meant by the term *desirable*?

10. A salesperson has to establish credibility with the customer. What does this entail, and how should the salesperson go about this job?

11. Why do you think sales executives feel the sales presentation should have some structure?

12. Discuss the reasons for using indirect rather than direct questions.

13. Research findings on communication effectiveness show that it is best if the salesperson uses a two-sided argument when the customer is aware of both sides. Why should the salesperson be encouraged to use two-sided arguments at all times? Explain why it is suggested that the salesperson always use the two-sided argument.

14. In planning a team presentation to a buying committee, how would you plan to get maximum interaction?

15. What is the best way to go about convincing a customer that as a salesperson you are not motivated to make invalid statements?

16. Explain the differences between the idea of participation in the need-satisfaction approach and the idea of balanced selling.

17. What are the differences between customer participation in the selling process and the idea of interaction?

18. It has been said that in selling to groups, interaction is much more complex. Explain.

19. Discuss why balanced selling is perhaps the best approach to the sales presentation.

20. Under what conditions would a salesperson-oriented approach be best in making a sales presentation?

CASE 7–1: THE DAYTON COMPANY

The Dayton Company is a firm that sells towels and other linens, such as sheets, pillowcases, and tablecloths, on a door-to-door basis. For the past two months, the featured product has been a hope chest of towels and linens priced at $275, $400, or $550. With the $275 order a plastic hope chest is provided free to the customer. The hope chest is made of wood for orders of $400 and $550

One evening, Leslie Carter, the company's top sales producer, is in a village just outside Dayton, Ohio. At 6 P.M., it is still light on a warm spring evening. Leslie says she does not feel appointments are necessary. Therefore she drives down a shaded street until she sees a man sitting on his porch. Then she approaches the man, and the following conversation takes place:

Carter: It certainly is a pleasant evening.

Man on porch: Yes, and it's been this way for the last week.

Carter: I was wondering if you could help me. I was supposed to see a young lady tonight who is getting married pretty soon. But you know what I did was up and leave Dayton and forget my notes with her name and address. Do you or your wife know a young girl around here who is getting married? It seems to me that the address was around here somewhere.

Man: I don't, but my wife will probably know. Jean, do you know anyone around here getting married?

Wife: Sure do; Jane, the Adams's daughter.

Carter: Could you tell me where they live?

Man: Go down two blocks to the stop sign and turn left. The Adams live in the third house on the right. Don't know the number, but it is a big white house.

Carter: Thank you very much.

A short time later Carter is talking to Jane Adams and her mother. She starts her sales presentation by giving Jane a gift of two guest towels, mentioning that she could get more free gifts. All she has to do is give her the names of some of her friends, and if they purchase a hope chest she will get a free gift. Jane is able to give Leslie four names, and her mother leaves the room to get the addresses for each of the girls.

Leslie starts to show Jane the quality of the towels, telling her that initials will be put on the bath and hand towels free of charge. When Jane's mother returns, Carter opens up her descriptive book on the hope chests.

Carter: Jane, your mother will tell you that now is the time to get your towels and linens. After you are married, there will always be something else you need.

Mrs. Adams: She is so right, Jane. Dad and I never had what I really wanted.

Jane: I guess you are right, Mother.

Carter: Our deluxe chest has everything you will need for many years to come. Jane, just ask your mother how many times she has wished she had another set of towels or sheets. It is pretty tough to have to wash the sheets and then put them right back on the bed.

Mrs. Adams: Jane, Miss Carter is so right. Don't forget, you will be working and won't have a lot of extra time.

Jane: I like the different colors for the towels.

Carter: Our deluxe chest gives you the opportunity to have a bath set in every decorator color. You also will have a set of sheets in each color.

Jane: The colors are pretty in the towels, but I don't think I would like them as sheets.

Carter: Our finance plan allows you to pay it off in a year or two years if you like. Remember seven bath sets, seven sets of sheets, fourteen pillowcases, and three table cloth and napkin sets. The big plus, don't forget, is the free chest you can use for storage.

This sales interview goes on for about 15 minutes, with Jane finally deciding to buy the deluxe chest. Her mother writes out a check for $100 and says they will pay the balance, $450, upon delivery. During the rest of the interview Carter continues to dominate, directing many of her questions to Mrs. Adams.

That same evening Carter goes on to sell three more hope chests. One of these is another deluxe chest, while the other two are special sets priced at $275. In addition she has the names of seven girls to call on the next night. In one sales call Leslie did not get a sale; the mother of the girl was not at home.

Questions

1. What approach to the sales presentation is Carter using?
2. In paying a lot of attention to the girl's mother, do you feel she is making a mistake? Explain your answer.
3. Do you feel Carter would be as successful if she used a balanced selling approach to the sales presentation?

CASE 7–2: COSMOPOLITAN TRAVEL, INC.

Carol Brumley had worked for Cosmopolitan Travel for two and a half years. In that time she had built up a solid base of satisfied clients. Most of her customers were businesspeople who travel for their firms. However, Carol typically got their business when they needed tickets for personal or family trips. She was also adding to the list of clients on a steady, methodical basis. In short, she was pleased with how things were going in her short career in the travel business.

Late one Tuesday, Carol had just gotten off the telephone when Roger Vanderbilt walked in the office. He took a seat next to her desk.

Vanderbilt: Hi, Carol. How are you today? I happened to be downtown when I remembered that I needed some tickets for a trip next week. Rather than call I thought I'd just stop in and pick them up.

Brumley: Great. Where do you want to go and when?

Vanderbilt: New Orleans and I have to be there in time for a dinner engagement at 7:00 P.M. on Wednesday.

Brumley: Alright, how about returning?

Vanderbilt: Anytime after 5:00 P.M. on Thursday would be fine but I'd prefer a direct flight.

Carol excused herself while she put the necessary information into the computer terminal setting on her desk. After a few moments she had two flights that satisfied Vanderbilt so she had the computer print up the ticket. After putting the sale on his credit card, Carol gave him the ticket and leaned back in her chair.

Brumley: What are you doing for Thanksgiving?

Vanderbilt: We're going to drive up to Philadelphia to see my wife's sister and her husband. They have lived there for two years already and we have yet to visit them; it's embarassing.

Brumley: Sounds like you'll need some diversion. Why don't you and the family fly up to New York for one full day, see a play, visit some museums, have a nice dinner and return to Philadelphia the next night?

Vanderbilt: You sure know how to spend my money! Frankly, my wife was thinking the same thing. But getting to New York costs a fortune for the five of us. On top of that, we'll need a hotel and food. I don't see how I could swing it.

Brumley: Let's look at Amtrak. They have some great family fares, especially if you can go on the weekend. And there's a hotel called the Piccadilly which has a family weekend special. It's not too far from the Whitney Museum.

Vanderbilt: What do you think the whole thing would cost?

Brumley: Let me do this. I'll do some investigation and call you in a day or two at your office. I'll have a complete tentative budget, food, cabs, tickets, everything. How does that sound?

Vanderbilt: OK to me, but tell me first and not Mary or the kids.

Brumley: Fair enough. I'll need some information about your daughters. What are their ages and do they have any special interests? Have they been to New York before? Does your wife have any special interests? I know she gets there on business every so often, but have you and she gone there just for fun, together?

Vanderbilt: Let me talk this over with Mary and the girls and call you tomorrow with some of those answers. Maybe this is a pretty good idea. We could use a day away from our normal routine in the Big Apple.

Brumley: I'll wait until you call. Do you need any other tickets?

Vanderbilt: Not right now, thanks. I'll talk to you tomorrow.

Questions

1. What type of approach is Brumley using with Vanderbilt?
2. Would you have done anything different if you were Brumley?
3. Was Brumley too aggressive?
4. Would a canned or standard presentation work in this business?

KEY POINTS

- Demonstration provides opportunities to appeal to all the customer's senses.

- The primary emphasis in demonstration is on the customer's sense of sight.

- Demonstration enhances interaction with the customer.

- Demonstrations are advantageous in selling to groups and team selling.

- Mobile demonstrators help to show large and complex products.

- Demonstrations aid the salesperson's customer orientation.

- Demonstrations are helpful in showing how to use the product, creating a good impression, and giving the salesperson confidence.

- Sales aids used as part of the demonstration focus on key points, develop credibility through reinforcement, and create a favorable impression.

- Sales aids used in demonstration include the product itself, visual aids, and audio visual aids.

- Rules for effective demonstrations deal with preparation, the actions of the salesperson, and what the salesperson has to say.

Chapter

8

DEMONSTRATION

Frank Brady, a manufacturers' representative specializing in housewares, has been able to attract clients in large part because of his ability to turn housewares departments and speciality stores into exciting retail carnivals.

"Ever tasted fresh strawberry juice?" he asks a passing customer he has buttonholed. "This is just fantastic! You have to try some," he enthuses as he presses the Dixie cup full of pink liquid into the customer's hand.

He sells excitement rather than the products themselves. Demonstrators working for him create six-foot-long hero sandwiches to "prove" the benefits of a slicer. Four different chicken dishes are baked simultaneously to lure hungry customers to an oven. All types of taste-tempting drinks are created to enhance the appeal of juicers and coffee makers.[1]

DEMONSTRATIONS SUPPLEMENT SALES PRESENTATIONS

Demonstration, in its many forms, gives the salesperson an opportunity to appeal to the customer through all applicable senses. Obviously a customer cannot smell or taste a machine, but he or she can see it and operate it while listening to a discussion of its benefits. Selling cookware presents a unique opportunity for the salesperson to appeal to all five senses by making the sales presentation the preparation and eating of a meal, while also affording ample opportunities for the salesperson to talk about product benefits. Demonstrations play a major selling role for Stanley Home Products, for example. Instead of just telling people at a demonstration party about a particular brand of soap, the representative will pass around a bar and asks each one to smell it.[2]

The sales presentation is not simply a conversation between a customer and a salesperson. If it were, salespeople could be pictured as attempting to interact with customers who cannot see, feel, smell, or taste. The salesperson in such a situation could not hope to be as effective as one who makes use of as many of the customer's senses as possible, particularly sight. Today's salesperson can be equipped with a vast array of selling tools—ranging from a simple presentation using slides or transparencies—to a remote portable terminal that can plug the salesperson into a computer at the home office.

Several questions must be answered concerning demonstrations: (1) how demonstrations can help sell, (2) what types of sales aids are available, and (3) what must be done to make sure demonstrations are successful.

Demonstration affords the salesperson a greater chance of successful interaction with the customer. This is true in selling to individual customers and particularly so with groups. Demonstrations are a must in team selling, where interaction is difficult. Another reason for using demonstration is the uniqueness it gives the sales presentation. This helps to build a customer orientation that indicates the salesperson's concern with the customer's special needs or wants.

Demonstrations are also helpful in showing how to use a product. For potential customers to see value in a product, they have to be shown how to use it, see the output from the product, and be convinced that they can use the product to their advantage. As an example, compare the selling impact of kitchen knives in an attractive display case with a demonstration in which potential customers are allowed to use the knives on various food products.

Another advantage of demonstrations is the impression they can have on potential customers. Demonstrations are tangible evidence of the efforts of the salesperson and his or her company. This is very important in marketing to resellers. At trade shows, for example, it is not uncommon for audiovisual aids to be used extensively not only to show the product in operation but also the future advertising planned for the product.

"Whattya mean, do I have a different style? They're the first shoes ever invented."

Reprinted by permission The Wall Street Journal.

Not all demonstrations are successful!

Repeated demonstrations also give the salesperson confidence during the sales presentation. Finally, demonstrations provide uniformity in the content of the sales presentation. Individualization is still practical through selection of what is included in the demonstration and what is emphasized in the sales presentation by the salesperson.

Improved interaction

According to the Better Vision Institute, we get 83 percent of our knowledge from our sense of sight.[3] Psychologists have estimated that 87 percent of our impressions come to us through our eyes, 9 percent through our ears, and the rest through the other three senses.[4] Both figures indicate that the sense of sight is too important to overlook in selling. The salesperson needs to show as he or she talks (Table 8–1).

Suppose the product is the "Kitchen Wonder," a hypothetical utensil capable of doing 14 different jobs in the kitchen.[5] To mention a few, the Kitchen Wonder can chop, slice, dice, and cut food; squeeze oranges; blend milk shakes; and beat eggs and batter. If the salesperson just explains everything the product can do, it is doubtful that the customer will be able to remember many of the features by the end of the sales presentation. And in not remembering, the customer misses the main selling point—the many uses of the product.

If the salesperson shows the machine and demonstrates how it does each of the 14 jobs, the customer gets a much better idea of the many product uses. More important perhaps, the customer is not being asked to believe anything but is shown what the product can do. Hence, a demonstration increases the credibility of both the sales presentation and the sales representative.

In demonstrating the Kitchen Wonder, the salesperson might also appeal to the sense of touch by letting the customer operate the product. The customer who is encouraged to try out the product has added

**Table 8–1
Helpfulness of audiovisual sales aids**

Degree of helpfulness	Percentage of salesmen reporting
Extremely helpful	15 ⎫ 42
Helpful	27 ⎭
Not very helpful	9
Of no help	12
No answer	37
Total	100

Source: Reprinted by permission of *Sales Management, The Marketing Magazine.* © 1973 Sales Management, Inc.

conviction and intensified desire for the item. Conviction is important because the customer must feel that a product is worth the asking price.

The salesperson could present the Kitchen Wonder three times in making the sales presentation. The first time he or she shows and explains the machine and each individual attachment, being alert to what features seem to be of interest to the customer. The second time through, the salesperson demonstrates what jobs each attachment can do, giving particular attention to features the customer seems interested in. The customer may remark about how useful a blender would be in mixing drinks, for example, and this clue tells the seller to spend comparatively more time demonstrating the blender attachment. The third time through, the salesperson lets the customer operate the Kitchen Wonder, starting with the product use that has the greatest customer interest. If the customer still seems to be most interested in blending, he or she should be encouraged to try this feature first.

There are several advantages to demonstrating a product several times during the course of a sales presentation:

1. Repetition helps the customer remember the many uses of the product, particularly those in which interest is highest.
2. Appeals are made to the sense of sight.
3. Appeals are made to the sense of touch.
4. The customer is given an active part in the sales presentation.

While the customer's sense of sight is the primary target in the demonstration, the possibilities of appealing to other senses should not be overlooked. In selling what they describe as diverse, hard-to-define capabilities, Garlock sellers combine an appeal to the sense of touch with a "show and tell" presentation. In this part of the presentation, a representative goes through a flip chart of color photos showing Garlock facilities. The wording of sales messages on the pages of the flip chart is brief and benefit-oriented. The use of the flip chart to describe capabilities gets the idea across to customers, who frequently comment: "I didn't know you were in that." To accompany each chart the representative has trays of products that the customer can feel and inspect. Here again the emphasis is on Garlock's capabilities to solve the customer's problems. In the six months after Garlock sales personnel started using the flip chart and the trays of products in their sales presentations, quotations increased 300 percent.[6]

Helpfulness in special selling situations

Some sort of demonstration is a necessity in selling to a group of customers or in team selling. Just talking will not make an adequate impression in these circumstances.

The fact that demonstration holds the attention of the customer is important in selling to a group, because individual participation is likely to be limited. In one-on-one selling, a salesperson can hold the attention of the customer by answering and asking questions. The opportunities for this interaction are decidedly fewer in group selling situations.

Selling teams find demonstrations valuable because they hold the customer's attention for longer periods of time. Generally, sales presentations by teams run longer than those delivered by individuals. The demonstration focuses the attention of the customer on the product, thus offsetting the time involved and the distraction of having to listen to more than one person. Demonstrations are also a good way to tie together what is said by the various members of the selling team.

In group selling, demonstration can give each customer a part in the presentation. When each customer can handle and inspect the product, or if feasible, operate it, the customer participation that is so often lacking in groups is provided. With a selling team, demonstration provides a good opportunity for salespeople to pair off with customers. Suppose a selling team makes a sales presentation of data processing equipment to the administrative staff of a local hospital. One representative makes a presentation to the entire group, showing what the equipment will do and how it can be operated. At the conclusion of this formal part of the presentation, each salesperson pairs off with one of the hospital staff to discuss the equipment and help each one actually operate it.

A means of customer orientation

One way to tailor the sales presentation to individual customer needs or wants is through demonstration. The uniqueness the demonstration gives a sales presentation helps the salesperson convince the customer of his or her orientation to the customer's requirements.

Customer orientation in demonstrations can be evidenced by an elaborate color-slide presentation especially developed for a particular customer or a standard form that the salesperson fills out on the customer before or during the sales presentation, such as the estate planning forms used by life insurance agents. The potential size of the sale will usually determine the complexity of the demonstration.

When the demonstration is of a general nature, the salesperson can achieve some individualization by focusing on those product features that are of primary interest to the customer. Often company filmstrips are made to show the various products offered. Because all product features will be shown in such presentations, the salesperson should be familiar with the film so as to be able to stop it after a product feature of particular interest to the customer. The representative can then make relevant comments, ask for questions, and perhaps rerun the portion of the film dealing with that feature.

Demonstrations can create a favorable impression upon customers in several ways.

Effect on customers

1. Demonstrations are tangible evidence to resellers of the efforts of the salesperson and his or her company. A wholesaler can see the TV commercials to be run on a product.
2. Demonstrations permit the potential customer to "star" or participate in a show of product use.
3. Demonstrations help create customer confidence in product use prior to purchase.
4. Demonstrations help create an atmosphere of honesty about what the product can and cannot do.

All of these effects are important in conveying the overall message that the salesperson seeks to present. Circumstances dictate the priorities that the seller should assign to each in setting up an effective demonstration.

Sales aids are part of the demonstration phase of the selling process. These include the product itself, visual aids, and audio visual aids.

TYPES OF SALES AIDS

Sales aids can provide emphasis by focusing on key points in the sales presentation. Equally important is the fact that sales aids can add credibility to the presentation. The customer is more likely to believe what the salesperson says if it is reinforced by a sales aid. Another important reason for using a sales aid is the impression it makes on the customer. Generally, the greater the amount of money involved in the product sale and/or the higher the level of management taking part in the purchasing decision, the greater the need for a sales aid. One steel company reported spending nearly $4,000 on a sales presentation to a firm involving a potential sale of $140,000. Growing awareness of the impact from sales aids plus increasing technological advances (such as computer-based graphic systems used to make slides and transparencies) should broaden acceptance of sales aids.

Product use   Demonstrations often make use of the actual product or service offered. Most salespeople prefer to use the products they are selling, but characteristics such as physical size may prevent demonstration at the customer's location. A seller cannot demonstrate a computer in a customer's office, but arrangements can be made to take the customer to a location where the computer has been installed and is working.

Plant visits to the seller's headquarters are helpful to show such product benefits as company capabilities and quality control. These visits should be more than guided tours. In visiting the Learjet plant in Wichita, Kansas, customers can see and talk with anyone they wish. Questions are answered and explanations are provided.[7]

A *mobile demonstrator* or clinic that can be moved to the site of the presentation is one way to demonstrate products that are too big or too complex to be carried into a customer's office. Many sales personnel believe mobile demonstrators are the best way to provide the proof of performance demanded by today's customer of technical products. For example, representatives for American Dockbridge of Milwaukee, Wisconsin, found customers were extremely suspicious of a change in mechanical dockboards, being unable to visualize it from the photographs carried by the salesperson. A mock-up demonstrator was not much help either, because it did not offer proof of the value of the change. To solve the problem, a trailer demonstrator was built that could be operated anywhere; all the representative had to do was pull it up to the customer's place of business and give the demonstration. In the next 10 months, more than 50 percent of the demonstrations ended in sales, representing a significant increase over the record for the original product.[8]

An industrial distributor, C. W. Marwedel of San Francisco, makes use of mobile demonstrators because changing customer needs have ruled out catalog selling or demonstrations involving a single product. Formerly, it was not uncommon for a salesperson to take a tool to a plant for a demonstration only to discover that more equipment was needed to make the demonstration meaningful. The company also found that customers are increasingly unwilling to go to seller display rooms for demonstrations.[9]

Product demonstrations that take place away from the customer's location are seldom attempted on the first or even the second sales call. The customer has to be partially sold before an outside demonstration is arranged, particularly if considerable time and money are involved.

The sales presentation comes first in selling the Learjet, then a demonstration flight in the plane. The vice president of marketing is quoted as saying, "We never give a demonstration unless the customer knows what he needs in an airplane. The demonstration is the last thing we do."[10]

Visual and audio visual aids

In addition to using the actual product, there are two other basic types of sales aids for demonstrations.[11] Both are visual aids. The *illustrator* type is a simple, straightforward visual dealing with one aspect of the sales presentation. The seller uses an illustrator to supplement or support what is said to the customer about a particular product feature. The illustrator should be convenient to use and carry. For example, it is now possible for a salesperson on the road to make transparencies with the use of a kit. Examples of visuals that can be used as illustrators are transparencies, filmstrips, slides, flip charts, models, photographs, manuals, and charts (Table 8–2). A list of audio visual equipment available to salespeople would include:

Projectors
    Super 8mm sound movie.
    16 mm sound movie.
    35 mm slide.
    35 mm slide with synchronized tape deck.
    Rear screen 35 mm film strip with self-contained, synchronized tape deck.
    Opaque projector.
    Overhead projector.
    Remote control filmstrip.
Tape recorders
    Cassette.
    Reel to reel.
Video equipment
    Nonproduction recorders and players
        Black and white.
        Color.
    Cameras
        Black and white.
        Color.
    Receivers
        Black and white.
        Color.

Bearings, Inc., of Cleveland, Ohio, developed a sales presentation that includes three illustrator visuals. A flip chart introduces and explains the firm's system for reducing customer purchasing costs, a brochure gives a more detailed explanation of the system, and a reprint of an advertisement further promotes it.[12] The Gates Rubber Company produced a 90-second film on the use of a new snow tire which is one of the most effective sales aids because, like a television commercial, the story is "short and sweet."[13]

Table 8–2
Visual materials used
by salesmen

Visual aid	Percentage of salesmen reporting use
Exhibits	80
Chalkboard	60
Color slides	60
Flip charts	50
Recording	20
Videotape	10
Film	10
Other	30

Source: Reprinted by permission of *Sales Management, The Marketing Magazine.* © 1973, Sales Management, Inc.

The second type of visual is called the *organizer*. The organizer provides most of the sales presentation. What the salesperson has to say during the presentation personalizes it. Some insurance companies use comprehensive brochures to describe their product. Having the visual organizer tell the complete sales story has three advantages:

1. The seller keeps talking about what he or she should be talking about, namely customer benefits.

Cut the babel

A Los Angeles-based marketer of fuel distribution systems, E. B. Wiggins, now sends prospects located abroad a cassette tape with information about its products, in the prospects' own languages. A blank tape is provided, notes sales manager Roc Lane, so that the recipient can ask the company questions. For top-level prospects, Lane includes a cassette recorder with a built-in mike to make the two-way communication that much easier.

Reprinted from *Sales & Marketing Management,* © 1977. Used by permission.

2. The seller can concentrate on interaction with the customer rather than on what to say next.

3. The seller has a better chance to achieve the objective of the sales call.[14]

Demonstrations do not automatically make a sales presentation more successful. Certain rules must be followed to produce effective demonstrations that have a positive impact on sales presentations. These rules can be summarized as follows:[15]

RULES FOR DEMON-STRATING

1. Make advance preparations. Mistakes can be disastrous to the sales presentation, so make sure you know what you are doing. Go over your demonstration again and again until you get it perfect.

2. Personalize your demonstration. Avoid relying too heavily on visual aids, which may make the sales presentation too slick and impersonal. Go over each sales point in the customer's own words.

3. Position yourself so the customer can see what is going on in the demonstration. You should have nothing to hide, so do not turn your back or in any way cover up the demonstration.

4. Make sure the customer sees what you want him or her to see in the demonstration. You need to double check each sales point by either asking a question or giving a more detailed explanation.

5. Do not talk too fast or rush through your presentation. Talking too fast and rushing through the presentation makes it difficult for the customer to follow the buildup in the sales presentation. It also gives the customer less opportunity to ask questions and participate in the sales presentation.

6. Try to get the customer into the demonstration. This is a good way to get the necessary interaction with the customer. The customer not only hears and sees, but also touches. Salespersons have found, for example, that getting the customer to write down certain words or make computations is helpful in developing interaction.

7. Make demonstrations as short as possible. The customer is liable to become bored or confused by a demonstration that is too long.

The use of demonstration as part of the sales presentation allows the salesperson to appeal to more than just the customer's sense of hearing. The primary emphasis in demonstration is on the customer's

SUMMARY

sense of sight, but other senses may be involved as well. These include touch, smell, and taste.

There are a number of reasons for using demonstrations. The first is that better interaction is possible because the salesperson is appealing to more than one sense. Demonstrations tend to increase the credibility of both the sales presentation and the salesperson. Second, demonstrations are a big help in special selling situations because they hold the attention of the customer better than just talking can. They also provide the possibility of getting individual customers involved in the sales presentation. Third, demonstrations provide an opportunity for tailoring the sales presentation to the individual customer. Other reasons include showing the customer how to use the product, impressing customers, giving confidence to the salesperson, and providing uniformity to the sales presentation.

If possible, most salespeople prefer to use the product itself as a sales aid in demonstrations. Mobile demonstrators are a solution to the problem of showing large and complex products. The illustrator type of visual sales aid deals with only a part of the sales presentation. The organizer type of visual sales aid takes over the sales presentation, leaving the seller with the supplementary role of personalizing the sales message.

The salesperson should follow certain rules to make demonstrations effective: (1) prepare in advance, (2) personalize the demonstration, (3) position yourself so the customer can see everything, (4) make sure the customer sees what you want him or her to see, (5) do not talk too fast or rush through the demonstration, (6) give the customer a part, and (7) keep it short.

REVIEW QUESTIONS/DISCUSSION QUESTIONS/EXERCISES

1. Briefly identify the following:
   a. Plant visit.   c. Illustrator.
   b. Mobile demonstrator.   d. Organizer.

2. Discuss why it is important to appeal to the customer's sense of sight.

3. You are preparing a sales training session on demonstration. What reasons can you give sales personnel for using demonstration as part of their sales presentations?

4. How does a demonstration make what you are saying more believable?

5. Lanier Business Products of Atlanta used the Westar satellite to present a three-hour introduction of a new line to 2,000 employees in 11 cities.[16] Relate this marketing effort to the concepts presented in this chapter.

6. Pick a product you are familiar with and plan a sales presentation using demonstration.

7. Why are demonstrations an absolute must in selling to groups of customers?

8. How would you explain the seeming contradiction between the rule that the demonstration must be personalized and the fact that the demonstration focuses the attention of the customer on the product?

9. How do demonstrations improve the salesperson's customer orientation?

10. Discuss why salespeople prefer to use the product itself in demonstration.

11. How would you keep plant visits from becoming simply guided tours?

12. Why do you feel customers are less willing to go to the salesperson's place of business to see demonstrations?

13. Defend the statement: The more products a salesperson has to sell, the more likely he or she is to use some form of demonstration.

14. In what situations would you use an illustrator rather than an organizer?

15. How would you explain the lack of popularity for recordings as a sales aid?

16. List the advantages claimed for the organizer sales aid.

17. Why should you position yourself so the customer can see everything?

18. Why is getting the customer involved more important when selling to a group?

19. How does a salesperson achieve repetition in demonstrations?

20. With several products to sell, how can salespeople keep their demonstrations short?

CASE 8-1: THE WOOD COMPANY

The Wood Company manufactures a line of personal care products including hair dryers, razors, curling irons, manicure sets, and massagers. Recently they have introduced a new product called the "Shaper." Using the Shaper, a person can trim, shape, or thin his or her hair. Two heads are provided—one called a "long cut" and the other a "short cut." The Shaper is available in a variety of colors—brown, black, blue, green, and yellow. The advertising theme emphasizes the maintenance of a well-groomed appearance between trips to the barber or hair stylist.

For nearly two months the sales force has been calling on large retailers with little success. This is very disappointing, since Wood must take back all unsold merchandise and it has provided substantial advertising money for the new product. Clay Wood, the president, is concerned about the poor market reception for the Shaper. He sees the product as being very useful, with no direct competition. The results of a focus group research project back up his opinion of the product.

Questioning Walter Jones, the sales manager, Wood learns that his salespeople are finding it difficult to convince buyers for the chains that consumers will see a need for the Shaper and then buy it. The price (suggested retail of less than $20) is not a problem. The buyers also see the Shaper as a substitute for home barbering kits that have only a small market. Pamela Wozniack, director of marketing research, tells Wood that the biggest question raised in focus group interviews was the consumers' inability to see themselves using the product. She added that consumers had no problem understanding the benefits from using the product.

Clay Wood remains convinced that the Shaper has great potential and could become a top seller for the company. Wood feels that the sales force is just not doing its job. He believes that the sales presentation now being used fails to get major selling points across to buyers.

Questions

1. Can a demonstration help in the sale of the Shaper to buyers for retail stores?
2. Could the same demonstration be used in retail stores to sell the Shaper? If not, what would be the best type of demonstration?
3. Identify the best sales aids to take to the annual housewares show to introduce the new product to buyers.

CASE 8–2: LAKE CHEMICAL COMPANY

The Lake Chemical Company recently developed a new silicon-based plastic material called LAKSIL. The advantages of LAKSIL are its durability, high resistance to extreme heat and corrosion, and low competitive cost. The principal markets for LAKSIL are industrial machinery, wheeled vehicles (cars and trucks), appliances, and electrical transmission equipment.

Despite these advantages, sales representatives for Lake Chemical Company have experienced a great deal of apathy among customers in regard to the new product. Tom Roman, a relatively new sales representative, has done the best job in selling LAKSIL accounting for nearly 60 percent of the total volume. However, most of his sales have been to small customers with a limited need for the product. Only a scattering of those considered prime prospects are located in Roman's territory.

In a meeting with top management, Peter Serro the marketing manager proposed that Tom Roman be assigned exclusively to the selling of LAKSIL, regardless of sales territory. The advertising manager, Sally Kasko, while acknowledging that Tom Roman has done the best job so far, brought up the point that he made at least two plant visits in making every sale. If the cost of these visits were related to the dollars generated by the specific sale it would be doubtful if any of the sales of LAKSIL were profitable. Her counter proposal is to develop a slide presentation with sound that could be used by all of the sales reps. She went on to add that the printed sales information on LAKSIL was fairly good, but customers have to be shown the superiority of the product.

Questions

1. If you were a member of top management, who would you agree with? State your reasons.
2. Contrast a plant visit with a slide presentation for selling effectiveness.
3. Suppose Tom Roman is assigned to sell LAKSIL. What rules would you set up in regard to plant visits by customers?

A Profile of Professional Selling

Eric W. Goldman

A million dollars isn't what it used to be, thanks to inflation, but it is still the kind of fortune not everyone can amass in a lifetime. At 23, Eric W. Goldman has piled up a net worth that he figures at three times that, and he expects to make close to $300,000 this year from salary, bonuses, and return on investments. He flaunts his wealth: a penthouse apartment on Manhattan's fashionable East Side, a 14-room country house with five fireplaces on a 62-acre spread in Woodstock, New York, 60 suits, and three sports cars—a Mercedes, a Porsche, and a BMW.

Goldman started his life of high finance as a go-fer in a Wall Street investment firm. He kept his eye out for the main chance and found it in 1977 in the booming oil and gas business. He is a founder of XOIL Energy Resources, a corporation devoted to putting rich investors into energy tax shelters.

An observant child, he was aware that in his neighborhood on Sundays everybody breakfasted on bagels, lox, and cream cheese. Why not offer home-delivered fresh bagels? At age 10, he set up his bagel route, serving 50 customers. Eric netted about $25 a week that summer.

A few years later, he observed runners and joggers coursing the streets of Far Rockaway. He found his way to New York's garment district, where he bought odd lots of sweat suits at low prices. He then sold his wares for double what they cost him and made enough to buy his first car. He was 16. The car was an Alfa Romeo. He paid $8,500.

On salesmanship alone Goldman would surely rate a Ph.D. He sells with the zeal of an evangelist and he conveys his faith—especially in oil and gas deals. Looking for deals, Goldman toured oil fields, talked to roustabouts and roughnecks, petroleum engineers and geologists, lawyers and bankers. His clients prospered. The obvious next step was to get into the business of promoting oil and gas deals.

Along with two senior partners, Goldman set up XOIL in August 1977. One was named president and chief executive; the other was made chairman. Goldman got no title at first—the older men feared investors might look askance at a company with an officer who was only 20. The next year, at 21, he got a title: vice president in charge of sales!

Source: Used by permission from Eleanor Johnson Tracy, "Oh to be Rich and 23," *Fortune*, October 20, 1980, pp. 99–100. © 1980 Time, Inc. All rights reserved.

SECURING SALES TODAY AND TOMORROW

KEY POINTS

- Sales resistance is anything the prospect does or says to stop, postpone, or hinder the salesperson from successfully closing a sales interview.

- Objections are a logical and expected part of any sales presentation.

- Prospects raise objections for several reasons: (1) desire to avoid the sales interview, (2) failure of the salesperson to prospect and qualify properly, (3) objections as a matter of custom, (4) resistance to change, (5) failure to recognize a need, (6) negative reaction, and (7) lack of information.

- There are six major classifications of objections: (1) objections to delay action, (2) product objections, (3) source objections, (4) service objections, (5) price objections, and (6) objections related to the salesperson.

- There is no one correct time in the sales interview to deal with an objection.

- Methods of handling objections include (1) rebuttal, (2) the "Yes, but . . ." approach, (3) counterquestions, (4) testimonials, (5) restating the objection, (6) positive conversion, and (7) warranties and guarantees.

- The best response to a price objection is to sell the quality features of the product. Other techniques for minimizing price objections include (1) do not invite price comparisons, (2) do not quote a price without a supporting statement, (3) do not postpone responding to a price objection, (4) break the price quotation into small units, and (5) describe the price in terms of an investment or profit.

- A systematic approach to handling objections includes the following steps: (1) anticipate the objection, (2) prevent the objection, (3) classify the objection, (4) control the sales interview, (5) handle the objection, (6) secure agreement from the prospect, (7) attempt a trial close, and (8) continue the presentation.

Chapter

9

SALES RESISTANCE AND OBJECTIONS

Texan Red McCombs has built a $50 million fortune in convenience stores, the NBA's San Antonio Spurs, radio stations, oil exploration, real estate, automobile dealerships, insurance, and numerous other ventures. But McCombs began by selling Fords. In fact, much of his success has been attributed to his sales ability. His first employer recalled how McCombs would handle sales resistence at the Ford dealership:

> When we had a prospect walk in the dealership, and the fellow would tell him he'd have to go talk to his wife before he decided, why, Red went to talk to his wife with him. If he had to go to the banker, Red would go explain the deal to the banker. He never let a customer say "Let me think about it." Red doesn't like mañana. What happens, happens today.[1]

Clearly, Red McCombs appreciated the importance of overcoming customer objections, and then moving to close a sale.

THE CONCEPT OF SALES RESISTANCE

Sales resistance is anything the prospect does or says to stop, postpone, or hinder the salesperson from successfully closing a sales interview. It is a logical and expected aspect of any selling situation. People typically resist, avoid, or delay buying decisions. This reaction must be anticipated and dealt with by the professional salesperson.[2] One source, in fact, puts it this way:

> Many sales managers suggest that selling has not really begun until the prospect voices objections. They believe that many potential salesmen prove to be effective only until the buyers object—then the poor salesman loses heart and considers his efforts to be fruitless. Salesmen who succeed, however, prove their merit and their abilities under the actual test of meeting and overcoming a good percentage of the objections they encounter.[3]

Objections are the outward expression of sales resistance. The ability to identify, analyze, and correctly adjust to customer objections is often the key to successful selling. A study of sales personnel in a business machines company found that those who are comparatively successful understand more of the prospect feedback to which they are exposed, are better able to summarize this feedback consistently, and can select responses that are more appropriate for the prospect.[4]

The prospect's sales resistance is an inherent part of the sales interview. It is usually based on lack of knowledge about the product, the salesperson, or the seller's company; the conditions of the proposed sale; or any of the other factors in the personal selling process. The salesperson should treat sales resistance as a normal aspect of any sales interview, and one that can allow the presentation of a more complete sales story. If handled correctly, sales resistance can actually improve the overall likelihood of securing an eventual sale.

As an integral part of the buyer's role in the sales process, objections are one aspect of the communication interface between buyer and seller. The salesperson should study in detail the reasons for the various types of objections that are raised in the normal pattern of sales work.

REASONS WHY PROSPECTS RAISE OBJECTIONS

The numerous reasons for objections advanced by the customer include the seven discussed below.[5]

1. The prospect wants to avoid the sales interview. In many cases, the prospect is actually "too busy" or too concerned with other matters to grant such an interview. A merchandiser who is in the middle of calculating a monthly open-to-buy figure would be a poor candidate for even the best sales presentation. A supermarket manager who is preparing for the periodic inspection by the regional manager is another unlikely prospect, as is a person with a migraine headache, an executive on the way to an important industry conference, or a university purchasing agent awaiting budget passage by the state legislature. All prefer to avoid or delay a sales interview. In such cases the salesperson should maintain the prospect's goodwill and withdraw courteously, if possible, setting up a future appointment before leaving.

2. The salesperson has failed to prospect and qualify properly. Often it is actually the salesperson who is responsible for customer objections because he or she has not identified a properly qualified prospect. Objections such as "I really like the car, but the monthly payment would be equal to two paychecks a month" or "While it looks like you have a fine product, we just don't use that type of grinder in our operation" indicate that the salesperson has failed to qualify the prospect and must move back to one of the earlier steps in the sales process.

3. Objecting is a matter of custom. To many customers, objections are a matter of custom or habit. It is second nature for some people to object to any sales presentation, even if they have already decided to purchase the item. The traditional ritual associated with selling calls for at least token sales resistance. Generally, this type of objection will not block the salesperson from eventually closing the sale.

4. The prospect resists change. The prospect may object because the salesperson seems to be requesting a change in one's normal behavior or pattern of life. This is the situation encountered by current sellers of condominiums, and vacation homes. Many people naturally resist change and any proposal suggesting it, and it follows logically that they will resist many types of sales presentations and products. A package of benefits must be presented that will indicate to the buyer the need for change and the benefits it can bring.

5. The prospect fails to recognize a need. Some prospects do not see a need for the product or service being offered. They do not recognize how it could help in their manufacturing operations, make their lives easier, or lend status to their families. This often happens with the selling of technical industrial equipment. In most cases in which the prospect does not recognize the need, the salesperson either has failed to qualify the prospect or has made an ineffectual sales presentation.

6. The prospect has some negative reaction. Prospects can have negative reactions toward a salesperson, the product, the company, the industry, or certain conditions surrounding the suggested sale. Such reactions put the prospect in an adverse frame of mind, and the outcome is strong sales resistance. The prospect may have an unfavorable opinion of the salesperson's personal appearance, may be biased against a firm linked to a water pollution incident, or may believe that the entire industry has ignored the needs of certain buyers. Any of these factors can create the negative attitude that is responsible for many sales objections.

7. The prospect lacks information. The prospect may not understand a certain feature or characteristic of the product and may use an objection as a method of soliciting additional data on it. Information about the product's qualities, how it works, the guarantee or warranty, performance characteristics, and the like can be secured in this way. From the seller's viewpoint, this is the most desirable type of objection, since it is a natural lead to an expanded sales presentation. This type of objection allows the salesperson to modify, correct, expand, or improve the sales story to help the buyer better understand the product and its benefits. It also opens up several additional closing opportunities.

These reasons why prospects typically raise sales objections logically stem from the prospect's role expectation. Sales personnel who understand the reasoning behind sales resistance can better cope with the objections they will meet during their workday.

TYPES OF OBJECTIONS

Howard Valentine, the purchasing director at a New Orleans hospital, posts a monthly report card for sales personnel who call on him. Valentine's "Objectivity Chart" is based on nine criteria: (1) number of back orders, (2) ability to deliver in emergencies, (3) follow-up on special requests, (4) sales call frequency, (5) salesperson honesty, (6) number of invoice problems, (7) local warehousing ability, (8) price, and (9) quality.[6] While some sales representatives may not like their grades on Valentine's Objectivity Chart, they have to admit that he has taken a concrete approach to defining his objections to a particular product, company, or salesperson. Professional sales personnel would probably benefit if Valentine's method were widely adopted. Salespeople cannot handle customer objections until they understand what the person objects to in the sales process.

Customer objections are varied, but most can be classified as one of six major types: (1) objections to delay action, (2) product objections, (3) source objections, (4) service objections, (5) price objections, and (6) objections related to the salesperson.[7] In many cases, prospects advance two, three, or more objections during a sales presentation. It is helpful for the salesperson to classify each objection as it is put forth. This procedure permits the development of strong, effective answers to a limited number of objections.

We do not mean to imply, however, that every objection should be met with a canned response. Flexibility is a vital characteristic of the professional salesperson, and it is maintained by salespeople who handle objections effectively.

The initial step in handling an objection is to recognize it. To suggest how salespeople can treat objections as a natural part of the sales process, the National Cash Register Company has used a film entitled *The Engineering of Agreement* in its sales training program.[8] In the film a salesperson makes a presentation thought to be very effective, but the proposal is rejected by the prospect. The salesperson responds with counterarguments rather than determining the basis for the objection and then answering the prospect's doubt. Eventually, the seller does take the correct approach to the situation and a sales agreement is reached.

Objections to delay action

Some typical objections to forestall action on the sales proposal are the following:

Yes, I really like those new models, but I think I should talk it over with my wife.

I'll come back next payday.

I'm in a hurry now, but I will come back for a test drive when I have more time.

A good salesperson should anticipate that the prospect will attempt to avoid action on the sales proposal. These objections are attempts to delay the purchase decision and usually mean that the prospect is uncertain about the benefits to be obtained from the product.

Product objections

Some objections concern the product itself. The prospect may be generally unwilling to buy certain types of products, brands, or particular items in a product line. Examples of product objections include the following:

Yes, the new models are very attractive, but I can remember that my uncle bought one in 79 and the car fell apart in six months.

I agree that the Caribbean cruise would be nice, but I think I would prefer to vacation in Europe.

Why should I use dealership maintenance when the gas station on Jackson will do it for about 60 percent of what your service department will charge?

Product objections usually mean that the prospect has failed to see the value of a sales proposal. The salesperson must be able to stress the advantages of the product being offered. Furthermore, the salesperson must believe in the product and be able to defend it in a realistic manner.

Source objections

Source objections include the following examples:

Yes, it does appear that you have a fine product, but we have been dealing with Morehead Pharmaceuticals for years.

Your company sent me a cheap form letter when I complained about a delivery schedule last year.

I really like the drill, but where will we be able to get replacement parts? Your firm is so small I am worried about your parts supply system.

(Prospect to an Allied sales representative) Let me see . . . wasn't
Allied Manufacturing accused in a price-fixing scandal last year?

Source objections are sometimes unclear. The prospect may indicate a negative impression of a firm and yet not clearly state the
reasoning behind this objection or the supporting logic for it. Salespeople faced with source objections should be certain that they understand the real cause of such objections before attempting to deal with
them. Probing questions such as "Tell me why you feel that way
about my company" are extremely helpful in assessing the basis of
source criticism.

Once the salesperson understands the source objection, he or she
can proceed to answer the prospect. A salesperson must always be
positive about his or her company, its products, and its business integrity. Buyers have little respect for salespersons who "pass the
buck" by blaming their own firm's management or policies.

Service objections are numerous. A Louis Harris poll found that 70
percent of American consumers believe that industry does not pay
sufficient attention to service.[9] Many Americans honestly believe that
sellers quickly forget them once the transaction has been concluded.
In some cases, this admittedly has been the case. But for the vast
majority of all sellers, servicing is an important and often very profitable part of their business. Good service means repeat customers for
the company and the salesperson involved.

Salespeople must be able to confidently assure prospects that their
service needs will be met. They must believe in the product they are
selling and the servicing arrangements that support it.

Price objections may be the most critical questions with which the
salesperson must deal. Typical comments in this category are:

I can't afford to spend that much on merchandise that gives only a
33 percent return.

We really love that house on Crescent Drive, but we just can't
swing a $162,500 home for a couple of years.

The dealer over in Jacksonville quoted a price $200 under your
price.

Hello Mr. Frasier . . . before we get started, what is your price
quotation for the lubricant? There is no use wasting each other's
time unless you are competitive with Bayshore's price.

Such comments can be indicative of both uncertainty on the part of the buyer and an attempt to get a lower price. Prospects sometimes use price resistance to point out that the salesperson has failed to demonstrate product value equal to the asking price. This objection calls for an expanded sales presentation. In contrast, the price objections that a tourist raises in a Mexican marketplace suggest an interest in the item and a willingness to negotiate the matter of price. Methods of handling price objections are discussed further later in this chapter.

"I *warned* you that it was going to be a ROUGH estimate, Mr. Withers."

Reprinted by permission The Wall Street Journal.

Price objections are commonplace.

Objections related to the salesperson

Some consumers prefer not to deal with certain types of sales personnel or particular salespeople. The following comments are typical of this objection:

I never deal with door-to-door salespeople.

I don't think you are representative of the type of people with which we do business.

My husband and I prefer to buy from mail-order companies.

The last Universal representative that called on us tried to go over my head to get an order. Are you any different?

In dealing with these objections, sales personnel are forced to sell themselves before they can hope to close the sale. Reliability and a reputation for honest dealings are probably the most important ingredients in successfully handling this type of objection.

Objections can be considered at various times during the sales interview. Proper timing depends on the type of objection, the prospect's personality, and the environmental conditions surrounding the sale. In short, there is no one correct time to handle an objection.

WHEN TO HANDLE OBJECTIONS

A salesperson might choose to ignore an objection such as: "I am not sure this is the best color for a new car." The prospect has indicated that he or she is thinking about the purchase decision, and the objection concerns a relatively minor point. The salesperson may reason that once the agreement to purchase has been secured, the matter of color can be decided. Minor objections are sometimes ignored, since a response may tend to confuse the sales presentation and make the objection appear more important than it really is. If a salesperson ignores an objection that is important to a prospect, it most certainly will be raised again later in the interview.

Strong objections should be dealt with immediately so as to assure the maintenance of the salesperson's credibility. Prompt handling of an objection shows that the salesperson is sincere in his or her effort to meet the prospect's needs. In some cases, a direct response is used to handle the objection: the salesperson offers information, data, or arguments counter to the objection raised by the prospect. Other situations call for an indirect approach whereby the seller initially offers affirmative agreement and then proceeds to present the counter viewpoint. This approach, which is typically called the "Yes, but . . ." approach, is discussed in the next section.

Some objections are handled by delaying the response to the prospect. Typical remarks with which the salesperson can delay response are:

That is a good question, but I'll cover it a little later in the presentation.

Right . . . we'll come to that in just a minute.

Yes, I can show you how the machine will work in that set of circumstances, but first let me demonstrate. . . .

Such responses illustrate how objections can be postponed until a later, more advantageous point in the sales interview. Delaying objections has the advantage of letting the salesperson set the tempo of the interview, responding to objections at the most opportune time.

Timing responses to buyer objections is an important part of the technique of countering sales resistance. Correct timing comes from field experience and constant practice; all good salespeople know when to handle a particular type of objection, for each type of customer, in a given set of circumstances.

METHODS OF HANDLING OBJECTIONS

Literally dozens of methods for handling objections have been developed by sales personnel over the years, and more are being created everyday in response to particular objections. While no list of these methods can be all-inclusive, the following section describes the most common methods of handling objections: (1) rebuttal, (2) the "Yes, but . . ." approach, (3) counterquestions, (4) testimonials, (5) restating the objection, (6) positive conversion, and (7) warranties and guarantees.

Rebuttal

The rebuttal approach, also known as the denial method, is useful in answering direct questions that call for an immediate response. Consider this dialogue:

Prospect: Yes, Mr. Henderson, your company does offer some beautiful shirts, but my question is: Why should I switch from the Maddox line that I now carry in the store? After all, they also make a fine shirt.

Salesperson: I am glad you asked that question, Mr. Swerle! The answer is simple—we provide a markup of 42 percent while the Maddox line gives you only 37 percent. As a retailer you know that you must get the maximum possible return from each foot of shelf space. We give you a 5 percent greater return than the line you now carry . . . and, profit is the bottom line in your business, isn't it?

A rebuttal should be used only when the salesperson believes the prospect's objection is serious and important enough to merit an immediate response. There is no reason to risk a direct confrontation with the prospect over a minor objection that may later be forgotten or adequately handled by the rest of the presentation. In making a rebuttal, it is important to use a positive tone of voice. An argumentative rebuttal may give the appearance of high-pressure selling and, consequently, lead to increased sales resistance.

In the "Yes, but . . ." approach, the salesperson in effect agrees with the prospect's objection but then counters it with additional information:

> Yes, I agree that our economy is not in the best of shape, but inflation and high income taxes make home ownership a must today.

This approach has the advantage of putting both prospect and seller on the same line of thought. The salesperson indicates initial agreement with the prospect's opinion and reasoning. As an indirect response to objections, the "Yes, but . . ." approach avoids the adversary position that sometimes characterizes the rebuttal technique.

A simple *why* is often an effective way of dealing with objections. In effect, the seller reverses roles with the prospect. A counterquestion puts the prospect in the position of justifying why he or she objects to a certain point in the sales presentation. Consider the following example:

Prospect: What you say about your product may be true, but I am just not sure that your chemicals could hold up under the heat generated by our particular operation.

Salesperson: Why do you feel that way, Mr. Carpenter? I've shown you the lab reports that indicate the durability of our product.

Prospect: Yes, I know you have, Mr. Blake. I guess that what really worries me is that the last time we bought something from your company, the order was two weeks late.

In the example, the seller's use of the *why* question forced the prospect to identify the primary concern—the delivery schedule. Thus the prospect's original objection to the product's durability was a defense mechanism to avoid a discussion of an earlier experience with the seller. Now that the problem has been uncovered, the sales representative can proceed to deal with the prospect's true misgivings.

The 3M Company has taught its sales force that when a prospect brings up only factors that are negative to their case, they should counter with a question that adds positive factors to the discussion. The director of education and training for 3M Company has noted: "We feel that this is a significant addition to the question-asking process and is very effective in changing the climate of the prospect's negative response."[10]

Testimonials   Testimonials from satisfied users or independent evaluators are often a good way to refute an objection raised by a prospect. If the buyer can be shown that people with similar circumstances (or an independent evaluator) are favorably impressed with a product, the objections usually tend to fade or diminish in importance. Here is an example of how a testimonial can be used in handling an objection:

Prospect: The house has everything we want . . . and it is beautifully landscaped. But, we are concerned about the school system. I am just not sure that it is as good as the one at Quarry Point.

Salesperson: That was the same thing that concerned Mrs. Foraker, who bought that trilevel over on the next block. Before she made an offer on the house, she investigated the school system in the area and found that it is rated in the top 15 percent in those statewide student assessment tests. She told me just the other day that her children were extremely happy in their new school. If you would like to visit the school, I'd be glad to drive you over there.

Prospect: No, that won't be necessary. But I *am* glad to hear about the high standing of the school system.

Restating the objection   One of the simplest techniques for handling objections is to restate the objection. This approach has several distinct advantages. First, the salesperson can soften a prospect's criticism by rephrasing the question and shifting the emphasis to a more favorable posture. Consider these comments:

Prospect: I like the style, but I certainly object to seeing myself every time I walk down the street. Look at those dresses . . . they're all the same style.

Salesperson: Do you mean that you would prefer to look at some of the more mature styles? I assumed that someone like you would be more interested in these youthful fashions.

Prospect: Yes, I guess I really am interested in this type of dress.

This salesperson, by rephrasing the objection, has complimented the prospect and converted her to a positive attitude about the dress.

A second advantage of restating the objection is that the salesperson can sometimes make the objection seem unjustified to the prospect.

Prospect: I think your company has the worst customer service arrangement in the industry.

Salesperson: Did you say we had the *worst* customer service arrangement in our industry?

Prospect: Well, maybe it isn't the *worst,* but I have had some problems with your customer service people. For instance, last August. . . .

Upon hearing the objection restated with emphasis on the word *worst,* the prospect begins to modify the criticism and to specify actual reservations about the selling firm. This step will allow the salesperson to answer the prospect's doubts, and this will improve the likelihood of a purchase.

Positive conversion—sometimes referred to as the boomerang technique—takes an objection and offers it as a reason for buying. The following sequence of remarks is illustrative:

Positive conversion

Prospect: This is a tremendous piece of property. The lakefront is absolutely beautiful . . . but I am afraid real estate prices have made it a luxury we cannot afford now.

Salesperson: That is just the reason you should buy this property now. Real estate prices have been rising about 10–12 percent a year in this area. You can't afford *not* to buy the lot now . . . it certainly isn't going to get any cheaper.

The positive conversion method has to be implemented carefully, but in the hands of an experienced salesperson it can be an extremely effective approach to dealing with an objection. As illustrated above, positive conversion is particularly useful in countering price and expense objections.

Warranties and guarantees can be useful in answering objections about the serviceability of products. Examples are:

Warranties and guarantees

I really like the sports car, but I wonder if it will hold up during a Minnesota winter.

The merchandise meets our needs, but suppose a customer has some trouble with it. What do we do then?

Are you sure the machine is capable of stamping 140 pieces an hour?

A warranty or guarantee is an excellent weapon to use in combating objections about product quality, durability, performance, or service policies. When the prospect's doubts are resolved, a positive sales environment is stimulated.

As was noted earlier, price objections are often the most critical questions with which salespeople must deal. But sales personnel must

THE PRICE OBJECTION

be certain that they are dealing with a price objection rather than a prospect's comment about price that is really a product- or service-related objection. Retail salespeople often encounter remarks such as "That seems like a lot to pay for a dress." In this situation, the prospect wants to be assured of the item's quality and value and is not offering a price objection per se.

Price objections can suggest uncertainty on the part of the buyer or an attempt to get a lower price. In earlier days many firms had *flexible price policies,* which left the company's sales agent relatively free to negotiate the specific price with the buyer. In recent years, however, manufacturing industries have tended to move toward a *one-price policy* such as is common in retailing, and most salespeople do not have the authority to negotiate price. Any price concessions are usually under the control of the sales manager, and industrial sales personnel are seldom asked to negotiate price reductions. Flexible price policies, however, still characterize such fields as automobile and real estate sales.

Sales personnel are called upon to explain their company's price and to justify it in relation to value received by the buyer. The salesperson should treat a price objection as a sign that the prospect has not yet been sold on the sales proposal. Renewed selling effort is required to show that the price level is justified for the product package that is being offered. Certainly sales people should never apologize for the product's price. If they really believe in what they are selling, they also believe that the product is worth the asking price.

A salesperson's response to a price objection should be to show the value provided by the product.[11] Empirical studies have consistently

---

Test your knowledge

The domestic automobile industry's downsizing effort to compete with the imports has created its share of sales resistance on the part of some consumers. *The Wall Street Journal* quoted a retired railway worker as saying: "How can they raise the prices and give you less car? If you sit near the door in the back seat, your fanny hangs over the edge, and that's not very comfortable. I may buy a used car this year."

Questions
1. How would you handle this prospect's objections?
2 If you were a dealership salesperson, how would you respond to these comments?

shown that there is a relationship between price and the consumer's perception of the product's quality.

Two examples that take this approach are given below.

> You're correct, Mr. White, in saying that our product/service is not the cheapest. However, did you know that last year our company did over $_____ worth of business at these prices? Doesn't it seem reasonable to believe that, unless we gave our customers something extra, something of real quality, value, and performance at the right price, we could not have achieved this sales record? Let me show you a partial list of our customers who feel the price is right.

> Yes, Mr. Smith, I'll agree we're not the cheapest, and there's a good reason for it. The secret of making a cheaper product/service is well known to every manufacturer. In fact, every company can make two choices in establishing their produce/service line: (1) They can make a quality, value-laden product/service and market it at a fair, mutually beneficial price, or (2) they can make a cheaper, short life, less efficient product/service and sell it at a deceptively low price. Now my company has selected the first route. Isn't that the kind of company you'd like to do business with, to buy from?[12]

Price objections can be minimized, or in any event dealt with, in many other ways. Some of these techniques are discussed below.[13]

1. *Do not invite price comparisons.* A salesperson should not cite a whole list of prices such as "We have this model for $10, this other one for $20, model XL–407 for $30, and finally this one for $40." This type of approach invites price objections, since the seller has failed to identify the customer's needs before citing the various prices.

2. *Do not quote a price without a supporting statement.* In other words, do not say "It is $39.50"; say "It is $39.50 and has a Viewtronic lens that assures you of a sharp picture every time you click the shutter."

3. *Do not postpone responding to a price objection.* Give the prospect the information he or she seeks—now! Postponing the response arouses suspicion and causes the customer to lose confidence in the salesperson.

4. *Break the price quotation into small units.* Quote the product's price in terms of weekly or monthly payments, cost per mile or work hour, or some similar quantity. Most good salespeople never state the total price without also citing the price per unit.

5. *Describe the price in terms of an investment or profit.* For example, "The cost of this display unit is $4,000, and it will give you a return of $5,200 during the first year of use." A comparison of this nature allows the prospect to see the real value of the item.

Regardless of the technique or combination of methods used to handle price objections, it is important to handle them promptly. To do otherwise is to court failure in this most critical area.

A SYSTEMATIC APPROACH TO HANDLING OBJECTIONS

The proper handling of objections calls for a rational, systematic approach to the problem.[14] The eight-step sequence outlined in this section is suggestive of the format that should be followed in handling objections. The actual selection of steps varies with each particular situation, but the sequential arrangement is essentially the same. The steps are:

1. Anticipate the objection. An effective salesperson should be prepared to handle all questions and should anticipate the objection. Remember that objections are a natural part of the selling sequence.
2. Prevent objections. This step is best handled by preparing a complete sales presentation that considers nearly all the prospect's possible questions.
3. Classify the objection. Regardless of the exact wording, most objections fall into certain categories. Classification of objections is a tremendous aid in answering doubts and questions.
4. Control the sales interview. A salesperson who cannot adequately handle objections soon loses control of the sales interview. Unanswered objections tend to encourage other objections. In order to control the sales interview, the salesperson must deal with objections efficiently, and as promptly as feasible. The salesperson must express a positive approach to the sales interview, and avoid potential disagreements with the prospect.
5. Handle the objection. Numerous techniques for dealing with objections are available to the salesperson. A given set of selling circumstances dictates the techniques that might be used. If the first attempt at handling an objection is unsuccessful, the salesperson should turn to alternative approaches.
6. Secure agreement from the prospect. The salesperson should be sure to secure the prospect's agreement that the objection has been dealt with properly. A simple "Does that answer your question?" can be useful.
7. Attempt a trial close. Trial closes are discussed in detail in Chapter 10. They are low-keyed closes that can be helpful in determining the prospect's readiness to buy.
8. Continue the presentation. Assuming that the prospect's objection

has been answered but the individual is not yet ready to buy, the next logical step is to continue the sales presentation. This allows the salesperson to put forth additional selling arguments and provides an opportunity for closing the sale.

The above steps are a rational progression in handling sales objections. Their effective implementation will go a long way toward removing the obstacles to a successful sale.

SUMMARY

Sales resistance is anything the prospect does or says to stop, postpone, or hinder the salesperson from successfully closing the sales interview. Sales resistance usually takes the form of objections raised during the course of the sales presentation. This is a logical and expected aspect of any selling situation.

Prospects raise objections for several reasons: (1) the prospect wants to avoid the sales interview, (2) the salesperson has failed to prospect and qualify properly, (3) objections are a matter of custom, (4) the prospect resists change, (5) the need is not recognized, (6) the prospect has a negative reaction, or (7) information is lacking.

There are six major types of customer objections: (1) objections to delay action, (2) product objections, (3) source objections, (4) service objections, (5) price objections, and (6) objections related to the salesperson.

Objections can be handled at various times during the sales interview. Proper timing of the handling depends on the type of objection, the prospect's personality, and the environmental conditions surrounding the sale.

The most common methods of handling objections are (1) rebuttal, (2) the "Yes, but . . ." approach, (3) counterquestions, (4) testimonials, (5) restating the objection, (6) positive conversion, and (7) warranties and guarantees.

Price objections usually suggest uncertainty on the part of the buyer or an attempt to get a lower price. A salesperson's response to a price objection should be to demonstrate the value provided by the product. Studies have shown a relationship between price and the consumer's perception of the product's quality. Techniques for minimizing price objections include:

1. Do not invite price comparisons.
2. Do not quote a price without a supporting statement.
3. Do not postpone responding to a price objection.

4. Break the price quotation into small units.
5. Describe the price in terms of an investment or profit.

The chapter concludes by outlining an eight step systematic approach to handling objections: (1) anticipate the objection, (2) prevent objections, (3) classify the objection, (4) control the sales interview, (5) handle the objection, (6) secure agreement, (7) attempt a trial close, and (8) continue the presentation.

REVIEW QUESTIONS/DISCUSSION QUESTIONS/EXERCISES

1. Briefly identify the following:
   a. Sales resistance.   f. Restating the objection.
   b. Rebuttal.   g. Positive conversion.
   c. "Yes, but . . ." approach.   h. Warranties and guarantees.
   d. Counterquestion.   i. Flexible price policies.
   e. Testimonials.   j. One price policy.

2. List and explain the reasons prospects raise objections during a sales interview.

3. Identify and discuss the six major classifications of objections.

4. Why is it helpful for salespeople to classify each objection as it is put forth?

5. There is no one correct time to deal with an objection. Comment on this statement.

6. Describe the seven common methods of handling objections.

7. One of the authors once heard a salesperson remark: "How can you sell a product that has a significant price disadvantage? They (prospects) love it until it comes down to the price. That is where we lose them. . . ." How would you reply to this discouraged salesperson?

8. This chapter outlines a systematic approach to handling objections. Discuss this procedure for dealing with sales resistance.

9. Assume that you are a real estate salesperson. How would you handle the following objections?
   a. Yes, I think we want to buy your listing on Oakmont. However, I think I will buy it through another real estate office . . . an old friend, Jim Stapleton, sells for Penn-Jersey Realty.
   b. The location and price are right, but this is the dirtiest house we have seen . . . and most of the rooms need to be painted.
   c. I am pretty sure we will act on that listing in Fairmont Acres, but I want to be *very* sure before I make an offer, since I hear that your firm is very strict about forfeiting deposits. . . .

10. Describe your two most recent purchases. Did you offer any sales resistance? How did the salesperson handle your objections?

11. Practice the various methods of handling objections. One way would be for a friend to pretend to be a prospect, while you assume the role of the seller. Your friend can present objections to buying a predetermined product, and you can practice handling the objections. Then reverse the prospect/salesperson roles and try another type of product.

12. Develop a list of 20 to 30 objections, putting each on a 3″ × 5″ card. Write the type of objection that the statement represents on the opposite side of the card. Shuffle the cards, and practice identifying the various types of objections.

13. Consider the following statement: Salespeople never win arguments with prospects. Explain what is meant by this observation.

14. Match the objections in the left-hand column with the type of objection in the list at the right.

_____1. I don't have time to look at the coats now, but I'll stop back later.

a. Objections to delay action.

_____2. Why should I switch my business after a 15-year relationship with Oregon Products, Inc.?

b. Product objections.

_____3. Quite frankly, I prefer to do business with the fellow from Consolidated—Larry Henly!

c. Source objections.

_____4. I can't believe you'd want $10.50 per dozen for that item.

d. Service objections.

_____5. I hear that rust is a serious problem for this model.

e. Price objections.

_____6. Do you mean that if something goes wrong with the clock, I have to mail it back to the factory?

f. Objections to the salesperson.

15. Comment on the following viewpoint: You only get what you pay for these days.

16. Consider the following objections facing a steel sales representative:
    a. You fellows produce good steel, but I have some real reservations about your delivery schedule.
    b. Is it true that the Pollution Control Board has sought an injunction against your plant in Center City?
    c. Are you sure this is the right steel for this type of operation?
    Cite at least *two* methods that could be used to handle these objections. Write your responses on a sheet of paper, then briefly explain why you selected these methods of dealing with the objections.

17. Price objections may be the most critical questions with which the salesperson must deal. Discuss this statement.

18. The classification of various types of objections is dangerous to the selling profession, because it has the tendency to lead to canned responses. Comment on this statement.

19. Explain the salesperson's role concerning pricing in a firm that has:
    a. A flexible price policy.
    b. A one-price policy.

20. List and discuss five methods for minimizing price objections.

CASE 9–1: PACIFIC PHARMACEUTICALS, LTD.

After graduation from a state college in Colorado the previous spring, Howard Jennings accepted a position as a marketing representative for Pacific Pharmaceuticals, Ltd. Following a two-month training session at Pacific's San Francisco headquarters, he was assigned a territory in Los Angeles.

Jennings is entering the office of Dr. Joan Tilghman, a family physician in the Los Angeles area.

Jennings: Good morning, Dr. Tilghman. I am Howard Jennings with Pacific Pharmaceuticals. I know how busy you are, so I am glad you could take a few minutes to see me.

Tilghman: Nice to meet you, Mr. Jennings. How long have you been with Pacific?

Jennings: Just since July, I graduated from college last spring. In fact, you are my first sales call.

Tilghman: Oh, that is interesting! Well, tell me, what new products does Pacific have that would be appropriate for my practice.

Jennings: As a matter of fact, we have a new pain reliever that might interest you. Here is a brochure about it. What do you think?

Tilghman: Yes I heard about this one. It looks like something I would be interested in. And I have certainly prescribed a lot of Pacific Products over the years. But I see that there a couple of side effects. What can you tell me about these effects?

Jennings: Not too much really . . . but I would be glad to have one of our inhouse specialists call you and answer any questions.

Tilghman: Well, I don't have time for a lot of phone calls. I also heard that this item is going to sell for a 50 percent premium over its competition. I always try to keep the cost of prescriptions as low as possible for my patients. Many of them don't have insurance you know. . .

Jennings: I am sorry about the higher cost, but you know how expensive it is to develop a new product like this one.

Questions

1. Evaluate Jennings' first sales call. How could he have improved his efforts?
2. Analyze the reasons for Tilghman's sales resistance?
3. What type of objections did Tilghman raise?
4. Did Jennings handle the objection adequately? Discuss.

CASE 9–2: JERSEY PRODUCTS, INC.

Jersey Products, Inc., is a large producer and distributor of commercial chemicals. It is located in an industrial city in northern New Jersey. About 65 percent of its sales volume came from the New York City metropolitan area last year.

Fred Lindsey, Jersey's director of purchasing, has been with the firm for seven years. Before that he was in the purchasing department of a major steel company in Pittsburgh.

One day last January, Lindsey had granted an appointment to Carl Burlchek, a sales representative for a well-known office equipment manufacturer. Lindsey and Burlchek had never met before, and Jersey had never bought equipment from Burlchek's company. About 20 minutes before the scheduled 10:30 appointment, Lindsey received a long-distance call from Burlchek in which the conversation went as follows:

Burlchek: Mr. Lindsey, I'm sorry that I will not be able to make the appointment I set up last week. I am having some car problems here in Philadelphia . . . and I won't be able to get the car out of the garage before 2 P.M. It just cut out yesterday morning.

Lindsey: Oh, that is a shame. . . .

Burlchek: I am sorry we won't have a chance to meet, since I have to be in Hartford tomorrow morning. But could we set up an appointment next month, when I'll be in your area?

Lindsey: Yes, that would be OK with me. Let me transfer you back to my secretary, who can get you on the appointment book.

Burlchek: That's great.

Lindsey: However, if you run into any more car trouble, please give me a little bit more notice. This upsets my entire schedule today.

Burlchek: Don't worry about this happening again. . . . I am scheduled for a new company car in two more weeks.

Consequently, another meeting was scheduled between the two men in late February. At the appointed time, Burlchek enters the purchasing director's office.

Burlchek: Good morning, Mr. Lindsey, I am glad we finally have a chance to meet. Let me apologize again for missing that appointment last month.

Lindsey: That's OK. Now, let me see, as I recall you wanted to tell me about that new line of desks your company has brought out.

Burlchek: Yes, I do! We've had sensational success with these desks. It seems that just about everyone is ordering them. . . . We think that they will end up with 35 to 50 percent of the market.

   The company did some very careful research on matching desks to the physical characteristics of the individuals who use them. As a result, we came up with three *common sizes* or types of users. We call these our Alpha, Beta, and Delta user profiles. Our studies show that people using the right size desk are more productive. Let me show you how these desks work.

Burlchek shows Lindsey booklets and graphic displays of the new product. After an extensive sales presentation, during which Lindsey sits and listens quietly, Burlchek concludes:

Burlchek: Great idea, huh? Like I said, we think it will revolutionize the industry.

Lindsey: Maybe. . . .

Burlchek: Mr. Lindsey, we would like to have you come down to Philadelphia . . . at our expense . . . to look at the new desks. I'm sure that once you see them, you will agree that they are just the thing for those brand new offices you are going to be opening.

Lindsey: Well, I don't think I'll have a chance to get down to Philadelphia for another month or so. Besides, I kind of like the padded stuff offered by Conover Designs. In fact, their representative was in here to see me last month . . . same day you had that car trouble.

Questions

1. What is the reason for Lindsey's reaction to the new product?
2. What type of objection(s) has he raised?
3. If you were Burlchek, how would you proceed?

KEY POINTS

Closing is that point in the sales interview at which the salesperson secures the desired agreement from the prospect.

Closing is the ultimate goal of every salesperson.

There are several causes of closing failures: (1) fear, (2) improper attitude, (3) verbal overkill, and (4) failure to ask for an order.

There is more than one best moment to close a sale.

The salesperson should watch for closing cues from the prospect. These may be either verbal or physical.

Several closing techniques can be used: (1) assumptive close, (2) direct approach, (3) alternative decisions, (4) summary and affirmative agreement, (5) balance sheet approach, (6) emotional close, (7) critical feature close, (8) extra inducement close, (9) SRO method, and (10) silence.

After a successful close, salespeople should show their appreciation for the business, reassure the customer about the decision, and solicit sales leads.

Not all closings concern the actual sales of a product; some are to obtain appointments or set up demonstrations. However, the techniques and procedures used are the same.

Chapter

10

CLOSING: THE SALESPERSON'S ULTIMATE GOAL

Joe Girard always did know how to close a sale, according to those who saw him in action. Girard is listed in *The Guiness Book of World Records* for selling 1,425 trucks and automobiles during a single year. He has since relinquished his position at East Detroit's Merollis Chevrolet to his son. Girard now heads his own firm that promotes his talents for sales meetings, as well as marketing films and cassette tapes used in sales training activities. He has also published two books on selling.

His former colleagues recalled the dynamic closing techniques Girard used. Humorless prospects often burst into laughter when Girard would strip the proverbial shirt off his back. When one prospect failed to respond, Girard even took off his trousers and completed the sale dressed only in his underwear. Associates also recall Girard throwing his sports coat across a puddle for a woman who had resisted his sales presentation and was leaving the dealership. As usual, Girard eventually ended up with the sale.[1] Like other successful salespeople, Joe Girard knew the importance of an effective closing technique.

CLOSING—A DEFINITION

President Truman was fond of the saying "The buck stops here!" So it is with the closing phase of the sales process. Closing a sale is the salesperson's ultimate goal; in fact, it is the only reason for his or her role. *Closing* can be defined as that point in the sales presentation at which the salesperson secures the desired agreement from the prospect.

While the other aspects of the sales process—prospecting and qualifying, preapproach and approach, presentation, demonstration, handling objections, and building future sales—are all important, the actual process of closing is the salesperson's primary objective. A salesperson who cannot close, cannot sell. Unless the salesperson can sell the product or service to a prospect to the mutual satisfaction of both, the sales process cannot be completed. Closing is both the climax of the sales interview and the acid test of how well a salesperson can sell. Over the long run, success in closing also determines the salesperson's level of income and material success.

THE CAUSES OF CLOSING FAILURES

No salesperson is able to conclude every sales interview successfully. The "100 percent effective" salesperson has not been found in any industry. While *closing failures are sales failures,* they are to be expected and should not discourage the salesperson from trying again. Missed sales should be treated as a learning experience to be carefully analyzed and studied so as to improve future sales performance. Every salesperson should devote some time to assessing the effectiveness of each sale attempted. Such an effort will pay dividends in the future.

The causes of closing failures are diverse. Four will be discussed here: (1) fear, (2) improper attitude, (3) verbal overkill, and (4) failure to ask for an order.

It is natural for salespeople to fear the possibility of failure. Herbert D. Eagle, former president of Sales and Marketing Executives International, puts it this way:

Fear—the sales killer

> The salesman gets paid for the number of times he hears "no." The well-adjusted salesman knows in advance that he may close one sale out of 25 calls. He is mentally prepared to suffer those 24 turndowns. Still it takes its toll. So he gets paid for hearing "no."[2]

An industrial sales representative who becomes discouraged over the number of failures to close a sale should contemplate the problems faced by sales forces employed in direct-to-home marketing systems. Consider the following statistics for the encyclopedia seller, who "may approach 10 doors before being admitted. Once admitted, he may complete only one of three presentations. Only one of six presentations may be converted into a sale. Therefore, the salesman may suffer 179 turndowns in order to acquire one sale."[3]

Fear of failure is a leading reason why salespeople are sometimes unable to close a sale. Sales personnel operate in a fiercely competitive environment that requires tremendous personal drive and initiative. A sales turndown dampens enthusiasm and the desire to try again with the next prospect. The classic warning—we have nothing to fear but fear itself—is appropriate in this case. Generally, the best way to cope with this fear is to become an expert in the field and to know more than any customer could possibly learn about the firm's products or services. Fear of sales failure is inappropriate in the demanding field of professional selling.

Closely related to fear of failure is an improper attitude, which can be observed in the way the salesperson attempts to close, speech patterns, and personal mannerisms. Some salespeople have so little confidence in their presentations that they dread the closing stage; they fear failure because they have failed in the earlier steps of the sales process. They could profitably recall Henry J. Kaiser's remark that "impossibles are as impossible as thinking makes them so."[4]

Improper attitude

Other salespeople may appear too aggressive or overly eager to close. Buyers interpret this approach as high-pressure selling or evidence of the salesperson's inexperience, overconfidence, doubts about the product, conceit, or disrespect. The interpretation is unimportant, since the end result is the same: a missed sale.

In attempting to close a sale, the salesperson must be confident of both the product and his or her sales presentation. Someone who exhibits a positive, respectful, sincere, and helpful attitude toward the prospect is likely to secure the prospect's confidence and trust.

Verbal overkill

Another danger in completing a sale is verbal overkill by the salesperson. As one writer has remarked, "The old story that Samson slew 10,000 Philistines with the jawbone of an ass and that salesmen have killed thousands of customers exactly the same way appears to have some merit."[5]

Verbal overkill is characteristic of the salesperson who continues to extol the virtues of the product long after the prospect is ready to purchase. In some cases, the guilty salesperson simply lacks confidence in his or her ability to close; in others, the prospect's apparent willingness to close is not perceived. These perceptual problems have been described as the seller's "failure to equate the importance of listening with the importance of talking."[6] Both lack of confidence and failure to perceive a prospect's willingness to close are costly mistakes.

Verbal overkill is a real danger. The salesperson must watch for cues indicating when to attempt to close and then must be confident of the ability to do so. Various types of closing cues will be discussed later in this chapter.

Failure to ask for the order

The tale is often told of a salesperson who has been trying to sell product X to ABC Corporation with numerous sales calls over a prolonged time. One day the representative is surprised when ABC's purchasing director signs an order for several months' supply of product X. The dazed salesperson, who has kept going through patience and persistence, overcomes shock to ask why the purchasing director had finally decided to buy, after so many sales calls. The buyer's answer typically is "Today is the first time you ever asked me to give you an order."

True or not, the story illustrates the fact that the eventual completion of a sale interview comes when the salesperson asks the prospect for an order. The number of salespeople who never attempt to close is amazing to any trained observer. Some salespeople (a loose application of the term) do not appear to know that they are supposed to close; others seem to forget about this most crucial step. Completion of a sale requires the salesperson to initiate and conclude the closing process. Few buyers will ring up their own sales or voluntarily draw up and sign purchase orders. Even if the prospect actually seeks to buy an item, he or she will rarely proceed with the purchase unless the salesperson initiates the closing.

The red coats are coming

Atlanta's airport is the scene of a fiercely competitive battle between Delta and Eastern. The two carriers have a combined 87 percent share of Atlanta's annual 30 million travelers (the second busiest airport in the world). Nine other airlines compete for the remaining customers.

The competition is marked by major promotional blitzes. Eastern and Delta customer-service agents are also an important part of the contest. Delta's representatives in red blazers (known as the red coats) are everywhere, and have played a significant role in keeping the airline's 3.6 million passenger lead over Eastern.

Richard T. Price, a Delta red coat, figures that he persuades eight or more Eastern customers to switch to Delta on a "good day." This tactic is known as passenger diversion in the trade. How does he do it? According to Mr. Price:

You just ask them if they've ever been asked for their business. Ninety-five percent of them say no. So they're grateful when you offer to change their tickets and get their baggage transferred and maybe save them a long walk down the other guy's concourse.

Source: Jim Montgomery, "Eastern Airlines Fires New Salvos in Attempt to Slow Delta's Gains," *The Wall Street Journal*, April 12, 1978, pp. 1, 19.
Reprinted by permission of *The Wall Street Journal*, © Dow Jones & Company, Inc. (1978). All Rights Reserved.

WHEN TO CLOSE A SALE

It used to be believed that there is *one best moment* for a closing in a sales interview. The effective salesperson, it was believed, is the one who can spot this moment and then close effectively. This way of thinking has long since been discounted in the professional selling field.

Current thought is that there are *several* good moments to close the sale. While there are some points at which a close would be totally inappropriate, the correct point could occur at anytime during the sales presentation. Consider the following remarks by customers:

Customer upon entering a retail store: Hi Jack—listen, I want to get one of the new razors they have been advertising on TV.

Purchasing director to a sales representative entering his or her office: I'm sure glad you were able to stop back here this week. Lance, we've evaluated those samples you left with us, and our technical people say they are just what we need in the shop. And the price is right too!

Prospect to a real estate agent: Duane and I just love the house over on Linden Street. It has everything we have been looking for these past several months.

In the above situations, the salesperson would be foolish to do anything other than to attempt an immediate close. The customers have clearly indicated their acceptance of the products and their willingness to buy. All that is needed is some effort on the part of the salesperson to close. In such cases the close can occur very early in the selling process—perhaps during or right after the approach.

**Figure 10–1
Closing opportunities exist at various points in the sales process**

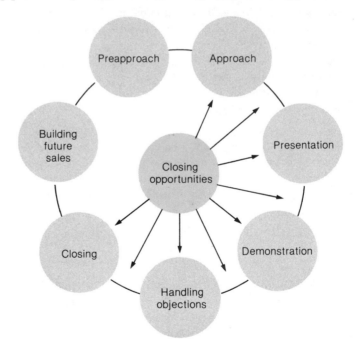

It is up to the salesperson to identify the exact points of the sales interview at which the customer might be amenable to a closing technique. Figure 10–1 shows likely points for such closing opportunities.

Closing cues

Closing cues are comments and body language that suggest a buyer may be ready to purchase the product. Good salespeople study their prospects carefully for these signals to indicate when they should attempt closing. A salesperson who can correctly perceive such cues has a significant advantage over one who attempts to close indiscriminately throughout the selling process. The customer sees the former type of salesperson as being helpful and the latter as resorting to high-pressure tactics.

The ability to spot closing cues comes from experience and practice. Acquiring this skill takes time. Nevertheless, all successful sales personnel have it, and the effort is well worthwhile.

Closing cues can be classified as either verbal cues or physical cues. *Verbal cues* include the following observations or questions:

Yes, I agree that your plan really solves our marketing problem.

Did you say 30 days is the same as cash?

When could you deliver the refrigerator?

Physical cues are actions, such as:

The prospect nods in agreement to a sales presentation.

The prospect puts on a coat and admires its fit in a mirror.

The prospect begins to study, in earnest, an insurance policy.

The meaning of both verbal and physical cues should be obvious to the salesperson. The customer has expressed an apparent interest in the product, and the correct moment for a closing attempt has arrived.

Other examples of closing cues include such verbal cues as:

What other colors do you have available?

I have always wanted an RX-7.

Can we pay for this over three years instead of two?

What is the approximate installation time for the machine?

This is a beautiful piece of property.

Your company has always been fair to us in the past.

Do you have this particular model in stock?

Where would I get replacement parts?

Let me taste one of your new snacks.

I really feel great in this dress.

I need the table for a bridge party tomorrow evening.

The base price is great, but how much do the accessories cost?

You say it has a two-year guarantee?

Well, I'd have to rearrange the shop somewhat. . . .

How would I contact your service department?

Of course, there are many more verbal closing cues. The examples that have been given show that verbal cues are usually in the form of a question or a positive expression about the product or service.

Other physical cues include these actions:

The prospect begins to reexamine the merchandise more carefully.

The prospect begins to read the contract, agreement, or application.

The prospect begins to use or sample the product

The prospect smiles upon hearing the contract terms.

The prospect tenses up and watches the demonstration intently.

The customer steps back and admires the water bed.

The purchasing agent begins to check competitive prices in other catalogs.

Physical cues to closing opportunities are numerous and varied. A good salesperson will carefully watch the prospect's activities and behavior so as to spot these signals.

Trial closes

Another method of assessing when to close the sale is the *trial close,* an attempt to determine the prospect's attitude towards the product and the sales presentation. The salesperson may hope to consummate the sale as a result of a trial close, but the expectations of doing so are not high. Therefore, it is best to view a trial close as a probe to determine the buyer's current state of buying intention.

A trial close should be indirect and low-keyed. *The salesperson wants to leave plenty of opportunity to continue the presentation and make additional closing attempts.* If the seller were to say "This car is an excellent buy at $8,350. When do you want to pick it up?" early in the interview, he or she might lose credibility with the customer and ruin any future chance for the transaction. Instead, the seller might say, "How would you like to handle the financing?" or "Do you like the blue or green best?" In both cases, sufficient opportunity remains to pick up the conversation and to close at a later point in the presentation. The buyer was not asked to say yes or no to the actual purchase. If the response was: "I think I would prefer to handle the financing through my credit union. In fact, they have cleared me for a loan up to. . . ." or "I think the green Reliant is the better choice," then the salesperson might launch into a final closing technique. The trial close has shown that the prospect is sincerely interested in making such a purchase and has made some tentative choices regarding the product.

Not all trial closes are verbal; some are based on a movement. The salesperson might pick up an order book, walk toward the cash register, or start to wrap the purchase. Some salespeople have mastered the art of the *silent trial close*. They simply stop talking and gaze intently at the buyer, hoping the decision to purchase the item will be announced. If the buyer does not respond as hoped, the salesperson breaks the silence by picking up the sales story again.

Regardless of the method used, the trial close is an excellent way of determining where a buyer stands in regard to a proposed purchase. All successful salespeople realize its value and practice it in virtually every presentation they make.

FINAL CLOSING TECHNIQUES

The first step in a successful closing is for the salesperson to be alert to possible closing cues. The second is to attempt one or more trial closes during the course of the interview. In most cases, a final closing technique is used only after these earlier steps have been accomplished.[7]

A salesperson does not expect to close every sale or to conclude most sales with just one closing technique. Fortunately, a variety of closing methods are available.[8] The salesperson's task is to select the technique that is most appropriate for each sales interview. Typically, each salesperson relies upon two or three that are practiced extensively until the individual is comfortable with them.

The exact titles of the different approaches vary, depending upon the source consulted. This text will use the following terminology:

1. Assumptive close.
2. Direct approach.
3. Alternative decisions.
4. Summary and affirmative agreement.
5. Balance sheet approach.
6. Emotional close.
7. Critical feature close.
8. Extra inducement close.
9. SRO method.
10. Silence as a closing technique.

These 10 approaches are the primary closing techniques used to-day. The effective salesperson continually strives to refine and perfect those methods that apply to his or her own sales interviews.

Assumptive close

In the assumptive close technique it is assumed that the buyer has decided to purchase the product or service offered. The salesperson could sign the contract, pass it to the prospect with a pen, start to ring up the purchase (this technique occasionally results in some voided cash register tapes), or pick up the phone and start to arrange delivery details.

An assumptive close can be used where the sales interview has concentrated on or been narrowed down to just one product and the salesperson is reasonably confident of the prospect's willingness to buy. The technique then is used to get the buyer to actually commit to the purchase—usually by his or her inaction. An assumptive close forces the prospect who has not decided to buy to interrupt the sales-person and indicate an unwillingness to conclude the purchase. Peo-ple who do desire the product are reluctant to interrupt.

Direct approach

An obvious way to close a sale is simply to ask the prospect for the order. This is known as a direct approach, and it should be used only when (1) the seller is reasonably confident of the outcome, or (2) sev-eral other closes have failed and the direct approach may be the last chance to conclude the purchase.

James Schlinkert of Olivetti Corporation of America recalls a sale of an accounting system to a small corporation of five people:

> We had them at our office one evening and presented our solution to their problem. They were a hard-nosed lot that had evaluated every other accounting system available. After a couple of hours of haggling over a $15,000 sale, I finally shut off the machine, put the key in my pocket, and virtually threatened to throw them out of my office. Imme-diately, they became very docile and signed a contract. I shocked my salesmen when I did that. But I had to take a calculated risk. The need and solution had been established.[9]

Schlinkert certainly chose a direct close in this situation. The cus-tomer's sales resistance argued against trying other techniques, so Schlinkert selected the direct approach as a reasonable risk.

Other less dramatic methods of using the direct approach include:

> Well, I guess that about covers all the details, Arnold. How many do you want to order for shipment next week?

I know that you are busy, Mrs. Abrovnik, so if it is all right with you I'll start to get this order written up.

It looks as if you prefer the Fiesta—I'll get some temporary license tags for you. You have certainly made a wise selection.

Even if the buyer resists the direct approach, the person is forced to clarify his or her position on the matter. This gives the seller a starting point for picking up the sales presentation again or a chance to answer possible objections. Eventually, it allows the salesperson to try another closing technique.

The elementary technique that proposes alternative decisions is one of the most commonly used approaches to closing. The alternative decision technique asks the prospect to make a choice in which either alternative is favorable to the seller. The decision may concern a major point (as with an automobile model): Do you prefer the Granada or the Fairmont? or a minor point: Which color would you like for the bedroom draperies?

The alternative decision technique can actually pose a choice: Will

Alternative decisions

"Your little girl will love this doll house—now, will that be cash or will you take out a mortgage?"

Reprinted by permission The Wall Street Journal.

Alternative decisions is a common closing technique.

that be on VISA or Master Charge? or it can raise a related question: Will two dozen be enough?

By requesting the buyer to make an alternative decision, the salesperson has forced the basic purchase decision. The buyer may affirm a particular choice in response to the above questions:

I think I'd like to have the Fairmont.

Green would probably look best in that bedroom.

VISA, I guess.

No, we're having company, so you'd better give me three dozen.

This type of choice commits the person to the actual purchase. If the person fails to make a choice, he or she usually identifies doubts about the product or some reasons for not concluding the sale at this point. In both cases, this provides the salesperson with an opportunity to expand the original sales interview by suggesting other models or additional uses of the product. The Rocky Mountain Casket Company of Whitefish, Montana, for example, sells caskets for use as wine closets, liquor cabinets, and coffee tables.[10]

Summary and affirmative agreement

The summary and affirmative agreement method is sometimes divided into two separate techniques, but it is logical to combine them into a uniform approach that is particularly useful when:

1. The product under discussion has many separate and difficult-to-remember features.
2. The customer seems to be impressed with particular features of the item.
3. The buyer may be forced to justify a purchase decision to a third party, like higher management or one's spouse.

In this technique the salesperson closes by summarizing the major features, benefits, and advantages of the product.[11] The seller pauses at each point and seeks agreement from the prospect, with comments such as:

I think you said that this feature would really help your loading operation.

Didn't you say that guaranteed insurability was very important to you?

The Chevette is certainly in the price range you mentioned earlier.

This is the exact thing you said you were looking for in a uniformed security service! Isn't that correct?

The summary and affirmative agreement technique has the dual advantages of reinforcing the key selling points in a sales presentation while at the same time building a series of acceptances about the need for, and importance of, these features. It is an extremely effective approach, particularly when the summary ends with some more direct closing technique.

One way to close a sale that stresses logic and analytical decision making is the balance sheet technique, sometimes known as the T-account, the two-sided, or the advantage/disadvantage close. Essentially, this approach presents the negative factors of a product, as well as the benefits related to it. The method can be used separately or with a summary of the major product characteristics.

Balance sheet approach

The salesperson may actually draw up a balance sheet for the product, such as the following:

Assets	Liabilities
Most comprehensive warranty in the industry. 15 percent lower operating costs. A complete service facility located only 10 minutes away.	The initial price is 3 percent higher than the competition.

When the salesperson starts by listing a liability or disadvantage of the product, the buyer is likely to appreciate the fact that the seller is acknowledging that the product is not perfect. The balance sheet approach establishes the salesperson's credibility in the mind of the prospect. If the salesperson is handling a reliable product, it should be possible to list many more advantages than disadvantages. The objectivity of this technique appeals to many buyers. Advertisers have also used two-sided promotional messages that tell both positive and negative features of a product. This approach has proven particularly successful among better-educated consumers.[12]

After listing assets and liabilities, the salesperson would conclude with a statement such as:

> There it is in black and white, Frank! While our initial price is a little higher, a 15 percent savings in operating costs more than makes up for the difference during the first year you use the machine. Then, when you consider that we have the best warranty in the industry, and the ready availability of our service facility, I don't see how you can make any other choice. Do you?

Emotional close   An emotional close seeks to motivate the person to buy through appeal to such factors as fear, pride, romance, or the need for peer group acceptance. Insurance agents may attempt to close by stressing the need for the bread-winner to provide financial protection for the family should he or she die or become disabled. An emotional close can be a very potent weapon in the hands of a qualified salesperson.

For the most part, emotional closes are used only when several other approaches have failed or when the salesperson believes the prospect is particularly susceptible to this technique. However, the opportunities for using an emotional close may be more numerous than is usually believed. For example, one source has noted:

> Even purchasing agents working for larger organizations appear to be more human in their buying habits than industrial marketers have realized. Emotional factors such as fear of disapproval of superior executives, personal friendships with particular selesmen, and the prestige of the merchandise resource all affect the professional buyer.[13]

Emotional closes should probably be avoided in situations where there is a high repeat-sale potential. This type of close relies on stimulating an impulsive purchase on the part of the prospect and should be carefully considered before being used in closes where long-term seller-buyer relationships exist or are sought. Continued reliance on this technique may injure this relationship.

Critical feature close   Sometimes it is possible to close by stressing a critical feature of the product. The seller's product may have a characteristic not found in any competitive product. This provides a significant advantage that can be emphasized in a close such as: "Now, isn't that exactly what you said you always wanted that grinder to do?"

Another possible use for the critical feature close arises when the prospect appears extremely impressed with a particular product feature. The salesperson goes back and highlights this point and then asks for the order directly.

Critical feature closes are effective only if the buyer agrees with the seller's assessment of the feature. Many salespeople have been embarrassed in using critical feature closes when the prospect did not view the characteristic as particularly pertinent or relevant. The salesperson must make the buyer see the importance and need for such a feature. If this cannot be accomplished, then the salesperson should switch to another closing technique immediately.

All good salespeople hold at least one selling point in reserve. These are known in sales terminology as *clinchers*. The salesperson holds back one or more clinchers to assist the close or to help pick up the thread of conversation should the close fail.

Clinchers typically take the form of an extra inducement to buy the item. This may be a lay-away option, a quantity price discount, a waiver of delivery charges, or a special servicing capability. Special inducements of this nature can have a significant impact on the sales interview. When the salesperson has offered a "special favor" to the buyer, many prospects feel obligated to close the sale.

The disadvantages associated with this technique are:

1. This type of clincher may encourage the customer to seek additional favors from the seller.
2. Special inducements must be applied uniformly to all buyers. Discriminatory behavior is unethical at least, and often illegal.

Extra inducement close

A technique known by several names has lately been designated the standing room only (SRO) method. With this method the salesperson tells the prospect that the purchase should be concluded at the present time because the merchandise probably will not be available later. The real estate agent might say:

> This is the last lot in Acorn Acres. We had two people look at it yesterday, and a couple more are supposed to come out this evening. I am sure we will sell it by tomorrow morning, so if you want it, now is the time to act!

SRO method

An automobile salesperson might apply the SRO technique this way:

> As you know, this is a limited-production sports car, and this is the last one we'll get until January. I'd suggest you move pretty fast on it, since our other sales rep has a professor up at the college who is interested. In fact, Professor Maxwell is supposed to come down here this afternoon.

The SRO technique works only when the availability of a product is limited or some future event may change the terms of the deal. Automobile, real estate, and many industrial supply sales personnel can legitimately say, "You'd better buy it now because we expect prices to increase in the weeks or months ahead." These salespeople use an impending event that threatens the current sales terms as a closing device. This can be very effective during times of inflation.

Another modification of the SRO technique is to ask for a deposit to hold the item being considered. Rarely do customers ever forfeit their deposits and decide not to buy the product.

Silence as a closing technique

Silence was discussed earlier as a method of attempting a trial close. It can also be used as a final closing technique, but it is suggested that silence be used sparingly in this way. It is an aggressive close, and the salesperson may find it difficult to continue the presentation should this close fail.

The only essential difference between using silence as a trial close and as a final close is the amount of time involved. During a trial close, the silence is just a brief pause in the conversation, while it is a longer, more definite break when used as a final closing technique.

A word of caution about closing

In addition to knowing and practicing the various techniques of closing, the seller should also keep the closing segment in perspective to the entire sales process. One way of doing this is to consult a checklist of things *not to do during closing*. The Photo Marketing Association—International has prepared such a list, and it is reprinted in Figure 10–2.

Figure 10–2 Don'ts in closing

1. Don't rush the customer. The customer is the most important person in the store, and rushing him or her to a decision often means high-pressure.
2. *Ifs* and *hopes* are signs of weakness. Be positive. Convey your sales points with assurance. Don't say, "I think maybe you will like it, if you try it."
3. Don't stand around with a look of indifference. Sure, you've told her a lot about the merchandise, but you're the salesman—your job is to sell.
4. Keep interested. *Don't appear bored* because the customer pauses a few seconds to make up her mind.
5. Don't attempt to close until all voiced objections are answered. By not answering questions, you arouse suspicion. Suspicion often leads to high pressure—and high pressure means lost sales and customers.
6. Don't oversell. You can talk too much about the item! Watch your customers' reactions.
7. Don't leave the customer in a state of indecision.

Source: *Seven Steps in Selling for Retail Photographic Salesmen* (Jackson, Mich.: Photo Marketing Association–International, 1970).

Another type of closing

Some interviews between salesperson and prospect are not intended to result in a closed sale. Neither the seller nor the buyer may expect to complete the transaction at the end of an interview. An IBM or Burroughs sales representative may work with a prospect for many months before a sale is actually completed, for example, and other high-value items requiring capital expenditures are sold in a similar fashion.

In some cases, a salesperson-prospect discussion may be designed entirely to:

1. Discover who the salesperson should contact in a company about a particular product.
2. Secure an opportunity to make a sales presentation at a later date. Insurance agents typically set up presentations when both husband and wife are available.
3. Obtain an interview with the technical or operating personnel who will actually be using the product.
4. Set up a time to conduct a product demonstration for the prospect.

The important thing is that the closing techniques discussed above are also applicable to these types of buyer-seller interfaces. A sales representative has successfully *closed* in these situations if he or she has determined the correct buying contact, set up another appointment with a prospect or other interested parties (such as a company's technical personnel), or confirmed a time for a product demonstration. The same closing techniques and procedures are applicable.

POSTSALE ACTIVITIES

The sales process does not end when the buyer signs the contract or says "I'll take it." Once the buyer agrees to the purchase, the salesperson must proceed with the concluding details of the sale: fill out the appropriate forms, arrange payment terms, and consult the buyer about delivery. The key to success at this stage is to be efficient, polite, and reassuring. Too many salespeople linger with the buyer after a sale has been completed. Most buyers appreciate those who conclude their business carefully yet quickly and then leave. The sales adage "Get in, get the sale, get out, and get on to the next prospect" holds true.

Postsale activities are necessary to buyer satisfaction and enhance the salesperson's likelihood of securing future business. Sales managers suggest the following guidelines to postsale activities.

1. Show appreciation. The salesperson should let the customer know that the order is appreciated. The seller must avoid excessive expression of satisfaction (perhaps glee) at the successful completion of the sale. The proper attitude is restraint and dignity, since there has been an exchange that is mutually beneficial to both parties. A simple thank you or "We really appreciate the business, Jim" is appropriate.

2. Reassure the customer. During the time between the purchase agreement and the end of the interview, the salesperson should seek to reassure the customer that the buying decision was the correct one. The following remarks are examples of how this might be done:

> I know you will really enjoy wearing this sweater.
>
> Leonard, this was a good decision on your part.
>
> Wait till you see the first efficiency rating after our system is installed!
>
> Boyd, the air conditioning option you chose will sure make your vacation driving more pleasant next week.

3. Solicit sales leads. Sales representatives must always be alert for sales leads. A new customer is a likely source since most people will tend to reduce their doubts about a purchase by promoting it to their friends and associates.[14] However, the salesperson must avoid any suggestion of high-pressure tactics in seeking these leads. A simple request is adequate: "Jack, do you know anyone else in your area who might be interested in this type of policy?"

4. A future sale versus a lost sale. Not all sales interviews conclude with a closed sales agreement, as was noted above. In these cases, it is essential that the salesperson build toward future sales rather than writing the interview off as a lost sale. The salesperson must strive to keep the prospect's door open to future sales presentations by thanking the person for the time and maintaining goodwill.

SUMMARY

Closing can be defined as the point in the sales presentation at which the salesperson secures the desired agreement from the prospect. Closing the sale is the goal of every salesperson.

The causes of closing failure include (1) fear, (2) improper attitude, (3) verbal overkill, and (4) failure to ask for the order. This chapter points out that missed sales should be treated as a learning experience to be analyzed and studied in order to improve future sales performance. They should not discourage salespeople in future sales presentations.

There are several points in the sales process at which the salesperson might attempt to close, rather than only one best moment. The salesperson should watch the prospect for closing cues—verbal or physical—that suggest a readiness to purchase the product. Then a trial close, or an attempt at closing to determine the prospect's readiness to buy, should be tried.

Ten closing techniques are identified and discussed: (1) assumptive close, (2) direct approach, (3) alternative decisions, (4) summary and affirmative agreement, (5) balance sheet approach, (6) emotional close, (7) critical feature close, (8) extra inducement close, (9) SRO methods, and (10) silence.

These techniques and procedures also apply in closing situations that are not concerned with the actual sale of a product. Some are to obtain appointments or set up demonstrations, for example.

The manner in which postsale activities are handled is also important, because repeat-sale potential can depend on it. After a successful close, salespeople should (1) show their appreciation for the business, (2) reassure the customer about the decision, and (3) solicit sales leads. If the salesperson is unable to close, he or she should be sure to maintain the option of a possible sale in the future.

REVIEW QUESTIONS/DISCUSSION QUESTIONS/EXERCISES

1. Briefly identify the following:
    a. Closing.   d. Silent trial close.
    b. Closing cue.   e. Clincher.
    c. Trial close.

2. Explain the following statement: A salesperson who cannot close, cannot sell.

3. List and discuss the various reasons why salespeople fail to close some sales.

4. Cite some examples of closing cues for which a salesperson should watch.

5. There is more than one best moment to close a sale. Comment on this statement.

6. Identify and explain each of the 10 closing techniques discussed in the chapter.

7. When is the appropriate time to close a sale? Discuss.

8. What should the salesperson do after closing a sale? What should the seller do if he or she has failed to close the sale?

9. Can closing techniques be used in any buyer-seller interface other than an actual sales transaction? Explain.

10. Match the remarks by sellers (designated a–e) in the left-hand column with the correct closing technique (designated 1–5) in the list at right.

    a. There you are, Homer. While the policy doesn't contain the dread disease clause, it has all of the other five features you said were important to you. That is better than our competition . . . and our policy is cheaper.

    _____1. Extra inducement close.

    b. Would you prefer to use VISA or Master Charge?

    _____2. Alternative decision.

    c. I know you want to get back to the loading dock, Earl, so why don't I get this order written up for you?

    _____3. Balance sheet approach.

    d. Mrs. Merriam, if I can have your order today, we will be able to give you a special barbeque set absolutely free!

    _____4. SRO method.

    e. Mr. Lambrowski, this is the last floor model we have. If you like the set I would suggest you give us a deposit, these floor model sales never last more than a couple of hours.

    _____5. Direct approach.

11. List two or three closing techniques that would be appropriate for each of these types of salespeople. Justify your choices.
    a. Stockbroker.
    b. College textbook salesperson (calling on college professors).
    c. Used-car salesperson.

12. Describe your two most recent purchases. What closing technique did the salesperson use in each of these?

13. Marvin A. Jolson, in *Consumer Attitudes toward Direct-to-Home Marketing Systems* (New York: Dunellin Publishing Co., Inc., 1970), p. 49, reported that:

    Most direct selling firms proudly claim that almost one hundred percent of their sales are obtained on the salesman's first call. Such believers in "one-call" closing have statistics to support the fact that less than 5 percent of all callbacks result in sales. One sales manager of a national direct selling firm in his orientation of new salesmen says "We don't sell a *product;* we sell a reason for people to buy today."

Evaluate this statement. What does it mean to professional selling?

14. Assume you are a sales representative for a carpet-cleaning franchise. The prospect has just said, "Yes I definitely want to get your people in here to clean this carpeting, but I really think I should consult my husband about the price, and he is on a week's business trip." How would you handle this objection, and then proceed to close?

15. A salesperson in one automobile dealership has a blanket authorization to negotiate up to a $300 discount from the original price quotation for any model. In a sales interview, a prospect says she will purchase the automobile if the seller reduces the original quotation by $150. The salesperson replies:

Well, I don't know whether we can go that far. Let me check with my sales manager. (He returns to the prospect five minutes later.) This is your lucky day . . . the sales manager says we can cut it by $150, provided this special discount is kept just between the three of us. Let me write that up right now.

Evaluate this closing technique. Are any ethical considerations involved?

16. Practice the various closing techniques. One method would be for a friend to pretend to be a prospect for a product, while you assume the role of the salesperson. Then reverse the prospect-seller roles and try another type of product.

17. Which closing techniques would probably be used by the following sales personnel?
    a. Life insurance.
    b. Home remodeling.
    c. Office furniture.
    d. Cemetery lots.

18. Identify and describe two or three situations (other than an actual sales transaction) in which you might be required to use a closing technique.

19. Develop a list of about 20 to 30 closing statements. Put each on a 3″ × 5″ card. Write the closing technique that the statement represents on the opposite side of the card. Shuffle the cards and practice identifying the type of close.

20. One of the authors has had a salesperson tell him, "How do I close? Well, I just keep coming at them until they buy. I close by never quitting on a prospect until I have sold him." Evaluate this salesperson's approach.

CASE 10–1: BADGER LAKE ESTATES (A)

Foster-Johnson, Inc., is a developer of a second-home resort community located on a large lake in northern Wisconsin. The development—Badger Lake Estates—consists of over 600 lots priced at $20,000 and up. An 18-hole golf course; large clubhouse with dining room and cocktail lounge; extensive recreational facilities such as shuffleboard, tennis, and racquetball courts; and snowmobile and horse-riding trails are provided for residents. Skiing is available within a 10-mile drive.

Badger Lake Estates has a *quality* image because of its location advantage, the variety of recreation that is available, and a sales contract that specifies only second homes in the $80,000 and above category may be constructed on the property. Approximately 30 percent of the lots have already been purchased, and on nearly half of these either construction is underway or there are finished residences. Foster-Johnson, Inc. has a subsidiary operation—Northern Wisconsin Construction Company—that builds a majority of the homes at Badger Lake.

The developer's promotional program starts with advertisements in Milwaukee, Chicago, and Minneapolis newspapers which provide a mail coupon for additional information. Since over 80 percent of lot sales come from these three metropolitan areas, there is a Foster-Johnson sales office in each city.

When a newspaper coupon is received by a sales office, an attractive packet of sales information is mailed the same day. One week later, a sales representative calls the prospect. If the prospect appears to be a potentially qualified buyer, the salesperson seeks an appointment to discuss the property. If the appointment is refused, the sales office mails a stamped, self-addressed postcard saying that Foster-Johnson will be happy to supply additional information about the development at any time. All the prospect has to do is check the appropriate box and return the card.

If the prospect does approve the representative's call, an appointment is arranged at which both husband and wife are present. When the salesperson arrives, he or she immediately tries to confirm their interest in a second home and their ability to purchase such property. If satisfied on this count, the representative begins an extensive presentation that uses slides to highlight various features of Badger Lake Estates. The prospects are also given an expensive, well-produced booklet on the development.

Brian Sullivan, a sales representative in the Chicago area, has just finished such a presentation at the home of Dr. and Mrs. Raymond Albright. Albright is a dentist in an exclusive Chicago suburb.

Sullivan: You both appear to be very interested in establishing a vacation home in Wisconsin. Is that correct?

Mrs. Albright: Yes, I think we would be interested. Ray and I have always liked that section of Wisconsin. In fact, we spent a week there last summer.

Albright: The lakes in that area are certainly an attraction for someone who likes to fish like I do.

Sullivan: Great! I am glad to learn that you like our location. We think it is one of the most beautiful spots in the entire country. Now I guess the only thing we need to decide is when you will tour the property. Of course, we pay for lodging and meals. Would next weekend suit your schedule, or would you prefer to come up the following weekend?

Questions

1. What type of closing technique has Sullivan used?
2. Why didn't Sullivan attempt to close an actual lot sale at this time?
3. What is your assessment of Foster-Johnson's promotional strategy?

CASE 10–2: BADGER LAKE ESTATES (B)

It is 9:30 A.M. on a Saturday morning, and Dr. and Mrs. Raymond Albright have just arrived at the sales office of Badger Lake Estates. They are greeted by Hal Skorski.

Skorski: I trust that the accommodations Brian Sullivan and I arranged for you over at the Brookside Inn were OK?

Albright: Yes, they were fine. We had a very nice room.

Skorski: Good! Well, I know you want to see the many fine lots available here at Badger Lake. But maybe we should look at this map first . . . so I can point out where we will be going as well as the development's proximity to the other lakes and communities in the area.

Skorski points out the various points of interest on a large wall map and discusses them. Then he says:

Skorski: Let's get started. It is a beautiful autumn day, and I know you will enjoy the pleasant drive. The property has all the features of the best fall color tour.

After two hours of touring the property, the Albrights indicate some interest in a wooded corner lot. Skorski invites them to examine the lot.

Skorski: I can see by your faces that you agree with me that this may well be one of the most beautiful lots in Badger Lake Estates. This is just the type of prestige location that is right for people like you.

Albright: What do you think, Susan?

Mrs. Albright: I love it! The entire development is just lovely, but this is the best pick as far as I'm concerned. But maybe we should look at some other developments in the area.

Questions

1. How should Skorski respond to Mrs. Albright's comment?
2. Suggest two or three closes that Skorski might use in this situation.
3. Assume the Albrights decline to buy the property at this time. What should Skorski do in this case?

KEY POINTS

- Sales to established customers are the foundation of successful sales careers.

- Experienced salespeople retain current customers by: (1) building goodwill, (2) handling complaints, (3) processing requests for rush delivery, and (4) handling requests for other kinds of special treatment.

- The best prospects for increasing sales are current customers, not new prospects.

- Sales to current customers can be increased by either obtaining a larger portion of their purchases or increasing the customers' sales levels.

- Reclaiming lost sales is one way of increasing sales volume that is overlooked by many salespeople.

- Past sales activities are an excellent source of ideas for new prospects.

- Past sales activities should be studied to learn how to sell more efficiently in the future. Sales reports are the primary source of information for this purpose.

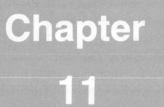

Chapter
11

BUILDING FUTURE
SALES

Milton Bradley had a problem. Its new electronic games—Simon, Big Trak, and Microvision—were instant winners in the toy market. But as orders poured in, the firm had to find a way to deal with an industry-wide shortage of electronic chips. And then to make matters worse, the chip manufacturers overestimated their output.

The Springfield, Massachusetts, toy firm decided to allocate its popular electronic games so as to be as fair as possible to its customers. Milton Bradley also wanted to be sure that the games were available in the markets where they were to be advertised. The company called upon its sales force to explain the difficult situation to its accounts— a tough job at best! But as George Ditomassi, Milton Bradley's senior marketing vice president, put it, "We and our customers will live to do business together next year, and problems must be handled intelligently."[1]

This chapter discusses the last step in the sales process which in this book is called *building future sales* because this phrase stresses the importance of the final step in selling. The last step is viewed as a first step, the initial step toward future sales. Selling is an ongoing activity, without a beginning or an end.

Many interrelated activities are involved in building future sales. It is helpful to divide these activities into three categories: (1) maintaining current sales volume, (2) expanding sales volume, and (3) increasing selling efficiency.

MAINTAINING CURRENT SALES VOLUME

Too often, salespeople act as if the last step in the selling process is closing the sale. Once an order is obtained, they move on to the next prospect. Any order follow-up or customer service is minimal.

This is a shortsighted attitude toward selling, for it fails to consider the importance of developing and maintaining good customer relationships. Experienced salespeople recognize that to continually increase their sales volume, they must first build a solid foundation of sales to current customers. With such a base, sales to new customers can make up the increases. Without this base, sales to new customers only replace those that are lost in the normal course of events.

There are many ways salespeople can maintain sales to established accounts and convert new customers into established ones. Those that will be discussed here are (1) building goodwill, (2) handling complaints, (3) processing requests for rush delivery, and (4) handling other special requests. All involve convincing customers that their purchases are wise ones. One selling expert says:

> The most important thing I've learned is that selling a man something means doing something for him. Not just describing benefits, but delivering them. In fact, the word I've come to like best is *installing:* taking out your screwdriver and pliers and actually meshing the operating benefit with one of your customer's key processes. This means you don't just take the order; you don't just oversee delivery; you don't just handle complaints. You accept responsibility for *making the benefit happen* in the customer's plant. Most important, you make sure the customer realizes he is better off, not because of the benefit per se, but because of *you*.[2]

Building goodwill among customers is a simple matter; all that is necessary is to attend to the customer's interest. This is the marketing concept in action, but putting the marketing concept into action is easier said than done.

Building goodwill

In a survey of automobile buyers that sought to determine the real reasons why people had not returned to the dealerships where they had bought their last car, 68 percent of the respondents said they left because the salesperson was indifferent. In short, over two thirds of the business was lost because it appeared to the customer that the salesperson did not care![3]

Indifference to new customers is particularly harmful. New customers usually have taken their business from someone else, probably because they were not satisfied with their previous supplier. Now they are trying a new supplier to see if he or she is any better. Imagine what indifference can do in this situation!

What can salespeople do to protect themselves from falling into the indifference trap? First, they can keep in touch with customers. And second, they can recognize that customers—new or old—are a company's most important asset.[4]

Scheduling calls. Keeping in touch with customers is primarily a matter of scheduling. With proper planning, a salesperson can visit new customers and established accounts on a regular, recurring basis. To assist in this planning, it is helpful for a salesperson to maintain a *tickler file*—a reminder of things to be done. Some salespeople keep warranty cards and call their customers just before the warranty expires to ask them to bring their purchase in for a final check. Some appliance salespeople accompany the service people when they install the new appliance. Others use calendars on which they mark the dates of sales or sales reports; these will be described later in this chapter. Whatever method is used, all professional sales representatives see their customers regularly. They have learned from experience that the best way to get repeat business is to stay in touch with customers.

It is not easy to generalize about how often a customer should be visited. For some types of selling, even the most important customers require a visit only once every several weeks, although telephone contact should be more frequent. In other cases, customers should be seen weekly or even more often. Sometimes a representative visits very large accounts every day of every week and may even maintain an office on the customer's premises.

It is also difficult to suggest the proper amount of time to wait before first visiting a new customer after a sale. Frank Lawrence of GO, Inc., recommended that International Harvester truck salespeople should make their first call on a new customer 3 days after the delivery of a new truck, their second call 10 days after delivery, their third after 17 days, and then one call every 90 days thereafter for as long as the customer owns the truck, or until the customer "buys or dies."[5] Quite obviously, this would be much too often for a product like an automatic washer and dryer, carpeting, or even a new car.

It is also true that different customers require different frequencies of salespeople's calls, or *callback schedules*. How often each customer should be visited will depend on the importance of the customer, special problems, the relative newness of the account, and other similar factors. It is common for salespeople to divide their accounts into categories so that each customer in a given category has the same callback frequency. All customers in category 1 might be contacted every week, all those in category 2 once a month, and the remaining customers might be contacted at least once every half year. Account classification is described in greater detail in Chapter 12.

Recognizing the customer's importance. The second aspect of avoiding indifference and building goodwill is recognizing that customers are a firm's most valuable asset. This is more than a mental attitude; it is a prescription for action. Most firms carefully protect expensive laboratory or production equipment with regular maintenance routines to ensure that necessary maintenance is performed as required. Yet many customers are serviced on a time-available basis—if there is time, they get serviced; if not enough time is available, they do not.

Such an attitude prevails when the salesperson views customer service narrowly, seeing it as little more than reasonable delivery time and accurate order fulfillment. But to customers, customer service "involves every point of contact with the supplier . . . [sales] calls, order placement, engineering advice, shipping notification, processing of claims, the invoice itself and other matters."[6] And even though sales personnel are not normally responsible for many of these activities, professional salespeople involve themselves enough with each of these activities to ensure that their customers are always served adequately. Jorgensen Steel Company attributes much of its 185 percent increase in sales over a 10-year period to just such an approach to customer service.[7]

Customer service plays an important role in minimizing customer dissonance (see Chapter 3). For many products, service after the sale is a major part of the purchase decision. If the service is good, the decision is viewed favorably; if it is bad, the buyer regrets the purchase.

There are many things salespeople can do to minimize dissonance. A telephone call to see if the customer is pleased goes a long way in this regard. The clothing salesperson who compliments the customer on her appearance performs the same service. And the new-car salesperson who chats with the customer during the first trip to the service department under warranty also makes the customer feel good about the purchase decision.

One of the most difficult aspects of ensuring repeat business is the problem of handling complaints. Something is wrong when a customer complains, and the complaint might be serious enough to affect the customer's purchase decision the next time the product is needed. The salesperson who is going to build a long-term relationship with customers must be able to handle complaints.

Handling complaints

The best way to handle complaints is to avoid them. Any complaint represents a failure of the product or the company to fulfill the customer's expectations. This situation can arise in one of two ways: (1) the performance of the product or firm is poor, or (2) the expectations of the customer are too high.

The salesperson's presentation plays a major role in the development of the customer's expectations for the product or firm. It is not only ill advised to give the customer impossible expectations, it is wrong. A salesperson with *integrity* has been described as "one who helps the customer to have a valid set of expectations regarding how well the product will solve his problem."[8] Integrity in selling also makes good sense from a pure business standpoint. If the customer's expectations are too high, the product cannot possibly meet them, and the customer will be unhappy with the purchase. The customer whose expectations are met, however, will be satisfied with the purchase and more inclined to buy the product again. The salesperson must remember that a customer's expectations are formed before the purchase is made, not afterward. It is up to the seller to see that the customer's expectations are consistent with the proven performance of the product. Telling the customer that there was a misunderstanding after a complaint has been registered does little good.

If the reason for the complaint is a valid one and the product does not perform to a reasonable level of expectations, something has gone wrong in the product's manufacture. It is imperative that the firm make amends to satisfy the customer.

All too often, the inexperienced salesperson is willing to reimburse the customer for the extra costs incurred or to replace the defective product with a new one. This is a fast, easy solution. But these solutions are easy only to the salesperson. The firm incurs extra costs, the customer often has to wait for the delivery of the new item, and somebody in production will probably be reprimanded. It would be much better if the salesperson could rectify the situation with the product already on hand. This may mean taking off a coat, rolling up some sleeves, and showing how the defective part can be made to work with a small readjustment, or it may mean making a quick repair on the spot. If these solutions are not possible, the customer will have to be given a new item or rework charges will have to be paid, but these should be offered only if the other possibilities fail.

Processing rush delivery requests

When normal delivery time is insufficient to meet the customer's needs, a rush delivery request is made. This often means that the product has to be specially handled in production and packaging, a speedier and more costly mode of transportation has to be used, and expedited delivery service is required. All of this costs money, and someone has to pay the bill.

If the customer requests rush delivery and offers to pay the extra charges, the salesperson has little trouble handling the request. It is only necessary to see that the proper paper work is issued and that everyone in the firm understands the importance of speedy delivery and expeditious handling. Some additional internal handling charges may be incurred, but normally these are minimal and can easily be absorbed.

But if the customer requests special delivery and handling and suggests that the salesperson's firm absorb the cost difference, a decision must be made. Should the deal be accepted and the additional costs absorbed? If the answer is yes, all of the firm's customers will be paying for the extra delivery service because the firm's costs are going to increase, and ultimately these increases will be reflected in higher prices. On the other hand, if the extra costs are not absorbed and the customer is required to pay the bill, there is a risk of losing the customer. Acceptance of the deal depends on several factors. Is this the first time the customer has asked for special consideration, or is it standard practice? How important is the customer to the firm? Is there a possibility of getting special consideration from the customer on a later occasion? Will the customer recall the extra service, or will it be expected? Answers to these and similar questions will determine whether or not the charges should be absorbed.

In general, it is best if all customers receive the same service and delivery. If special service is required, the customer should be prepared to reimburse the firm for the extra costs incurred. In the short run, this may be a very difficult course to pursue, especially when a very good customer starts to apply pressure. But in the long run it works, because each customer realizes that the salesperson is treating every customer fairly and respects him or her for it.

Customers can make many requests for special treatment besides expeditious delivery. They can ask for special packaging, tighter quality control, extra product tests, design changes from the standard specifications, and other exceptions to the normal processing of the product. They may request particular financing arrangements, discounts, or payment terms.

Handling other special requests

Special requests should be handled virtually the same way as rush delivery requests. The same considerations apply, and the same problems will result if the customers' demands are met too easily. But there is an additional dimension to handling special requests that does not affect rush delivery requests. Requests for rush delivery are so common that a salesperson quickly learns from experience which requests are reasonable and which are not, approximately how much each rush delivery will cost, and what the reactions of the people in the firm will be to the request. This is not the case for other special requests. These requests may be totally new to the salesperson, or the salesperson may not be familiar with the effects the special treatment can have on the firm's normal operations. Accordingly, the salesperson is in a precarious position in negotiating with the customer.

To help in this regard, many companies insist that all salespeople spend some part of their sales training working in the plant. Each salesperson becomes acquainted with the effects special requests can have on the operation of the production facility. Without this experience the salesperson may make unreasonable requests, which accounts for the antagonism often found between production and sales forces. As J. J. Arntz, manager of operations at Ohio Steel Tube Company, said, "The sales and production departments of a typical corporation get along about as well as Adolf Hitler and Joseph Stalin after they signed their nonaggression pact."[9] To forestall the harmful effects of such an atmosphere, Arntz made some changes:

> I told our people: "We're not going to be a sales-oriented company; we're not going to be a production-oriented company; we're going to be a customer-oriented company." . . . The point is that sales and production have to cooperate better—to serve the customer better.[10]

The salesperson who recognizes the possible effects of each special request on the firm's operations is in a better position to consider the request on its individual merits. This knowledge also makes it easier to negotiate a fair arrangement with the customer.

EXPANDING SALES VOLUME

The successful salesperson must be able to maintain current sales volumes. But it is not enough to simply maintain current levels of sales. Successful salespeople increase their sales volumes year after year. In fact, it is this growth in sales that often distinguishes the mediocre salesperson from the outstanding one.

There are three ways of expanding sales volume: (1) expanding sales to current customers, (2) developing new customers, and (3) reclaiming lost sales.

Expanding sales to current customers

The best prospects for increased sales are current customers.[11] If the salesperson has successfully built goodwill and if customers are satisfied with their purchases, they are likely prospects for additional sales. New prospects have to be found, sold, and cultivated, whereas all this has been accomplished with satisfied customers. It is much simpler to look to current customers for increased sales than it is to look for new customers.

There are two methods of increasing sales to current customers; through a larger share of the customers' business and through increased sales of the customers' end products.

"I'm not kidding around anymore, Mrs. Whitman.
You have our book, we have your son."

Reprinted by permission of the Saturday Review

Nonprofit organizations must also ensure that
customers are served.

Obtaining larger shares.   When a firm provides only a portion of a customer's total needs, the most obvious way to increase sales is to increase its share of the currently available business. To do this, the salesperson must convince the customer that more benefits are obtainable from his or her product than from a competitor's. The best way to convince a customer of this is to make it true—that is, to actually provide better service and products. Then the promise of greater benefits is a fact that the customer readily recognizes.

Ultimate success in this area occurs when the customer makes the supplier the *sole source* of a product (see Chapter 3). Many buying firms are reluctant to grant a supplier this privilege, however, because it often results in a reduced level of service and performance. Some suppliers become complacent without competition. This accounts for the axiom in marketing which holds that the toughest position for a supplier is to be a sole source. The firm in this position must work twice as hard to maintain it as it did to attain it.

The discussion up to this point has been based on the assumption that each customer's total needs for a product are fixed and cannot be increased. In the next section, it will be shown how suppliers can help their customers increase their total levels of sales. Another way of increasing a need for a particular product is to show customers new uses for the product in their current operations. During the past several years, the amounts of aluminum and plastics used in American cars have been increased. These industries have increased their share of the automobile companies' business by replacing other materials. Alert salespeople recognize this possibility and are constantly looking for opportunities to increase the use of the products and services they offer.

Expanding volume to current customers in a cocktail lounge

A good cocktail waitress can increase the sales volume of a cocktail lounge substantially, earning up to $25,000 annually in the process. But the U.S. Bartenders Guild president estimates that a mere 5–10 percent of all cocktail waitresses are really competent in their work.

Peg Dameron offers a solution to this problem with her Southern California Cocktail Waitresses, Inc., a school to train people interested in their occupation. Students learn about 200 or so drinks, the industry's trade jargon, and how to present orders to a bartender in the order in which glassware and stocks are arranged. The students are taught to memorize drink orders, rather than writing them down, so as to save time and maximize efficiency.

The aspiring cocktail waitresses also learn how to increase sales volume in a lounge. Students are taught to always be on the lookout for near empty glasses. If one member of a party finishes a drink sooner than others, a waitress's comment that "You're not going to let him [her] drink alone, are you?" can often stimulate further sales. Waitresses also learn to inquire whether they can "freshen" a cocktail rather than asking if the person wants a second round. Increasing the customers' level of sales is an effective way of expanding volume to current customers—even in a cocktail lounge.

Source: G. Christian Hill, "Toppers and Tipplers Tend to Be Tippers, Wowing Waitresses," *The Wall Street Journal*. April 5, 1978, pp. 1, 37.

Increasing the customer's level of sales. Firms that sell their products through distributors, wholesalers, retailers, and other middlemen can increase sales by increasing their customers' sales. Anything the supplying firm can do to help its customers increase their sales will automatically increase its own sales also. Training the customer's sales force to use better selling techniques and providing product information; supporting the customer's advertising, both financially and creatively; and showing customers new uses for the product are some of the ways suppliers have found to increase customer sales.

Existing customers are an ideal source of sales leads because satisfied customers will be willing to share their pleasure at having made the right decision with friends and acquaintances. Many customers will provide the names of other good prospects. For example, a new-truck buyer will, on the average, give the salesperson the names of three to five good prospects.[12]

Developing new customers

Satisfied customers also can give the salesperson ideas of how the product could satisfy the needs of other potential customers. The technique of *clue management* can help the salesperson uncover a whole new market for a product. Clue management has been called "paying great attention to early indications of change."[13] Skillfully used, it can suggest to the salesperson not only new markets for existing products but ideas for new products as well.

Finally, professional salespeople go beyond using customers as a source of sales leads; they ask existing customers to help them *sell* the product. They ask if other prospects may see the product in operation at the customer's plant, if the customer would write a brief letter recommending the product, or if the customer would endorse the product in advertisements. Activities of this sort use the customer as a salesperson, and this is one of the most effective means of promoting a product. There are few sources more credible than satisfied customers, and the professional salesperson knows it.

Since sales to established accounts is the foundation of successful selling, losing business from existing customers is particularly detrimental to long-term success. Business is usually lost because something has happened to upset the status quo. Either the products or services the salesperson is offering have deteriorated, or else competitors have introduced better products, increased services, or lowered prices enough to encourage some customers to switch their business. In either case, the salesperson has not done the job if the loss of business comes as a surprise.

Reclaiming lost sales

As the firm's contact with its market, the salesperson is relied on to alert the firm to changes in the market that could adversely affect sales. If this is not done, unexpected changes in competitors' products or services will catch the firm by surprise, and it may take years to regain an advantage the firm once enjoyed. The same is true for changes in the firm's operations. It is easy for a firm to become complacent and fail to notice slight changes in the quality of its products or services. Customers notice, however, and, even more important, so do competitors. If the deterioration continues long enough, it may become so bad that reconstruction is almost impossible. All of this can be avoided if the firm's sales force is continually monitoring the market to determine if conditions are changing and, if so, how they are changing.

INCREASING SELLING EFFICIENCY

Sales managers are responsible for increasing the efficiency of the sales organization. This requires them to carefully monitor the activities of sales personnel in order to take corrective action when necessary. This is the reason most salespeople must complete expense, activity, and call reports on a regular basis.

Unfortunately, filling out reports is one of the more tedious aspects of selling. Most salespeople view it as a necessary evil, but it is one of the most important aspects of the selling process. Suggestions for handling such paper work are outlined in Chapter 12.

Reports are required by the sales manager to increase selling efficiency. If the sales manager can use these reports for this purpose, so can the salesperson. To illustrate this point, the reports that a Blue Cross–Blue Shield of North Carolina sales representative completes regularly and sends to a sales manager are discussed below. In each report, there is information that is useful to the salesperson as well as to the firm.

Expense reports and activity reports

Figure 11–1 is a copy of the summary page from the weekly report form used by Blue Cross–Blue Shield of North Carolina. There is one page for each day of the week, Monday through Saturday, and one for the week's total. This is a combination expense report and activity report.

Expense report. The expenses section of the weekly report form includes (1) auto mileage, (2) cost of meals, (3) room expenses, (4) miscellaneous expenses, and (5) number of calls grouped by type of call. Several things can be learned from this section of the report.

Once a salesperson determines what expenses for a "typical" week should be, each week's expense report can be studied to determine if expenses are out of line or within reason. If expenses are more than expected, then the salesperson either is more extravagant than necessary or is inefficient in travel planning. If, on the other hand, ex-

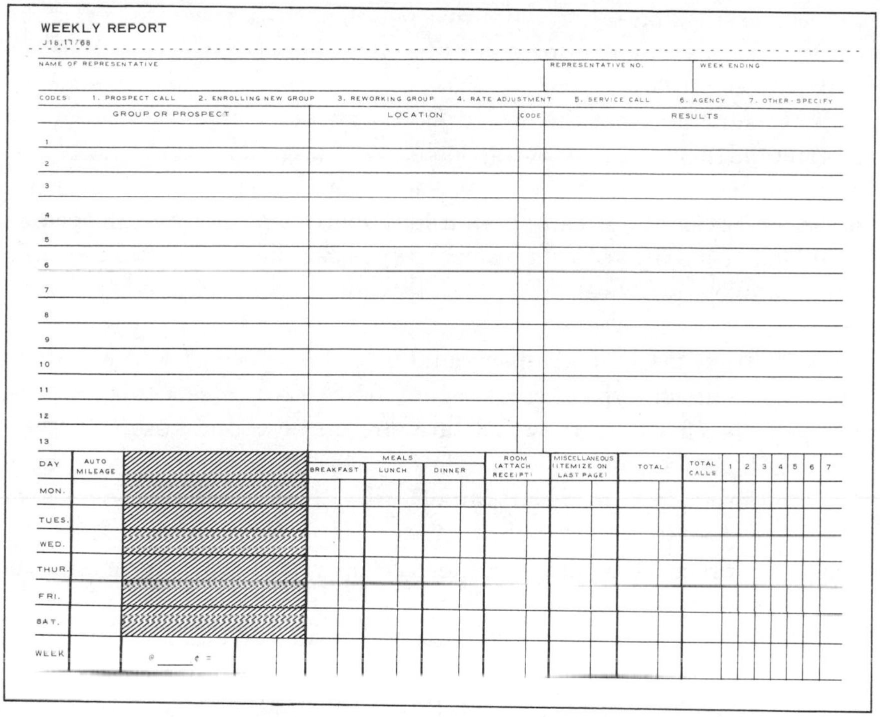

WEEKLY REPORT
J18,11/68

NAME OF REPRESENTATIVE	REPRESENTATIVE NO.	WEEK ENDING

CODES: 1. PROSPECT CALL 2. ENROLLING NEW GROUP 3. REWORKING GROUP 4. RATE ADJUSTMENT 5. SERVICE CALL 6. AGENCY 7. OTHER-SPECIFY

GROUP OR PROSPECT	LOCATION	CODE	RESULTS
1			
2			
3			
4			
5			
6			
7			
8			
9			
10			
11			
12			
13			

DAY	AUTO MILEAGE		MEALS BREAKFAST	MEALS LUNCH	MEALS DINNER	ROOM (ATTACH RECEIPT)	MISCELLANEOUS (ITEMIZE ON LAST PAGE)	TOTAL	TOTAL CALLS	1	2	3	4	5	6	7
MON.																
TUES.																
WED.																
THUR.																
FRI.																
SAT.																
WEEK		@ ____ ¢ =														

Figure 11–1
Blue Cross–Blue Shield weekly report

penses are lower than expected, the salesperson may be spending too much time in the office and not enough time in the field.

The record of the total number of calls made (by type of call) can also be instructive. A salesperson can tell from this data whether much time is being spent making some types of calls and not enough time making others. While the number of each type of call made each day or week will vary greatly, the salesperson knows whether the variation is normal or whether difficult calls are being avoided.

Activity report. The top portion of the weekly report records activity. Here the salesperson reports the name and location of each sales call, the type of call, and a brief description of the result of the call.

By reviewing the order of calls by location, salespeople can determine if their sales-call planning is effective. For example, if the first three calls on Monday were in Charlotte and the last two in Greensboro, the trip was better planned than if the order of calls required trips back and forth between Charlotte and Greensboro.

The report also shows at a glance whether certain types of calls are successful and other types are not. If this is the case, then the salesperson can reexamine the differences between the two types of calls.

Since summaries of the activities reports of all sales personnel are distributed periodically, salespeople can learn how their activities compare with those of the most successful salespeople in the company. For example, it can be seen how more experienced salespeople split their time between the various types of calls and how many calls they complete each week.

Call reports

In addition to expense reports and activity reports, call reports are the third common type of sales report. Almost all salespeople prepare call reports on which they indicate the purpose and result of each sales call. Some firms use a single form for all types of calls; others use a different form for each. Blue Cross–Blue Shield of North Carolina uses the latter approach, with special forms for (1) prospect reports, (2) proposal reports, (3) new-group reports, (4) group underwriting transmittal reports, and (5) group cancellation reports.

Other examples of call reports appear in the section, Handling Paper Work, in Chapter 12. Some of the problems encountered with call reports are also noted in Chapter 12.

Prospect report.   When a Blue Cross–Blue Shield of North Carolina representative completes a call on a new prospect, a prospect report is prepared. Figure 11–2 is a copy of the form used for these reports.

If the first call does not result in a sale, the salesperson completes only the top portion of the form and the Remarks section at the bottom and indicates the date of the planned callback. All of this information is useful for subsequent sales calls. The data at the top of the form indicate up-to-date pertinent information about the prospect. The information in the Remarks section is usually more personal; if something unusual happened during the first visit or if the prospect revealed some particular interests or hobbies, these would be noted there. Information of this nature makes the second call more personal and convinces the prospect of the salesperson's orientation to his or her interests. Requiring salespeople to indicate the planned callback data forces them to plan future sales calls and travel plans. It also serves as a "tickler" to remind them that another call is needed on this particular prospect and when it should be made.

On occasion, the sales call may not result in selling Blue Cross–

FIRST REPORT ☐ SUPPLEMENTAL REPORT ☐

PROPOSAL REPORT ☐ PROSPECT REPORT

☐ FORMAL PROPOSAL ☐ GROUP BOOKLET

ALWAYS COMPLETE TOP LINE.

D-U-N-S NUMBER 1-7	NAME OF ESTABLISHMENT 8-31		COUNTY NO. 32-33	REPRESENTATIVE NO. 34-37
STREET ADDRESS 38-56	CITY 57-69		TOTAL EMP. 70-74	
NAME AND ADDRESS OF PRESENT CARRIER		GROUP NUMBER 8-17		
NAME AND TITLE OF CHIEF EXECUTIVE 18-36	LINE OF BUSINESS 37-55			

HOME OFFICE USE

SIC CODE 75-78		79	80 1
CARRIER CODE 56-59		UNION CODE 60-62	
TYPE 63		79	80 2

TYPE OF GROUP-CHECK ONE

☐ NATIONAL ACCOUNT ☐ ASSOCIATION ☐ STATEWIDE ☐ REGULAR

NAME OF UNION

PERSON CONTACTED AND TITLE	DATE CONTACTED
HEADQUARTER CITY	ANNIVERSARY DATE

BENEFITS		BC & BS	COMMERCIAL	BENEFITS		BC & BS	COMMERCIAL
ROOM				MAJOR MEDICAL	MAXIMUM		
DAYS					DEDUCTIBLE		
EXTRAS					COINSURANCE		
OUTPATIENT BENEFITS	ACCIDENT				PRIVATE ROOM LMT.		
	SICKNESS				RATES - IND.		
MATERNITY - HOSPITAL					RATES - FAMILY		
ROUTINE NURSERY CHARGES				TOTAL RATES	INDIVIDUAL		
SURGERY BENEFITS	MAXIMUM				FAMILY		
	NORMAL DELIVERY			COMPANY CONTRI-BUTION	INDIVIDUAL		
	APPENDECTOMY				FAMILY		
	TOTAL HYSTERECTOMY			COB			
MEDICAL				STUDENT COVERAGE			
WAIVER	SEMIPRIVATE LEVEL	RATE TABLE		DENTAL COVERAGE			

BENEFITS	GIS	COMMERCIAL	BENEFITS		GIS	COMMERCIAL
LIFE			A & H	WEEKLY BENEFITS		
AD & D				NO. OF WEEKS		
RATES				DAY BENEFITS BEGIN		
[illegible]				RATES		
RATES						

REMARKS

PLANNED CALLBACK DATE	REPRESENTATIVE	DATE

J19.1/71 WHITE - MARKET RESEARCH PINK - SALES DEPT. CANARY - DISTRICT OFFICE GOLDENROD - REPRESENTATIVE

Figure 11–2
Blue Cross–Blue Shield prospect report

Blue Shield's services, but the salesperson may have learned a great deal about the prospect's present health insurance coverage. In such a case the salesperson also completes the middle portion of the form, recording all of the pertinent information about the prospect's current insurance, such as the name of the insurance company, the nature of the benefits provided, and the rates charged. If the salesperson plans to make a proposal to the prospect on the next visit, this information will be extremely useful. The proposed Blue Cross–Blue Shield coverage can be designed to meet or exceed the coverage presently provided.

Proposal report.   Once the salesperson has made a proposal to a prospective client, a proposal report is completed. The form used for the proposal report is the same as the one for the prospect report, but the entire form is filled out. The proposal report is useful as a "tickler" to remind the representative that a proposal has been made and that after a reasonable amount of time a callback is necessary to close the sale.

The proposal report should include any pertinent remarks made by the prospect during the proposal presentation, including objections or concerns expressed about the proposal or things the prospect specifically liked about it. It could also include information about who is involved in the purchase decision and when the prospect expects the decision to be made. This information will be helpful in closing the sale.

New-group report.   Once a sale has been made, the representative obtains the necessary information to put the new policy into effect, and a new-group report is completed. Figure 11–3 is a copy of the form used for these reports at Blue Cross–Blue Shield. This may be one of the most important reports for the sales representative.

The new-group report shows the coverage purchased by the client, the coverage it replaced, an evaluation of the major weaknesses of the replaced coverage, the major strengths of the new coverage, and the sales technique used to obtain the sale. In a sense, it is the salesperson's blow-by-blow description of the sale—what happened, why it happened, and how it happened.

Not only is the information contained in the new-group report useful for review purposes, but the salesperson learns a great deal by preparing it. A complete reassessment of the sale is required, and this forces an examination of past selling behavior. Mistakes are recognized and can be avoided in the future, and things that worked well can be noted for future use.

Group underwriting transmittal.   As pointed out earlier in this chapter, an excellent way of increasing sales volume is to expand the sales volume to existing customers. This is also true at Blue Cross–Blue Shield. Calls on existing clients can often result in increased insurance benefits or the enrollment of additional employees. When a

Figure 11-3
Blue Cross–Blue Shield new-group report

NEW GROUP REPORT

NAME OF GROUP | LOCATION | GROUP NO.

DISTRICT OFFICE | RATE TABLE | NO. EMPLOYEES | NO. EMP. COVERED | EFF. DATE

NAME OF PREVIOUS CARRIER

BENEFITS		BC & BS	COMMERCIAL		BENEFITS	GIS	COMMERCIAL
ROOM				LIFE			
DAYS				AD & D			
EXTRAS				RATES			
MATERNITY				DEPENDENT LIFE			
MAXIMUM SURGERY				RATES			
MEDICAL				WEEKLY BENEFITS			
MAJOR MEDICAL	MAXIMUM			A & H	NO. OF WEEKS		
	DEDUCTIBLE				DAY BENEFITS BEGIN		
	COINSURANCE				RATES		
	PRIVATE ROOM LIMIT						
OTHER BENEFITS							
RATES	INDIVIDUAL			COMPANY CONTRIBUTION	INDIVIDUAL		
	FAMILY				FAMILY		

ANALYSIS OF GROUP SALE

What do you feel was the dominant weakness in the former program which brought about the cancellation?

What do you feel was the dominant strength in your program or relationship?

State sales techniques used to sell this group (approach used, etc.)

REPRESENTATIVE'S SIGNATURE | REP. CODE NO. | DATE | DISTRICT MANAGER'S SIGNATURE

J25.8/69 | WHITE – SALES DEPARTMENT | CANARY – DISTRICT OFFICE

salesperson calls on an existing client to protect or increase current levels of sales–an activity known as *reworking*–a group underwriting transmittal form is completed to report on the results of the visit (Figure 11–4).

To complete this report, the salesperson must learn: (1) the total percentage of all potential employees covered by the policy, (2) whether other coverage is available to the group, (3) whether existing coverage could be increased, and (4) whether all branches of the firm are included under the existing policy. This information is important for sales planning purposes. It shows the salesperson which customers are the best prospects for expanded volume and whether an increase in the number of employees covered or in the extent of the coverage, or both, should be covered in the sales presentation.

Group cancellation. As in everything else, failure occurs in selling, even though lost sales are avoided by all salespeople to the best of their ability. Nevertheless, the professional salesperson learns

**Figure 11–4
Blue Cross–Blue Shield group underwriting transmittal form**

GROUP UNDERWRITING TRANSMITTAL

☐ NEW GROUP
☐ REWORK   REWORK CYCLE _____   EFF. DATE _____   DATE SUBMITTED _____

NAME OF GROUP _____   GROUP NUMBER _____

A STATISTICS

1. EMPLOYEES ALREADY SUBSCRIBERS IN THE GROUP* _____	7. N.G. OR OTHER NCBCBS GROUP _____
2. SPOUSE EMPLOYEES NOW IN THE GROUP* _____	8. OVER AGE _____
3. NEW APPLICANTS _____	9. REFUSALS _____
4. SPOUSE EMPLOYEES NEW _____	10. INELIGIBLE _____
5. TRANSFERS TO GROUP _____	11. TOTAL EMPLOYEES _____
6. TOTAL COVERED _____	*Not applicable to new groups.

12. SPONSORED DEPENDENTS _____
13. COLLATERALS* _____
14. TOTAL ELIGIBLE EMPLOYEES (6+9) _____
15. % OF NET POTENTIAL ENROLLED (6÷14) _____

Complete only when No. 14 has 21 or more eligible employees listed.

B COVERAGE CHANGE

CHANGE ALL SUBSCRIBERS TO SAME COVERAGE   CHANGE IN CLASSIFICATION

CHANGE APPLICATIONS ATTACHED ☐ YES ☐ NO   CHANGE APPLICATIONS ATTACHED ☐

☐ LIST OF SUBSCRIBERS CHANGING ATTACHED (SHOW NAMES, CERTIFICATE NUMBERS, PRESENT AND NEW COVERAGE)

C ANALYSIS

NOT ELIGIBLE ☐ RETIRED ☐ PART TIME ☐ TEMPORARY

OTHER COVERAGE IN GROUP ☐ YES ☐ NO

IF YES, GIVE DATA BELOW AND AT RIGHT

NAME OF CARRIER _____   DATE INSTALLED _____

BENEFITS	EMPLOYEES CONTRIBUTION	DEPENDENTS CONTRIBUTION
HOSPITAL	$	$
EXTRAS	$	$
SURGERY	$	$
OTHER	$	$

D BRANCHES INCLUDED

_____

_____

_____

_____

E COMMENTS - EXCEPTIONS

_____

_____

_____

_____

_____

_____

_____

_____

SIGNATURE OF REPRESENTATIVE _____   REP. NO. _____

C3 2/69   WHITE - UNDERWRITING   CANARY - GROUP   PINK - SALES   GOLDENROD - DISTRICT OFFICE from losing sales to competition. Blue Cross–Blue Shield of North Carolina provides for this kind of learning experience by asking its sales force to complete a group cancellation report whenever a client cancels a policy (Figure 11–5).

Examination of Figure 11–5 shows that the salesperson can learn a great deal just by completing this form. The salesperson must not only give the information necessary to formally effect the cancellation but must also determine the nature of the policy that replaced Blue

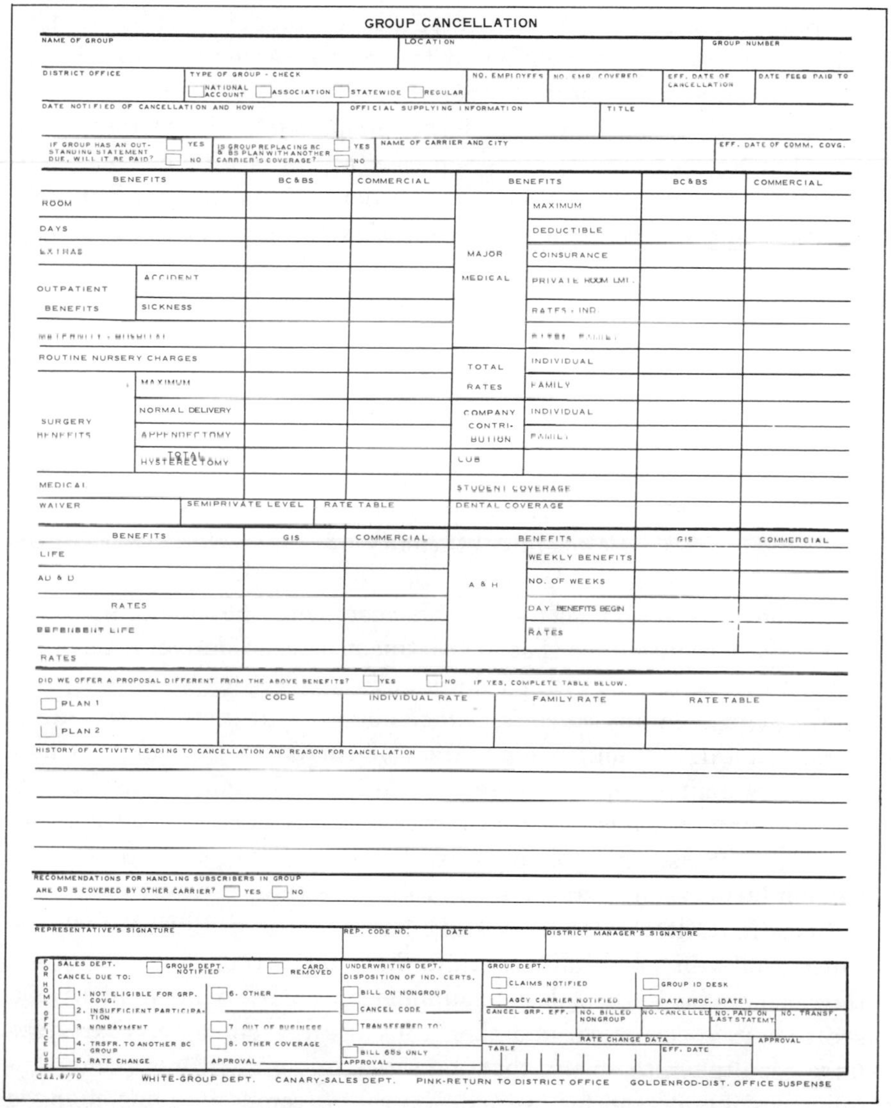
GROUP CANCELLATION
NAME OF GROUP | LOCATION | GROUP NUMBER
DISTRICT OFFICE | TYPE OF GROUP - CHECK: NATIONAL ACCOUNT, ASSOCIATION, STATEWIDE, REGULAR | NO. EMPLOYEES | NO. EMP. COVERED | EFF. DATE OF CANCELLATION | DATE FEES PAID TO
DATE NOTIFIED OF CANCELLATION AND HOW | OFFICIAL SUPPLYING INFORMATION | TITLE
IF GROUP HAS AN OUTSTANDING STATEMENT DUE, WILL IT BE PAID? YES / NO | IS GROUP REPLACING BC & BS PLAN WITH ANOTHER CARRIER'S COVERAGE? YES / NO | NAME OF CARRIER AND CITY | EFF. DATE OF COMM. COVG.
BENEFITS | BC & BS | COMMERCIAL | BENEFITS | BC & BS | COMMERCIAL
ROOM; DAYS; EXTRAS; OUTPATIENT BENEFITS: ACCIDENT, SICKNESS; MATERNITY - HOSPITAL; ROUTINE NURSERY CHARGES; SURGERY BENEFITS: MAXIMUM, NORMAL DELIVERY, APPENDECTOMY, TOTAL HYSTERECTOMY; MEDICAL; WAIVER | SEMIPRIVATE LEVEL | RATE TABLE
MAJOR MEDICAL: MAXIMUM, DEDUCTIBLE, COINSURANCE, PRIVATE ROOM LMT., RATES - IND., RATES - FAMILY; TOTAL RATES: INDIVIDUAL, FAMILY; COMPANY CONTRIBUTION: INDIVIDUAL, FAMILY; CUB; STUDENT COVERAGE; DENTAL COVERAGE
BENEFITS | GIS | COMMERCIAL | BENEFITS | GIS | COMMERCIAL
LIFE; AD & D; RATES; DEPENDENT LIFE; RATES
A & H: WEEKLY BENEFITS, NO. OF WEEKS, DAY BENEFITS BEGIN, RATES
DID WE OFFER A PROPOSAL DIFFERENT FROM THE ABOVE BENEFITS? YES / NO. IF YES, COMPLETE TABLE BELOW.
| CODE | INDIVIDUAL RATE | FAMILY RATE | RATE TABLE
PLAN 1
PLAN 2
HISTORY OF ACTIVITY LEADING TO CANCELLATION AND REASON FOR CANCELLATION
RECOMMENDATIONS FOR HANDLING SUBSCRIBERS IN GROUP
ARE 65'S COVERED BY OTHER CARRIER? YES / NO
REPRESENTATIVE'S SIGNATURE | REP. CODE NO. | DATE | DISTRICT MANAGER'S SIGNATURE
FOR HOME OFFICE USE
SALES DEPT. | GROUP DEPT. NOTIFIED | CARD REMOVED
CANCEL DUE TO: 1. NOT ELIGIBLE FOR GRP. COVG. 2. INSUFFICIENT PARTICIPATION 3. NONPAYMENT 4. TRSFR. TO ANOTHER BC GROUP 5. RATE CHANGE 6. OTHER 7. OUT OF BUSINESS 8. OTHER COVERAGE APPROVAL
UNDERWRITING DEPT. DISPOSITION OF IND. CERTS.: BILL ON NONGROUP, CANCEL CODE, TRANSFERRED TO:, BILL 65s ONLY, APPROVAL
GROUP DEPT.: CLAIMS NOTIFIED, GROUP ID DESK, AGCY CARRIER NOTIFIED, DATA PROC. (DATE)
CANCEL GRP. EFF. | NO. BILLED NONGROUP | NO. CANCELLED | NO. PAID ON LAST STATEMT. | NO. TRANSF.
RATE CHANGE DATA: TABLE | EFF. DATE | APPROVAL
C22.9/70 WHITE-GROUP DEPT. CANARY-SALES DEPT. PINK-RETURN TO DISTRICT OFFICE GOLDENROD-DIST. OFFICE SUSPENSE

Figure 11–5
Blue Cross–Blue Shield group cancellation report

Cross–Blue Shield, whether or not a counterproposal was offered, a history of the events leading up to the cancellation, and the main reasons for the cancellation. To prepare the report adequately, the salesperson must examine in detail the whole sequence of events leading up to the cancellation. The salesperson also has a permanent record of cancellations that can show whether there is any sort of pattern to them. If there is, steps can be taken to prevent further cancellations.

The five different call reports forms discussed here are also used by Blue Cross–Blue Shield's corporate marketing group to prepare summary reports of the activities of all the company's sales personnel. These reports are distributed to every salesperson so each can learn from the experiences of others.

This discussion of the various forms completed by Blue Cross–Blue Shield of North Carolina sales representatives is intended not as a recommended reporting scheme but rather to illustrate the valuable information contained in a typical set of sales report forms. It should be clear that completing such forms is not a burden but an opportunity to study past sales activities and to learn from them. Such a review is impossible without these types of reports.

SUMMARY

Chapter 11 has described the last step in the selling process, with emphasis on the importance of building future sales. This step includes: (1) maintaining current sales volume, (2) expanding sales volume, and (3) increasing selling efficiency.

To maintain existing levels of sales to current customers, the salesperson must build goodwill with customers, handle complaints, and process requests for special treatment or rush delivery. Such attention will be repaid with a solid foundation of sales to existing customers, and then any sales to new customers will increase the salesperson's total. Without a foundation of current sales, sales to new customers simply replace those that are lost. Beyond simply maintaining current levels of sales to existing customers, the salesperson can also increase sales to them by obtaining a larger share of their current business or increasing the volume of their own sales.

Reclaiming lost sales to existing customers is a difficult task because it often means that something has gone wrong. In order to get the business back, the salesperson must first learn what went wrong, see that it is corrected, and then convince the customer that steps have been taken to ensure that the same problem will not recur. Another possible reason for lost sales is that a competitor has changed some aspect of its product offering. Here also the salesperson must learn what change has taken place and what must be done to reclaim the business lost.

By studying past sales activities the salesperson can learn how to improve selling efficiency. The reports most salespeople must prepare on a regular basis are an ideal source of information that can be used to learn more about their own performance.

REVIEW QUESTIONS/DISCUSSION
QUESTIONS/EXERCISES

1. Briefly identify the following:

   a. Tickler file.   e. Activity reports.
   b. Callback schedule.   f. Expense reports.
   c. Sole source.   g. Call reports.
   d. Clue management.   h. Reworking.

2. Is building future sales the last step or the first step in selling? Explain.

3. Briefly describe the four aspects of maintaining current sales volume.

4. Ask a salesperson you know to show you the various sales reports he or she regularly completes. Determine which information provided to management is also useful for the salesperson's own purposes. Could the forms be improved?

5. Professional car salespeople know that a call to a new-car buyer a short time after the delivery of the car goes a long way toward building a lasting relationship. List five different ways that a car salesperson could develop a tickler file useful for this purpose.

6. What are the various factors that ought to be taken into account in the development of a customer callback schedule?

7. How can customer complaints be avoided? Are there things a salesperson can do to help in this regard?

8. How are rush delivery requests and special requests alike? How are they different?

9. Should a salesperson always try to meet a customer's requested delivery date? Explain.

10. Show why current customers are the best source for increases in a salesperson's current level of sales.

11. Could a salesperson obtain a larger share of a customer's business by helping a customer firm increase its own level of sales? Explain.

12. Using clue management, prepare a list of four courses that would be successful if added to your school's curriculum: Describe your reasons for adding each course to your list.

13. Satisfied customers are a company's best salesperson. Show how this

sales axiom could be used by the owner of a local restaurant.

14. How can a sales manager use reports from the field sales force? Discuss.

15. Do sales reports provide useful information to individual salespersons? Discuss.

16. List and briefly describe the two basic ways of increasing sales to current customers.

17. The dangers of a sole-source arrangement to the buyer are quite obvious, but the dangers to the seller are not quite as obvious. What are some of the dangers to the seller in a sole-source arrangement?

18. Sales managers know that more sales calls result in more sales. Does this mean that a salesperson should be encouraged to continually increase the number of calls made each week? Explain.

19. Describe the nature and purpose of the three most common types of sales reports.

20. Can a salesperson learn from sales that are lost? Explain.

CASE 11–1: THE TAILOR HOUSE

The Tailor House is an exclusive ladies's shop located in University Park, Virginia, home of the University of South Virginia. Clientele at the Tailor House ranges from high school students who live in University Park to wealthy matrons from the surrounding area. The Tailor House has always carried a traditional style of dress common to Southern college towns, today known as the "preppie" look. Also, the store carries an extensive array of fancier clothing for more formal occasions.

Many of the store's clerks are drawn from the University. These clerks work for modest wages in exchange for considerable discounts on the merchandise they sell. All are well-dressed with a good sense of what the clientele expects from a store like the Tailor House. Other clerks are middle-aged women from the community who have worked in the store for several years. One of these women, Mary Beth Grant, has worked for the Tailor House for seven years, purchases most of her clothes there, and makes sure that her friends at the country club know that she does. She is also the assistant manager of the store.

One day Grant was straightening a pile of sweaters on a sale table when Beth Perreault, the 15-year-old daughter of one of the professors at the university, walked in with a package under her arm. She approached Grant and opened the package.

Grant: Can I help you?

Perreault: Yes, I hope so. I purchased this sweater here three weeks ago and have worn it twice since I bought it. Earlier this week I hand-washed the sweater and look what happened. There are yellow streaks all over the white. I would like to exchange it for another sweater.

Grant: But you're only supposed to dry clean that brand of sweater. I'm quite sure that washing these sweaters will damage them.

Perreault: But it says right here on the label that the sweater may be either dry cleaned or washed by hand.

Grant: Oh, it does, doesn't it. Still I think you better get it dry cleaned first.

Beth left the store a little angry and a little hurt. She had saved a long time to buy a $45 sweater from her meager earnings as a baby-sitter and in the snack shop at the faculty club pool. She had bought the sweater at the Tailor House because her parents had always told her she was better off buying a few high quality items than several low quality pieces. Now she was afraid that she would be stuck with a sweater she couldn't wear.

She went straight to the drycleaners and gave them the sweater to clean. Three days later she picked it up and saw that the streaks were still there. She was sick. She went home and asked her mother to go with her to the Tailor House to talk to Grant since she felt intimidated the first time.

Mrs. Perreault and Beth walked into the Tailor House and asked for Grant. They were told that this was her day off and were asked if anyone else could help them. Another clerk, Terry Meyers, a student at the university, came over to them to see if she could be of assistance. Mrs. Perreault told Terry what had happened and showed her the streaks in the sweater.

Meyers: What cleaners did you take this to?

Beth Perreault: Sam's in the mall. Why?

Meyers: Remind me never to take any of my things to Sam's!

Mrs. Perreault: What does that have to do with anything? I'm getting angry! Clearly there is something wrong with the sweater. Why don't you either give Beth her money back or another sweater?

Meyers: I'm sorry. I didn't mean to make you angry. But I can't make exchanges. Only Mrs. Grant or the manager can do that. You'll have to come back tomorrow.

Mrs. Perreault: This is the poorest excuse for service I've ever run into!

The next day Beth and her mother successfully exchanged the sweater for another. Although no angry words were exchanged, the atmosphere was clearly icy.

Questions

1. Should Grant have handled the situation differently? How about Meyers?
2. Was there anything in the store's policies that you would change?
3. Would you buy a sweater at the Tailor House knowing Perreault's experience? Do you think Beth and her mother will tell their friends about their experience?

CASE 11–2: GLENRIDGE COMPANY

Bud Coley of Glenridge Company has just received a call from Dick Phillips, purchasing agent for Holsten Crankshaft, Inc. Phillips wants to know how soon he can get 35 grinding wheels made to special specifications. They are needed as soon as possible.

Holsten Crankshaft, headquartered in South Boston, Virginia is a company that finish-machines crankshaft forgings for several large truck engine manufacturers. Considerable grinding is done in the course of its operations. Although most of the grinding wheels it uses are of standard sizes and materials, there are some that require special processing.

For years Phillips has purchased all grinding wheels from Einhorn Abrasives Company. This company has served Phillips well over that period, and its prices have remained very competitive. Accordingly, Coley had never been able to get any business from Phillips, even though he was sure that Glenridge could serve Phillips as well as Einhorn Abrasives did. Coley reasoned that if Phillips gave some business to Glenridge he would be far less susceptible to the problems inherent in a sole-source arrangement. But Phillips had always been concerned about Glenridge's ability to serve him and had elected instead to give all of his business to Einhorn Abrasives.

In this particular case, Phillips had called Einhorn Abrasives first, but it was unable to get the 35 grinding wheels to Phillips in less than three weeks, which was totally inadequate for his needs. If he does not get the wheels within a week, the production line is going to shut down, so he decides to call Glenridge and see what it could do. The phone conversation goes like this:

Coley: Glenridge Company, Bud Coley speaking. Can I help you?

Phillips: I certainly hope so! This is Dick Phillips at Holsten Crankshaft and I've got a problem I need some help with.

Coley: Oh, hello, Mr. Phillips. It's been a while since I've seen you. How have you been?

Phillips: Fine, thank you, and it's nice to talk to you again.

Coley: What's the problem?

Philips: Do you remember that special grinding wheel we use to finish-grind the flange on the Black Motor 6 shaft?

Coley: Yes, we have a blueprint of it in our files. I gave you a quote on that item a few months ago, as I recall.

Phillips: That's the one; I need 35 of those as soon as possible. How soon could you get them to me?

Coley: Hmmmmm. Let me put you on hold a minute and see if we have the necessary materials in stock and how soon we could break into our production cycle. Hold on.

After a pause, Coley resumes:

Coley: I checked with our production control people and they say that if you approve and are willing to pay for a special setup, we could ship the wheels in three days. Air freight should get the wheels to you in about one or two days. But that assumes that I have a purchase order in hand, so you would have to add however long it would take you to get me a purchase order.

Phillips: How much extra do you think the special setup will be?

Coley: I'm just guessing, but I am quite sure that it won't be more than $1,000.

Phillips: Go ahead. Make the wheels and send me the bill. If this is typical of the kind of service you provide, I think I'd like to reconsider our past purchase policies concerning your company.

Coley: But I can't go ahead without a purchase order.

Phillips: Look! I'm authorizing you to start making those things. If you want me to clear this with your boss or his boss or the president or anybody else, put him on the phone!

Coley: My boss is out of town and I'm sure the president doesn't want me to concern him with this problem.

Phillips: Well then, go ahead, for goodness sake!

Questions

1. What should Coley do?
2. Would you pass on the cost of the special setup or would you absorb the cost? Why?
3. Should Coley agree to this request but make it conditional upon the receipt of more business in the future, or should he just fulfill this request without any conditions attached?

KEY POINTS

The purpose of time management is to assure that salespersons spend as much time as possible in front of customers.

Time management together with the preapproach make up the all-important self-management.

Salespeople differ widely in terms of selling costs per call.

Time for a salesperson is valuable and of varying potential.

The basic ingredients of time management are account classification, routing, and paper-work management.

The guiding principle in account classification is that salespersons should practice selective selling and concentrate on the customers who are the most profitable.

Self-management is essential to the success of salespersons.

Routing plans are concerned with reducing the time it takes to go from sales call to sales call in covering the assigned sales territory.

Oftentimes, selling costs such as travel can be reduced without a loss of selling effectiveness.

Some paper work is an essential aspect of the sales job.

A salesperson, to be successful, must be self-motivated.

Chapter 12

TIME MANAGEMENT AND SELF-MOTIVATION

George Metropolis, a representative selling supplies and equipment to restaurants in New Jersey states his objective as increasing the net profit per sales call. Using net profit as a yardstick helps him to discipline himself automatically and eliminate or minimize unproductive effort and time. He does this by taking a cost-accounting approach to analyzing his activities, keeping in mind the economic realities of the various situations. Some of the questions he asks himself:

1. Am I calling on the right person?
2. Am I making more personal visits than necessary?
3. Am I getting maximum mileage out of the mail and telephone?
4. Am I prospecting enough? Too much?
5. Which accounts are definitely profitable; which are borderline; which are submarginal?
6. Which accounts could I drop and thereby boost overall profit performance?
7. How much time am I wasting?
8. How many functions and tasks could I delegate?[1]

THE SELF-MANAGEMENT CONCEPT

In Chapter 6 it was learned that the purpose of the preapproach is to optimize the effectiveness of the salesperson in the eyes of the customer or, in other words, to accomplish the selling objectives. The emphasis in the preapproach is on preparation and anticipation as opposed to solely reacting to customers. The purpose of time management is to optimize the amount of time a salesperson spends in front of a customer. This is done chiefly by minimizing all demands on the salesperson's time that are not directly related to the objective of the sales call. The emphasis in time management is on spending as much time as possible on selling as opposed to traveling, waiting, and calling on people who are not available.

Together, preapproach and time management make up what might be called *self-management*. Self-management is important to the salesperson for several reasons.

1. Unlike other jobs, a salesperson's success and growth as a professional are due almost entirely to his or her own efforts.
2. For the most part, salespersons work on their own with only arm's-length supervision.
3. Without self-management an individual salesperson will find it difficult to develop the all-important traits of self-discipline and self-motivation.

"For $100 you can buy 15 seconds to sell me life insurance."

Reprinted by permission The Wall Street Journal.

Many buyers also understand the importance of time management

Self-management is also important to the company.

1. The overall sales performance of the company is upgraded with more effective and efficient salespersons.
2. The opportunities for incentives other than the traditional financial rewards tied to sales volume are greatly increased.
3. The steadily increasing costs of supporting a salesperson in the field (car expenses, lodging, food, and the like) can at least be partially offset by efficiency and effectiveness.

SALES CALLS AND EXPENSES

Taking a look at Table 12–1 we can see considerable differences between salespeople in their utilization of time. Account representatives and sales engineers calling on customers who are concentrated in a metro area may make only half as many calls as either a detail or service salesperson operating in the sales territory. Within a category, salespeople may differ by as much as 4 calls a day or 956 calls over a period of a year using 239 working days.

Combining this information with that contained in Table 12–2 it is obvious that the profitability of salespeople can vary widely. First of all, it stands to reason that the more sales calls a salesperson makes, the more he or she will be able to produce in terms of sales volume. An increase of just one sales call a day translates into 239 more sales calls over a period of a year.

Second, more sales calls will mean a lower cost per call or in other words, a lower cost of contacting customers. Referring to Table 12–1 we see that detail salespeople will make anywhere from 6 to 10 calls a day in a metro area. From Table 12–2 we know that median costs for a detail salesperson are $33,200. This means that a detail salesperson by increasing the number of sales calls per day will produce the following savings assuming the additional calls do not increase total costs.

Increase in calls per day	Decrease in cost per call		Percentage decrease
6 to 7	($23 to $20)	$3	13
7 to 8	(20 to 17)	3	15
8 to 9	(17 to 15)	2	12
9 to 10	(15 to 14)	1	7

These savings in most instances will offset the costs of increasing calls and the steadily increasing costs of selling.

**Table 12–1
Typical salespeople's
call patterns**

Type of salesperson		Average calls per day		Estimated days in field per year	Average calls per year	
		Territory A	Territory B		Territory A	Territory B
Account	R	4–6	2–3	239*	956–1,434	478–717
representative	M	5	2.5		1,195	598
Detail	R	6–10	4–6	239*	1,434–2,390	956–1,434
salesperson	M	8	5		1,912	1,195
Sales	R	4–7	3–4	190†	760–1,330	570–760
engineer	M	5.5	3.5		1,045	665
Industrial	R	6–8	3–5	239*	1,434–1,912	717–1,195
products	M	7	4		1,673	956
salesperson						
Service	R	8–10	4–6	239*	1,912–2,390	956–1,434
salesperson	M	9	5		2,151	1,195

Notes:
R: Range of calls.
M: Mean number of calls.
Territory definitions: A—Usually a metro area where customers are concentrated, the salesperson can make several calls at one location, or the sales manager's philosophy emphasizes maximum calls per day. B—Customers are dispersed and longer sales calls are required to sell a product or service.
*Based on 5 days, 52 weeks per year, less 6 holidays, and less 15 days for vacation and sickness.
†Based on 239 workdays less 1 day per week in office (49 days)
Source: Reprinted by permission from *Sales & Marketing Management* magazine's *1980 Survey of Selling Costs.* Copyright 1980.

Type of salesperson	Median direct sales costs 1979	Percent change 1978–79	Compound annual percent increase 1974–79
Account representative			
Total	$37,800	+ 6.5%	14.2%
Compensation	28,750	+ 8.5	12.4
Auto and T&E	9,050	+ 0.6	20.9
Detail salesperson			
Total	33,200	+ 7.1	14.3
Compensation	25,000	+ 8.7	12.3
Auto and T&E	8,200	+ 2.5	22.3
Sales engineer			
Total	39,100	+10.1	7.3
Compensation	27,500	+ 7.8	6.1
Auto and T&E	11,600	+16.0	10.6
Industrial-products salesperson			
Total	35,800	+ 8.5	9.7
Compensation	26,000	+ 8.3	8.2
Auto and T&E	9,800	+ 8.9	14.4
Service salesperson			
Total	37,250	+ 3.5	11.6
Compensation	27,000	+ 8.0	9.1
Auto and T&E	10,250	+ 2.5	20.7

**Table 12–2
How direct sales
costs are changing**

Note: T&E: Travel and entertainment, including food and lodging.
Source: Reprinted by permission from *Sales & Marketing Management* magazine's *1980 Survey of Selling Costs*. Copyright 1980.

Salespeople need to carefully consider their use of time because time equals money. A salesperson who works 239 days a year and eight hours a day will have 1,912 hours available during the year. At various earnings levels, the value of a salesperson's time can be calculated as follows:

**THE VALUE
OF TIME**

Earnings level	Per working hour
$15,000	$ 7.85
18,000	9.41
20,000	10.46
25,000	13.08
30,000	15.69
35,000	18.31
40,000	20.92

Looking at it in another way, a salesperson on a 5 percent commission would have to sell over $156 worth of products every working hour to equal a salary of $15,000 for the year. For a salary at the

$20,000 level, sales production would have to be over $208, or an additional $52 per working hour.

Estimates are that a salesperson will spend anywhere from one third to one half of his or her time in actual selling situations. Therefore, a salesperson making $15,000 a year is paid $5,000 to $7,500 for face-to-face selling and the remainder for driving, waiting, and other nonproductive activities. Looking at it in terms of only the time spent in face-to-face selling, the appropriate hourly figures in the above table would have to be doubled or perhaps tripled. This means that a salesperson making $20,000 a year is paid from $20.92 to $31.38 for every hour spent productively in front of customers.

Nine tenths of wisdom consists in being wise in scheduling time.

Theodore Roosevelt

Source: Courtesy of the Economics Press, Fairfield, New Jersey.

ANALYSIS OF SELLING ACTIVITIES

For a salesperson to make the most efficient use of available time, the first step is to determine how the working day is spent. One way to do this is to use a form similar to the one suggested for insurance agents (Figure 12–1). The emphasis is on getting the salesperson to think about both the number of sales calls or interviews and the amount of time spent selling.

A salesperson will then probably want to make a more detailed analysis of his or her own activities. This can be done by dividing up what goes on during the normal working day into productive and nonproductive activities. Some of the specific activities that could be included under *productive* are:

1. Making sales presentations.
2. Handling customer complaints and problems.
3. Checking the customer's want list.
4. Taking inventory of the customer's stock.
5. Setting up sales promotional displays.
6. Making telephone calls to maintain customer contact and to make appointments.
7. Making collections and adjustments of customer accounts.
8. Checking with other company personnel on customer requirements and delivery schedules.
9. Developing customer sales plans and selling aids.
10. Studying product literature.

Figure 12–1 How many selling calls do you make each week? How much of your time is spent selling?

Preliminary statement: It should be alarming to most agents to realize what a small percentage of their time or total working hours is spent in SELLING situations. If you're not afraid of the results and want to improve, fill out this form for just two months. One of two things will happen: (1) You'll see you're having a large number of SELLING interviews but making few sales or—and more likely—(2) You are spending 10% or less of your time SELLING. If (1) is true, then you'd better upgrade your prospects, merchandise your programs better and learn better closing methods. If (2) is the situation, you'd better analyze your time and try to curtail nonproductive activities and develop better methods of getting selling interviews. This may mean streamlining your proposals so you have more time to be in front of your prospect and less time at your desk with your calculator. REMEMBER: You only get paid when you are SELLING.

Month of _____

Day	How many selling interviews	How many selling hours	Day	How many selling interviews	How many selling hours
1			16		
2			17		
3			18		
4			19		
5			20		
6			21		
7			22		
8			23		
9			24		
10			25		
11			26		
12			27		
13			28		
14			29		
15			30		
			31		

Month of _____

Day	How many selling interviews	How many selling hours	Day	How many selling interviews	How many selling hours
1			16		
2			17		
3			18		
4			19		
5			20		
6			21		
7			22		
8			23		
9			24		
10			25		
11			26		
12			27		
13			28		
14			29		
15			30		
			31		

Note: Don't count fact-finding interviews, cold calls, delivering policy, phone calls, etc. Count only the time you have made an appointment and are in front of the prospect with a specific proposal.

Reprinted with permission. © by James S. Harding, CLU, The Harding Company, Portland, Oregon

The latter two activities are often considered an extra job requirement to be completed outside normal working hours. Completing company reports such as the call report is a nonproductive activity that, in many companies, the salesperson is expected to do on personal time.

Some of the activities that fall under the heading of *nonproductive* are:

1. Driving an automobile or traveling to the customer.
2. Waiting to see a customer.
3. Calling on someone who is not a customer or purchasing influence.
4. Engaging in general conversation.
5. Conducting a broken interview.
6. Calling on customers who are unavailable.
7. Completing paper work.

Once the different types of activities are identified and categorized, the next step is to determine how long the salesperson should keep a record of how the working day is spent. While it is not possible to give an exact answer to this question, it would seem reasonable that a salesperson who does a lot of repetitive selling to the same group of customers should maintain a record for two complete trips through his or her territory. For a salesperson who does a substantial amount of development work and has to make numerous cold calls, the time period for analysis will have to be longer in order to capture the work pattern.

In reviewing their activities salespeople will want to:

1. Eliminate those activities that need not be done at all.
2. Set activity priorities by importance saleswise rather than urgency.
3. Determine ways of increasing productivity in important activities (shorten time involved, group similar activities together, set deadlines, standardize).
4. Develop daily and weekly schedules.

By concentrating one's attention on the problem, the salesperson will start to make changes in the approach to the job of selling. One common change is to lengthen the working day and spend more hours on the job. Salespersons in highly congested urban areas, for example, may start their days earlier to get ahead of the traffic and come later after the traffic has lessened. Waiting time in the morning might be used to review customer selling plans; and time spent waiting for traffic to lessen in the evening can be used to complete company reports. Salespersons whose customers are spread out over a wide geographic area start to travel at times other than when customers are open for business. It is not unusual to find salespersons leaving home on Sunday rather than Monday morning.

While working longer hours helps a salesperson to become successful, it is not the objective of time management. Time management is aimed at more efficient use of time. After analysis of the typical working day, regardless of its length, the salesperson will undoubtedly find that he or she wastes a great amount of time. While there are several obvious changes that can be made, earnest efforts to reduce nonproductive time are based on four practical ideas: (1) not all hours in the working day offer the same potential for productive efforts; (2) all customers are not alike—some offer a better chance for sales than others; (3) there can be more efficient coverage of the salesperson's assigned territory; and (4) better ways can be developed for taking care of the paper work burden.

VARYING POTENTIAL OF TIME

One of the most important ideas in time management is that not all hours of the day have the same potential for productive efforts. Buyers may be available only during certain hours, or by the very nature of the customer's business it may be better to visit a customer during certain hours. A salesperson calling on a doctor would want to avoid, if at all possible, the hours set aside for seeing patients. Then, too, the salesperson's level of energy will vary throughout the day.

Knowing which hours are more valuable and which are less valuable permits the salesperson to allocate activities accordingly. The more important tasks, namely selling activities, are allocated to valuable time periods, and the less important or nonproductive to less important hours. While this sounds good, it may not work out in practice. One obstacle is that almost all customers may limit the hours a salesperson can see a buyer to the same narrow range, perhaps from 1 P.M. to 4 P.M. on Monday through Wednesday.

In such situations, the salesperson should make use of the telephone, making appointments and calling in advance to check on an appointment and the availability of the customer. If the customer will not make appointments, the salesperson will have to use his or her imagination in getting to see the customer. The customer might be invited to breakfast or dinner occasionally rather than the overworked lunch. Another approach might be to have the customer visit the facilities of the seller.

Also, the salesperson should take a traffic count of other salespeople during the time set aside by the customer. There is a good chance that there will be fewer salespeople on certain days and at certain times, thus increasing the chances of seeing and spending the necessary time with the customer.

In utilizing time to the best advantage, it is often helpful to set up a schedule such as the one shown in Figure 12–2. This helps develop the self-discipline so necessary in a salesperson. At the same time it highlights the necessity for good habits as part of time management.

**Figure 12–2
Scheduling selling
activities**

Weekday time period		Activities
7:30–8:30	....	Reviewing sales plans
8:30–9:30	....	Phoning to make and confirm appointments
9:30–3:30	....	Conducting field work: selling, providing customer assistance, deliveries, handling collections
3:30–5:30	....	Phoning to make appointments, planning the next day's work, completing company and personal reports*

*On Fridays the emphasis should be on completing one week's activity and planning the next week. It may prove helpful for the salesperson to summarize accomplishments in relation to what was planned.

Test your knowledge

Answer yes or no to the following statements.

1. I am definitely time-conscious.
2. I plan for more sales time.
3. I plan to spend most time with the best prospects.
4. I plan to make early morning calls.
5. I plan to make Saturday calls.
6. I plan off-day calls.
7. I spend my time with the person who has authority to buy.
8. I balance calls between active and prospective accounts.
9. I plan when to terminate an interview.
10. I set up appointments in advance.
11. I turn social time into action time.
12. I resist stereotyped thinking about calls.
13. I do not plan excessive office, floor, or paper work time.
14. I use basic selling methods.
15. I regard time as my chief asset.

Source: Adapted by permission from James R. Robeson, H. Lee Mathews, and Carl G. Stevens, *Selling* (Homewood, Ill.: Richard D. Irwin, 1978), p. 325. © 1978 by Richard D. Irwin, Inc.

Not all customers will buy the same amount or have the same potential to buy from a salesperson. Sellers should practice selective selling and concentrate on a limited number of accounts with clearly evident profitability. Sometimes the firm will help the salesperson in classifying accounts, but often the task is left to the salesperson. The proportion of unprofitable accounts is usually greater than one would suppose. One company, for example, found that 76 percent of its customers could be classified as unprofitable. These customers were switched to catalog buying. With the reduced number of accounts, the company was able to reduce its sales force and, more importantly, drastically decrease the number of accounts for each salesperson.

The approach a salesperson takes to screen customers depends upon the makeup of the territory. For existing customers, company sales records are the primary source of information. Additionally, the salesperson should try to determine the share he or she is receiving of each customer's business. For new customers, the evaluation has to be based on potential alone, using the same standards applied to existing customers. If an existing customer who purchases $500 or more a month is classified as a major account, a new customer with this potential should be rated similarly until proven otherwise.

A two-way classification scheme (good–poor, major–minor) is simple and easy to understand. However, a three-way classification scheme, such as the one described below, may be more suited to many sales territories.

ACCOUNT CLASSIFICATION

"A" accounts

These are existing and potential customers who are or will be the best customers of the firm. Usually purchase volume and the type of products purchased are considered in classifying a customer. For example, a dental supply wholesaler defines "A" accounts as key accounts that purchase $400 or more of dental supplies a month on a yearly purchase plan, and buy at least one major item or two minor items of dental equipment a year. A new dental account that buys all its equipment from the firm is automatically an "A" account, even though the purchases do not equal the required minimum.

"B" accounts

These existing customers are not good customers of the firm but have the potential to be so. Sometimes, a customer will split his or her purchases among a number of suppliers or buy only a part of the seller's line of products. This in effect reduces their purchases below the minimum for an "A" account.

"C" accounts

These are existing or new customers that do not or are not likely to buy a quantity of merchandise that will make them profitable accounts.

Selective selling

After customers are classified, the salesperson should give priority to making calls to the better customers. Not only should they be worked first, they should also be seen more frequently than less important customers. Sales calls on new customers should be limited to those with the potential to be "A" accounts.

It is obvious that selective selling as a means to more efficient utilization of time and in turn greater profitability contradicts many traditional selling philosophies. One of these is that the way to increase sales is to make more calls. Companies that adopt this philosophy know from past records that a certain number of calls will result in a certain sales level. They fail to recognize that the salesperson should not make calls just to increase the probability of a sale. The seller should direct his or her efforts toward those customers that are clearly profitable and will continue to be so.

Another traditional viewpoint is that all customers should be worked the same. The basis for this idea is that the particular business was built on customer loyalty and any changes would disrupt this relationship. What is overlooked is that only a small proportion of customers are profitable and it is to these customers that the firm owes its major selling efforts.

ROUTING

Routing plans are concerned with reducing the time it takes to go from sales call to sales call in covering the assigned sales territory. One of the easiest ways for the seller to waste time is to spend more time than necessary in getting from one customer to another. It also adds to selling costs in excessive mileage.

Sales-call patterns can be broadly defined as routine or regular and variable or irregular. With a routine call pattern, there is very little turnover in assigned customers. The salesperson sees the same customers on a regular basis. In fact, customers learn to expect the sales call and this can be an advantage. Once a routing plan is set up, the salesperson can use it over and over again.

There is a greater problem for the salesperson who has to make calls on an irregular basis. The routing plan will then be built around the call and the customer's location. The salesperson will route calls on the way to, and back from, the customer, as well as calls to customers located in the same town as the primary call.

Routing helps the salesperson become more efficient in the use of time by focusing on customer locations and the time distance between customers. Locating customers on a map will often reveal some obvious routing patterns. It is not unusual to find customers clustering near each other. This cluster provides a convenient division of the sales territory.

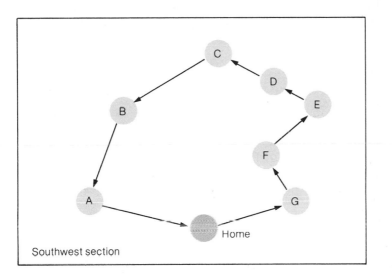

**Figure 12–3
Routing diagram—
typical loop**

The next job is to gather information on the amount of time it takes to get from one customer to another in each of these divisions. Probably several times should be included to reflect the time of day a salesperson will be traveling. In Figure 12–3, the salesperson starts the loop with customers located at *G, F, E,* and *D* because of traffic and the subsequent delays encountered in the mornings in moving toward *A* and *B*—which would keep him or her from completing the loop in a day.

Another way to develop a routing plan is to key it to the customer that the salesperson wants to call on that particular day. In the example in Figure 12–3, suppose the salesperson keys a routing plan to the customer located at point *D*. Suppose further that the salesperson has an appointment for 9:00 A.M. Assuming it will take about 40 minutes to reach the customer at this time of day, this will undoubtedly be the first call of the day. Using point *D* as a starting point, the seller will then proceed to a routing plan that will end at home. Obviously the routing will cover other geographic areas of the sales territory (Figure 12–4).

**Figure 12–4
Routing diagram
using key call as
the basis**

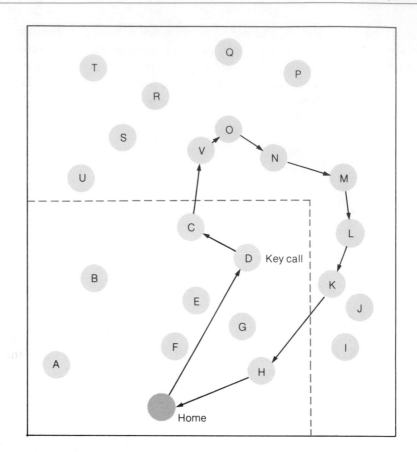

Frequently a conflict will arise between account classification and efficiency in routing. The most efficient call pattern will include customers who should not receive the same frequency of sales calls. Since account classification seems to be more important, the best approach to the problem would be to have separate routing plans for each account classification. Another approach might be to increase the number of calls made in a day and cover these customers or some portion of them on trips to "A" customers.

Time restrictions on seeing a customer, account classification, and routing information should all be kept as part of the sales records on customers. While these records add to the paper work burden for the salesperson, they are essential to time management. Time management in turn builds a successful career in selling. It follows that handling paper work efficiently is a vital and often overlooked part of sound time management.

Frequently overlooked by salespeople are the possibilities of reducing selling costs, particularly travel, without a loss of selling effectiveness. A significant contribution to cost reduction is made by substituting mail and phone contacts for personal visits. A special corporate rate from a hotel or motel chain is another way to reduce costs. Reasonable spending habits in regard to food can be developed with accompanying cost reductions.

REDUCING TRAVEL COSTS

Completing paper work, primarily the preparation of reports for management, is part of every sales job. All salespeople complain about it and feel it is the least desirable aspect of a selling career, but it is necessary in today's sales environment. We have also seen that sound self-management will add to the paper work burden.

HANDLING PAPER WORK

Paper work for the salesperson can be divided into two categories. One category includes those reports, notably the call report, required by the company. The range of these reports is illustrated in Chapter 11. The other category includes those records needed by the salesperson for effective self-management of his or her territory. The most basic of these is the customer sales plan.

While a call report is nothing more than a summary of a salesperson's activities on a day-to-day or week-by-week basis, each company will design its own form to provide certain specific information. To illustrate this, note the obvious differences between the reports for Aeroquip Corporation and International Silver Company shown in Figures 12–5 and 12–6, respectively.

Call reports

Some of the problems encountered with call reports are:

1. Salespeople may use call reports for purposes other than those intended.
2. Salespeople may be inaccurate or biased in their reporting.
3. Salespeople may include too much detail.
4. Salespeople may not like to make out reports of any kind.
5. Salespeople may find that excessive time is required to fill out reports.
6. Salespeople may be late in turning in their reports.
7. Salespeople may focus too much on the past as opposed to the current or future status of an account.[2]

Figure 12–5 Aeroquip Corporation call report

Aeroquip | Sales Contact Report Form No. 81-351

TERRITORY No. ____

AEROQUIP CORPORATION

CALLS MADE FOR WEEK ENDING ____ SALES ENGINEER ____ (Name)

DATE	CUSTOMER NAME NAME & TITLE OF PERSON CONTACTED	CITY	Cust. Type: OEM	Dist.	User	PRODUCTS CHECK ALL DISCUSSED: Reus	Crimp	Freon	Coup.	Adp.	RR	Mar.	Other (Describe)	COMMENTS

PROJECT CODE — INDUSTRIAL DIVISION PRODUCTS

Reus -------- Reusable hose & fittings
Crimp ------- Crimped hose & fittings
Freon -------------- Freon couplings
Coup. -------------- Other couplings
Adp. --------------------- Adapters
RR Railroad Hose Fittings & Couplings
Mar. ---------- Navy Hose & Fittings

Distribution: White - District Office Pink - Sales Engineer Yellow - Van Wert - Accounting

Source: Reprinted by permission of Aeroquip Corporation

Other reports

In addition to the call report, a salesperson may be required to fill out reports on account status, exceptions, dealer inventory, loss of business, new accounts, and dealer termination. As might be imagined, these reports are completed on an irregular basis as the occasion demands. A regular report required in several companies is an estimate of future sales by customer. Not to be overlooked in any section on paper work is the selling expense report discussed in Chapter 11.

Customer sales plan

The customer sales plan such as the one shown in Figure 12–7 may or may not be required by the company. In any case, the sales-

Figure 12–6 International Silver Company call report

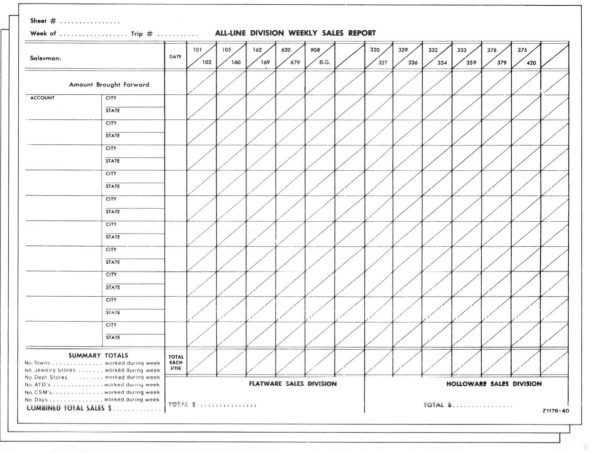

Source: Reprinted by permission of International Silver Company

person will find it desirable to keep such plans for at least the key customers. These plans are basic to any customer file.

A salesperson will want to have a time management card for every customer, with its respective account classification plus information on the travel times between customers. What a salesperson needs in the way of routing sheets depends upon whether the pattern of territory coverage is regular or irregular. With a regular route, the salesperson will set up daily routings and follow them until a change is indicated. A salesperson following an irregular pattern will need to fill out a routing sheet during preparation for the next day's work.

Time management records

**Figure 12–7
Example of customer
sales plan**

Customer sales plan (For *major* customers & prospects)										

Date of preparation   Customer & prospect profile   Salesperson

1. Customer (or prospect) and location   Birthday _____
2. Kind of business _____
3. Buyer _____   Phone No. _____
4. Other contacts _____   Birthday _____
5. Calling days & hours (or other pertinent information) _____
6. Estimated (or exact) purchases for past year $ _____

Hosiery	Watches	Watchbands	Sunglasses	Clocks	Lighters	Flashlights & Batteries	Pipes	Billfolds	Other	Other
$	$	$	$	$	$	$	$	$	$	$

Source: Reprinted by permission from *Sales & Marketing Management* magazine. Copyright 1980.

Information on the time management card would possibly include:

1. Customer restrictions on times for sales calls.
2. Best times for seeing customers.
3. Length of sales interviews with customers.
4. Delays experienced in calling on customers.

**Efficiency in
paper work**

Doing paper work is unproductive in comparison to time spent in front of customers and it is burdensome to salespeople. Yet a certain amount of paper work is a requirement of salespeople in nearly every firm. It can also increase the efficiency as well as the productivity of the salesperson.

The following suggestions may help the salesperson to handle paper work efficiently.

1. Think positively about paper work. The salesperson should remember that much of the paper work will increase productivity and enhance a sales career.

2. Do paper work now. Salespeople should not allow paper work to accumulate. Right after a sales interview or while waiting for the next interview, notes should be taken of what happened during the previous sales interview. Dictation tapes can be mailed periodically to the home office.

3. Set aside a block of unproductive time for working on reports and records. Interruptions can drag out any project and cause the salesperson to spend more time than necessary on report writing. Unproductive time is the best time for scheduling paper work. A salesrep in Los Angeles, for example, completes the day's paperwork before starting for home and in this way is able to miss much of the heavy traffic on the freeways.

4. Set priorities on paper work. The due date for a particular report is one type of priority. Another is the relative importance of the paper work to the salesperson's performance. For example, it is not logical to spend all the time with a report that has no due date and neglect the necessary planning for the next sales day.

A successful salesperson has to be self-motivated. This self-motivation is achieved by attaining goals such as sales results and efficiency in selling performance. Among the terms that are applied to this self-motivation are *self-starter*, *inner drive*, and *self-discipline*. The salesperson must supply the bulk of his or her own motivation. It is one area in which the salesperson cannot depend on company management for more than encouragement.

SELF-MOTIVATION

Undoubtedly the biggest obstacle is the fact that the salesperson will hear the word "no" a lot more times than the word "yes." It is a natural part of the sales job and must be expected. Another obstacle to effective self-motivation is over-pacing. The salesperson becomes discouraged when everything planned for a given day is not accomplished. This can be offset by planning, setting realistic goals, and possibly delegation of certain routine tasks.

The goal of salespersons is obvious; they must operate in such a fashion as to produce sales results. Their pay plan helps provide direction as does the customer sales plan. Motivational support can come from making the salesperson feel a part—indeed a vital part—of the marketing team. The way to do this is to provide (*a*) advertising support that ties directly to the salesperson and what he or she is doing; (*b*) up-to-date information from marketing research on markets and individual customers as well as competitors; (*c*) continuous sales training; and (*d*) technical as well as costing counsel.

The opportunity for upward mobility in the company is also a motivating factor. Salespeople need to be made aware that the job of selling is not a dead-end, but rather a step in a career path. This can be reinforced in training and by seeing it happen in the firm. Time management introduces additional goals and reinforces the satisfaction a salesperson can obtain in doing a good job. Moreover, efficiency in using time gives the salesperson more opportunities to produce sales and receive greater financial rewards.

SUMMARY

Time management together with preapproach make up what is called *self-management*. The purpose of time management is to minimize all the demands on a salesperson's time that are not directly related to selling.

Just how important time management can be is seen from a look at selling costs per call, a calculation of the hourly value of a salesperson's time, and the observation that a salesperson may not spend more than half of his or her available time in front of customers.

Important ingredients of time management are analysis of selling activities into productive and unproductive tasks, and realization of the varying potential of time periods throughout the working day. Tools used in time management include account classification, routing, cost reduction, and paper work management.

With only arm's-length supervision, the successful salesperson must provide most of his or her own motivation. Time management adds to the goals for a salesperson and reinforces the satisfaction from the selling job. The firm needs to prepare the salesperson to accept turndowns. The firm should also provide marketing support, and insure the opportunity for upward mobility in selling and management.

REVIEW QUESTIONS/DISCUSSION QUESTIONS/EXERCISES

1. Briefly identify the following:
   a. Time management.
   b. Self-management.
   c. Productive selling activity.
   d. Unproductive selling activity.
   e. Routing plan.
   f. Call report.

2. Explain the value of account classification to time management.

3. List the reasons why self-management is important to salespeople.

4. If a salesperson receives a 2 percent commission on all sales, how much will he or she have to sell every hour to make $18,000 during the year, $30,000?

5. Defend the idea that the time spent in preapproach is productive.

6. For a salesperson who calls regularly on hardware stores in a three-state area selling a line of tools, list some of the possible productive and unproductive selling activities.

7. Why is it more difficult to analyze selling activities when the salesperson makes a large number of cold calls?

8. Criticize the statement: the more calls, the more sales.

9. Take a typical day at school and divide it up, showing the varying potentials for studying and attending class.

10. What are the advantages of a three-way classification of accounts as opposed to a two-way classification?

11. What are the arguments against the classification of accounts?

12. Describe the two different approaches to developing a routing plan.

13. Explain the conflict between account classification and routing efficiency.

14. What are the two types of paper work for a salesperson?

15. Look at the call report in Figure 12–5 or 12–6 and make suggestions on how it could be revised.

16. List the problems companies have had with call reports.

17. Some companies combine the selling expense report with the call report. List the advantages and disadvantages of such a combination.

18. What should be included in time management records?

19. Do you feel that upward mobility is a strong incentive?

20. Why is self-motivation so important to the success of the salesperson?

CASE 12–1: DeLUXE FOOD PRODUCTS

Janet Robinson, a veteran of seven years with Deluxe, was recently promoted from sales representative to marketing manager for the East Coast division. She was extremely happy with the promotion and the significant pay increase. However, she did feel it had taken too long.

Meeting with other marketing managers for the first time, she expressed the opinion that the delay in getting the promotion was because she was a woman in a man's world. Dick Vermell disagreed with this and told her it had taken him 10 years and Bob George 8 years to get promoted. Other marketing managers joined in the conversation and all felt that too much time was spent at the sales representative level. Another problem was the difficulty in hiring college graduates when opportunities for advancement were slow in coming.

The next day Janet made an appointment for lunch with the vice president of marketing. At the lunch she related what she saw as a problem, namely slow advancement. His reply was that maybe a maximum should be placed on the number of years an individual should remain in the job of sales representative. If the individual was not promoted at the end of so many years, he or she would be released.

Questions

1. Do you feel the suggestion of the vice president would have a positive motivational effect on the sales force?
2. How would you change his suggestion?
3. In what ways would you defend the concept of selling as a career without the need for advancement?

CASE 12–2: MID-AMERICA SUPPLY COMPANY

The Mid-America Supply Company located in Chicago, Illinois, is a wholesaler of hardware products in an eight-state area. Thirty salespersons call on retail dealers in Illinois, Indiana, Iowa, Kentucky, Michigan, Minnesota, Missouri, and Wisconsin.

Salespersons see each of their accounts once a month on a regular schedule. No distinctions are made between accounts on the basis of sales volume.

For the last two months an outside consulting firm has been studying how all 30 sales representatives spend their time. The average results are shown in Exhibit 1 for the eight best salespersons and the eight poorest in terms of sales volume.

Exhibit 1

| | Percent of working day | |
| | Best salespersons | Worst salespersons |
Activity		
Essential		
Face-to-face selling	28	18
Checking want list	20	14
Setting up displays	10	9
Helping with advertising	5	2
Handling adjustments	3	2
Handling billing and credit	3	5
Total	69	50
Nonessential		
Driving	13	18
Waiting for interview	7	12
Broken interviews	3	6
General conversation	2	10
Completing reports	6	4
Total	31	50

Questions

1. What conclusions can be reached from the results of the study?
2. How would you go about setting up a training program in time management?
3. How would you introduce the subject of account classification to top management of Mid-America Supply Company?

A Profile of Professional Selling

John W. Hanley

The career of John W. Hanley, president and CEO of Monsanto and formerly executive vice president with Proctor & Gamble, is a case study of how a sales career can lead to the top. He used his sales ability—first exercised on small orders from corner groceries—to blanket the Southeast with Tide. A talent for selling was transmitted into a talent for leadership.

While in high school, working at odd jobs such as soda jerk, he decided to see if people could be persuaded to do what he wanted them to do. For example, in convincing patrons to add an egg to their malteds for nutrition's sake, he would say, "Do you want one egg or two?" rather than, "Do you want an egg?"

He continued selling in college—everything from beer mugs to flowers. Graduating as an engineer from Penn State in 1942, he went to work for Allegheny Ludlem. Following World War II he went to Harvard Business School. Because of their sales training program, he signed on with Procter & Gamble as a salesman after Harvard.

After a year as a salesman, he ranked at the top in his district. Getting there took careful planning. He began by studying the work habits of his fellow salesmen. He figured he could get ahead by working an extra day a week and calling on 50 percent more stores.

As a salesman, Hanley was upward oriented. He enjoyed selling, but he didn't want to do it forever. His next level of responsibility was as a sales trainer, and then he became supervisor of 12 salesmen. Next came a district managership and then managership of a new division. He impressed his superiors with his planning and organizing. One said: "He organizes everything . . . so well that his capacity to perform is unbelievable."

At 33 Hanley became sales manager for the soap and detergent division which accounted for 70 percent of P&G's sales and 85 percent of the profits. He developed an environment for those reporting to him where they in turn could grow through candor and hard work.

As competition increased, he decided to skip several stages in product development. He accelerated test marketing and established manufacturing priorities for new products. Later he set up teams of sales, advertising, and research and development executives to mastermind new products and product improvements, and he split the sales force into two distinct groups.

Hanley next went to work for Monsanto. In switching from consumer products to chemicals, he has had to learn a new industry. Also, he is working to build an organization where (1) responsibility is pushed down to the lowest level; (2) there is a dedication to better management; and (3) individuals can utilize their abilities to the fullest.

Part

6

PERSONAL SELLING AS A CAREER FIELD

*A salesman is got to dream, boy.
It comes with the territory.**
ARTHUR MILLER
Death of a Salesman, Requiem*

KEY POINTS

The rewards of selling can be categorized as (1) financial rewards, (2) nonfinancial rewards, and (3) opportunities for advancement.

The starting point for any reward system is a good method of evaluation that relates compensation (or changes in compensation) to performance.

Financial rewards are quite generous in selling. Sales personnel receive compensation significantly above that of most other career fields.

A basic decision in establishing any compensation plan is the overall level of payment. Firms may decide to pay a competitive wage that is about normal for the industry, or compensation that is set above the competitive level.

Salespeople may be paid according to (1) a commission plan, (2) a salary plan, or (3) a combination or mixed plan.

Salespeople also receive other financial payments: (1) fringe benefits, (2) expense accounts, and (3) sales contest awards.

Several nonfinancial rewards accrue to salespeople: (1) personal satisfaction, (2) status within one's organization, (3) competitiveness, and (4) freedom of action.

Salespeople usually cite opportunity for advancement as a primary reason for their career choice.

A career path is a series of steps that sales employees go through in preparation for advancement. A selling career provides multiple career tracks: (1) sales management, (2) professional sales careers, and (3) marketing staff careers.

Chapter

13

THE REWARDS OF
A SALES CAREER

Syntex Laboratories realizes that many members of its 500-person sales force do not aspire to sales management or marketing staff positions. So in order to provide additional growth opportunities for its sales personnel, the California-based pharmaceutical firm has set up a professional development program with five separate growth levels.

1. Representative
2. Professional medical representative
3. Certified medical representative
4. Territory manager
5. Senior territory manager

The company requires varying amounts of course work for each level in the program. Progression through the different growth levels provides additional responsibilities as well as benefits like quarterly bonuses and incentive trips to places like Nassau.[1] A sales career at Syntex can truly be a rewarding experience thanks to the professional development program.

Professional selling has such a variety of rewards that any listing would be incomplete. The more obvious rewards of selling can be categorized as (1) financial rewards, (2) nonfinancial rewards, and (3) opportunities for advancement. This classification forms the outline for the bulk of this chapter.

THE NEED FOR AN EVALUATION SYSTEM

The starting point for any reward system is a good method of performance evaluation. Rewards need to be planned and allocated systematically rather than on a haphazard, uncoordinated basis. Salespeople and sales managers alike should perceive the rewards as being fair and should have a clear understanding of the conditions for them and the rationale supporting them.[2]

In the search for an effective evaluation program that realistically reflects a salesperson's actual performance, Dow Chemical uses what it describes as a "pay for performance" plan. Dow sellers receive a salary that is adjusted annually according to their respective ratings. Other firms may evaluate on a semiannual, quarterly, or even monthly basis. The key to a good compensation plan is a system of relating compensation (or changes in compensation) to performance. In other words, the salesperson who does the best job will receive the greatest reward.

A lack of adequate evaluative measures forces the sales manager to rely on subjective opinions as to a particular salesperson's worth. In such a situation, a salesperson may become disillusioned and discouraged, and excessive turnover of qualified sales personnel may result. Sales personnel expect to be evaluated on standards they understand and upon which they can agree; if they meet those standards, they expect to be compensated accordingly.

Financial rewards are quite generous in selling; in fact, it is often noted that sales is one of the most lucrative of all career fields. A successful salesperson can earn more than most of his or her contemporaries. Unfortunately, the above-average earnings potential tempts some people who are not qualified to enter the field. Such people eventually fail and turn to another occupational endeavor for which they are better suited.

FINANCIAL REWARDS

High earnings are the reward for qualified personnel who are willing to invest the time and effort required for success in the field of selling. A Dartnell survey reported that experienced sales personnel on commission averaged $32,135. Those on a salary and commission plan earned $28,456. And experienced sales people paid on a straight salary basis averaged $22,265. Another source reported entry-level salaries averaging about $16,000 in a recent year.[3]

Certainly, salespeople are well rewarded for their efforts. But no one should enter any field simply because of its earnings potential. Nonfinancial rewards for work are also important if one is to be truly content with one's job and lifestyle. Further, all rewards have associated costs, and the financial remuneration of a sales career is no exception. In the case of selling, long hours and sincere, diligent effort are required for success.

There are two major types of financial rewards: (1) compensation plans and (2) fringe benefits, expense accounts, and sales contests. Both affect the overall level of financial rewards the salesperson will receive, as well as the salesperson's motivation.

Compensation plans can be used to accomplish a variety of sales management objectives. Oakite Products, a specialty chemical sales company, once switched from a commission plan to salaries as a cost-cutting move. Later, the firm changed its sales strategy and its compensation plan again. This time Oakite introduced a variable commission plan designed to improve its market coverage, cut marginally profitable sales, and control the firm's 30 percent annual turnover among sales personnel. The new plan guaranteed a sales representative $500 per month, and tied commissions to gross margins and order size.[4]

Compensation plans

Compensation levels. The first basic decision the company must make in establishing a compensation plan is the overall level of payment to be made. Some firms may decide to pay a *competitive wage,* or compensation that is about standard for the industry. Others deliberately pay *high salaries* (or commissions) that are above those of the competition. Some firms use a high salary level to attract experienced sales personnel from other companies. All good sales personnel command at least competitive salaries, but many companies fail to review their compensation plans periodically, allowing their compensation scale to slip below a competitive level, a situation that calls for prompt corrective measures when it is recognized.

Selection of a compensation level is a company policy that should be subjected to rigorous analysis because of its far-reaching effects on sales productivity. The compensation level should be a deliberate management decision designed to accomplish particular company objectives. For instance, a small industrial goods firm may decide to hire only experienced salespeople currently working for competitors, a decision prompted by the alternative of having an expensive training program for inexperienced trainees.

One possible influence on the level of sales compensation can be the presence of a labor union. While unions are not widespread in contemporary selling, there is some trend toward unionization among white-collar workers in general. This will undoubtedly have an influence on the field of selling in the future.

Compensation methods. In addition to their overall level of compensation, the firm must also decide on how sales personnel will be paid. There are three basic options: salary, commission, or some type of combination plan. Table 13–1 presents the results of one survey of sales compensation methods.

Commission or straight salary? The original method for compensating salespeople was the commission plan. Its primary advantage is that straight commissions link the amount of pay directly to sales productivity. The greater the amount of sales for a salesperson, the higher his or her earnings. Commissions provide maximum sales incentives. Historically, commissions were limited to sales volume, but many firms now try to link them to the relative profitability of the item sold.

A straight salary plan is at the opposite end of the compensation

Table 13–1 Type of compensation by industry.

Industry	Number of companies	Salary	Commission	Combination
Aerospace	5	60%	—	40%
Appliance (household)	8	25	25%	50
Automobile parts and accessories	12	34	16	50
Automobile and truck	10	30	30	40
Beverages	6	50	—	50
Building materials	23	17	13	70
Casualty insurance	5	20	20	60
Chemicals	13	23	23	54
Cosmetics and toilet preparations	9	33	34	33
Drugs and medicines	12	25	25	50
Electrical equipment and supplies	19	26	10	64
Electronics	21	19	9	62
Fabricated metal products	26	26	19	55
Food products	14	43	14	43
General machinery	26	19	15	65
Glass and allied products	8	60	20	20
Housewares	12	25	25	50
Instruments and allied products	10	30	20	50
Iron and steel	10	20	—	80
Life insurance	5	20	20	60
Nonferrous metals	6	50	—	50
Office machinery and equipment	7	14	29	57
Paper and allied products	12	33	—	67
Petroleum and petroleum products	4	50	25	25
Printing	17	24	47	29
Publishing	14	10	30	60
Radio and television	7			100
Retailing	4	50	25	25
Rubber	8	25	—	75
Service industries	21	15	40	45
Textiles and apparel	6	33	33	34
Tobacco	4	—	100	—
Tools and hardware	11	18	36	46
Transportation equipment	5	100	—	—

continuum. In this plan salespeople are paid a given amount at specified times. This allows sales management to maintain maximum control over the selling effort. If management decides that sales personnel should allocate greater effort to market research, account servicing, or the like, the salary plan will not penalize the salesperson, as would be the case with a commission plan. A recent study by the Research Institute of America found that there was an increased use of commissions and other incentives, while the percentage of manufacturing firms offering straight salaries had declined.[5]

Mixed plans. Between the extremes of straight commission and straight salary are a variety of mixed compensation plans. These mixed approaches try to achieve the advantages of both sales force control and selling incentive. Mixed compensation plans include (1) drawing accounts, (2) combination plans, (3) salary plus bonuses, (4) point systems, and (5) the smorgasbord approach.

Drawing accounts are advances against commissions earned by the sales representative, who "draws" a set amount each pay period which is charged against the commission account. Then periodically (say quarterly), the balance of the commissions is paid to the individual. A modification is the *guaranteed draw,* whereby the seller is not liable for repayment if the draw is more than the commissions earned in a given time period.

A *combination plan* is one that has a set salary as well as a commission component. The exact mix varies from industry to industry. Combination plans are probably the most common mixed compensation method.

Salary plus bonuses is another approach to sales compensation. Bonuses differ from commissions in that they are rewards for achievement that is not directly related to sales. Bonuses might be given for a substantial number of new accounts, feedback about special account servicing efforts, or general overall selling performance.[6] Bonuses are usually paid annually, as contrasted to the monthly or quarterly payment of commissions.

Point systems award points or credits for achievement in a certain area. Salespersons receive points for each level of sales volume garnered, new accounts opened, specific servicing activities, number of calls made, and the like. Some systems include penalty points as well as credit points, and the net point total is converted to a compensation payment on a periodic basis. If each point is equal to 35 cents, then someone who earns 6,400 points in a particular month will receive a check for $2240 (minus deductions).

Another compensation program utilizes the *smorgasbord approach,* which allows employees to select the mix of salary, commissions, bonuses, and fringe benefits that best suits their needs.[7] A younger person might elect cash to furnish a new apartment, while an older one might concentrate on increased insurance or pension payments. Most smorgasbord plans have a limited number of options and require that the individual's selections remain set for a given period of time. These rules cut the costs of administering such a plan. While the smorgasbord approach has not been widely implemented, it may become a standard feature of future compensation plans.

Sales personnel also receive financial rewards that are not directly tied to the firm's compensation plan, including substantial *fringe benefits*. These include life insurance, disability insurance, health insurance, vacations, pension plans, stock options, and the like. When salespeople were commission agents, they had few of these benefits. But times have changed and so has sales compensation. Today's salesperson receives a full range of fringe benefits. For example, 75 percent of the sales force at Black and Decker Manufacturing Company have become stockholders through a stock purchase plan.[8] Similar examples can be found in many other firms.

Most sales personnel also have *expense accounts* to cover the legitimate costs of fulfilling their job requirements. An expense account is not a reward for selling, since a salesperson should not make money (or lose it) as a result of an expense account. A good expense account policy is to pay all realistic selling expenses and disallow all those of a personal nature. Legitimate sales expenses include business travel, lodging, meals, and work-related entertainment.

Expense accounts are examined in this chapter because they are a *payment* to the sales force. However, a company should not allow an expense account to become a type of fringe benefit. Neither should the firm permit the person's expense allowance to dip below the actual costs incurred. A typical example of this failure is an organization that continues to pay 15 or 18 cents per mile for automobile travel, even though travel costs now are substantially higher.

Expense accounts can take various forms such as those discussed below.[9]

1. Periodic allowance. The salesperson is given a set amount to cover expenses. The salesperson keeps his or her own expense records. A common complaint is that sales management has a tendency to let the allowance fall below the amount actually required, and the salesperson may try to keep a portion of the allowance and thus limit useful sales activities.

2. Unlimited expense account. This plan pays all legitimate selling expenses. Various reporting systems can be used. Specifically, all lodging expenditures and entertainment costs over $25 require receipts. All expense reports should contain the names of persons entertained, dates, and business purpose.

3. Limited allowance. A standard example of this type is a per diem plan that allows salespeople a set amount—say, $60—for each day they are away from home. Similar plans might set weekly limits on various categories of expenses, such as room charges, meals, and entertainment.

Fringe benefits/ expense accounts/ sales contests

Salespeople also participate in special promotions that emphasize a particular line or product. These promotions, usually called *sales contests,* are used to support the introduction of a new product, stimulate lagging sales, and offset seasonal declines. The objective is to motivate the salesperson to market a particular item or product line more aggressively. The prizes used in sales contests include not only

**Table 13–2
Suggestions for implementing a successful incentive contest for sales personnel**

1. Set individual quotas.
2. Establish different quotas for different lines.
3. Base programs on two or more factors, not just on dollars or on units.
4. Analyze your markets and your sales programs before you set your sales-incentive goals and quotas.
5. Base goals on previous actual performance.
6. Set realistic goals.
7. Have measurable objectives.
8. Strive for maximum participation.
9. Make rules that are easy to understand.
10. Spell out requirements carefully before the program begins.
11. Report standings to participants on a regular basis.
12. Give field sales managers the flexibility to adjust for unusual circumstances.
13. Don't use lottery-type programs.
14. Always have more than one winner.
15. Evaluate your results, including salespeoples' and field sales managers' opinions of the program.

Source: Adapted by permission from Sally Scanlon, "Incentive Game Plan in 1980: A S&MM Survey," *Sales & Marketing Management,* April 7, 1980, p. 62. Copyright 1980.

The Hunt Club

When Hunt-Wesson—a division of Norton Simon—sought to improve its position in tomato product markets, it implemented a nationwide consumer promotion effort. And in order to gain the support of its 450-person sales force, the company set up a 36-member "Hunt Club" for personnel achieving superior performance during the promotion period. Sales volume, distribution, display, and cooperative advertising improvements were used to determine the membership. Hunt Club members are identified by their tomato-red jackets, related accessories, and engraved business cards. The exclusivity of the Hunt Club must have worked as a sales force motivator since the firm reported sales increases in excess of 25 percent.

Source: Reprinted by permission from "Joining the Club at Hunt-Wesson," *Sales & Marketing Management,* May 14, 1979, pp. 21–22. Copyright 1979.

money, but also items of merchandise, travel, and tickets to sporting events. A *Sales & Marketing Management* survey found an increased use of contest incentives during periods of high inflation. The magazine's report also suggested some tips on setting up such a program (Table 13–2).

Sales personnel are usually considered to be the most highly motivated employees, financially, in any organization. Any sales motivation effort would be foolish to subordinate the role played by an adequate compensation program. But it is important to realize that there are also nonfinancial rewards associated with a sales career that can be significant motivators in selling.

Perhaps the most important nonfinancial reward is the *personal satisfaction* a salesperson receives from knowing that he or she is fulfilling a vital need in society. The salesperson satisfies customer needs, participates in the efficient distribution of production, and creates jobs in other segments of the economy, as in manufacturing or the service sector. Salespersons can take pride in the fact that their work lubricates the machinery of modern economic life.

Another nonfinancial reward is the salesperson's *status* within his or her own organization. Because productive firms realize the importance of the seller's efforts in the field, higher average compensation and substantial opportunities for career advancement are offered. The advancement path for sales personnel is described in the next section.

Most salespeople sincerely enjoy the *competitiveness* of their occupation and regard it as an important nonfinancial reward. Selling is the most competitive activity in any business organization, and good sales representatives enjoy the chance to achieve in such an environment. The intense competition quickly separates those who will succeed in selling from those who would be well advised to seek employment elsewhere.

Freedom of action is one of the most important career advantages cited by professional salespeople, who are apt to say they hate being tied to a desk and really enjoy being able to get out among the people. The professional salesperson likes the opportunity to meet and interact with people with different personalities, goals, and problems and, for the most part, to come and go at will. Because selling is a results-oriented job rather than predicated on routine and procedure, freedom of action is one of the most enticing nonfinancial rewards in this career field.

NONFINANCIAL REWARDS

OPPORTUNITIES FOR ADVANCEMENT

Various surveys have shown that salespeople often cite opportunity for advancement as a primary reason for their career choice. This reasoning is logical and entirely consistent with the evidence, which indicates that effective salespeople are among the most promotable employees of any firm. Recent studies have shown that more chief executive officers have come from sales and marketing than any other functional area within industry.[10]

The opportunity for advancement may come in several ways. Salespeople can advance to increased sales responsibilities, become district managers, or step up to staff marketing positions in marketing research, product management, or market planning. The possibilities are endless for the salesperson who achieves a good track record in the field.

The career path concept

A management that realizes the contributions of a good salesperson is likely to move effective performers to areas where they can make the greatest impact on the success of the company. The concept of the *career path* as a series of steps employees go through in preparation for advancement is helpful in this regard.

Traditionally, many companies had the idea that sales management is the logical next step for the successful salesperson. This be-

"Simpkins, you've been traded to Consolidated Manufacturing for two sales managers and an account executive to be named later."

Reprinted by permission *The Wall Street Journal.*

Some career paths take funny twists.

lief, often called the "star salesperson concept," assumes that superior sales performance guarantees effectiveness as a sales manager. Nothing could be further from the truth! Selling and the management of a sales force are totally different jobs that require different skills. One consulting psychologist reported that evaluation of over 250,000 individuals revealed that "only one in eight really good salesmen possesses equally good management ability."[4] A common saying is that when you promote the star salesperson, the company loses two people—the star salesperson and the manager he or she replaced.

		Cash income*	Other income†	Total compensation
1.	Nicholas DiBari *senior v.p., marketing* Comdisco	$674,241	$ 12	$674,253
2.	John Slevin *v.p., sales* Comdisco	$600,862	35	600,897
3.	Irving L. Rousso *executive v.p., sales* *and merchandising* Russ Togs	499,000	32,700	531,700
4.	John G. Hill *v.p., sales* Storage Technology	145,000	201,658	346,658
5.	William S. McConnor *senior v.p., refinery* *marketing* Union Oil of California	306,921	32,745	339,666
6.	C.H. King *senior v.p. marketing* *& refining* Standard Oil (Ohio)	181,450	153,340	334,790
7.	David M. Tracy *senior v.p. and pres.,* *Fieldcrest Div. sales* Fieldcrest Mills	210,300	78,277	288,577
8.	Richard Barrie *senior executive v.p.,* *marketing & sales* Fabergé	259,917	22,668	282,585
9.	Benjamin O. Sampson *pres., marketing div.* Cone Mills	247,500	17,875	265,375
10.	Robert L. Lair *senior v.p., marketing* Cessna Aircraft	139,924	102,825	242,749

Table 13–3
The 10 top paid sales and marketing executives

*Salaries, fees, directors' fees, bonuses, commissions
†Securities, profit sharing, personal benefits
Source: Reprinted by permission from Thayer C. Taylor, "What Top Sales and Marketing Executives Earn," *Sales & Marketing Management,* September 15, 1980, p. 41. Copyright 1980.

Top sales and marketing executives are also paid handsomely for their work. Table 13–3 identifies the 10 top paid sales and marketing executives in a recent year.

Multiple career paths

Management positions, however, are not the only advancement opportunities open to salespeople. The 3M Company established the position of account executive for the successful career salesperson who is best qualified to maintain a direct sales responsibility. Promotion to this coveted classification requires approval of the division general manager, the group vice president, and the vice president of marketing. D.W. Mahmer, the corporate vice president of marketing, describes the plan as follows: "Advancement to account executive at 3M recognizes sales representation whose extended experience and highly developed skills in managing major account responsibility deserve special recognition for what can truly be called professionalism."[12]

The multiple career path is now widely accepted in industry. Figure 13–1 graphically demonstrates the three primary career paths for sales personnel within a company. Salespeople may be selected to

**Figure 13–1
The multiple career path concept for sales personnel**

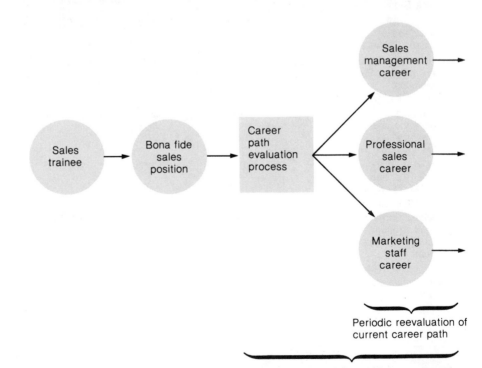

follow sales management careers, professional sales careers, or marketing staff careers.

Trainees are promoted to regular sales positions and gain meaningful field experience in that capacity before any career path decision is made. The length of the initial job assignment varies according to industry, company, product, and customer requirements. The actual career path evaluation process should involve the individual salesperson, the sales manager, and perhaps a staff person skilled in career consultation. The decision that results from this evaluation should be the one that best meets the needs of both the individual involved and the company.

Once a career path has been selected, it should be reevaluated on a periodic basis. A person's career objective is subject to change, and company planning should adjust.

Sales management career track

Salespeople who are eventually expected to enter sales management should be identified early. A formal program of job rotation could be set up once adequate field selling experience has been achieved so that the sales management candidate has experience in a variety of positions. In this way he or she will better understand the requirements, interrelationships, and responsibilities of a sales management position.

Surprisingly many firms do little to prepare future sales managers. The manager is often picked from the sales force and assumes the position after only a brief orientation session, perhaps conducted by the outgoing manager. One survey reported that only 29 percent of the respondents had programs to train field sales managers, and many of these programs were "informal" at best.[13]

Examples of firms that *do* provide for the internal development of field sales managers include National Starch and Chemical Corporation, General Electric Company, Sylvania Electric Products, International Business Machines, New York Telephone Company, and New York Life Insurance Company.[14]

Professional sales careers

Ample professional opportunities should be available to those who follow a sales career path. The Syntex Laboratories program is an excellent example of this type of action.

One way of motivating the professional salesperson is to use a sales force segmentation scheme. A plan of this type suggests segmenting the sales force on the bases of financial recognition, job title, personal recognition, communication differences, and peripheral ben-

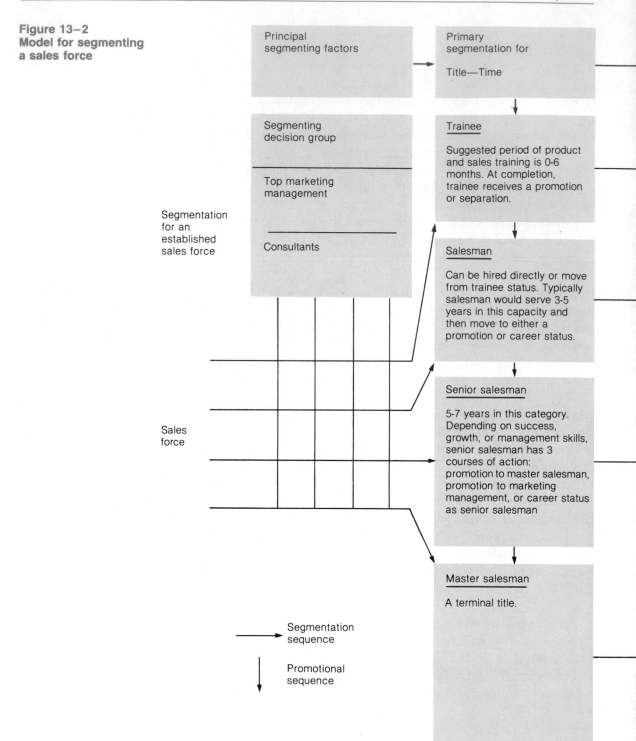

**Figure 13–2
Model for segmenting
a sales force**

| Principal segmenting factors | Primary segmentation for Title—Time |

Trainee

Suggested period of product and sales training is 0-6 months. At completion, trainee receives a promotion or separation.

Segmenting decision group

Top marketing management

Consultants

Segmentation for an established sales force

Salesman

Can be hired directly or move from trainee status. Typically salesman would serve 3-5 years in this capacity and then move to either a promotion or career status.

Sales force

Senior salesman

5-7 years in this category. Depending on success, growth, or management skills, senior salesman has 3 courses of action: promotion to master salesman, promotion to marketing management, or career status as senior salesman

Segmentation sequence

Promotional sequence

Master salesman

A terminal title.

Source: Herbert H. Mossien and Eugene H. Fram, "Segmentation for Sales Force Motivation." *Akron Business and Economic Review* 41:Winter 1973)8:–9.

Secondary segmentation for	Tertiary segmentation for
Salary Peripheral benefits	Recognition and Communication
Base hiring salary — no change while in this status. No bonus eligibility. 15% of sales force based on average turnover or promotions. Number hired relates directly to need. Uses basic car. Not eligible for trips, contests, or similar reward.	No vacation—primary contacts during training are through training personnel. Communications through trainers dealing with planning, sales techniques, role playing, competitive product, and formal progress reports.
Incremental raise on "graduation" from trainee status. Productivity raises while in this status. Bonus or incentive over salary limited to 10%. Represents 15% of sales force. Top of basic line car. Eligible for basic sales contests or special promotions.	Standard company vacation. Periodic home office sales meetings. Communications are basically routine as above, enhanced by more detailed competitive analysis. Advanced closing techniques, etc. Introduction to general company problems and actions.
Primary career level. 50% of sales force will have this title at any given time. Most fertile group for promotion to management. Salary plus bonus with 30% limit. Middle range car. Eligible for all routine contests plus special contests for senior and master only.	Standard company vacation. Periodic sales meetings plus special sessions with middle managers. As above in respect to communications, but more personally oriented and sometimes from upper management. Special peer sessions within the sales meeting. Receives broad-base bulletins dealing with growth, acquisitions, company profits, etc.
Top producers—strong sales talent. Makes up 20% of force. High salary—no limit on bonus. Premium cars. All base contests plus special competitive awards. Awards for husband and wife. Premium trips.	Managerial discretion on vacation, home office visits. Attend all routine sales meetings. Act as upper management resource for broad base planning and strategy. Presents successful sales experiences to other sales personnel. A periodic dinner for informal discussion with the president would be in order. On mailing list for middle and upper management bulletins. In general, treated with distinction.

efits.[15] A model for segmenting a sales force according to these bases is shown in Figure 13–2. This plan allows for substantial professional development within the sales career path. The emphasis is on maintaining the initiative and motivation of the firm's sales personnel.

Marketing staff careers

Marketing staff careers are also available to sales personnel. Many companies regard two to five years of field selling experience as a necessary prerequisite to a marketing staff position, reasoning that a person who has not had direct field sales experience cannot function effectively in a sales support area or a corporate staff position.

Numerous marketing staff functions are open to people with sales experience. These opportunities are in the areas of market research, advertising, distribution analysis, warehousing, traffic management, customer relations, systems planning, transportation, shipping, sales analysis, distribution cost analysis, dealer relations, and sales training. People with successful sales experience have proved their worth to the firm and are likely candidates for challenging staff positions. Such individuals are in demand, and in many cases staff departments actually bid for their services.

SUMMARY

The rewards of a sales career can be categorized as (1) financial rewards, (2) nonfinancial rewards, and (3) opportunities for advancement. Any reward system should be based on an effective method of evaluation that relates compensation (or changes in compensation) to performance.

A basic decision in establishing a compensation plan is to determine the level of payment. Firms may decide to pay a competitive wage that is about average for the industry or compensation that is set above the norm. Next, the method of payment must be established as a (1) commission plan, (2) salary plan, or (3) combination or mixed plan. Sales personnel also receive other financial payments such as fringe benefits, expense accounts, and sales contest awards.

Financial rewards are usually quite generous in selling. Salespersons receive compensation significantly higher than that of most other career fields. Nonfinancial rewards that accrue to the sales force include (1) personal satisfaction, (2) status within one's organization, (3) competitiveness, and (4) freedom of action. Sales personnel also have substantial opportunities for advancement through multiple career tracks: (1) sales management, (2) professional sales, and (3) marketing staff.

REVIEW QUESTIONS/DISCUSSION
QUESTIONS/EXERCISES

1. Briefly identify the following:

   a. Combination plan. d. Sales contest.

   b. Drawing accounts. e. Career path.

   c. Guaranteed draw.

2. Prepare a list of reasons why salespeople typically receive above-average compensation.

3. Describe a smorgasbord compensation plan. What types of compensation would you select?

4. Differentiate between commissions and bonuses.

5. How can a point system be used in a sales compensation program?

6. Discuss the major types of expense accounts:

   a. Periodic allowance

   b. Unlimited expense account

   c. Limited allowance

7. List and discuss the various nonfinancial rewards received by sales personnel.

8. Design a sales contest to motivate a sales force in the following circumstances:

   a Automobile dealership sales personnel who are going to be selling a new front wheel drive model.

   b. Sales representatives for a line of machinery parts that has not sold well. Assume that all sales quotas assigned have been met for the firm's other three lines.

   You will want to consider questions such as:

   a. How will the contest be administered?

   b. How long will the contest run?

   c. Who will be eligible to participate?

   d. What prizes are to be awarded?

9. Interview a sales executive at a firm in your community and ask the manager to describe the sales compensation program used. Then prepare a brief report for your class.

10. Why do sales personnel often cite opportunity for advancement as a primary reason for their career choice? Discuss.

11. Explain how a sales force can make effective use of the multiple career path concept. Discuss the various career track options available to a salesperson.

12. Interview some professional salespeople. Ask them to describe the rewards of their particular jobs. Prepare a list of these rewards and present them in a class discussion.

13. Interview a personnel executive of a firm in your area and ask him or

her to describe and contrast the compensation plans used for several professional occupations: (1) accounting, (2) engineering, and (3) production management. Then prepare a brief report comparing these compensation plans to those used in selling. What are the major differences? Similarities?

14. An expense account is not a reward for selling. Comment on this statement.

15. List and discuss the various mixed compensation plans that have been used in selling.

16. Prepare a paper analyzing the expense account policies for sales personnel within a given industry. What generalizations can be reached?

17. What are the advantages and disadvantages of commission and salary compensation plans?

18. Why would a company ever deliberately choose to offer its sales force a compensation program that is considerably higher than the competitive norm for that particular industry? Discuss.

19. The starting point for any reward system is a good method of performance evaluation. Comment on this statement.

20. Jan Vogel—an excellent salesperson—has just turned down a promotion to district sales manager. Here is the reasoning:

The managership paid only $2,000 more than I earned last year. And I know of two big accounts I am about to land. When they come through, I'll be making about $4,000–$5,000 in additional commissions every year.

Do you agree with Vogel's reasoning? What does this situation suggest about the firm's compensation plan for sales personnel? Sales managers?

CASE 13–1: COLUMBUS PRODUCTS, INC.

Judith Karansky is facing one of the toughest choices in her four-year marketing career. Karansky covers the Springfield, Ohio, territory for Columbus Products, an Ohio-based electronics firm with national distribution. She has recently been offered a product manager's job with Standard Electronics in Indianapolis. Karansky must give Standard an answer within a week.

Karansky had decided to interview for the Standard job after Alice Folsom, her district sales manager, had refused her request to join Columbus Products management internship program. Folsom noted that Karansky would be an excellent candidate next year but that she had never recommended anyone for the program with less than five years' service.

The management internship program involved a six-month stint serving as an assistant to a sponsoring manager. Karansky had asked to be assigned to a divisional sales manager, the level above Folsom. The program was widely recognized as the stepping stone to a management position within Columbus. Karansky was confident that she could do a good job in the program and that she would be appointed a district sales manager upon its completion. Only Folsom stood in her way.

Standard's job offer caused Karansky considerable anxiety. She liked Columbus and would prefer to spend her career with them. Her job as a sales representative was satisfying and she liked Springfield. But Karansky also sought new challenges. The unanswered question was whether a staff position at Standard Electronics was the correct move at this time?

Questions

1. Evaluate Karansky's career path decision?
2. What choice would you make? Why?

CASE 13–2: FEDERATED INDUSTRIES

Federated Industries based in Rockford, Illinois, is a medium-size manufacturer of equipment for the petroleum industry. Its products include lifts, hoists, drills, pumps, pipeline controls, and related items.

Federated sales representatives have always been compensated on a straight-salary basis. Last year, the salary range for field representatives was $27,000–$35,000. Employees with several years' service clustered in the $30,000–$35,000 range, while the range for less experienced personnel tended to be about $27,000–$29,000. Each of the 30 representatives is evaluated annually, and salaries are adjusted accordingly. Brownell granted salary hikes of 6 to 10 percent this past year.

Benton Avery, Federated's executive vice president, has long been concerned about turnover and the relative lack of incentive in the current salary structure. He blames the turnover on the compensation system, which he believes does not adequately recognize superior performance. Recently, Avery was heard to remark:

> It's crazy, some of our salespeople have become bureaucrats. They sit around and try to appease their sales manager, but do very little real aggressive marketing.

But, why should they? The highest earnings are reserved for those with the longest seniority in our sales organization. The reps know that they will get a cost of living increase, and that any merit pay is based more on internal politics than on sales performance.

Avery has since directed Scott Polner, the national sales manager, to develop a compensation plan that would provide greater incentive to good sales performance. Polner has been instructed to increase incentive compensation, but still retain enough of a salary base to cover basic living costs.

After several weeks of intense study, Polner and his staff are set to reveal their new sales compensation plan to Avery. An outline of the plan appears in Exhibit 1.

Exhibit 1

Revised sales compensation plan, Federated Industries

Salary component

0–5 years experience with Federated	$12,000
6–10 years experience with Federated	$13,200
11–15 years experience with Federated	$14,400
16–20 years experience with Federated	$15,600
Over 20 years experience with Federated	$16,800

Commission component

All products in the Federated line have been classified in commission categories identified A, B, C. The division was made on the basis of gross profits to Federated, with A representing the most profitable items and C the least profitable ones.

A commission schedule has been established for all sales over the assigned sales quota in each category. Initial sales quotas were set at 90 percent of the previous year's sales of each product group. The commission schedule is:

Category A = 10% of sales over quota for this category.
Category B = 8.5% of sales over quota for this category.
Category C = 7% of sales over quota for this category.

Bonus component

Annual performance reviews will be continued but will concentrate on activities not directly related to sales volume. Attention will be given to customer relations, new accounts, account servicing, cooperation in securing marketing intelligence, and the like.

The district sales manager, with approval of Mr. Polner, may grant annual bonuses of up to $5,000 for a salesperson.

Notes:
1. The salary component will be reviewed every two years and adjusted to reflect changes in the cost of living.
2. The national sales manager estimates that this plan will result in approximately the same level of compensation as currently exists for the salary plan.

Questions

1. Do you agree with Avery's criticism of the current compensation plan at Federated Industries?
2. How do you believe Avery will react to the proposed revision to the compensation plan? Why?
3. What is your own evaluation of Polner's plan?
4. What changes or modifications (if any) would you make to Polner's plan? Why?

KEY POINTS

The widespread implementation of formalized sales training is well documented in industry. Initial sales training deals with the preparation and orientation of new sales personnel. The emphasis is on forming proper selling habits so a field position can be assumed as soon as possible.

Continuous sales training involves refreshing, improving, and updating the selling skills of veteran personnel. The major benefits of sales training are: (1) increased sales productivity, (2) reduced turnover, (3) improved morale, and (4) lower costs of supervision.

Sales training techniques include: (1) lectures, (2) audiovisual aids, (3) role playing, (4) self-study, (5) on-the-job training, and (6) job rotation.

Continuous sales training programs are different from initial sales training operationally as well as conceptually: in the types of trainees involved, objectives, program content, and training methods.

Initial training programs will cover such subjects as product knowledge, selling techniques, market orientation, and company orientation.

The attitudes of experienced sales personnel are an important consideration in developing continuous training programs.

Chapter 14

SALES TRAINING: A VITAL LEARNING PROCESS

This chapter and the previous one consider two sales activities that are of particular concern to students considering a career in selling. In Chapter 13 the rewards of a selling career were considered. The development of sales personnel through training is the subject of this chapter.

Consider the situation confronting Squibb's introduction of Corgard, a new cardiovascular drug. The pharmaceutical firm had traditionally introduced new products via literature and workshops. Sales managers had only minimal responsibilities in the training program. But Corgard required a more comprehensive effort because (1) the firm intended to introduce related products later; (2) the sales force was unfamiliar with the particular market; (3) Corgard would be a difficult drug to explain to physicians; and (4) two competitive products were available, so the sales force would have to understand Corgard's major selling points such as once-a-day dosage.

Squibb's solution was the Corgard Core Sales Development Program, which began with a meeting of sales managers eight months before the product launch. The size and importance of the new market was explained, then sales managers were told that they were responsible for monitoring their personnel's progress in the self-paced training program that Squibb had developed. Sales personnel were to study the Corgard materials over the next several months, and the training effort would culminate with an examination at the national sales meeting, a few weeks prior to the launch.

Ten study modules had been developed to cover topics ranging from the physiology of the cardiovascular system to Squibb's marketing strategy for Corgard. The program employed both audio cassettes as well as printed materials. Judging from the 96.5 percent overall score on the final examination, and favorable field sales reports after the launch, the Corgard Core Sales Development Program can be considered a major sales training success for Squibb.[1]

TYPES OF SALES TRAINING

The principal objective of any sales training program is to develop selling proficiency, particularly in terms of increased sales production and establishment of long-term customer relationships. The specific objectives of training depend upon the type of training.[2]

Sales training can be classified as either initial or continuous. *Initial sales training* deals with the preparation and orientation of new sales personnel. The emphasis in initial training is on forming proper selling habits so that the salesperson can assume a field position as quickly as possible. The amount of preparation necessary depends on several factors, such as the recruiting source, technical complexities in the product and market, the amount of typical buyer knowledge, the organizational status of purchasing influences, the financial strength of the firm, and the attitude of sales management.

Continuous sales training involves refreshing, improving, and updating the selling skills and marketing knowledge of experienced personnel. Continuous training also helps to remotivate experienced sales personnel. The changes taking place in any market necessitate the retraining of experienced sales representatives so that all will have the latest sales techniques, and product as well as market knowledge at their command. Ford's Marketing Institute recognizes the need to keep employees abreast of the times:

> The rapid explosion of change everyday is testing the ability of people to keep up.
>
> Technology is virtually doubling our available knowledge every few years. Industrial retraining experts project that individuals will soon have to be completely retrained every five years as known techniques, equipment, and procedures become obsolete.
>
> Accompanying this rapidly accelerating rate of growth and new con-

"Honestly, Mildrip, do I look like the sort of fella that intimidates people?"

Reprinted by permission The Wall Street Journal.

Some sales managers adopt an autocratic management style in their training efforts.

ditioning is an unprecedented demand for more education. People have recognized the need for maintaining a knowledge level commensurate with the effect of change on their lives.[3]

BENEFITS OF A SALES TRAINING PROGRAM

Several major benefits can be gained by a company that adopts a good sales training program. The primary benefit is that sales productivity is improved through better seller-buyer relationships. Liberty Mutual Insurance reported significant improvements in sales performance when it adopted "Professional Selling Skills," a short training course developed by the Educational Division of Xerox Corporation. Controlled experiments at Liberty Mutual showed a 6.2 percent average increase in premium sales by groups that took the course over groups that did not.[4] Training also improves retail sales performance. When the Maytag Company conducted a special four-week program to train retail appliance salespersons for appliance dealers, enthusiastic reports were made by the dealers about 19 of the 23 participants.[5]

Another advantage of sales training is that it can reduce the turnover rate. A well-trained salesperson is better able to cope with the demands of the job and less likely to seek other employment. Because sales training builds morale among the field force, it helps to establish a positive attitude, which also helps reduce turnover.

Sales training also improves the efficiency of sales management and reduces the cost of supervision. A well-trained salesperson is self-motivated and requires less direction, control, and supervision from sales management.

Figure 14–1 illustrates how Phillips Petroleum explains the benefits of sales training to the new marketing hirees.

COSTS OF SALES TRAINING

The typical company spends thousands of dollars on developing a field sales representative. Just consider Squibb's expenditures to train its sales personnel to launch a single product: tape recorder, audio cassettes, printed materials, and the most precious item of all— the time of the sales force and sales management. Clearly, the costs of sales training must be considered in evaluating the potential benefits of such efforts.

The costs of initial and continuous sales training are really different in nature. Initial sales training involves considerable out-of-pocket costs, whereas the primary costs of continuous training are

Welcome to Phillips Petroleum Company. You have been selected as a candidate for our marketing team because someone believes you have above average potential in the area of salesmanship.

During the next few months, the Division/District Director of Training will be your supervisor as you progress through the initial training program with our company. It is his responsibility to guide your training by utilizing all facilities at his disposal. He will expose you to a variety of work assignments and call on various instructors to assist him in giving you the highest quality education available. In turn, it will be your responsibility to study and learn as much as possible in this short period of time. How fast you progress in the future will be affected by your individual desire and effort during these early months.

Your goals are our goals and we stand ready to assist you in reaching them. So again, welcome to Phillips Petroleum Company and to a long, mutually profitable future.

Marketing Department
Phillips Petroleum Company

Figure 14–1
Phillips Petroleum Company statement of purpose of sales training program for new company representatives

indirect ones such as the time sales managers devote to training salespeople under their supervision.[6]

Sales training is costly when considered as an expense item, but in relation to its results most firms consider it to be an extremely profitable expenditure of company funds. The key factor is developing the most efficient sales training program possible given company resources and personnel.

INITIAL TRAINING PROGRAMS

Length

The objective of initial training is to prepare the individual for a particular sales job. The amount of time it takes to do this will, of course, vary from company to company and from sales job to sales job. Typically training inexperienced sales recruits will take about three months.[7] For about two out of every three industrial companies, sales training will not last longer than six months (Table 14–1). The percentages are slightly higher for consumer products and services companies. The length of the sales training program should never be regarded as fixed, but rather it should always be under review in order to guarantee that enough time is available to cover current technology in the field of selling.[8]

Table 14–1
Length of training period for new sales personnel

	Type of company		
Time period	Industrial products	Consumer products	Services
0–6 weeks	27%	29%	60%
6 weeks to 3 months	27	14	5
Over 3 months to 6 months	13	29	10
Over 6 months to 12 months	33	28	10
Over 12 months	—	—	15
Total	100%	100%	100%
Median training period in weeks	12	15	6

Source: Adapted and reprinted by permission from *Sales & Marketing Management.* © 1977.

Content

Usually four subject areas are covered in initial training programs—product knowledge, selling techniques, market/industry orientation, and company orientation. From Table 14–2, it is obvious that product knowledge receives the most attention and company orientation receives the least.

Product knowledge. Regardless of the type of sales job, it is likely that sales trainees will spend a considerable amount of time in acquiring a knowledge of products and how they are used by customers.

Table 14–2
Distribution of
training time for
newly hired sales
personnel

	Percentage devoted to				
Values	Company orientation	Market/ industry orientation	Selling techniques	Product knowledge	Other
Mean value	13%	17%	24%	42%	4%
First quartile value	5	10	15	30	—
Median value	10	15	20	40	—
Third quartile value	20	20	30	60	—

Base: 152 sales units reporting.

Source: David S. Hopkins, *Training the Sales Force: A Progress Report,* Research Report—Division of Management Research (New York: The Conference Board, 1978), p. 6.

For many companies, the starting point is finding out how the product is made. Steel manufacturers might require trainees to spend up to a year in job rotation from one mill operation to another. Wholesalers or distributors often have the sales trainee work in their warehouses filling orders and learning the inventory before venturing into the field.

Factory experience may be supplemented by field observation of products at customer installations and/or placement of the trainee in other areas of the marketing channel. A manufacturer of earth-moving equipment, for example, makes it a practice to assign sales trainees to its largest distributor for three to four months.

The importance of acquiring product knowledge should be impressed upon sales trainees. A mastery of the product line is a prerequisite to a good sales presentation; without it, the salesperson soon loses control of the sales interview and the possibility of a closing is reduced.

Selling techniques. The emphasis here is on the selling process and various selling tactics. In some companies this may involve a series of rules or "how-to-sell" techniques such as are found with formula selling and canned presentations.

Other companies prefer training in sales techniques that encourage a sales trainee to think and react to different selling circumstances in his or her own way. The flexible approach is generally favored today for most professional sales jobs.

Another aspect of selling is self-management. This is very important in training field sales personnel because it provides information on how and where to apply the sales techniques that are learned as well as how to manage one's selling efforts. Field salespeople are usually regarded by their employers as territory managers, which means they have responsibility for a given group of accounts. *Self-management* refers to the way in which a salesperson covers a territory and serves a group of customers.

Market/industry orientation. The market/industry orientation portion of the training program deals with information about prospects, customers, and competition. A salesperson's knowledge must extend beyond the narrow confines of his or her own company. An effective salesperson knows who needs the product, why it is needed, and how the various purchasing decisions are made. But he or she must also know about the products and competitive strategies of the competition. Training programs should familiarize the salesperson with the ways in which other firms market their products, as well as the advantages and disadvantages of competitive products.

Company orientation. Most training programs start with an orientation to the company and its particular industry. Historical evolution, internal organization, basic product lines, corporate policies, and operating procedures are usually covered in this segment of the program. A good company orientation contributes to job preparation because it gives the salesperson confidence to deal with prospects and customers as a representative of the company and an informed participant in the industry.

TRAINING TECHNIQUES

The number and variety of training techniques are immense. But the key is to use the most appropriate training techniques for the particular material scheduled for presentation. Some aspects such as sales techniques are best taught through participative methods. Other material, such as company and market information, is best presented through techniques in which the trainee is not actively involved and thus can concentrate on absorbing the data being presented.

Some of the more widely used techniques in initial sales training programs are (1) lecture, (2) audiovisual aids, (3) role playing, (4) self-study, (5) on-the-job training, and (6) job rotation.[9]

Lecture

Lectures are an effective way to present information such as company history, corporate policy, and credit procedures to a large audience. The lecture method is ideally used in the company and market orientation sections of the sales training program. Advantages include a relatively small cash outlay and speed in presenting the material. Disadvantages include the following.

1. The method is poorly suited to teaching selling techniques or presenting certain types of product knowledge.
2. Trainees' retention rates for lectures may be somewhat lower than those for other training techniques.

Audiovisual aids

The aids used in sales training range from simple classroom blackboards to closed-circuit television presentations. While they are often expensive and sometimes require preparation by outside firms, visual aids have the advantage of expanding the dimensions of sales training, and thereby increasing interest and attention levels. In fact, the increased use of colored slides and transparencies in sales training and elsewhere has led to Xerox and General Electric's development of computer-based systems capable of producing these items quickly and efficiently.[10]

Visual aids can be used in all segments of the training program. Dow Chemical U.S.A. uses videotape playback and role playing as well as taped situations and response mechanisms to teach correct selling techniques. Other firms use audiovisual tapes of sample presentations by veteran salespeople. These tapes typically contain several costly mistakes that the sales trainees are asked to identify and discuss.[11] Chesebrough–Ponds used a film featuring some of its sales force to teach other personnel how to sell Rave hair spray.[12]

Role playing

An effective method of teaching the firm's selling techniques is role playing, in which a sales situation is set up and the trainees assume the roles of salesperson, prospect, and others involved in the case. Initially a trainee may feel uncomfortable in role playing, but eventually most are impressed with the realism possible through the use of this technique.

Role playing is an excellent way of involving trainees in the training program. It is a participative technique that usually generates considerable interest and enthusiasm.

Some role-playing situations are simple buyer-seller interactions. Others are more elaborate and may even introduce environmental considerations into the situation. American Parts, a manufacturer and distributor of automotive parts, has developed a training program for its jobber's sales personnel that simulates the environment of a modern service station, the setting in which these sales representatives most often operate. In the American Parts simulation,

A large screen simulating a typical busy service station projects the common sights and distractions that seep into today's service station while a recording of actual noises blares out added interruptions.

During this time a trainee is attempting to make his sales pitch to the dealer (played by the sales training manager).

The interruptions are familiar: an attendant yelling at the dealer, driveway bells ringing, a kid wanting change, a man asking directions, and another salesman also vying for attention.

After this realistic environment is simulated, the trainees see the futility of the situation. Using the unique teletrainer, the sales training manager demonstrates how much better it is to phone the dealer and make an appointment that will afford some privacy in the dealer's office, his station, or over a cup of coffee in a restaurant.

Each student gets a chance to use the teletrainer, which records the conversation, and to critique his conversation along with the class and the sales training manager.[13]

Self-study

Self-study programs are usually designed to supplement or reinforce other instructional techniques. Self-study is particularly useful in improving or updating the salesperson's product knowledge. The Corgard Core Sales Development Program described earlier is an excellent example.

This technique can use correspondence courses, programmed instruction, or audio teaching systems. While the exact approach varies, one study found that about 45 percent of the firms responding used some form of self-study to supplement their sales training.[14]

Programmed instruction is the self-study technique that has received the most attention in recent years.[15] Users of programmed sales training materials include Schering Corporation; Spiegel, Inc.; Eastman Kodak; AT&T; Prudential Insurance Company; Mead Johnson; Humble Oil Company; Shell Oil Company; and Warner Brake and Clutch Company.[16]

In programmed instruction the material is divided into short sections of discussion and review items. This approach is an effective way of reviewing previously presented material or dealing with complex product knowledge problems. For example, it might be used in the pharmaceutical industry to teach detailers (with no pharmacy background) the necessary terminology and names of drugs. Similarly it could be used in any technical industry in which sales typically depend on extensive product knowledge. A disadvantage of programmed instruction is that it must usually be prepared by an educational specialist and this can be costly.

An on-the-job training experience is included in nearly every initial sales training program. In many cases it is the final step in the initial training program. Dow Chemical, however, puts on-the-job experience in the middle of its training program, and other firms base almost their entire program on this type of training.

On-the-job training

All on-the-job training has the following results:

1. It provides a transition from what is to how to do it under actual conditions.
2. It introduces the trainee to his or her field assignment.
3. It provides a degree of trade-off in actual sales production during the course of the training.[17]

Successful implementation of on-the-job training depends on the skill and qualifications of the person responsible for supervising the trainee. A successful salesperson may make a good training supervisor, but this is not always the case. Some salespeople are reluctant to supervise or coach trainees because they believe their own sales will suffer, and others may have developed shortcuts that are not advisable for entry-level salespeople. The selection of supervisors for on-the-job training is an important sales management decision that should not be slighted.

Job rotation

Initial training may have the trainee spending fixed amounts of time in various departments of the company and/or with different types of customers. There are two major advantages of job rotation. One is that the sales trainee gains a greater appreciation of the contributions of other departments to his or her effectiveness in the field. Another is that the trainee can see how the sales job is viewed by others. A disadvantage is that not all of the learning is directly related to professional selling and is therefore of less immediate value to the company.

CONTINUOUS SALES TRAINING PROGRAMS[18]

Continuous sales training can be differentiated from initial sales training on operational as well as conceptual grounds. In addition to the types of trainees involved, there are differences in objectives, program content, and training methods. There may also be a difference in the attitudes of trainees. While experienced sales personnel can grasp sales training material more easily, they are sometimes resentful of intrusions into their selling time and possible criticisms of the sales approaches they may be currently using.

The attitude of experienced sales personnel suggests some basic guidelines for structuring continuous training programs:

1. The immediate and personal value of the subject covered in a training session must be made apparent to the sales personnel in attendance. Actual case histories and pilot test results are helpful in demonstrating practical significance.
2. The concept of continuous training as synonymous with professional development must pervade every training experience of a salesperson.
3. The concept of continuous training must be visualized as guidance and motivation of sustained personal growth by trainee and trainer alike.[19]

Objectives

Continuous sales training has three primary objectives: (1) to provide refresher training, (2) to update marketing knowledge, and (3) to remotivate salespeople.

Refresher training deals with practical problems such as classifying prospects, handling objections, and closing. Mattel isolated 12 problem sales situations and then convinced four actual Mattel customers to conduct mock sales interviews with a group of Mattel district managers who impersonated salespeople.[20] These interactions were videotaped and presented at a sales meeting. The mock interviews are designed to have maximum training impact. For instance, one segment ended with the buyer saying:

> Charlie, you get a guy like me in here, you beat him to death with the presentation; you get through with the presentation and you want to write. You know damned well there are other lines I still want to look at.

Continuous training also provides an *updating of marketing knowledge*. In too many cases, this aspect of continuous training involves only information about the introduction of new products or selling strategies. This type of training is critical to the salesperson's success, but marketing knowledge also needs to be updated. New selling strategies and techniques are an example. Eastman Kodak Company sends its technical sales representatives through a three-day program entitled "Selling by Objectives." And the Bank of America required more than 4,000 of its personnel to go through counselor selling training sessions to learn how to market customer services.[21]

Another important objective of continuous training is to *remotivate* experienced sales personnel. Salespeople operating for the most part on their own must continually be motivated to accomplish company objectives. The two most popular themes in seller remotivation are the importance of selling to the company and society and the firm's concern for the salesperson as an individual. There are good reasons for stressing these particular themes. Salespeople have at best only arm's-length supervision and therefore must provide almost all of their own motivation. Social criticism and the competitive buffeting of the marketplace may cause sales personnel to doubt the role they play within the company and in society as a whole. The sales representative is also often physically separated from the rest of the firm and seeks a way to relate to the parent organization. Remotivation is an important factor in keeping the sales organization healthy.

Program content

The content of continuous sales training programs is essentially the same as that for initial programs. The differences are in greater attention to time management and in the emphasis and level of sophistication. While historical information about the company might be appropriate in an initial sales training program, it would probably fall on deaf ears if presented to an audience of veteran salespeople.

Variations in program content can be related to the sales task model presented in Chapter 2. If service skills are considered more important than creative skills, continuous training tends to emphasize the subjects of selling skills and time management. If creative selling skills are rated more important, the training usually stresses product and market knowledge. In any case, program emphasis and sophistication should be based upon an assessment of the skills and knowledge currently possessed by the sales force.

Training methods

Sales managers can be expected to have a larger role in continuous training. Many continuous training programs can be classified as on-the-job training, and many companies ask experienced sales personnel to assist in this task. A temporary or part-time training assignment is often considered desirable for salespeople on a management career path.

There are four principal methods of providing continuous sales training: (1) joint sales calls, (2) sales meetings, (3) sales seminars, and (4) self-instruction.

Ongoing training programs usually involve a *joint sales call* by the salesperson and a supervisor or critic, after which the latter evaluates the salesperson's performance and offers suggestions on improvement. It is the most common application of on-the-job training for experienced sales personnel.

Sales meetings are a form of group training. Most firms conduct at least an annual sales meeting. Table 14–3 shows the frequency of sales meeting attendance by experienced sales personnel.

**Table 14–3
Frequency of sales
meeting attendance
by experienced sales
personnel**

Number of meetings per year	Sales units	
	Number	Percent
Fewer than 1*	4	3%
1	24	16
2 to 4	72	47
5 to 12	39	26
More than 12	13	8
Total sales units reporting	152	100%

*Such meetings scheduled on average less often than once a year.
Source: David S. Hopkins, *Training the Sales Force: A Progress Report*, Research Report Division of Management Research (New York: The Conference Board, 1978), p. 16.

One of the basic reasons for the common use of sales meetings as a continuous training technique is their wide support from sales managers. Three quarters of the marketing executives questioned in a Dartnell survey thought that the meetings they attended were worth the expense and effort.[22]

Sales meetings have the advantages of being an economical method of presenting training information and providing opportunities for association of sales management and other sales personnel. To some extent these advantages are offset by the costs of transportation and housing and the opportunity lost by pulling the sales organization out of the field. The impact of these disadvantages is somewhat reduced by scheduling sales meetings during slack sales periods.

Sales seminars or workshops usually revolve around a discussion of critical selling problems in the field. Seminars are relatively unstructured compared to sales meetings. The primary purpose of seminars or workshops is to provide veteran sales personnel with a forum for sharing mutual problems and sales experiences. Seminars and workshops should be relatively narrow in scope to provide participants with intensive training in specific aspects of selling.

Self-instruction is another method of continuous sales training. Programmed learning was described above as a self-study technique in which the material is divided into small segments of information and a self-checking device such as review questions. Cassette units are often used as a self-study mechanism in such areas as new product information. While self-instruction as used in sales training programs sometimes lacks motivation and professional guidance, it is a relatively inexpensive way of providing continuous training in field locations.

SUMMARY

The use of formalized sales training programs is widespread in American industry. These programs can be classified as either initial or continuous. The initial sales training program deals with the preparation and orientation of new sales personnel, with emphasis on the formation of proper selling habits. Continuous sales training involves refreshing, improving, and updating the selling skills of experienced sales personnel to assure that all have the latest sales techniques and product knowledge at their command.

A good sales training program benefits a company by (1) improving sales productivity, (2) reducing turnover, (3) building morale, and (4) improving the efficiency of sales management and reducing the cost of supervision. Sales training can be extremely expensive, often costing thousands of dollars for each trainee.

The format of an initial sales training program can be divided into three issues: (1) program length, (2) internal organization, and (3) educational content. The training period for inexperienced sales personnel is usually divided among four different aspects: (1) product knowledge, (2) selling techniques, (3) market orientation, and (4) company orientation. The actual educational content of these four segments varies according to the company and the type of sales job.

Widely used training techniques include. (1) lecture, (2) visual aids, (3) role playing, (4) self-study, (5) on-the-job training, and (6) job rotation.

Continuous sales training programs differ from initial sales training operationally as well as conceptually. The objectives of continuous sales training are: (1) to provide refresher training, (2) to update marketing knowledge, and (3) to remotivate salespeople. Continuous training makes use of the following techniques: (1) joint sales calls, (2) sales meetings, (3) sales seminars, and (4) self-instruction.

REVIEW QUESTIONS/DISCUSSION
QUESTIONS/EXERCISES

1. Briefly identify the following:
   a. Initial sales training.
   b. Continuous sales training.
   c. Self-management.
   d. Role playing.
   e. .Programmed instruction.
   f. Job rotation.
   g. Refresher training.

2. Outline the benefits and costs associated with initial sales training. What would you conclude from this analysis?

3. Explain why sales training programs may differ in length between two companies.

4. All salespeople need retraining. Comment on this statement.

5. Effective training programs may reduce the turnover of sales personnel. Comment on this statement.

6. Describe the internal organization of an initial sales training program.

7. Contact the sales training executive at a firm in your locality and ask to be allowed to observe a day's activity in the training program. Then prepare a two- to three-page paper on what you observed.

8. Contact some salespeople you know. Ask them to describe the sales training efforts in their companies. Report what you have learned to the class.

9. The class is divided into three or more groups and each is asked to prepare a training session. The session can involve company orientation, market orientation, sales techniques, or product knowledge. Each group presents its session, using the remaining groups as trainees. When each session is concluded, the "trainees" should constructively criticize their "trainers."

10. What is meant by *self-management?*

11. Invite a local sales training executive to speak to your class on the subject, What a Beginning Salesperson Can Expect in the Training Program.

12. The emphasis in initial training is on forming proper selling habits so that the salesperson can assume a field position as soon as possible. Comment on this statement.

13. Contact a recent graduate of your college who has entered a sales career and ask him or her to describe the sales training received.

14. Discuss the following statement: Continuous sales training programs are different from initial sales training on operational as well as conceptual grounds.

15. List and identify each of the six sales training techniques discussed in this chapter.

16. Which training techniques are most effective for presenting:
    a. Company orientation.
    b. Market orientation.
    c. Sales techniques.
    d. Product knowledge.

17. Cite examples where sales training would be helpful to organizations involved in activities other than business. What type of sales training would be appropriate in each of the cases?

18. Sales training is a useless expenditure of company funds, since you can-

not teach someone to sell. People are either born with this ability, or they are not. Comment on these statements.

19. Given the high cost of visual aids, all companies should carefully consider their use. Comment on this statement.

20. At your library review several sources of information on teaching techniques. Are any of these techniques (other than the ones noted here) applicable to sales training?

CASE 14–1: PORTLAND MUTUAL INSURANCE COMPANY

Oregon-based Portland Mutual Insurance Company offers a variety of insurance coverages and financial packages. A sales force of 88 representatives are spread across the United States. These representatives report through a comprehensive field sales management organization headed by district and zone sales directors.

Portland Mutual is judged to have one of the best initial sales training plans available in the insurance industry. Beginning sales personnel are trained for a full year in a series of classroom, on-the-job, and office assignments. Management has always been justly proud of the quality standards maintained in its initial sales training program.

Robert C. Bowman, Portland's president, is discussing the training function with the company's newly appointed national sales manager, Ann McNeil.

Bowman: We have always been proud of our training of new sales representatives but, you know, there is one aspect we have consistently neglected.

McNeil: What is that, Bob?

Bowman: Continuous training for our experienced sales personnel! What do we do for these people? I'll tell you . . . very, very little! The district sales managers work with them about two weeks each year to identify trouble spots, and we hold a national sales meeting each July. I have always thought that insufficient product knowledge is one of our company's problems. Most of these people came on board long before we offered Keogh Plans, mutual funds, tax deferred annuities and the like. Most of them were trained to sell life insurance—period! I just don't think spending a couple of hours at the national sales meeting is enough to cover the complicated new financial packages we are offering. Also, very little is done to introduce new selling techniques or market information.

McNeil: Yes, I agree that we don't do much to help the professional development of our experienced sales people. Let me start working on next year's sales meeting; maybe I will be able to come up with an improved format to meet our continuous sales training needs.

Bowman: Good idea. . . . .Why don't you get back to me on this in two weeks.

Questions

1. Identify the various deficiencies in the continuous training plan of Portland Mutual Insurance Company.
2. Can a continuous training program be based on an annual sales meeting and an occasional visit by the district sales manager? Explain.
3. What format would you use for the next Portland Mutual sales meeting? Prepare a brief outline for McNeil's report on this subject.

CASE 14–2: LEVIN'S FASHIONS

Levin's Fashions is a chain of 20 stores specializing in medium-priced women's wear. Levin's has seven stores in Washington, six in Oregon, five in northern California, and two in Idaho. The chain was founded by Harold Levin, who opened the first store in downtown Seattle in 1938. Since that time the firm's management has been family-dominated, with the exception of some long-time employees in operational areas such as credit and accounting. Olin Levin is currently president of the firm.

One of Olin Levin's first actions since taking over for his father last August was to hire four young graduates for management trainee positions. Levin believes that the firm's rapid expansion necessitates the acquisition of additional managerial talent to build for the future. Marilyn Adams and Thomas Manshek are two of these management trainees. After an initial orientation to the chain's history, policies, procedures, and market position, the trainees are being rotated through a series of staff assignments to familiarize them with the firm's operations and problems.

Adams and Manshek have been assigned to review the firm's training program for retail sales personnel. The outline for this program is shown in Exhibit 1.

Except for welcoming comments and a 45-minute session on store history and policies, all of the formalized training is handled by Porter Slade, the personnel director. Slade is a long-time employee who had spent 20 years as the chain's general office manager before being named personnel director two years ago. He is considered totally devoted to the firm and is an above-average public speaker.

Exhibit 1
**Retail sales training
at Levin's Fashions**

	8:30–8:45	Welcome	Store manager
	8:45–9:30	Store history and policies	Store manager
Day 1	9:30–10:15	Market, competition, products	Personnel director
	10:15–10:30	Coffee break	
	10:30–12:00	Charge accounts, layaways, cash control procedure, markdowns, and markups	Personnel director
	12:00–1:00	Lunch	
	1:00–3:00	Explanation of the product lines and work of the various departments	Personnel director
	3:00–3:15	Coffee break	
	3:15–5:00	How to sell	Personnel director
Days 2–5	The trainee is assigned to a position on the floor and is under the direction of an experienced salesperson who provides on-the-job counseling.		

Questions

1. Do you see any possible trouble spots in the sales training at Levin's?
2. Do you believe Slade should handle the bulk of the formalized training?
3. What suggestions could you offer to improve the format of the training program?

A Profile of Professional Selling

Alexander Brodie

Due to the recession, many tire dealers have reported falling sales. But not Alexander Brodie. His dealerships, one in Honolulu and another in Waipahu do $5 million worth of business annually. He sells 70,000 new tires a year, accounting for about 14 percent of the local market.

When a customer buys a tire from one of his dealerships, his or her name is entered into a computer along with such information as make and model of car and customer driving habits. Customers receive a postcard every year as a reminder that it is time for a free tire checkup. Drivers who have experienced problems with their tires or drive a lot will receive phone calls.

It is estimated that more than one out of every three customers take advantage of the free checkups, contributing to Brodie's base of 80 percent repeat business. Free wheel-alignment checks are used to attract owners of new cars. New business is solicited by television commercials starring Alexander Brodie. About one half of the commercials are concerned with proper tire maintenance.

The Brodie sales approach also features the dangers of poor tire maintenance. New customers are given a cup of coffee and ushered into a waiting area decorated with battered tires, a warning about the dangers of poor tire maintenance. If the individual is a repeat customer, the salesperson will have his or her file in hand in minutes.

To motivate his sales force Brodie has installed two profit-sharing plans, one with monthly cash payouts and the other deferred. There is also a "service" commission that is separate from the normal sales commission. A record is kept of each salesperson's contact with a prospective customer. At the end of each month, salespeople divide up a pool equal to 0.5 percent of the gross sales for the month in proportion to the number of contacts.

Used by permission from William R. Wood, "Hawaiian Firm Salesman Profits from Fervor for Record Keeping," *The Wall Street Journal*, August 25, 1980, p. 13.

Part

7

ADDITIONAL DIMENSIONS OF SELLING

We pride ourselves in knowing our markets and our customers.

KENNETH H. OLSEN
President, Digital Equipment Co.

KEY POINTS

- Retail selling and service selling are unique and important types of selling.
- Retail selling is different from other sales situations in that customers who already have some idea of what they want come to the salesperson.
- Two major problems faced by retail salespeople are their inability to select customers and the need to maintain their stores' image.
- The primary attributes of a successful retail salesperson are pride, knowledge, and a service orientation.
- The retail process is composed of the following steps: (1) approaching the customer, (2) determining needs and wants, (3) presenting merchandise, (4) meeting objections, (5) closing the sale, and (6) suggestion selling.
- Service selling is primarily the function of salespeople handling retail, wholesale, or industrial accounts, and of detail personnel.
- Service selling responsibilities differ considerably, depending on the type of customers serviced.
- The most important aspects of successful service selling are an enlightened attitude toward service and extensive knowledge.

Chapter

15

RETAIL SELLING AND SERVICE SELLING

Retail and service selling are two unique, important types of selling. In spite of their uniqueness from other types of selling, they both require similar selling skills. To be successful in either field the salesperson must have a customer service attitude and extensive product knowledge.

William Stephenson of the Uniroyal Chemical Company was chosen one of 1980's top 10 salesmen by *Purchasing* magazine. Stephenson combines good ideas with a willingness to help the customer implement the ideas in the customer's operations. The buyer who nominated Stephenson for the award says of him, "We get first-class reps up here in general and he's still head and shoulders above the rest." The buyer also says that if tests are necessary to prove out one of Stephenson's ideas, Stephenson will sit in on the tests in the customer's lab—and he might even bring in chemists from his own firm to help out if necessary.[1]

RETAIL SELLING

Retail selling is the sale of goods and services to consumers for their own or other's personal use. Most retail selling is done in establishments such as department stores, drug stores, automobile and truck dealerships, discount stores, boutiques, and restaurants. Some retail selling, however, is done outside retail establishments. Examples of this kind are selling life insurance in a prospect's home, door-to-door selling, and telephone selling.

Only *in-store retail selling* will be discussed in this chapter. The sales process in which a retail salesperson goes to the customer was discussed earlier. When the customer comes to a store, the seller's task is considerably different, requiring changes in the sales approach. Before discussing in-store retail selling, however, it is helpful to consider the importance of the retail selling function.

The role of retail selling

Retail selling is treated as a separate topic in this book because it occupies a unique and vital position in our economy. The importance of retail selling is apparent in light of its role in the overall economic structure and its financial importance in our free-enterprise system.

Peter Drucker has described marketing as "the process through which the economy is integrated into society to serve human needs."[2] The marketing system in a free-enterprise economy such as ours distributes the output of production to the consumer. Without an efficient marketing system, the goods that are produced might never reach the consumer or might be too expensive for the consumer to buy.

The country's *standard of living* refers to the quantity and quality of goods and services that average consumers can purchase with their financial resources. The standard of living of each family or household rises with an increase in income or a decrease in the cost of the items consumed. An efficient marketing system can increase the standard of living by minimizing the costs of distributing goods and making them readily available to consumers.

Retailing is crucial to the marketing function because it is the final step in the marketing process and has a direct effect on the level of the standard of living in a society. It has been said, "In a product's long journey from the producer to the customer, the last two feet are the most important." That "last two feet" is the distance across the sales counter.

The importance of retail selling can also be shown by its magnitude in dollars. Table 15–1 is a summary of retail sales data from 1972 to 1979. During this time retail sales increased 101 percent and always amounted to more than 50 percent of disposable personal income. Per capita retail sales increased more than 90 percent, while retail sales per retail employee, many of whom are salespersons, increased 52 percent to nearly $59,000.

Year	Retail sales ($ millions)	Retail sales per Employee	Capita	Retail sales as percentage of disposable personal income
1972	$440,222	$38,752	$2,108	54.9%
1973	503,317	44,283	2,392	55.7
1974	537,782	46,602	2,538	54.6
1975	584,423	45,572	2,736	53.9
1976	651,884	48,536	3,030	55.5
1977	724,020	52,484	3,339	55.6
1978	800,890	54,957	3,662	54.9
1979	886,047	58,811	4,017	54.5

**Table 15–1
Retail sales in the United States, 1972 1979**

Source: *Survey of Current Business* (Washington, D.C.: U.S. Department of Commerce, Bureau of Economic Analysis, appropriate issues).

The retail salesperson's job

Generalizations about the duties and responsibilities of retail salespeople are difficult to make. Salespeople have different responsibilities because they sell widely different products and services. Figure 15–1, a job description for a retail motor truck salesperson for the International Harvester Company, stipulates the following duties, among others: (1) selling trucks, (2) appraising used or repossessed equipment, (3) promoting the sale of service and parts, (4) assisting customers in their analysis of truck operating costs, and (5) recommending ways to lower these costs. Compare these responsibilities with those of a salesclerk in a large department store. Besides selling merchandise, salesclerks are expected to (1) maintain the appearance of their departments, (2) assist customers with complaints or returns, (3) prevent thefts, (4) wrap merchandise, (5) help customers locate particular items, even if they are in other departments, (6) provide customers with the service required, and (7) maintain records for billing and inventory replenishment purposes. In spite of the differences in the duties of retail salespeople, two things are expected of all—they must sell and keep the customer coming back. Their other activities help them do this job more effectively.

Certain characteristics are common to all in-store retail selling, making this type of selling distinct from all others. The most distinctive feature is that customers come to the store, instead of salespeople

**Figure 15–1
Description of a
salaried position in
the sales organization
of the International
Harvester Company**

INTERNATIONAL HARVESTER COMPANY
SALES ORGANIZATION
Salaried Position Description

RETAIL SALES REPRESENTATIVE (SALARY & INCENTIVE)
RETAIL MOTOR TRUCK SALESMAN (SALARY ONLY)

Typical Duties:
   Sell motor trucks, auxiliary equipment, parts, service and accessories in a specified section comprising a portion of the retail territory and/or among persons or firms on a definitely assigned list of accounts. Contact prospective new and used truck customers, recommending the type, size and model of truck best suited to their requirements, making demonstrations, quoting prices, terms, specifications and related data, making sales for cash or credit subject to required approval and preparing various forms and documents required in the sale. Assist customers and prospective buyers in analyzing truck operating costs, recommending means of improving costs and efficiency. Appraise or assist in the appraisal of used or repossessed equipment. Promote and stimulate the sale of service and parts and the use of Company operated service facilities, developing new sales prospects and making regular follow-up contacts with all potential customers. Prepare and furnish records and reports required in the maintenance of prospect system. Keep thoroughly informed of all important developments in the local truck market and in the application of sales and service features of trucks, parts, accessories and allied equipment. Perform related work as assigned.

Source: International Harvester Company, Chicago, Ill.

seeking them out. Because of this, in-store retail salespeople are not bothered with prospecting, and preapproach. Customers who enter a retail store have some idea of what they desire and are further along in the buying process. The retail salesperson merely helps customers complete the buying process, which began before they ever entered the store. Other sales personnel have to start the buying process by showing customers they have unsatisfied needs which the product or service offered can help satisfy.

The retail salesperson faces two major disadvantages. First, he or she is unable to select customers, because the customer does the selecting. The salesperson therefore must sell to a large variety of customers, which is more difficult than selling to customers with similar problems and buying habits. In selling to customers who are alike, the salesperson's experience accumulates as sales situations occur over and over, and much can be learned from previous successes and failures. This also happens with a large variety of customers, but the learning process takes much longer and is more difficult.

Second, when customers select the store and the salesperson, the burden of attracting customers falls on the store's advertising, displays, physical characteristics, and, most importantly, its salespeople. Research has shown that a retail store's image is primarily determined by the personality of its salesclerks. In a sense, "the personality of the employees becomes the personality of the store."[3] The resulting image affects the likelihood that a customer will shop in the store.[4]

Pierre Martineau once described the position of the salesperson in retailing as follows:

> It is ironical that at the very time when a better educated and discriminating shopper expects more from the store and the clerk, management is dragging its feet in upgrading salespeople. The stores are more beautiful and interesting; they have buyers ranging far and wide to offer the broadest merchandising selection. But what about the salespeople?[5]

Requirements for the retail salesperson

Unfortunately, the situation has changed little. Too many retail salespeople consider themselves clerks or order takers, instead of selling professionals capable of affecting the buying decisions of their customers.

Two qualities of a salesclerk that seem to influence a customer are attractiveness and credibility.[6] The difference, then, between an order taker and a sales initiator is that the latter is appealing and informative whereas the former will usually lack these qualities. For example, shoe sales personnel that are well-dressed (with special attention to their own footwear) and have good merchandise knowledge will likely be more effective than sales personnel who lack these qualities. It is also important for the salesclerk to establish identity and rapport with consumers.[7] At this point, the woman or man interested in becoming an effective retail salesperson might well ask, "What personal qualities and skills do I need to develop to become a more effective salesperson?" The sections below suggest answers to this question.

Pride.   The primary requirement for professional retail selling is belief in oneself, in the merchandise, and in the store. Without this pride, the sales presentation is unconvincing, transparent, and uninspiring; with it, the sales presentation is dynamic, convincing, and informative.

Knowledge.   The second basic requirement is knowledge of the store, the merchandise, and, most importantly, the customer. An effective retail salesperson must know a great deal about the store to be able to serve customers properly. He or she must be well acquainted with such information as:

1. How refunds, exchanges, and sales adjustments are handled.
2. Where other departments are located and what merchandise each carries.
3. Procedures for credit sales, delivery, installation, and other special customer services.
4. What advertisements the store is currently running and whether there are any special promotions in the department.
5. When the store is normally open and what the hours are during special seasons.
6. Whether any future special promotions are planned and when they will be held.

Customers also expect salespeople to have extensive knowledge about the merchandise they sell. Customers often ask retailers questions about the merchandise. A clothing salesperson, for example, may be asked if a garment is washable, guaranteed not to shrink or fade, or appropriate for formal occasions; some customers even ask salespeople for their opinions and preferences. Other customers might want to know how the store's merchandise compares with that of the competition. If the sales representative is unable to answer such questions, sales will be lost.

The retail salesperson must also have enough knowledge about customers to be able to understand them. In retail sales as in other selling, the salesperson must be able to ascertain the customer's needs and how they can best be satisfied. The factors affecting the salesperson's ability to communicate effectively with customers must also be recognized. Unfortunately, because in-store retail salespeople face an endless variety of customers, they are limited in what they can learn about each customer. They must be good listeners, since they know nothing about the customers until they meet in the store and must learn as much as possible very quickly during the sales encounter. One way to learn is by observing customers' dress and mannerisms, but asking questions and listening attentively are most important. Customers tell a lot about themselves if the salesperson listens to what is said.

Service orientation. Any professional salesperson sincerely desires to serve customers. Salesmanship is not persuading people to buy things they do not want or need. Rather, professional selling is getting to know each customer, listening to and satisfying individual needs, and keeping the promises made.[8] Only by adopting this orientation can the salesperson expect to be successful in the competitive retailing arena.

Bait and switch: An unethical retail sales practice

Some retailers have used what is termed a "bait and switch" in their sales efforts. This unethical practice involves advertising low-priced items that build customer traffic ("the bait"). Once the potential buyer is in the store, retail sales personnel try to convince the person to buy a higher-priced model. Common "switches" include inadequate stock of the advertised item, comments on the inferior quality of the cheaper product, and attempts to make the purchase of the advertised item inconvenient to the consumer. "Bait and switch" selling is viewed as deceptive and unethical by most observers, and the Federal Trade Commission has taken action against it.

Source: See Joseph Barry Mason and Morris Lehman Mayer, *Modern Retailing: Theory and Practice*, rev. ed. (Plano, Tex.: Business Publications, Inc.,1981), p. 731.

The retail selling process

As with other forms of selling, the retail selling process can be divided into a series of steps. While such a division is helpful in describing the process, in practice the selling process is a smooth flow; some steps are not always required.

The basic steps in the retail selling process are: (1) approaching the customer, (2) finding out his or her needs and wants, (3) presenting the merchandise, (4) meeting objections, (5) closing the sale, and (6) selling by suggestion. It should be noted that the process for retail selling differs very little from the more general sales process described earlier.

Approaching customers.   Many retail sales are made or lost in the first few seconds after the customer arrives in the department. If the customer is treated warmly and the salesperson exhibits a helpful, courteous attitude, the process starts off well. But if the customer is neglected and treated indifferently or discourteously, then the sale is as good as lost. The salesperson should act as if the customer is a guest, to be attended to and pleased. The salesperson's personal appearance and the appearance of the department are important in the approach stage.

What the salesperson says in approaching and greeting customers can be a critical factor. A survey conducted in 100 retail clothing stores to determine what retail sales personnel say when greeting customers revealed that about nine out of 10 times the opening will be: "May I help you?" "Can I help you?" or something very similar (Table 15–2).[9] This is one of the most overworked and least effective approaches used today. Everyone knows the standard response to this: "No, thank you." Once the customer says this, the salesperson must either leave or risk offending the customer by staying around.

**Table 15–2
Opening remarks of 100 sales floor personnel in retail clothing stores**

Opening remark	Number of respondents
May I help you?	58
Can I help you?	19
What size do you wear?	5
May I be of assistance?	3
What can I do for you today?	2
What can I help you with today?	2
What can I show you today?	2
Can I help you, honey?	1
Can I show you something?	1
Have you seen our ad in today's paper?	1
Have you seen our sale merchandise?	1
I have something I want you to see	1
May I show you something?	1
What color did you have in mind?	1
What size were you looking for?	1
Would you like to try it on?	1

Source: William H. Bolen, "Customer Contact: Those First Important Words," *Department Store Management,* April 1970, pp. 25–26.

In either case, things have started out poorly. Some of the other approaches are much better.

Among the other phrases used were, "What size do you wear?" "What size were you looking for?" and "What color did you have in mind?" Note how all these are offers of assistance to which the customer cannot respond, "No, thank you." The retail salesperson who uses this approach is offering assistance without making the customer ask for it.

Two other approaches, "Have you seen our ad in today's paper?" and "Have you seen our sale merchandise?" are better still. Both show that the salesperson has the interests of the customer in mind and that he or she is willing and able to provide more information. It is hard to imagine a customer who would not appreciate this kind of assistance.

The best approach of all was the statement "I have something I want you to see." This makes the customer feel important. It conveys a desire to please and serve, an awareness of the customer as an individual, and a familiarity with the merchandise available. The worst thing a retail salesperson can do is to use a routine opening remark.

Determining customer needs and wants. To tailor the sales presentation to the customer's needs and wants, the salesperson must learn as much as possible about each customer. As noted above, this is one of the most difficult tasks for the retail salesperson, because of the variety of customers served. This does not make it any less important, however.

To learn the customer's needs and wants, the salesperson must be adept at observing customers. What kind of clothes is the customer wearing? What is the first thing the customer looked at or picked up? Are children along? Is the customer in a hurry or just browsing? Does the customer appear happy or sulky? Most of these questions can be answered by simply observing the customer's clothing, facial expression, and mannerisms.[10]

The retail salesperson can also ascertain the customer's needs by asking leading questions. What is the customer going to do with the merchandise? Do his or her tastes seem to be different from the salesperson's? Will the customer need the merchandise soon, or can she wait? Many questions can be answered only by asking the customer. Beginning salespeople often mistakenly assume things about their customers. If they see a woman with a little girl looking at a child's dress, they assume it is for the child, whereas it might be a gift. Or they assume that because they like green, the customer likes green also. If there is any doubt, the salesperson should ask the appropriate question.

To get to know the customer, the retail salesperson must learn to listen. The key to good listening is concentration on what the customer is really saying. This can be a help in understanding each customer's needs and wants.

Presenting merchandise. As in any kind of selling, product demonstration can be vital to a retail sales presentation. The merchandise should always be demonstrated if requested because it is immediately available and ready for presentation. Customers "experience" a product through merchandise demonstrations. They can taste a new flavored vitamin pill, see how a shirt looks on them, get the feel of a golf club, smell an expensive French perfume, or touch a satin bedsheet. In each case, the effect the use of merchandise has on the customer's senses is one of the primary reasons for purchasing the item.

From the salesperson's point of view, demonstration is vital because it puts the customer one step closer to purchase. It can convert a "looker" into a "tryer." Demonstration can also help the salesperson get the customer to trade up or to buy substitute merchandise when the merchandise sought is not carried by the store.

Customers *trade up* when they buy more expensive merchandise or more merchandise than they had intended to purchase. A demonstration shows customers the advantages of trading up by allowing them to see and experience the difference between the merchandise they intended to buy and more expensive merchandise. Reid R. Rogers, while director of training for Hudson Belk, a department store in Raleigh, North Carolina, told sales personnel: "Never show a customer the very top of the line or the very bottom of the line—if it can be avoided. This way there is flexibility for trading the customer up, or allowing the customer to trade down if the price is higher than the customer expected it to be."

Substitute selling is encouraging customers to purchase merchandise that is different from what they had requested. Usually this tactic is used because the store does not carry the requested merchandise. A retail salesperson also might suggest other merchandise such as another brand of the same item because the substitute merchandise is more suited to the customer's needs.

Both trading up and selling substitute merchandise can be dangerous selling techniques. The customer may become dissatisfied with the alternative merchandise and then blame the seller. These approaches should be used only if the salesperson honestly feels that the alternative merchandise will produce a more satisfied customer. If the salesperson does not feel this way, it is better to give the customers what they want, even if this means sending them someplace else to get it.

Avoiding and handling objections. Probably the most frightening aspect of retail selling to inexperienced salespersons is customer objections. There is a natural tendency for beginners to feel that customers raise objections because they do not want to buy the merchandise they are considering. This is not the case at all. Customers who do not want to buy, or who do not see what they want usually leave and do not stand around to discuss the matter. Customers who raise objections are still very interested in the merchandise, but they have doubts about the advisability of buying it. They may be concerned about its cost, some of its characteristics, or whether to buy now or sometime in the future. Occasionally a customer might object to the store itself. Normally this will relate to the store's reputation, a service policy such as delivery or installation, or the store's pricing policy.

Calming irate customers with "WHAT" questions

How do you calm down an irate customer?

That's the question Gimbels Bridgeport's Ken Andrews sought to answer. The technique he came up with is a series of questions which he calls "the WHAT questions."

Here is how Andrews describes the WHAT questions:

What would you think if I told you that there is a technique that, if you use it, would give you the power to calm down any irate customer and then allow you to deal with and handle that customer?

All you have to do is ask a WHAT question, that is a question that starts with the word WHAT, as in: WHAT would you like Gimbels to do? WHAT could we do that would bring you satisfaction?

Now you might ask, how is that going to calm down some nasty, unreasonable, irrational, and in general, unpleasant customer?

In order to answer, I have to ask another question. Are you aware that when a person speaks, two separate parts are talking and that both those parts can talk separately?

Want to know what the parts are? First, there is the mental part, which is the faculty that selects the words we speak. Second, there is the feeling part which selects our tone of voice and our facial and body language. Normally these two are in balance—that is, the feelings are in a normal

Continued

state and the mind is free to speak logically, calmly, rationally and nicely.

When an irate customer speaks, his or her feelings are in great turmoil. What happens is the mind part is virtually nonexistent. Hasn't it happened to you?

A person with upset feelings can't listen, can't be reasoned with, must be heard by someone, and does not require a direct answer.

When you encounter such a person, please be aware it is his internal problem and not yours; that his feelings are just trying to get out and are not directed at you; that you just happen to be in the way.

Okay—what can you do?

1. Understand that it is not your personal problem.
2. Listen. Most of the time upset feelings just need to be heard.
3. Especially, don't defend, argue or react.
4. Instead, ask only WHAT questions. Never ask WHY questions.

What is the reason for asking WHAT questions? WHAT questions can only be answered with a fact, not a feeling. Feelings can't deal with WHAT questions. As you ask a WHAT question—and you may have to ask several or repeat the question, however many times it takes, as if you were a broken record—the mind is forced to switch back on. As it does, the feelings will subside and the customer will calm down because you cared and you will be able to deal with and handle his or her problem. It even works in personal and social situations.

What would make you want to do this? What will you get out of it? I submit these things:

1. An upset customer, mad at Gimbels, is converted to a customer who sees Gimbels as a place that cares for his/her feelings and problems and who tries to satisfy him/her calmly and rationally.
2. Knowledge and therefore confidence on your part that you are able to convert a very negative situation into a positive one. And that's a good feeling.
3. Personal power and growth as a communicator who can function in the face of turmoil, adversity and abuse and be the better for it.

You could even use WHAT questions on the management!

Source: Reprinted from *Stores* magazine: © National Retail Merchants Association, copyright, 1979.

The best way to handle objections is to answer them in advance. The salesperson anticipates the objection and provides the information necessary to answer it before the customer can raise it. If it appears that the customer is concerned about the high price of the merchandise, the salesperson can describe and demonstrate the exceptionally high quality of the article during the sales presentation. In this way, the customer's potential objection is answered before the customer ever mentions the price.

However, even the best salesperson must face objections, because they are not always able to anticipate all the customer's concerns beforehand. When this happens, the professional salesperson depends on a variety of techniques for handling objections. These techniques are the same for retail sales as for any other sales process (see Chapter 9). It does not matter which approach is used in handling objections as long as the salesperson remembers that customers who raise objections still want to buy. The problem is they just need help in convincing themselves.

Closing the sale. Closing the sale is as important in retail selling as it is in other types of selling. Without a close, there is no sale.

The various approaches to closing sales described in Chapter 10 are applicable in retail situations. All salespeople must decide when to close and how to do it. The closing of a retail sale is the same as in any other kind of sale, but the timing of the close is distinctly different in retail selling. If retail customers are closer to purchase than most other buyers, then it logically follows that they are also closer to closing. A retail sale may take less than a minute, or it may take much longer. Since a retail sale can occur very quickly and it is impossible to predict in advance how long it will take, retail salespeople must always be ready to close, from the very moment they start the sales process. Too often sales are lost because the salesperson failed to close soon enough. It is far better to try to close too soon than too late. It is possible, and usually advisable, to try to close several times in a single sales presentation.

The only danger in trying to close too early is that the salesperson may appear to be overly aggressive, or the customer may feel the salesperson is trying to get rid of him so another customer can be served. Both of these dangers actually relate to how the closing is made rather than to when it is made, however. If care is taken not to make the customer feel pushed, it is possible to try to close half a dozen times or more in a single sale. After the sale is completed, of course, the salesperson should thank the customer for shopping at the store and ask him or her to return.

Selling by suggestion. After a retail sale has been closed, but before the sales ticket is written up and the merchandise wrapped, there is an opportunity for the retail salesperson to encourage additional purchases. This opportunity, which is unavailable to almost any other seller, is the chance to sell by suggestion.

When retail salespeople encourage customers to buy additional items or to buy larger quantities of the same merchandise, they are *suggestion selling*. Two forms of suggestion selling, trading up and selling substitutes, have already been described. In addition to these two there are others, such as:

1. Suggesting complementary items. Examples of this are suggesting a tie to go with a shirt or a blouse to go with slacks.
2. Suggesting merchandise never before available. If a man is buying deodorant, the salesperson may want to show him the soap and shampoo that is available in the same line.
3. Suggesting seasonal merchandise such as suntan lotion for the summer, electric hand warmers for the winter, or door wreaths for Christmas.
4. Suggesting sale merchandise. Often retail customers are unaware of a special promotion another department is running, and a suggestion is all that is needed to encourage them to go look at the items. Many customers appreciate such attempts to "save them money."

Incorrect suggestion selling can offend customers and make salespeople appear overly aggressive and forceful. But this does not mean that suggestion selling should be avoided. Rather, it emphasizes doing it properly. The best approach to use in suggestion selling is very similar to that used to close a sale. The salesperson must sincerely want to help the customer by offering additional information the customer might not have thought of or known about. Note how different the following two approaches are in suggesting that the customer buy an additional shirt. An inept salesperson might say, "Can I talk you into one more of these?" while the professional salesperson would say, "For the remainder of this month, you can buy two of these shirts for only $28, a savings of $3!" In the first case the customer is asked to do the salesperson a favor, while in the second the salesperson offers to do one for the customer. Obviously, the latter is the better approach.

There are three steps retail salespeople can take to improve their ability to sell by suggestion. First, the salesperson can develop a list of other items related to every item sold in a department. Every time an item is sold, the seller will automatically think of the related items and can suggest one to the customer. Second, the salesperson can make sure he or she knows about all the special promotions in

"During the last session of the 'Positive Selling' class, the teacher sold me on taking the advanced course."

Reprinted by permission of The Wall Street Journal

Suggestion selling can be found in unusual places.

the department, as well as in the others in the store. And third, retail sales personnel can make all sales suggestions specific instead of general. Instead of saying, "Will there be anything else?" for example, they can say, "Let me show you these new knit ties we just received."

If retail salespeople are aware of the needs of customers and consciously try to assist them, suggestion selling can not only increase sales but also contribute to the reputation of the store. If, on the other hand, they apply the selling by suggestion technique in an offensive manner, or if they try to sell customers things they neither want nor need, suggestion selling can give the store a bad image.

It has been suggested that personal selling as a merchandising tool is in its twilight years,[11] a conclusion based on the technological and institutional innovations that have been introduced in retailing in recent years. Today people can buy life insurance, magazines, books, handkerchiefs, golf balls, hot soup, and a host of other things from vending machines. Mechanical troubles in automobiles are diagnosed by testing machines instead of mechanics. Metal and plastic bank tellers give cash advances and credit deposits to accounts on week-

The future of retail selling

ends as well as evenings. Works of art are sold through the mail, and people join clubs to buy books and records.

Yet to conclude that retail selling will soon pass away is to disregard equally significant changes in today's customers. They are better educated, can afford more things, are more willing to be different, want better quality, and, most of all, are clamoring to be treated as individuals. Taking these and other factors into account, it can be concluded that (1) effective personal selling is critical to the survival of many retail stores[12] and (2) the best product these stores have to offer may well be the representative who sells it.[13]

SERVICE SELLING

Many sellers call on the same customers on a recurring basis. Although they may spend some time seeking potential new customers, most of it is devoted to maintaining sound relations with their regular customers. This is called *service selling*.

Service selling is directed primarily at organizations rather than individuals. It is done by salespeople who sell to wholesalers and retailers, by industrial sales personnel and by detail personnel. Salespeople who sell to ultimate consumers do very little service selling, although at one time in our country's history the traveling sales agent served such a function in many rural areas.

The service selling function

It is impossible to recommend a sequence of steps for service selling in the same way that Chapters 5 through 11 did for the sales process as a whole. But the primary tasks associated with service selling, which vary with the type of service selling and depend upon the customers served, can be listed.

Service selling to wholesalers and retailers. The primary responsibility in service selling to wholesalers and retailers is to maintain an adequate inventory of merchandise in each customer's place of business. Adequate inventories are dependent on orders and deliveries. The sales representative can help ensure timely orders by monitoring the customers' inventory levels and suggesting when orders should be placed to assure appropriate delivery time. Once the order has been placed, he or she should follow the order through the stages of order processing and delivery until it is received by the customer.

Salespeople serving retail or wholesale accounts can also be expected to keep customers informed of revisions in company policies and of new services or products being offered. Many firms use their account salespeople to assist in developing sales forecasts because they know the operations of each of their customers intimately.

Salespeople who sell to retailers have additional duties such as the responsibility for maintaining shelf displays and promotional materials, including end-of-aisle floor displays, mobiles, window signs, and checkout counter displays. They must encourage retailers to display their promotional materials prominently and to keep their shelf displays attractive and well-stocked. They are expected to check each of their products on the retailers' shelves to make sure it is getting enough display space and that an adequate mix of sizes and types is available.

Essentially, salespeople selling on a regular basis to retail or wholesale accounts will be expected to (1) maintain the level of sales to the accounts they service, (2) increase sales to these accounts where possible, and (3) add new customers to the customer list. Most of their time is spent on the first two responsibilities.

Service selling by detail personnel. Detailing is an unusual kind of selling in which the salesperson sells to someone other than the buyer of the product. One example of a detail salesperson is the drug company representative who calls on physicians instead of the patients who actually buy the drugs. If the detailer can convince the physician of the superiority of his or her company's drugs over competitive brands, the physician will prescribe the drug by brand name, not generic type. Thus the physician makes the brand choice, not the pharmacist or the patient.

Drug company detailers keep physicians aware of the drugs their company has available to treat various diseases and inform them of the side effects of drugs as they are discovered. Each new drug is thoroughly tested in the drug company's laboratories to determine the possible effects it may have on patients. For example, a cold remedy might cause nausea, create dizziness, or be ill-suited to diabetic patients. If the physician is not cautioned about the drug's possible side effects, a patient using it could suffer severe consequences.

Drug company detail personnel also perform a service to druggists by keeping them informed about their company's drugs. When a detail salesperson calls on a druggist, there are additional duties. Inventories must be monitored to ensure that supplies are adequate for the druggist's needs, and display materials must be installed and maintained.

Another example of detailing is that done by textbook sales representatives. They call on teachers instead of students because teachers determine which textbook will be used in each course. The primary duty of a textbook representative is to keep teachers aware of what textbooks the company has available. Even though a textbook salesperson may not know the exact contents of all the firm's books, he or she should be able to discuss the differences between the company's texts and those of its competitors. The effective textbook representative can also demonstrate how each book offered can be used in the context of various courses.

Textbook salespeople regularly visit the bookstores where their books are sold. They follow up orders, check inventory levels, and monitor the number of used textbooks available in each bookstore.

Service selling to industrial buyers.   Due to the nature of industrial buying, service selling is often the most important function of an industrial sales force. Negotiations for industrial purchases may take months or years, and much more is involved in the selling process than just an approach, a presentation, a demonstration, and a close. Industrial buyers expect much more from salespeople, and they usually get it.

Industrial sales personnel, especially those selling highly complex technical products, are expected to assist in installing the product and in evaluating its performance in the customer's operations. Anything related to the product is, in the opinion of the industrial buyer, the responsibility of the industrial sales representative. Accordingly, the industrial buyer is likely to hold the salesperson accountable for (1) product quality, (2) delivery performance, (3) technical information, and (4) total product cost.

Many technical products must pass an *acceptance test* procedure when they arrive at the customer's plant. If too many shipments of the product fail such tests, the resulting shipment rejections may cause costs to skyrocket or production to be delayed. In either case, the customer is unable to operate efficiently and economically. Industrial salespeople are expected to monitor their product's quality and to be able to intervene when things go wrong. In some cases poor-quality products pass the acceptance tests but cause delays in the customer's production operations because they require extensive reworking or special handling. Here again the salesperson is expected to help resolve the difficulties encountered with the product.

Prompt delivery is a very important factor for industrial buyers. When a particular product is needed to maintain manufacturing operations, late deliveries not only can be frustrating, but actually have severe economic consequences such as shutting down a production line, which can mean hardships for those who are unemployed. Industrial sales representatives, therefore, are expected to consider delivery a critical aspect of their selling.

Many buyers consider industrial salespeople to be a primary source of technical information.[14] For some technical products, however, it is unreasonable and unrealistic to expect the salesperson to both service accounts and provide technical expertise. In these cases, technical service representatives may assist salespeople in providing customers with extensive technical services and information. But when such assistance is not provided, the salesperson is expected to perform the technical service function.

Industrial buyers also believe that industrial salespeople ought to provide information on *total product cost,* which refers to the total cost of using the supplier's product in the buying firm's operations. It includes the price of the product, delivery and handling charges, special charges, and any other costs typically included in the out-of-pocket costs of a product. Other buyer's costs related to processing or using a product are also included. Certain products may require special jigs or fixtures, or one supplier's product might make it necessary to buy another article to use with it. All of these additional costs associated with actually using the product are included in total product cost. A total product cost is the cost to the customer of buying and using that product, taking into account any cost reductions that may result from using it.

Industrial buyers believe that sales representatives should know the out-of-pocket costs of their products and the effects these products would have on the operating costs of the firm. Often a higher-priced product is the most economical alternative because of its offsetting operating advantages. Salespeople who do not think in these terms are unable to measure the cost that is most important to industrial buyers—total product cost.

In service selling, salespeople call upon the same customers again and again. It is more important for them to be able to relate well to people in a close, personal way than to be able to get to know people quickly and relate to a large number of diverse individuals. They make cold calls much less frequently than other sellers, so the fear of rejection is relatively unimportant in service selling. There are two primary requirements for successful service selling: attitude and knowledge.

Skills required for service selling

Attitude.   There is an axiom of selling that maintains that "Selling is service; service is selling."[15] This attitude is required of all salespeople who wish to be successful in service selling situations. If they do not have this outlook, service will be rendered only when it is most expedient and not as a continuing responsibility.

Service salespeople must develop the proper attitude toward their own firms as well as toward their customers. Balance is the key to successful service selling. Saying that the customer is always right is as wrong as saying that the seller is always right. Sometimes the customer is right and sometimes the seller is right. Salespeople can help determine who is right by adopting the philosophy of representing the customer when in the company office and the company when out of the office. Thus both seller and buyer are fairly represented and the long-range interests of both are protected and enhanced.

The service attitude provides a way to enhance the long-term interests of both the seller and the buyer. If this philosophy is applied fairly, both parties benefit. Sellers maintain a profitable level of sales, and buyers are assured of continuing sources of supply.

Knowledge.   After proper attitude, knowledge is the most useful attribute for successful service selling. The industrial salesperson must know his or her products, the customer's operations, and the customer's quality and delivery requirements. And for the retail or wholesale salesperson, knowledge of the customer's operations and their relation to the firm's product line is crucial. In each case, the service selling function is impossible without a thorough knowledge of the many interrelated facets of each selling situation and the desire to develop a working relationship with each and every customer.

Many other characteristics of the successful service salesperson, such as persistence, ambition, and drive, could be listed here. Without the proper attitude and adequate knowledge, however, successful service selling is impossible, no matter what other qualities the salesperson possesses.

SUMMARY

This chapter has discussed retail and service selling, which are worthy of special attention because of their importance and uniqueness. Total retail sales are large and growing, and this trend is likely to continue. Retail selling occupies a unique position in our modern economy because it is the final link between production and consumption.

In-store retail selling differs from all other selling, including the retail selling done outside of retail establishments, in two respects: retail customers come to the salesperson, and they are closer to the purchase point than other customers. While these are distinct advantages, retail salespeople must deal with a larger variety of customers. They are key factors in the success of their employers.

Successful retail salespersons must have pride in themselves, knowledge, and a service orientation. The retail selling process has six distinguishable steps: (1) approaching the customer, (2) determining the customer's needs and wants, (3) presenting the merchandise, (4) answering objections, (5) closing, and (6) suggestion selling. While retail selling resembles the sales process described in Chapters 5 through 11, there are some special problems and opportunities inherent in the retail selling process.

Service selling provides service to established customers. Most service selling is done by sales forces responsible for retail, wholesale, or industrial accounts, and by detail personnel.

Retail and wholesale account salespeople are primarily responsible for maintaining current sales patronage. Retail account sales personnel also oversee in-store product displays and promotional materials.

Detailers sell to someone other than the buyer of the product. Drug company sales personnel sell drugs to physicians and textbook sales representatives sell textbooks to teachers, even though their products are bought by patients and students, respectively. Detail personnel sell to intermediate parties because these people determine which product will be purchased.

There are many facets to the service selling duties of industrial account salespeople. Industrial buyers expect sales personnel to (1) monitor product quality, (2) supervise delivery performance, (3) provide technical information, and (4) evaluate total product costs.

Although many skills are required for successful service selling, the two most important attributes are an enlightened attitude toward service and extensive knowledge.

REVIEW QUESTIONS/DISCUSSION QUESTIONS/EXERCISES

1. Define the following terms:
   - *a.* Retail selling.
   - *b.* Standard of living.
   - *c.* Trading up.
   - *d.* Substitute selling.
   - *e.* Suggestion selling.
   - *f.* Service selling.
2. Explain the role of retailing in this country's high standard of living.
3. How does in-store retail selling differ from other selling? Do these dif-

ferences affect the way retail sales personnel perform their jobs? If so, how?

4. Visit several local bicycle dealers and tell them that you are shopping for a new ten-speed bike (other products may be substituted). Observe the sales techniques used by each salesperson and later prepare a brief written summary of each encounter. Pay special attention to the sales techniques and potential pitfalls discussed in this chapter. Rate each salesperson on overall retail sales effectiveness. Compare your experiences and ratings with those of the other class members. How many sales personnel received high marks, and how many received low marks? Can you draw any conclusions from this experience?

5. What are two major disadvantages of retail selling when compared to other selling?

6. What are three major requirements for successful retail selling?

7. Why is closing a retail sale like suggestion selling?

8. What are some things a retail salesperson should look for, or questions that should be asked, to determine the needs and wants of a customer shopping for a new set of golf clubs? For a new car?

9. List and briefly describe the six major steps in the retail selling process.

10. Is suggestion selling an unethical practice used by retail sales personnel to simply increase sales, or is it a service that most customers appreciate?

11. Select one member of the class to act as a customer shopping in a large department store. The rest of the class is to assume the role of retail salespeople. In turn, have the "shopper" enter each "salesperson's" department. Each seller must greet the customer without using the phrase "Can I help you?" and must not repeat an approach already used. Continue until the list of approaches is exhausted—or, more likely, quit when the class is exhausted.

12. Make a log of your contacts with retail sales personnel. At the end of a month, prepare a report on which salesperson impressed you the most and which impressed you the least, and why.

13. Describe four different types of suggestion selling and show how each can be used by a salesperson selling paint and wallpaper.

14. List three businesses in which retail selling is likely to become more important in the future, and three businesses in which it is likely to become less important.

15. Is there a difference between service selling and the selling of services? Explain.

16. How does service selling to wholesalers or retailers differ from the service selling done by detail personnel?

17. Why are different skills required for successful service selling and successful retail selling?

18. Are there times when the customer is wrong?

19. What is total product cost? How does it differ from the price of an item?

20. The following test appeared in the November 27, 1972, issue of *Sales Management*. Do you agree with the suggested scoring system? Explain.

Here's how to tell if you're sold on retailing

1. You prefer sitting to standing.   Yes _____ No _____

2. You can't stand interruptions when you're talking.   Yes _____ No _____

3. Computing sales commissions is sexually stimulating.   Yes _____ No _____

4. People with bad breath should be told.   Yes _____ No _____

5. People who don't know their own size make you vomit.   Yes _____ No _____

6. People who don't know their own size give you an opportunity to measure them, which in turn can help your evening plans.   Yes _____ No _____

7. When someone asks you the difference between two models of the same item, you look at the price tag.   Yes _____ No _____

8. To be taken is human, to take divine.   Yes _____ No _____

9. If a product is heavily advertised, there's probably something wrong with it.   Yes _____ No _____

10. It is better to work on salary than on commission.   Yes _____ No _____

11. When a customer you've just met tries on a garment you should dance up and down and shout "It's you, It's you!"   Yes _____ No _____

12. People who shop on their lunch hour are interfering with yours.   Yes _____ No _____

13. When a customer complains, it's a good idea to say, "We hear a lot of that lately."   Yes _____ No _____

14. It saves time to ask for credit references before the customer makes a selection.   Yes _____ No _____

15. If you ever take a job in retailing, you will tell friends you can get it for them wholesale, then sell it to 'em retail.   Yes _____ No _____
                                                                        Maybe _____

Source: Reprinted with permission from *Sales Management, The Marketing Magazine,* © 1972, Sales Management, Inc.

Scoring: If you said "Yes" to more than five questions, it's a good thing you didn't go into retailing. A score of 10 means you probably shouldn't even be in selling.

CASE 15–1: WARMGLOW WOODSTOVES

Kip Ward, a graduate of the local college with a degree in philosophy, had recently opened a store specializing in the sale of energy-saving devices. His primary merchandise was a line of well-known, high-quality woodstoves. Accordingly, he had chosen the name Warmglow Woodstoves for his store.

He had found an ideal location in a mall which had been opened in a converted old factory. The mall had a unique character, consisting of a large number of massive exposed beams in the ceiling and brick floors under foot. Kip was confident that his business would be a resounding success. This pleased him because he felt he was also contributing to a significant social problem—the energy crisis.

One day Kip was sitting behind the counter reading a textbook entitled *Professional Selling* he had borrowed from a friend of his in the business school. He was particularly interested in the chapter on retail selling. As he sat there, he noticed a young couple come in the door and walk over to the woodstoves.

Ward: May I help you?

Young man: Yes, I hope so. We've been doing some reading about the cost savings associated with using a woodstove; we think we might want one installed in our home.

Young woman: I also understand that they're very cozy. We keep our thermostat down quite low and it gets a bit chilly at times. I was hoping that the woodstove could help in this regard also.

Ward: It well might help you on both counts. Where would you put the stove? Do you have a good central location?

Young woman: Not really. Our fireplace is in the family room which is located to one side and to the back of the house. Also, it is separated from the rest of the house by the breakfast room.

Ward: I'm not sure that a woodstove will work very well for you then. They seem to work better when they are centrally located. Maybe you ought to look at some other ways of solving your problem. Does your house have storm windows?

Young man: No, do you sell those also?

Ward: No, I don't but they might help as much or more than the stove. How about a blower for your fireplace? I sell those. Or how about some insulated draperies for your windows? Those could help too. I also sell caulking to seal your windows and insulating plates to put behind your plugs and electrical outlets. And I sell. . . .

Young man: Hold it! I'm confused. How about this? Why don't you come out to our house, look it over and then tell us what you would advise us to buy?

Ward: I'm really not qualified to do that, but there are people available at the power company who are. Why don't you call them?

Young woman: Maybe that's the best idea. Let's do that.

Questions

1. Review the retail selling process used by Kip Ward. Cite instances of good retail selling techniques and instances of bad techniques.
2. How might Kip have handled the situation differently?
3. Would you have tried to sell the young couple the woodstove?
4. Has Kip learned anything about services or merchandise which he might add to his current offering?

CASE 15–2: JETEX CARBURETOR COMPANY

Jetex Carburetor—located in Grand Rapids, Michigan—manufactures automobile carburetors for original equipment manufacturers (OEMs) and for distribution through industrial distributors to automobile supply stores. OEMs, though, buy over two thirds of Jetex's entire output. Power Motors Corporation is Jetex's largest OEM account, accounting for over half of its OEM sales. Sharon Morgan, sales engineer for Jetex, has sole responsibility for the Power Motor's account, which is her only account.

Morgan receives a phone call from Pete Vinke, the manufacturing superintendent at Jetex. A fixture used for drilling a port in the carburetors made for Power Motors had loosened during the latest production run, and the entire batch had been made with one port a quarter inch out of alignment. Vinke estimates that Jetex could safely correct the mistake by welding and redrilling the hole. Total cost for this rework would put the month's production costs over the allowed variation, but he is more concerned with what reworking would do to delivery.

The job had been promised for the end of the previous month, so it is already one week late. Morgan had called Power Motors as soon as she learned that the shipment was going to be late. Power Motors reported it was able to work around the problem for one or two weeks, but no more. If it did not have the shipment by the middle of the month, its production line would be shut down. With the engine production line down, Power Motors could continue to ship cars for only two weeks. After that, its entire inventory of completed cars would be depleted.

Morgan goes to Power Motors to see Tom Alves, the purchasing manager. When Alves hears about the problem, he becomes very upset. He simply cannot understand how a company like Jetex, which has been making carburetors for over 40 years, could allow something like this to happen. He feels that Jetex has to fix the problem and do it quickly. He will not accept any solution that would cut off the shipment of automobiles.

Morgan sympathizes with Alves's position but says that there is no way Jetex can correct the problem and ship the carburetors in time to avoid shutting down Power Motors' production line. Looking at it realistically, she says, there is even a good chance that the shipment of cars will have to be halted. Alves will not listen to such a possibility.

Morgan suggests that they talk to John McCann, the manufacturing manager at Power Motors, to see if there is anything he could do. McCann, after reviewing several blueprints, decides that there is one way Power Motors could solve the problem. Another hole, which had to match the misplaced carburetor port, could be drilled off-center, thus eliminating the need for any reworking. However, an entire set of new drilling fixtures would have to be made before Power Motors' drilling operations could do this. After calling one of his cost estimators, McCann says that the cost of this tooling would be in the range of $100,000. Alves concludes, "No problem, go ahead. Jetex will just have to absorb the cost."

Questions

1. What should Morgan do now? Support your position.
2. Assume that Morgan has talked with one of Jetex's accountants and has learned that, if she accepts the $100,000 charge, it will be assigned to the cost of sales. Would you still advise the same action that you did in Question 1?
3. Do you feel Alves is being unreasonable?

KEY POINTS

- Real estate and insurance pose different selling situations for the professional salesperson.

- Educational achievement in the field of real estate is indicated by GRI.

- Selling real estate is actually two jobs in one—obtaining listings and matching up customers with property.

- Obtaining listings is considered the most important aspect of selling real estate.

- A significant change in selling real estate is the presence of national realty networks.

- Selling insurance will differ in terms of the type sold and the arrangement the salesperson has with the parent company.

- Considerations in selling insurance include the reduction of customer uncertainty, identification and solution of the customer's problem, and the salesperson's self-perception.

- Professional certification (CLU) and (CPCU) is available to salespeople in the life and health insurance field, as well as property and liability.

Chapter 16

SELLING IN THE REAL ESTATE AND INSURANCE INDUSTRIES

Marge Roman, a realtor-manager in Canfield, Ohio, feels that to be successful in selling real estate in today's highly competitive market an individual must:

1. Maintain an adequate inventory of homes. If you have no homes to show you have nothing to sell. At the other extreme too many homes means that some will not receive the necessary amount of attention and you are not treating the sellers fairly.

2. Gauge your customers and be able to work with them on their level. The days when a buyer dropped into your office and said I would like this particular piece of property are gone forever. Today an agent must not only search out customers, but be able to profile them and relate to them.

3. Be persistent and don't give up too quickly. Selling real estate is a tough job and one where you, the agent, have to fit into someone else's time schedule. If you honestly feel the deal benefits both buyer and seller keep working until the deal is consummated. I have worked as long as a year with sellers.

4. Follow up every sale because that is where your next sale in one way or another is coming from.

Roman's approach reflects the dynamic challenges faced by real estate sellers. Equally complex situations confront insurance sales personnel. These two types of selling are the topics covered in Chapter 16.

THE IMPORTANCE OF REAL ESTATE AND INSURANCE SELLING

Real estate and insurance selling require special consideration for several reasons. First, real estate was the first industry outside of retailing to accept women as professional equals of men in selling. On the other hand, few women have entered insurance selling, a situation that major insurance companies such as Equitable are correcting with organized recruiting efforts.

Unlike other salespersons, those in real estate are licensed under state regulations. These state regulations cover all activities of those engaged in real estate selling including the distribution of commissions. In addition, it is common for real estate agencies to require that their salespeople maintain memberships in the local board of realtors and the state real estate association. Each of these will have codes of conduct that salespeople must abide by in selling real estate.

The designation GRI (Graduate, Realtors' Institute) has come to signify educational achievement in the field of real estate selling.

In the life and health fields, insurance agents have the opportunity to obtain the professional designation of Chartered Life Underwriter

(CLU). This designation is based upon strict ethical, experience, and educational requirements. The American Institute for Property and Liability Underwriters has developed an educational program that leads to the Chartered Property Casualty Underwriter (CPCU) designation.

Finally, the structures of both industries are undergoing fundamental changes that affect the selling function. Typically a localized business, the selling of real estate has experienced dramatic changes with the development of national franchise networks. Meanwhile, the changes happening in the insurance industry seem almost in direct conflict with each other. Life insurance companies, for example, are adding property and casualty insurance in anticipation of broadening their respective customer bases. But within some of these same companies, salespeople are becoming more specialized, for example, a salesperson in an agency who will handle only product liability insurance.

THE UNIQUE NATURE OF REAL ESTATE SELLING

Real estate selling differs from other selling in a number of ways. First, and perhaps the most obvious difference, is that real estate selling is actually two jobs in one. The real estate salesperson must not only go through the process common to selling any product, but he or she must also obtain listings or build an inventory of homes to sell. Many real estate salespersons are of the opinion that the latter is the more important aspect of the job. They point out that you cannot sell what you do not have in stock.

Another difference is the degree of intrafirm competition. Real estate salespeople from the same firm will compete with one another to sell a particular piece of property. The use of sales territories makes little sense in selling real estate, although salespeople will tend to specialize in certain neighborhoods.

Prospecting also differs in real estate selling. Referrals are of upmost importance. Also, prospective customers see the firm's signs on property they may be interested in and contact the real estate firm. A third source of prospective customers is what could be called *walk-ins*. Regardless of the source, these customers are further along in the buying process in terms of identifying need than those one would expect to find in most other selling situations, with the exception of retail buying. The emphasis must therefore be on helping customers to clearly define their housing needs rather than selling them a piece of real estate.

Generally speaking, prospective home purchasers have little

knowledge of construction and how to determine value in a home. Therefore, not knowing what to look for, their attention shifts to the neighborhood in which the house is located. This buying motive tends to be emotional and, as such, beyond the control of the salesperson. As a consequence, salespeople need to know a great deal about housing and be able to show customers what to look for in a house. A good way to do this is to develop a list of strong and weak points about each house, as well as about each area.

There is also a good possibility that customers will be confused with all the details and complexities involved in purchasing a home and arranging financing. Consequently, the salesperson assumes an active role in handling all the paper work and guiding customers through the necessary procedures. The complexity of the housing purchase and its related procedures places greater emphasis on the reputation of the salesperson than would be experienced in many other selling situations.

It is not unusual for all salespersons to have to deal with multiple buying influences and decision makers. Usually their respective roles, however, are much clearer than those involved in the purchasing of a house. There is the family unit itself, with the husband and wife playing dominant decision roles. The impact of the children on the decision can vary widely from situation to situation. Complicating the buying process still further is the fact that friends, relatives, and business acquaintances can and do play influencing roles.

As a result, real estate salespeople continually talk about having to have everything "right" to sell a house. As an illustration, a realtor related an experience he had in getting the right environment to close a sale a few years ago.

> One young couple must have looked at a certain house five times, each time taking about an hour. I have been in the business over 20 years and I could tell they were in love with the house and the neighborhood. Yet there was something keeping them back from closing the deal and it wasn't price. I finally asked them whether they would like their parents to see the house. They agreed it might be a good idea, so the next Sunday after church the couple, their parents, and grandparents went through the house without me. On Monday we closed the deal.

Finally, the amount of money involved in purchasing a house makes the amount of risk seem overwhelming to some customers. In such situations the salesperson must step in as the primary source of additional information and not let the customer rely on past experiences. It is also imperative that the salesperson supply rational motives for buying the house to keep the decision from being based entirely on emotional motives. See Figure 16–1.

Customer	Salesperson
Lacks knowledge about real estate	Establish advisor role
	Highlight strong points
	Develop rational motives for purchasing
Confused by complexities of purchase	Handle the details
	Simplify by showing the procedure step-by-step
Multiple buying influences and decision makers	Do not ignore any possible influence
	Give each member of the family reasons for purchasing
Perceives high amount of risk	Establish credibility
	Be primary source of information

**Figure 16–1
Characteristics of real estate customers and selling rules**

As noted earlier, the selling of real estate is actually two jobs in one. The first job is acquiring listings, which is considered the most basic task in the industry. The second job is matching up customers and real estate. This job is very similar to other selling situations.

The job of obtaining an exclusive listing involves getting the owner of property to believe that the salesperson and/or the firm represented offer the best means of selling the property in question. The more credibility the salesperson has with the customer, the more likely the customer will take the advice of the salesperson and the better the listing. It follows then that the better the listing, the quicker the sale and the happier the owner.[1]

In offering his or her firm's services to owners who wish to sell their property, the salesperson must show what can be expected. These services normally include:

1. Collecting all the data pertaining to the property including correct lot size, room measurements, square footage of the house, extras such as fixtures and wallpaper, and exclusions.
2. Accumulating loan data and terms.
3. Relaying all the above data to the Multiple Listing Service for printing and dissemination to members.
4. Showing property to only qualified buyers who have been carefully screened.

TASKS IN REAL ESTATE SELLING

Obtaining listings

5. Acquainting all sales personnel in the firm with the property.
6. Placing ads for the property through the advertising program of the agency.
7. Obtaining loan commitments from various lending agencies.
8. Placing "For Sale" signs on the property.
9. Providing advisory service on a continuous basis.
10. Processing the sale once it is made.
11. Making a market analysis of the property as a guide in pricing and selling the property.[2]

Usually the question of price will enter into the listing negotiation. This can be a problem if the property owners have in mind a price that the market will not support. When this happens, the salesperson has to "sell" the property owners on his or her marketing knowledge. A market analysis of the property is invaluable to the salesperson in convincing the property owners to accept a more competitive but lower-than-hoped-for price.

A market analysis of property should include:

1. Competitive advantages of the property (location, extras, loan, and the like).
2. Drawbacks to the property.
3. General and area market conditions.
4. Reasons for selling (such as moving or buying another house).
5. Requirements of the seller (time, limitations, financial needs, and so forth).

Matching customers and real estate

This part of the selling job is very similar to the selling of other products. The salesperson is involved in showing the house to qualified buyers, arranging and coordinating advertising, and handling the negotiations between buyers and sellers.

Actually, the phrase *showing the house* is a poor one because the salesperson wants to make sure prospects are thoroughly familiar with the house and are aware of all the features of the house. Therefore, it is important for the salesperson to know the house thoroughly by going through it as many times as necessary with the present owners. The salesperson also needs to collect information about the house independently. Much of this information will probably appear on the market analysis form.

A common and practical way of showing a home is through the use of an *open house.* One disadvantage of the open house is the lack of opportunity to screen prospects. Another disadvantage is that when there are several groups of prospects scattered about the house, the salesperson cannot make his or her presentation to each group. An open house, however, does give the property exposure to a wide proportion of the market. Some real estate people look upon this technique as simply a form of prospecting.

Making a specific appointment to show the house has many more advantages than the open house. The salesperson can screen the prospects beforehand, prepare, concentrate his or her attention on just one group, develop two-way communication with prospects (driving to the house the salesperson may gain a great deal of information about the prospects, particularly the purchasing roles of each member of the family), and better timing between the buyer and the seller may be obtained. In regard to the latter it is vital that the house be shown only when the seller thinks it is in good enough condition to be shown.

Another responsibility of the real estate salesperson is to oversee when, where, and at what frequency advertisements are placed. The salesperson may be involved in writing up the descriptions of the property to appear in the advertisements.

Most veteran salespeople in real estate are of the opinion that if a salesperson experiences trouble in closing, the cause can be traced back to having done a poor job in pricing and market analysis. In other words, the property is either priced too high in relation to its market position as revealed by market analysis, or the salesperson has failed to match up buyers with the house.

Legally the real estate salesperson is bound to report all offers to the sellers. However, the salesperson might want to discourage buyers from making any offers that are not reasonable.[3] It is important for the salesperson to emphasize to buyers that he or she is acting as an agent of the sellers and representing their interests.

EDUCATION REQUIREMENTS

Licensing and professional designation for salespersons in real estate are closely allied to courses offered by accredited and approved institutions of higher learning and professional organizations. In Ohio, for example, Real Estate Principles and Practices and Real Estate Law are prerequisites to sitting for the real estate salesperson's examination. Two additional courses, Real Estate Finance and Real Estate Appraisal must be completed prior to the real estate broker's examination. These four courses plus Real Estate Brokerage and a course labeled Special Topics (e.g. condominiums and cooperatives, commercial estate, investment analysis) constitute eligibility for the Graduate, Realtors® Institute comprehensive examination.[4]

NATIONAL
REALTY
NETWORKS

A great change that has taken place in the selling of real estate is the development of national realty networks. Some of the more familiar franchise operations are Century 21, Electronic Realty Associates (ERA), Gallery of Homes, Red Carpet and Better Homes and Gardens. While each franchise will have a different method of operation, there are several advantages of being a member of a national franchise network:

1. Referrals.
2. National recognition.
3. Uniformity in marketing approach.
4. Sales training programs.
5. Advertising.

Local real estate firms have always had national systems for referrals, but national franchises have formalized and improved the system. It is even possible in some cases for customers to see pictures of homes in another city minutes after making the request to a local franchise.

National franchise networks provide all the advantages of national recognition to what has heretofore been a very localized business. Traditionally, real estate firms have built their all-important reputations over the years, but only in their local areas. Being a member of a national organization without losing local identity provides the firm with some unique advantages.

This new dimension to the real estate business permits customers to move from city to city or suburb to suburb and still be associated with the same organization. In one location, a member of the franchise network will be selling the present residence and providing information about homes in the new location. In the area where the customer is relocating, another member of the franchise network is supplying information on homes and making arrangements to help the customer in purchasing a home. This advantage takes on even more significance with today's highly mobile population.

Uniformity in clothing (blazers and pants suits), signs, forms, and various marketing tools helps to develop consumer recognition and familiarity. Many of these ideas were borrowed from the fast-food industry, so it is hoped that uniformity will do as much for real estate as the Golden Arches have done for McDonald's.[5]

Most, if not all, national franchisers offer sales training programs to local members of their network. An executive for Century 21 is of the opinion that the sales training programs offered by the company are a vital tool. The executive commented that, "all too often, real estate salespeople are inexperienced and poorly prepared, perhaps even working part-time. And yet homeowners must rely upon them to help with the most important purchase of their lives."[6]

Last, but certainly not least, is the advantage a member of a national franchise network has in terms of advertising. Actually, this advantage is twofold. First, advertising has a significant impact on consumer recognition. The names of several national realty networks are as well-known today as many consumer products on store shelves. Second, local real estate firms can benefit from advertisements by paying only a shared cost rather than the total cost.

THE UNIQUE NATURE OF INSURANCE SELLING

Insurance selling includes not only life insurance but a vast array of plans such as property and casualty, health, product liability, and retirement funds. The insurance industry also has two different types of salespersons or agents. One is an employee of the insurance company such as is typically found in the life and health insurance business and with large property and casualty firms like State Farm and Allstate. The other is the independent agent who is principally a seller of property and casualty coverage.

Another complication in insurance selling is that the approach dif-

"I want some no-double-fault insurance."

Some customers have unique insurance needs.

fers depending upon the product. Customers buy property and casualty insurance because it is a requirement. You have to have insurance on your car as well as your home. Consequently, the selling of this type of insurance is service-oriented.

On the other hand, the need for life insurance or retirement plans is less obvious. The salesperson in this situation is more likely to be, and in fact has to be, creative in his or her selling efforts. The necessary change from service to creative selling has proved troublesome when independent agents or companies have added various types of insurance to their product offerings.

The insurance salesperson must also acquire an ever-increasing amount of product knowledge just to keep pace with a varied list of product offerings. Insurance companies are developing dozens of new products ranging from savings plans with fixed interest rates to intricate term riders and variable annuities.

Insurance as an intangible product

Regardless of the type of insurance, the biggest differences between insurance selling and other forms of selling can be traced to the fact that insurance is an intangible product. Since the buying and selling of services or intangibles differ from dealing in goods or tangibles, sellers of the former need to keep three things in mind.[7]

1. A service (insurance) must make a direct contribution to the reduction of uncertainties.
2. A service (insurance) must come to grips with a fundamental problem of the customer purchasing that insurance.
3. A service (insurance) can only be purchased meaningfully from someone capable of rendering this service. Selling ability and personality by themselves are meaningless.

There are three reasons customers feel uncertain about purchasing insurance.[8] The first is whether or not the proposed insurance will reduce uncertainty or solve the problem of the customer. Typical problems are protection of dependents, protection of investment in property, and retirement.

A second source of uncertainty for the customer revolves around whether the salesperson and the firm can identify and solve the customer's problem. Questions concerning the amount of liability for driving a car, the reimbursement of medical costs, or the building of an estate can be overwhelming to the customer. This means that the salesperson must build confidence in the customer.

There are two possible approaches to building confidence.[9] The first is a general approach in which the salesperson concentrates on demonstrating to the customer the abilities of the firm and the particular salesperson to solve problems in an area of insurance. In this approach the salesperson is not concerned with the specific problems of the customer, but rather utilizes such selling techniques as:

1. Describing a generalized approach to problem solving ("persuasion by method").
2. Describing the abilities of the salesperson and his or her backup in the firm to solve problems ("persuasion by personnel").
3. Describing the success achieved for other clients ("persuasion by success story").

A second approach is to focus on the specific problems of the customer. In life insurance this might involve a review of present insurance arrangements plus study and development of a financial needs program. With such an approach the salesperson goes through a series of sales interviews and continually reinforces confidence in the customer. In selling a group retirement policy to a manufacturer, the salesperson must show that the program solves all the problems at lowest possible cost.

The third source of uncertainty for the customer is the salesperson. How the salesperson perceives himself or herself and how this is demonstrated to the customer are key factors in reducing uncertainty. In this regard there are two basic types of insurance salespersons.[10] One is the individual who perceives his or her professional strength in selling as separate from the insurance product. The other is the salesperson who combines professionalism in insurance and related problem solving with professionalism in selling, emphasizing the latter. This type of insurance salesperson will most likely produce a greater volume of profitable and sustaining business than the person who is strictly a professional salesperson.

In contrast to other industries, professional certification is available to sellers of life and health insurance as well as property and liability. This indication of professionalism is the designation Chartered Life Underwriter (CLU), and Chartered Property Casualty Underwriter (CPCU), bestowed on men and women by The American College and the American Institute for Property and Liability Underwriters respectively. The CLU and the CPCU are awarded on the basis of individuals fulfilling specified educational, ethical, and experience requirements.

Professionalism in insurance selling

Candidates for the CLU must be of good moral character, hold a high school diploma or equivalent, and have three years of relevant experience. In addition, they must pass a series of 15 two-hour examinations encompassing the following subject areas:[11]

1. Economic security and individual life insurance.
2. Life insurance law and mathematics.
3. Group insurance and social insurance.
4. Economics and modern management.
5. Accounting and finance.
6. Investments and family financial management.
7. Income taxation.
8. Pension planning.
9. Business insurance.
10. Estate planning and taxation.
11. Legal environment of business.
12. Advanced pension planning.
13. Advanced estate planning.
14. Accounting and business valuation.
15. Risk management of property—liability exposures

The admission requirements of the American Institute for the CPCU designation are basically the same as for the CLU, namely good moral character, high school education, and three years experience in the field. The curriculum includes eight subject areas:[12]

1. Principles of risk management and insurance.
2. Personal risk management and insurance.
3. Commerical property risk management and insurance.
4. Insurance company operations.
5. The legal environment of insurance.
6. Management.
7. Economics.
8. Insurance issues and professional ethics.

LIFE INSURANCE SELLING

Although there are some 1,800 companies selling life insurance today, the largest seem to dominate the industry (Table 16–2). One estimate is that the top 400 companies, or a little over 20 percent of the industry, write 95 percent of the business in force.[13]

The salesperson is indispensable in selling life insurance given the vast number of companies and their respective product offerings. As an example, suppose that each of the 1,800 companies averages 20 different policies. This means a total of 36,000 different policies, an impossible buying task for the customer without the assistance of the salesperson.

Company	Life insurance in force ($000)†	Percent increase in life insurance in force last year	Premium and annuity income ($000)‡
Prudential*	$367,283,576	11.2%	$8,007,951
Metropolitan*	323,588,876	12.5	5,934,722
Equitable Life Assurance*	183,491,377	10.7	4,576,910
Aetna Life§	127,618,848	13.7	4,729,187
John Hancock Mutual*	125,594,445	11.3	2,170,657
New York Life*	111,892,459	10.4	2,598,658
Travelers‖	95,652,561	9.0	3,642,396
Connecticut General Life	73,574,843	14.6	2,434,535
Occidental of California	62,827,919	11.7	1,044,851
Northwestern Mutual*	51,667,387	13.9	1,246,917

**Table 16–2
The 10 largest life insurance companies (ranked by insurance in force)**

*Indicates mutual company.
†Face value of all life policies as of December 31, 1979.
‡Includes premium income from life, accident, and health policies, annuities, and separate accounts, and contributions to administration funds.
§Company is wholly owned by Aetna Life & Casualty.
‖Company is wholly owned by Travelers Corp.
Source: Excerpted from "The 50 Largest Life Insurance Companies," *Fortune Magazine*, © 1980, Time, Inc. All rights reserved.

The job of the life insurance salesperson has become more difficult because of higher Social Security payments, employee benefits from businesses, and the inflationary spiral. As an example, sales of new group insurance have quadrupled in a recent decade and now stand about equal to the total of ordinary insurance in force. Also, two thirds of the employees in the private sector are now covered by private pension plans.[14]

While competitive pressures prevent raising the price of life insurance policies, salespeople find themselves having to sell more life insurance to keep pace with the rising cost of living.[15] Further complications are that a salesperson will make a limited number of sales in a year, thereby forcing a higher value of insurance per sale, and a reduction in sales of group policies because of the lower premiums. Interestingly enough, it now takes $1.25 million in life insurance sales to qualify for the prestigious Million Dollar Round Table.

Top management at Northwestern Mutual Life Insurance Company feels that the incomes earned by agents reflect three factors:

1. Personal effectiveness and effort—productivity.
2. Persistency of business—quality of clients and service.
3. Commission rates.[16]

At Northwestern Mutual Life Insurance, the top 100 agents in production averaged above $100,000 in yearly pay (Table 16–3).[17] For the Equitable Life Assurance Society, the top 10 agents average over $145,000 a year. The top 100 agents average over $75,000, and more than 1,500 agents average well over $25,000.[18]

Table 16–3
Compensation survey
of 1,500
Northwestern Mutual
Life Insurance
Company agents

The top 25 agents averaged $162,928 in earnings
The top 100 agents averaged $102,810 in earnings
The top 500 agents averaged $51,870 in earnings
The top 700 agents averaged $44,691 in earnings
The top 1,500 agents averaged $30,742 in earnings

Source: *The NML Career Agent in Focus,* Northwestern Mutual
Life Insurance Company, 1978, p. 14.

SUMMARY

There are several reasons to give special attention to the selling of real estate and insurance. One is the early acceptance of women as selling professionals in real estate. Another is the licensing and regulation of real estate salespersons. Still another is the opportunity for health and life insurance salespersons to obtain a professional designation. Significant structural changes are also taking place in both industries. These changes can affect the job of the respective salesperson.

Among the differences between real estate selling and other selling situations are (1) the addition of obtaining listings to the selling job, (2) the existence of competition between agents in the same firm, (3) the fact that salespeople do only minimal prospecting for customers, and (4) the type of customer.

The two basic selling tasks for the real estate salesperson are obtaining listings and matching customers with pieces of real estate. The job of obtaining listings involves establishing credibility with the customer and setting the price. The job of matching customers with pieces of real estate includes showing houses, arranging and coordinating advertising, and handling negotiations.

A significant change in the selling of real estate has been the development of national realty networks. The advantages of a local firm joining such networks are (1) referrals, (2) national recognition, (3) uniformity in marketing approach, (4) sales training, and (5) advertising.

In selling insurance, not all agents sell the same type of plan, nor do all have the same arrangement with the parent company. Agents selling such plans as life and retirement often have to be more creative than those selling required property and casualty insurance.

Insurance is an intangible product, so the salesperson makes sure that the plan reduces uncertainties, helps the customer with his or her specific problem, and builds confidence in the customer. A designation of professionalism (CLU) is available to salespeople in life and health insurance, while the CPCU is the designation for property and liability. The CLU and CPCU are granted on the fulfillment of specific educational, ethical, and experience requirements.

The large number of companies and the array of product offerings make the salesperson almost indispensable to the customer. The job of the life insurance salesperson has become more difficult with increasing competition from Social Security and business employee benefit programs. The life insurance agent finds it necessary to sell increasing amounts of insurance to keep pace with inflationary pressures.

REVIEW QUESTIONS/DISCUSSION QUESTIONS/EXERCISES

1. Define the following terms:
   - *a.* Listing.
   - *b.* CLU.
   - *c.* Open house.
   - *d.* National realty network.
   - *e.* Market analysis.
   - *f.* Showing.

2. Explain why every real estate salesperson must obtain listings.

3. Discuss why relatively few women sell insurance.

4. Imagine that you are trying to convince a homeowner that you and your realty firm can do a better selling job than they can themselves. List the reasons.

5. Visit a local realty association office and find out the requirements for obtaining a license and membership in the association.

6. In what ways does matching customers with pieces of real estate differ from other selling situations?

7. How would you discourage prospective buyers from making too low an offer?

8. How do customers for real estate differ from customers for other products?

9. Visit a local real estate agent who is a member of a national network and find out the principal feature of his or her organization.

10. Set up a program for real estate salespeople that they could follow in prospecting for buyers.

11. Discuss the ethical implications of agents from the same real estate firm competing with each other.

12. Give the reasons real estate firms have traditionally been local firms.

13. Discuss the reasons customers for any type of insurance may feel uncertain in purchasing it.

14. If you were selling pension plans, how would you go about building confidence in yourself and the company you represent?

15. Visit the offices of an independent insurance agent and an insurance company. Identify the unique characteristics of each type.

16. Develop the reasons why an insurance agent should become either a CLU or CPCU.

17. Describe the two basic types of insurance salespersons.

18. Are there any advantages to a life insurance agent's adding homeowners and auto insurance to his or her product offering?

19. Contrast selling life insurance with selling real estate.

20. Develop a selling plan for talking about insurance to a professional (someone like an engineer or college professor) who works for a large institution that is covered by Social Security and extensive employee benefits.

CASE 16–1: GREENVALE REALTORS, INC.

Janet Remy has been in the real estate business for 25 years. After leaving college she joined her father's firm and worked there until five years ago, when she left to form her own firm, Greenvale Realtors, in an adjoining suburb of a large eastern city.

During the last two years gross commissions have tripled for Greenvale Realtors. The business that Remy started with just herself and a secretary has grown to 10 full-time salespeople and 4 part-timers. The suburb of Greenvale is still growing at a rapid rate and the prospects for the real estate business look good.

In the past month Janet Remy has received an offer to join a national realty network. The other two major real estate firms in Greenvale are already members of national networks. In the meantime, Janet's father has announced his intention to retire. It is his wish that Janet buy him out and merge the two operations, one in Greenvale and the other some 15 miles away in Cartersville.

In discussing the various possibilities with other real estate people in suburbs around the major city, Remy discovers a great deal of interest in forming a local group of firms under common ownership. This ownership group which Remy might head up as president could include some 15 agencies.

Questions

1. Outline the various alternatives for Remy.
2. List the advantages for each alternative.
3. If you were Remy, what would be your decision and why?

CASE 16–2: JOHN PENDERGAST, INDEPENDENT AGENT

John Pendergast, an independent agent, has been selling property and casualty insurance for 40 years in a small Midwestern community of 25,000 people. The makeup of the community has been steadily changing for the last 10 years from a rural-based economy with a scattering of large estates and a population of 8,000 to a suburb of a major city some 20 miles away. As this change has been taking place John's business has fallen off, rapidly so in the last three years.

Reviewing his list of customers with his son who has recently joined him in business, they find that the number of new accounts (new business written in each year) represents only 10 percent of total business for each of the last five years. Further, there has been considerable turnover in new accounts making it rare for one to last as many as three years. John's son, Ray, feels that most of the newcomers are professionals or executives with national firms.

Questions

1. What do you feel are the reasons for the downturn in business for John Pendergast?
2. What sort of program would you suggest to attract new customers?
3. Several life insurance companies have approached the Pendergasts with the idea of taking on their line of life insurance. What should be their reaction?

KEY POINTS

- Three major changes are taking place in selling. These involve the customer, the selling function, and the salesperson.

- Professional selling will not remain static; it will continue to evolve and develop as a result of environmental influences and the actions of those who work in this dynamic field.

- Today's consumers are better educated, oriented to social activism, and expect greater professionalism from the salespeople with whom they deal.

- Trends in the sales function include: (1) consultative selling, (2) megaselling, (3) systems selling, (4) specialist selling, (5) computer-assisted selling, and (6) national account selling.

- Sales personnel are changing in the following ways: (1) sellers have become more socially responsible; (2) minority groups are beginning to choose sales as a career field; (3) the term *salesperson* has replaced *salesman* in our sales vocabulary; and (4) the further professionalization of selling will require the salesperson to continue to change.

Chapter

17

THE FUTURE OF
THE PERSONAL
SELLING FUNCTION

Not too long ago, Jim Perkins used to knock people down as a member of the Denver Broncos' offensive line. But when his football career ended, he became a consultative seller of adhesives. Perkins applied the knowledge of adhesives that he had acquired to the solution of specific customer problems. The ex-Bronco would study the customer's needs and develop a recommendation as to the correct application in each instance. Jim Perkins, who now heads his own adhesives firm, illustrates one of the most significant trends in professional selling today.[1] Perkins was engaged in consultative selling, where the sales representative assists the buyer in making the best decision to accomplish a given objective.

This chapter introduces the concept of consultative selling and other trends. While the exact philosophy and structure of personal selling in the future is unclear, we do know that three major changes are taking place:

1. The customer is changing.
2. The selling function is changing.
3. The salesperson is changing.

Each of these trends will have a pronounced effect on the salesperson of the next decade. One thing is known with certainty: *Professional selling will not remain static;* it will continue to evolve and develop as a result of environmental influences and the actions of those who work in this dynamic field.

CHANGES IN THE CUSTOMER

Willy Loman, the fictional salesman in Arthur Miller's *Death of a Salesman,* or a 19th-century drummer would scarcely recognize today's customer. For the most part, modern consumers are better educated, more socially active, and display more confidence in purchasing. As a result they expect greater professionalism from the salespeople with whom they deal. These factors have greatly influenced the manner in which today's salesperson presents his or her sales story.

Consumer education

Modern consumers are better educated and more knowledgeable about the products and services they buy than their predecessors were. Society has begun to recognize the need to improve consumer information and expand its availability. Young people are gaining more awareness of consumer economics through such programs as Junior Achievement, career education starting in the elementary grades, and Distributive Education Clubs of America (DECA). Professional associations such as Sales & Marketing Executives International and the American Marketing Association and consumer groups have improved the general level of economic literacy and consumer knowledge.

There is little doubt that sales personnel of the next decade will have to be prepared to cope with consumers who insist upon more detailed, factual, and timely product and service information than in the past. Richard O. Baily, Burroughs Corporation's business machines group vice president, has said: "Today, the marketer must know his product. If he represents a new laser product used in eye surgery, he'd better know what he's talking about. Particularly if the product also glazes teeth to prevent decay."

Sales personnel must also expect to be confronted with substantial consumer activism. The growth of the consumerism movement had its roots in the joining of forces by the "average consumer" and social critics to ask some hard questions about marketing practices. As a result, nationwide boycotts have been launched, the number of product liability suits has increased dramatically, consumer advocates have attracted standing-room-only crowds on lecture circuits, and lawmakers are competing to introduce proconsumer legislation.

Consumer activism

In part, the consumerism movement seeks a better deal for purchasers. Sales personnel, on the firing line for their companies, can expect to be held accountable for many of their firm's decisions, whether or not they are product related. Salespeople or companies that ignore this trend will alienate many of the "new" consumers and risk losing some of their market share to better-advised competitors.

Leo G. Wilsman, United Van Lines' assistant to the vice president of marketing, describes sales professionalism as follows:

Sales professionalism

> The last and most important attribute of a top salesman is *professionalism*. In the life of every great salesman I have studied, I've noticed professionalism. To become a professional and remain one, a salesman must do it instinctively and automatically. I hope I can make this distinction between doing certain things, and being a certain kind of salesman. To me this is the secret of being a professional, the formula we are all seeking. Once a man gets hold of this formula, once he makes it a part of his life so that in every thought, in every act, he thinks, acts and is a professional, being on top becomes expected, almost automatic.[3]

Sales professionalism assumes complete product, market, and competitive knowledge. But a sales professional is also one who treats prospects and customers in a dignified, intelligent manner by attempting to meet their needs rather than selling them anything that is available. The professional salesperson personifies the marketing concept by being consumer-oriented, dedicated, sincere, and possessing a long-run outlook.

CHANGES IN THE SALES FUNCTION

The personal selling process itself is changing as alterations in various aspects of the marketing system cause modifications in the way companies sell their products. No list of these changes could be complete, but the following trends can be identified: (1) consultative selling, (2) megaselling, (3) systems selling, (4) specialist selling, (5) computer-assisted selling, and (6) national account selling. It is reasonable to suggest that these trends will continue to accelerate during the 1980s.

Consultative selling

Many salespeople act as consultants to their clients rather than as marketers of particular products. The *consultative salesperson* helps the buyer select the necessary items to accomplish a task, whereas a *product salesperson* is concerned with obtaining a particular sale with a given customer.

The publisher of *Computer Marketing Newsletter,* Gerard G.H. Guyod, makes this comparison:

> In the old days, we used to shove iron—sell computers off of the floor. We'd say "my machine is three times as fast as his" and we used to call computer selling "hot hardware and a handshake." But as software became more important we got into selling solutions.[4]

Table 17–1 compares the performance requirements of the consultative salesperson with those of the product salesperson. The primary differences are in the areas of planning, customer relations, selling strategy, and sales support usage.

Megaselling

Megaselling is modern terminology for "big ticket" or "big order" selling. Sellers of comprehensive data processing systems are examples of sales representatives involved in this activity. Similar illustrations are abundant in other industries.

Companies will continue to stress the importance of large-scale sales. As sales costs continue to increase, the emphasis is on increased sales productivity from the field force. This can be accomplished by either improving the salesperson's *close rate* (closed sales

Performance requirements of the consultative salesman	*Performance requirements of the product salesman*	**Table 17–1** **The consultative sales approach versus traditional product selling**
1. Performs a long-term business-planning function for his customer-clients and their own key customers.	1. Performs a short-term account-planning function for his company.	
2. Helps customer-clients define their businesses, their markets, and their product-service systems.	2. Helps customers acquire and apply his company's products.	
3. Maintains wide, multifunction access inside client companies and their own key customers.	3. Maintains access principally with customer purchasing and engineering functions.	
4. Sells systems of services and products, with primary emphasis on services.	4. Sells products and closely related product-application services, with primary emphasis on products.	
5. Draws on the full complement of company functions and services for support.	5. Draws principally on sales and technical services for support.	

Source: Reprinted by permission of the publisher from *Consultative Selling* by Mack Hanan, James Cribbin, and Horman Hoieor. © 1970 by the American Management Association, Inc. All rights reserved.

divided by sales calls) or increasing the size of the orders that are obtained. Megaselling is an attempt to accomplish the latter objective.

The concepts of suggestion selling and trading up (see Chapter 15) can be helpful in megaselling. Henry R. White, executive director of the Sales Executive Club of New York, puts it this way: "With the cost of a sales call soaring each year, management will be compelled to use the most imaginative tools and techniques to stretch the salesman's time, enable him to make more calls—and to sell more on those he does make."[5]

Megaselling often involves various sales personnel as well as top corporate executives who coordinate their efforts to secure a substantial purchase agreement. In the defense industry, for example, the sale of a new fighter aircraft to an ally can involve many billions of dollars and a lengthy period of time. Top management will often be involved in the negotiations and others will assist in the sale as they are needed. Of course, a variety of government officials are involved. The product sometimes has to be adapted to the purchaser's unique requirements, such as the use of equipment manufactured by the purchasing nation or subassembly by a local industry. Defense contractors must engage in megaselling in order to survive economically.

Systems selling

Carborundum Corporation sells a complete grinding service instead of grinding wheels, and Dictaphone Corporation sells a complete automated office information system instead of a dictating machine.[6] Business forms companies offer to custom design the entire flow of office paper work. Computer manufacturers offer a complete system of peripheral equipment to supplement the basic installation. These firms have adopted the concept of systems selling, in which a company markets a complete service or product line rather than individual items.

The basic premise of systems selling is that the firm is marketing a product line or service that satisfies an identifiable customer need. A system (or method) of satisfying that need is what the buyer seeks and the seller offers. Systems selling is a logical extension of the consumer orientation, which is essential in adoption of the marketing

"Actually, we haven't quite decided whether your proposal will fly."

Reprinted by permission The Wall Street Journal.

Systems selling often involves the preparation of elaborate sales proposals. Not all of these proposals are well received. . . .

concept. Different types of systems include related products, related services, and combinations of products and services.

Perhaps the greatest single barrier to the implementation of systems selling is the lack of trained personnel. Salespeople who have been schooled in traditional marketing techniques often have difficulty in adjusting to systems selling. Thorough orientation and detailed training sessions are required to introduce systems selling to an existing sales force.

Specialist selling[7]

Waukesha Motor Company, a Bangor Punta Corporation subsidiary, has been a recent convert to specialist selling in the attempt to gain a larger market share for its line of internal combustion engines. The firm has divided its sales force into specialist groups that serve certain customer classifications, such as construction and industrial equipment, petroleum equipment, and marine products.

The origin of specialist selling is usually credited to International Business Machines Corporation. Other users include Uniroyal's Industrial Products Division and Xerox Corporation. Customer specialization allows the salesperson to make more knowledgeable buying recommendations. Consider the case of a curtain manufacturer, Louis Hand, Inc., of Fall River, Massachusetts, which was interested in a new office copier. In the course of presenting this product for sale, a Xerox specialist studied Hand's method of generating production tickets. As a result, the Xerox representative ended up selling Hand a machine to replace a two-person offset press, as well as the copier.

Specialist selling is impractical unless the firm's product range is broad enough to serve all sizes and kinds of companies in an industry. Waukesha Motor Company has set up a list of Key Target Accounts (KTA), a representative group of equipment manufacturers, and continually monitors the engine power required by these accounts. These requirements can be modified to meet other prospects' situations.

Computer-assisted selling

Marketing management has generally overcome its hesitation to accept computers as a means of aiding the sales force. Computers now determine many aspects of selling, such as territorial alignments and routing plans, and they are commonly used in promotional budgeting decisions and sales analysis. Certain types of sellers use them for specific purposes; real estate agents, for example, identify homes that meet the housing needs of particular prospects with computer print-outs.

Computer-based *marketing information systems* (MIS) are designed to produce relevant information helpful in making marketing decisions. A marketing information system can be a great help to companies when it is designed to produce the data on which selling decisions can be based.

One survey found that MIS were being implemented at 77 percent of the firms studied,[8] and further usage of computer-assisted selling is to be expected. Those who are considering a career in selling or sales management would be well advised to learn as much as possible about the use of computers in marketing.

National account selling

Instead of dealing piecemeal with a customer whose operations are found in several different geographic areas, a firm may consolidate its selling efforts and assign the responsibility to one salesperson. The biggest advantage of so-called national account selling is a coordinated approach toward important customers. Other advantages include the opportunity for specialization by customer, identification of sales responsibility (it eliminates the question of who is responsible—the salesperson who calls on the home office or the one who has a branch in his or her territory), and a promotional opportunity for professional salespersons.

CHANGES IN THE SALESPERSON

Sales personnel are also changing. The demands of expanded competition, technological innovation, increased government regulation, and rising costs have all played a part in modifying the salesperson's role. Many changes have been necessitated to enable salespeople to survive in the current business environment. Some of the ways salespeople are changing are discussed below.

1. *The salesperson has become more socially responsible.* It is evident that society is requiring all marketers to accept a higher degree of social responsibility, and salespeople are directly involved in this trend. Factual and reliable product information, better customer service, honest and consistent business dealings, and ethical selling conduct—these are the marks of a socially responsible salesperson.[9]

2. *Minority groups are entering sales as a career field.* Blacks, native Americans, Spanish-speaking Americans, and other minority groups are being encouraged to see sales as an area of equal employment opportunity. Sales forces have traditionally had a poor record

in minority hiring, and salespeople from these groups face some challenges in the field.[10] Traditional racial and ethnic barriers have largely disappeared, however, and selling has become a vehicle for improving the professional and career status of millions of disadvantaged employees. The professionalism of the individual salesperson's approach must be the only criterion for determining his or her effectiveness.

3. *The term* salesperson *has replaced* salesman *in the vocabulary of marketing.* Field selling is no longer exclusively a man's world. The government now reports that women hold 17.1 percent of all sales positions in manufacturing industries.[11] Selling offers unlimited possibilities for women who choose this career field; in addition to its direct rewards, it is an excellent stepping-stone to other business careers. This has always been true for men, and it is becoming equally true for women.

4. *The further professionalization of selling will require the salesperson to continue to change.* An increasingly professionalized sales function will require the salesperson to be alert to changes in the way he or she sells. There seems little doubt that *professionalism* will be a characteristic of selling endeavors in the years ahead. Business can be expected to demand professionalism in selecting the next generation of sales personnel. It has to, if the marketing system is to continue to prosper.[12]

SUMMARY

This final chapter has examined three major changes taking place in personal selling: (1) the customer is changing, (2) the sales function is changing, and (3) the salesperson is changing.

Today's consumers are better educated and more knowledgeable about the products and services they buy than their predecessors were. In addition, sales personnel can expect to be confronted with substantial consumer activism. These developments will require increased professionalism on the part of salespeople.

The following trends in the modern sales function can be identified: (1) consultative selling, (2) megaselling, (3) systems selling, (4) specialist selling, (5) computer-assisted selling, and (6) national account selling. These trends will probably continue to develop.

Sales personnel are also changing in the following ways: (1) the salesperson has become more socially responsible, (2) minority groups are entering sales as a career field, (3) more women are seeking sales occupations, (4) the further professionalization of selling will require the salesperson to continue to change.

REVIEW QUESTIONS/DISCUSSION QUESTIONS/EXERCISES

1. Briefly identify the following:
    a. Consultative selling.   e. Close rate.
    b. Megaselling.   f. Marketing information systems (MIS).
    c. Systems selling.   g. National account selling.
    d. Specialist selling.

2. Interview two or three sales managers in your community. Ask them how their companies use systems selling, megaselling, consultative selling, specialist selling and/or national account selling. Then prepare a report for the class.

3. Prepare a list of examples of systems selling. Can you think of any other firms that could use this concept?

4. Describe how customers are changing.

5. Discuss how the selling function is changing.

6. Discuss how the salesperson is changing.

7. What is the current status of the consumerism movement? How is it expected to affect the sales function in the years ahead?

8. Differentiate between a consultative salesperson and a product salesperson.

9. Explain how the concept of key target accounts used by Waukesha Motor Company (as described in this chapter) could be used by other firms to implement specialist selling.

10. Prepare a report on how companies use computers to assist their sales forces.

11. Prepare a report on minority hiring for sales positions, and develop a bibliography to accompany your report.

12. Prepare a report on women in selling and develop a bibliography to accompany your report.

13. Develop a list of reasons why more and more women are exploring sales careers.

14. Interview several local firms to determine how affirmative action concepts are being implemented in their sales recruiting program. A starting point would be to prepare a brief one- or two-page report on the meaning of affirmative action. Upon completing the interviews, make a class presentation on what you have learned.

15. Review the textbook and identify possible trends in personal selling other than those discussed in Chapter 17.

16. Various writers have suggested that selling should have a generally accepted code of professional ethics. Can you find any examples of such codes? Try to develop a code of ethics that would be accepted by most salespeople.

17. Make a list of what you consider to be *professional* occupations. How does selling compare to each of the occupations on your list? Explain.

18. Ask five salespersons to define the following terms:
    a. Consultative selling.
    b. Megaselling.
    c. Systems selling.
    d. Specialist selling.
    e. National account selling.

    Record each definition carefully. Then compare the various definitions you have collected. Do they differ substantially? If so, why?

19. Arrange a panel discussion involving three sales managers for your class. The topic is "What Does the Future Hold for Personal Selling?" Prepare a short critique of what is said.

20. Prepare a brief report on how you think you will be able to apply the concepts presented in this book to your future career plans.

CASE 17–1: WESTERN ENTERPRISES

The scene is a cocktail lounge at the Tucson Airport. John Artero, a sales representative of Western Enterprises is involved in an intense conversation with Billy Watson, the division sales manager. Artero has brought Watson to the airport for a six o'clock return flight to the division office in Dallas. As the two wait for Watson's plane, Artero remarks:

> Well, I suppose there is nothing I can do about the restructuring of my territory. I have put too many years into Western to quit over this change, but, Billy I wish you could get somebody to listen to us old-timers before they start making such sweeping changes.
>
> Frankly, I was flabbergasted to hear that a computer at Houston (Western's corporate headquarters) had decided to rearrange my territory by "clustering accounts according to sales potential." Does management think I have just been skimming the cream off the top of my area? Or worse yet, is that damn computer running Western Enterprises?
>
> Remember last year when we received an edict from the national sales manager to change the reporting forms for market and competitive information, so that the Houston office could make greater use of our computer facility for sales analysis purposes? I can tell you, that move cost me an extra two hours a week in paper work.
>
> Billy, what do you think? Am I wrong about this?

Questions

1. If you were Watson how would you respond to the questions raised by Artero?

2. Does this discussion suggest some of the problems involved in using the computer in modern selling?

3. Does Artero have a valid criticism of Western's operation? If so, how would you remedy it if you were national sales manager?

CASE 17–2: EAST COAST AIRLINES, INC.

East Coast Airlines is a Miami-based domestic and international air carrier. The company serves most major cities along the Atlantic Seaboard, including Boston, Hartford, New York, Philadelphia, Baltimore, Norfolk, Charleston, Atlanta, Jacksonville, Miami, and Washington, D.C. East Coast also services major Caribbean islands, which have become popular vacation spots, and it operates several aircraft for charter travel to points in its service area.

Edward Kronwald is the manager of the firm's Charter Sales Group. Kronwald directs a field force of eight charter sales representatives who maintain liaison with the travel agents in their territories and contact various groups and organizations that use air charters. At a staff meeting, Kronwald suggests that his group implement the concept of systems selling. Here is the way he explains it:

> As you all know, East Coast has recently made two significant acquisitions. First we bought Funtime Travel, a chain of 13 travel agencies along the Atlantic seacoast. Then only last week we acquired major hotels on three Caribbean Islands, two of which are now serviced by our regular flights.
>
> This would be an ideal time to introduce the concept of systems selling to the Charter Sales Group. We could develop some vacation packages using these hotels, and our regular stops as well as charter flights. Then we could market the packages through Funtime Travel.
>
> It seems to me that the key will be to put together a dynamic, hard-hitting sales presentation. What do you people think?

Questions

1. What is your opinion of Kronwald's idea?
2. Can you cite examples in which systems selling has been used successfully in the travel industry? Have there been any failures?
3. Develop a sample vacation package for East Coast Airlines. Make any necessary assumptions about the location and room rates of the three vacation hotels.
4. Outline a sales presentation to a group or organization interested in charter travel for the package you have developed.

Appendixes

Appendix A

How to Get a Job in Selling

This text has described professional selling—what is required of the individual on the job as well as the possible rewards from selling. At this point you probably have a good idea of whether or not you want to consider selling as a career or as a starting point in pursuing another business career.

The next question is: How do you get a job in selling? The answer is a plan beginning with self-preparation and ending with closing the employment agreement. Your plan should recognize that getting a job is in itself a selling job.

The first step in seeking a job is taking care of all the details in regard to dress and grooming. This might include buying a suit, some shirts, a dress, or taking clothing to the dry cleaners. Footwear is important in that it should complement the suit or dress and be in good condition (shined shoes are a must).

Step one: Self-preparation

Good grooming is also a must for any job applicant. There are two questions an individual must ask with regard to grooming. The first is: Is my personal appearance appropriate for the selling job I will be seeking? The second is: Does my appearance project a neat, well-groomed look?

In the second step the individual analyzes himself or herself and develops career and monetary objectives. The key is know yourself in terms of not only strengths and weaknesses but also aspirations.

Step two: Self-analysis

Of the traits sales and marketing managers look for in job applicants, personal ones appear most important compared with marketing skills, nonmarketing skills, outside activities, and school characteristics (Table A–1). Six of the eight highest-rated characteristics are personal in nature, with maturity the most important. Personal selling/sales management skills are the highest-rated marketing skills and are ranked second overall.

In self-analysis, individuals should consider how best to project those traits that appear most important during the job interview and in their respective resumes. Previous job experience might be emphasized as evidence of maturity and personal selling skills. It should

**Table A–1
Hiring criteria as seen
by managers**

		Rank, characteristic, and variable*	Mean score
1.	P	Maturity	3.68
2.	M	Personal selling/sales management skills	3.67
3.	P	Appearance	3.60
4.	P	Cooperativeness	3.54
5.	N	Communications/public speaking	3.45
6.	P	Disposition	3.34
7.	P	Punctuality	3.30
8.	P	Mannerisms	3.28
9.	M	General marketing skills	3.21
10.	N	English/writing skills	3.14
11.	N	Management skills	2.89
12.	P	Extroversion	2.74
13.	S	Marketing department reputation	2.60
14.	M	Product development/management skills	2.59
15.	N	Finance skills	2.55
16.	M	Market research skills	2.51
17.	M	Market logistics skills	2.49
18.	N	Personnel management skills	2.48
19.	O	Civic functions	2.48
20.	N	Management science skills	2.47
21.	M	Advertising/advertising management skills	2.45
22.	M	Consumer/industrial buyer behavior skills	2.38
23.	S	School reputation	2.38
24.	M	Pricing skills	2.36
25.	N	Accounting skills	2.36
26.	S	Internship program	2.34
27.	O	Social functions	2.30
28.	S	Recruiting success with school	2.21
29.	N	Internship training skills	2.19
30.	O	Sports participation	2.10
31.	M	Retailing/retail management skills	1.99
32.	O	Home hobbies	1.99
33.	O	Fraternal organizations	1.99
34.	N	Social sciences/arts skills	1.93

*P: personal traits; M: marketing skills; N: nonmarketing skills; S: school reputation; O: outside activities.
Source: Kenneth C. Schneider, "Personal Traits Most Important to Potential Employers," Reprinted from *Marketing News* published by the American Marketing Association, January 31, 1978, p. 5.

also be remembered that the purpose of the resume is to secure an interview.

The inner drive to succeed is all-important no matter what career path an individual pursues. Therefore, as part of self-analysis an individual should set forth goals, in terms of both jobs and finances. A convenient classification is after 2 years, 5 years, 10 years, and 15 years.

Step three: Market research

The individual needs to be familiar with all the sources of information about jobs. Emphasis is placed on all sources because it is estimated that only 20 percent of the available jobs are public knowledge or publicized in some fashion.

Different types of sources include newspaper advertisements, college placement offices, professional publications, state employment offices, professional placement firms, and professional organizations such as Sales & Marketing Executives International and the American Marketing Association. College professors can often provide valuable insights into the job market, and specific jobs that might be available in the local area.

Step four: Contact strategy

In this step the individual develops a strategy for contacting prospective employers. Direct contact is twice as effective as other techniques, but a direct-mail approach will have to be used with many prospective employers. Attention should be directed to a well-constructed resume that highlights an individual's strong points.

Step five: Sales promotion

This step involves contacting and arranging the initial interviews with prospective employers. Important points to remember in the interview are:

1. Project important personal traits.
2. Obtain vital information about the job and working conditions.
3. Determine the key contact who will make the hiring decision.

Often a candidate for a sales job will be asked to sell some object on the interviewer's desk to the interviewer. The purpose is to see how the job applicant handles himself or herself in a selling situation.

Step six: Contact

This step involves the interview or usually interviews for the position. As a candidate for a position, an individual will very likely be interviewed by several different people. The first interview will be part of the preliminary screening of the individual along with the resume. Just as a prospect is qualified, the candidate will be screened initially to determine:

1. His or her level of interest in the position.
2. His or her qualifications as matched against the job description.

Subsequent interviews provide an opportunity for different people to meet the individual and develop certain areas in depth. Some of the key factors interviewers will be interested in are:

1. Motivation of the individual. Is the individual really interested in the job and will he or she perform well on the job?
2. Ability of the individual to handle himself or herself in meeting different people and facing different situations.
3. Ability of the individual to espouse his or her strong points.
4. Attitudes of the individual.

It is very likely that the candidate will be given a test with questions such as those listed at the end of this appendix. The results of the test along with some form of grading for the interviews will be used in determining whether or not a position is offered the candidate.

Step seven: Negotiation

This step corresponds to a sales presentation, only in this case the product is the individual. Salary, expenses, working conditions, fringe benefits, and possibilities for advancement should all be covered at this time.

Step eight: Closing

Uppermost in this step is knowing this is the job you, the applicant, really want! Getting an offer in writing and confirming in writing are essential. Company policy may dictate a visit to the home office in this step or Step six and such a request should be viewed positively.

A final word of advice seems appropriate. Once you are hired, do everything possible to learn your function as quickly as possible. You should strive to make yourself as valuable as possible to your new employer. When you have learned your job well and are a productive member of the sales organization, start planning the next step in your career path. In short, the personal sales cycle starts all over again! Good luck!

Preparation

1. As a salesman of complex industrial equipment, which of the following would be most important to you?
   a. A full understanding of the equipment.
   b. An ability to cite exact figures about the equipment's efficiency, life span, production capacity, etc.
   c. Information about companies that have used this equipment.
   d. Memorizing a standard sales presentation covering all important features of the equipment.

2. The salesman should try to understand his prospect in order to (check the *worst* answer)—
   a. Show that he is interested in the prospect.
   b. Make the sale as fast as possible.
   c. See the prospect's viewpoint regarding the product.
   d. Quickly establish rapport with the prospect.

Opening

3. Prior to your presentation, your prospect, whom you have just met, is talking to you about something not related to your product. While this is going on, the worst thing you could do is—
   a. Listen attentively.
   b. Mentally review your presentation but appear attentive.
   c. Attempt to politely interrupt so that you can start your presentation.
   d. Try to get some clues about his personality.

4. You have found out that your prospect wants very much to impress his boss. The best way of establishing your relationship with your prospect would be to—
   a. Mail him a news clipping in which his boss is mentioned.
   b. Put in a good word for him to his boss.
   c. Give him ideas he can present to his own management.
   d. Ask him what you can do to help him impress his boss.

Presentation

5. When presenting information about your product, advertising material is best used—
   a. As an initial attention-getter.
   b. In the middle of the presentation to break up whatever boredom there may be.
   c. As a visual aid, to be referred to from time to time.
   d. At the end of the presentation, and left with the prospect.

6. During the course of a presentation, a prospect inquires about his competitor's plans, with which you are familiar since the competitor

Continued

is also one of your customers. Which would be the worst course to take?

 a. Show how ethical you are by refusing to answer such a question.

 b. Help the sale along by telling what you have learned.

 c. Avoid answering by saying that you are not aware of the plans.

 d. Impress your prospect with the idea that he wouldn't want you to divulge such information about his organization.

Overcoming objections

7. When a prospect points out that in certain areas your competitor's product is better, the worst thing you can do is—

 a. Show how your competitor's product is lacking in other areas.

 b. Point out that this is only a very minor advantage compared with the advantages of your product.

 c. Point out the benefits of your own product.

 d. Subtly deny that his statement is valid.

8. Your prospect is a "yes" man who agrees with every point you make. However, when the close is attempted, he says that he needs more time to think it over. When you call on him again, the same situation occurs. What should you do on the third call?

 a. Continue your presentation, but inform him that you can't call again.

 b. Attempt to close the sale, but if this is not successful, leave and forget this prospect for the time being.

 c. Make a far-fetched claim about your product to see if your prospect is listening.

 d. Ask your prospect directly why he is not giving you the order.

Closing

9. What should you do if a company's buyer constantly refuses you?

 a. Alter your presentation.

 b. Study the methods of your competition.

 c. Don't call on him for a while.

 d. Attempt to influence his subordinate personnel.

10. After completing a rather lengthy presentation which included most benefits and features of your product, you should (check both the best *and* the worst action)—

 a. Summarize the features in which the person has shown interest.

 b. Suggest that he think a minute before making a decision.

 c. Ask him when he thinks he can make a decision.

 d. Ask him how much of your product he wants to order.

Answers: 1. (A) 2. (B) 3. (C) 4. (C) 5. (C) 6. (B) 7. (D) 8. (D) 9. (A) 10. (A Best), (C Worst).
Source: Reprinted by permission of Sales Aptitude Corp.
The best score is 11 (the final question requires a double answer); the worst possible score is 0.

Appendix B   Selected Readings

The following list of readings, arranged alphabetically by author, represents a cross section of the vast amount of material that one could study on this subject. Some of these articles illustrate a historical perspective. Others are quite contemporary. Some selections are easy, pleasurable reading; others are very complex and technical. The sources also vary from popular to academic to regional publications.

Your authors hope that you will find the list a useful resource as you explore the concept of professional selling. Continuous reading is a vital part of any self-improvement program.

Ash, Mary Kay. "Lady: Have I Got a Job for You!" *Marketing Times,* January–February 1978, pp. 26–28.

Carruth, Eleanore. "New Arms for an Army of Insurance Agents." *Fortune,* April 1977, pp. 132–34.

Caust, Daniel. "A Plan for Every Customer." *Sales & Marketing Management,* July 7, 1980, pp. 36–37.

Doyle, Stephen X., and Benson P. Shapiro. "What Counts Most in Motivating Your Sales Force?" *Harvard Business Review,* May–June 1980, pp. 133–40.

Dreyfack, Raymond. "A Guide to Profitable Salesmanship." *Sales & Marketing Management,* April 7, 1980, pp. 35–37.

Hahne, C. E. "How to Measure Results of Sales Training." *Training and Development Journal,* November 1977, pp. 3–7.

Halvorson, Paul J., and William Rudelius. "Is There a Free Lunch?" *Journal of Marketing,* January 1977, pp. 44–49.

Haugh, Louis J. "Detailmen—Salesmen Who Don't sell." *Advertising Age,* February 13, 1978, pp. 67–68, 70.

"Hyster, Getting a Lift from Operation Turnaround." *Sales & Marketing Management,* January 1979, pp. 14–15.

Kanuk, Leslie. "Women in Industrial Selling." *Journal of Marketing,* January 1978, pp. 87–91.

Lynch, Dudley. "Getting 'In Sync' with the Customer." *Sales & Marketing Management,* May 19, 1980, pp. 42–46.

Menzies, Hugh D. "The New Life of a Salesman." *Fortune,* August 11, 1980, pp. 172–80.

Morner, Aimee L. "Jack Hanley Got There by Selling Harder." *Fortune,* November, 1976, pp. 162, 166, 171, 173, 175, 177–178.

Nash, Henry W. "Origin and Development of Personal Selling." *Mississippi Business Review,* January 1977, pp. 6–8.

O'Hanlon, James O. "Even a Millionaire Couldn't Buy Something Like That." *Forbes,* November 1, 1977, pp. 88, 90.

O'Hanlon, James O. "The Rich Rewards of the Salesman's Life." *Forbes,* October 16, 1978, pp. 155–62.

Pletcher, Barbara. "Memo to: Saleswomen Re: Problems and Opportunities." *Marketing Times,* January–February 1979, pp. 26–29.

Putinski, Donald. "3 Aces: Planning, Goal-Setting, Delegating." *Marketing Times,* September–October 1978, pp. 22–24.

Reetof, Walter G. "How to Find Meaning in all Those Statistics." *Marketing Times,* September–October 1978, pp. 26–27.

Scanlon, Sally. "Every Salesperson a Psychologist." *Sales & Marketing Management,* February 6, 1978, pp. 34–36.

Stepanak, Steven H. "Educate Your Customers to Appreciate Service." *Business Horizons,* August 1980, pp. 21–22.

Stephenson, P. Ronald; William L. Cron; and Gary L. Frazier. "Delegating Pricing Authority to the Sales Force: The Effects on Sales and Profit Performance." *Journal of Marketing,* Spring 1977, pp. 21–28.

Swan, John E; Charles M. Futrell; and John T. Todd. "Same Job—Different Views: Women and Men in Industrial Sales." *Journal of Marketing,* January 1978, pp. 92–98.

Taylor, Thayer C. "A Letup in the Rise of Sales Call Costs." *Sales & Marketing Management,* February 25, 1980, pp. 25–34.

Teresko, John. "Bridging the Gap between Trade Shows and Sales." *Industry Week,* January 9, 1978, pp. 39–42.

Thornton, Jack. "Honing Sales Techniques." *Industrial Marketing,* June 1980, pp. 68, 72.

Thornton, Jack. "Republic Steel Selling to Declining Markets." *Industrial Marketing,* June 1980, pp. 74–78.

Uttal, Bro. "How Ray MacDonald's Growth Theory Created IBM's Toughest Competitor." *Fortune,* January 1977, pp. 94–99, 102, 104.

Young, George. "Owens-Corning Incentive Plan Woos Distributors—and Sales." *Industrial Marketing,* January 1978, pp. 99–100.

Appendix

C

Salesmanship: The Time-Is-Money Game

By STEWART A. WASHBURN
Vice President & Director of Special
Projects, Porter Henry & Co.

Ask any salesman this question: What's the difference between a good salesman—a good producer—and one who just gets by?

The chances are he'll tell you that the good producer is the one with the more persuasive communication skills. Maybe he'll tell you that the good producer is the one who knows his customers and products best. Rarely, however, will you hear that the good producer is the one who invests his time where the money is.

Yet of the three things that make for sales productivity—
☐ **effective two-way communication skills**
☐ **knowledge of customers and products**
☐ **prudent investment of available sales time—**
the way a salesman invests his time may well be the most critical.

Salesmen can always improve their selling skills. They can always learn more about their products, their customers, and their prospects. But there is nothing they can do to expand time. There are only 250 business days per year. Most salesmen can make only five calls a day. With careful attention to routing, some salesmen can squeeze in one additional call per day. That means only 1,250 calls per year for most salesmen and 1,500 for a fortunate few. (Some consumer packaged goods salesmen are able to make 10 calls per day. With luck, they may even be able to squeeze in another call, for a total of 11. That means, for them, only 2,500 or maybe 2,750 calls per year.)

There is no way in heaven or on earth that the time budget can be increased. Yet most salesmen tend to spend about the same amount of time with all customers and prospects, invest the same amount of time with buying influences as with decision makers. And they spend sales calls as if they were limitless.

Making salesmen aware that salesmanship is a real time-is-money game is a continuing challenge for us and for anyone managing or supervising salesmen. One of the easiest ways we've found for convincing salesmen that time is indeed money is a simple paper-and-pencil game. The chips are half-hour increments of time. The game board is a territory complete with prospects, customers, and less-than-ideal transportation facilities similar to those in thousands of territories. The rules and method of scoring reflect the facts of life that salesmen face every day.

Salesmanship: The Time-is-Money Game has taught hundreds of salesmen the importance of investing available sales time wisely, as well as how to find just a little more time. We offer no money, no savings bonds, no trading stamps as an inducement to play. All we offer is an opportunity to become familiar with a device that will show your salesmen how to manage their time effectively.

Who Can Play This Game

This game is designed for any field man—manager or salesman—who may play it either alone or in competition with his peers.

Source: Reprinted by permission from *Sales & Marketing Management* magazine.

Centerville Sales Territory

This is the situation:

You represent the Great American Corp.; you are a general line salesman. Yours is the Centerville territory. You have worked the territory for several years and know it quite well.

You are about to plan your itinerary for the last four weeks of the quarter. Your quota for the quarter is $300,000. Sales for the first two months of the quarter total $280,000, leaving you only $20,000 short of your nut. It is important that you meet your quota because Great American has big plans for you if you do.

You have 14 regular customers for your products in the Centerville territory. So far during the quarter, they have bought $280,000

worth. However, you know that among them they have the potential for an additional $27,500 during the remaining month of the quarter.

You have also identified 10 nonbuying prospects in the territory. They represent an additional $39,800 in potential sales during the remaining month of the quarter. Your job is to plan the itinerary that will generate the most sales for you during the remaining four weeks of the quarter.

Details of your customers and prospects, identified by name and number, follow, as does a map of the Centerville territory showing the location of your accounts and the travel time between them.

Here Are The Rules

1. Available Selling Time

Sales time is limited to the period from 8:30 a.m. to 5:00 p.m. for five days, Monday through Friday, during the four-week period for which you are to plan the itinerary. Use the planning form. You'll need four copies, one for each week. A sample, partly filled in.

Sales time is reduced by the following factors:

Travel—the amount of time it takes to travel from one account to another

Waiting time—the amount of time you must wait to see a prospect or a customer if you do not have an appointment.

Telephone time—the amount of time you spend on the phone making appointments.

Paper work—each day of selling activity generates one hour of paper work, which must be completed before the beginning of the next week.

Lunch time—unless the lunch hour is used to entertain a customer or a prospect, effective selling time is reduced by a one-hour lunch period sometime between 11:30 and 1:30.

Don't forget holidays—your territory celebrates them all.

2. Travel Time

Travel in the Centerville territory is mostly by car. Facilities for air travel are limited.

North Town Airways has an early morning turnaround flight between Centerville and North Town and a late evening turnaround flight. Service between Easton and North Town and Weston and North Town is quite frequent during the day. The current North Town Airways schedule is shown.

If you travel by air, it will take you ½ hour after your arrival to rent a car and drive to town. For example, if you fly to Easton, it will take you ½ hour to rent a car and drive to Alpha Transformer. However, if your first call after flying to Easton is to be made on the Air Conditioning Corp., it will take you ½ hour to rent a car and travel through Easton plus one hour of travel from Easton to the Air Conditioning Corp. Except in the case of air travel to North Town, travel to the first call each day may be completed by 8:30.

Hotel or motel accommodations are available within ½ hour's travel of all accounts. It is not necessary to return home each night. See travel map.

3. Making Appointments

Calls can be made cold or by appointment. Appointments can be made by phone only on the day before the call is scheduled. Three appointments can be made by phone per ½ hour. Phone calls to make appointments can be made only during normal selling/business hours; that is, from 8:30 to 5:00. Separate appointments must be made with each individual.

Calls can be made without appointments, but ½ hour of waiting time will be consumed before the person can be seen.

4. Length Of Each Sales Call

No sales call on an individual can exceed 1½ hours. However, if lunch is included, a sales call may be extended to 2½ hours.

5. Value Of Sales Time

Each half hour of sales time with a decision maker or a key buying influence increases the probability of making the sale as follows.

Calls On Present Customers

	First Call			Second Call			Third And Succeeding Calls		
	1st ½ hr.	2nd ½ hr.	3rd ½ hr.	1st ½ hr.	2nd ½ hr.	3rd ½ hr.	1st ½ hr.	2nd ½ hr.	3rd ½ hr.
Decision Maker	10	7	5	8	5	2	5	3	0
Key Buying Influence	6	4	2	5	4	3	4	3	2

Calls On Prospects

	First Call			Second Call			Third And Succeeding Calls		
	1st ½ hr.	2nd ½ hr.	3rd ½ hr.	1st ½ hr.	2nd ½ hr.	3rd ½ hr.	1st ½ hr.	2nd ½ hr.	3rd ½ hr.
Decision Maker	5	4	3	6	7	8	10	11	12
Key Buying Influence	4	3	2	4	5	6	7	4	3

5. (Continued)

If you make an hour-and-one-half first call on the design engineer of Handwound Coil Co. and a first call on the general foreman, you will increase the probability of making the sale by 34% (10 plus 7 plus 5 plus 6 plus 4 plus 2). You will have consumed three hours of sales time. However, if you make a one-hour first call on both the design engineer and general foreman plus a half-hour second call on each, you will have consumed the same amount of time, three hours, and will have increased the probability of making the sale to 40% (1st calls: 10 plus 7 plus 6 plus 4; 2nd calls: 8 plus 5).

6. Entertainment

You can entertain only one person at a time, only at lunch, and for only one hour. Entertainment increases the probability of making the sale by a percentage equal to the value of the second half-hour of the call. You can entertain a prospect or a customer only after spending one-half hour of selling time with him in his office. With entertainment (lunch), a call may extend to 2½ hours, with extra credit for the lunch hour.

7. Scoring

For sales time to count, the probability of making the sale must be greater than 50%. To calculate the value of sales time with an account, simply multiply the total probability of making the sale (provided it is greater than 50%) by the total remaining potential of the account. Use the score sheet.

8. Winning

The winner will be the salesman who follows the rules and generates the greatest sales volume.

Customers	Sales To Date	Remaining Potential	People To See
1. Handwound Coil	$75,000	$3,000	Design Engineer* Gen. Foreman Foreman Purchasing Agent
2. General Dymo	63,000	1,500	Purchasing Agent* Design Engineer #1 Design Engineer #2
3. Superior Electric	34,000	4,000	Purchasing Agent* Design Engineer
4. Herman Transformer	28,000	1,000	Purchasing Agent*
5. Alpha Transformer	24,000	2,000	Purchasing Agent* Design Engineer
6. Circle D. Centrals	9,500	3,000	Purchasing Agent* Design Engineer
7. Easton Motors	8,000	1,500	Design Engineer*
8. Fractional Motors	7,000	3,000	Design Engineer* Foreman Purchasing Agent
9. Acme Motors	7,000	2,500	Design Engineer* Purchasing Agent
10. Bartlett Transformer	6,500	1,000	Purchasing Agent*
11. Zip Electric	6,000	3,000	Purchasing Agent* Design Engineer
12. Taft Electric	6,000	500	Purchasing Agent* Design Engineer
13. Macro Electric	5,000	500	Purchasing Agent*
14. Roth Motors	1,000	1,000	Design Engineer*
Prospects			
15. ABC Transformer	—	3,000	Purchasing Agent* Design Engineer Foreman
16. Ace Motors	—	1,500	Design Engineer* Foreman Purchasing Agent
17. Air Conditioning Corp.	—	5,000	Purchasing Agent* Design Engineer
18. Amp Motors	—	3,500	Design Engineer* Foreman Purchasing Agent
19. Eastern Windings	—	1,500	Design Engineer*
20. Holmes Electric	—	3,000	Design Engineer* Purchasing Agent
21. Manual Electric	—	1,800	Purchasing Agent
22. Micro Electric	—	2,500	Design Engineer* Foreman Purchasing Agent
23. Twister Coil	—	3,000	Purchasing Agent* Design Engineer
24. U.S. Lyndon	—	15,000	Design Engineer* Foreman (1) Foreman (2) Purchasing Agent

Decision Maker

Centerville Territory

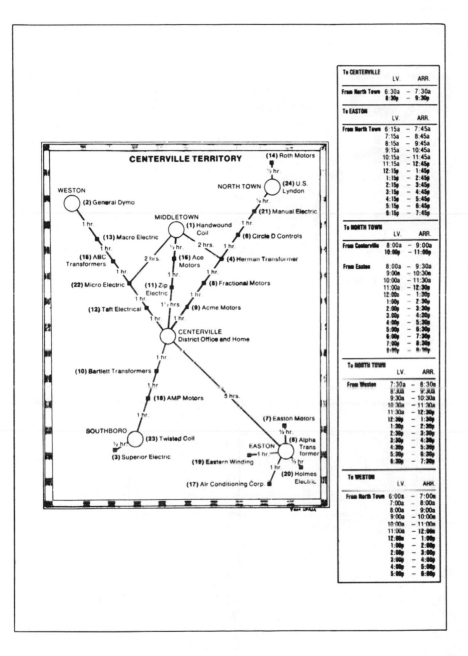

The schedule tables on the right side:

To CENTERVILLE	LV.	ARR.
From North Town	6:30a – 7:30a	
	8:30p – 9:30p	

To EASTON	LV.	ARR.
From North Town	6:15a – 7:45a	
	7:15a – 8:45a	
	8:15a – 9:45a	
	9:15a – 10:45a	
	10:15a – 11:45a	
	11:15a – 12:45p	
	12:15p – 1:45p	
	1:15p – 2:45p	
	2:15p – 3:45p	
	3:15p – 4:45p	
	4:15p – 5:45p	
	5:15p – 6:45p	
	6:15p – 7:45p	

To NORTH TOWN	LV.	ARR.
From Centerville	8:00a – 9:00a	
	10:00p – 11:00p	
From Easton	8:00a – 9:30a	
	9:00a – 10:30a	
	10:00a – 11:30a	
	11:00a – 12:30p	
	12:00n – 1:30p	
	1:00p – 2:30p	
	2:00p – 3:30p	
	3:00p – 4:30p	
	4:00p – 5:30p	
	5:00p – 6:30p	
	6:00p – 7:30p	
	7:00p – 8:30p	
	8:00p – 9:30p	

To NORTH TOWN	LV.	ARR.
From Weston	7:30a – 8:30a	
	8:30a – 9:30a	
	9:30a – 10:30a	
	10:30a – 11:30a	
	11:30a – 12:30p	
	12:30p – 1:30p	
	1:30p – 2:30p	
	2:30p – 3:30p	
	3:30p – 4:30p	
	4:30p – 5:30p	
	5:30p – 6:30p	
	6:30p – 7:30p	

To WESTON	LV.	ARR.
From North Town	6:00a – 7:00a	
	7:00a – 8:00a	
	8:00a – 9:00a	
	9:00a – 10:00a	
	10:00a – 11:00a	
	11:00a – 12:00n	
	12:00n – 1:00p	
	1:00p – 2:00p	
	2:00p – 3:00p	
	3:00p – 4:00p	
	4:00p – 5:00p	
	5:00p – 6:00p	

Scoring Sheet

The information on this page completes all you will need to know to play this game. Record your solution, week by week, on the copies of the form on the opposite page. Before you do, make eight photocopies of the form—four for practice, four for record. GOOD LUCK.

Account	(Remaining Potential)	x	(% Probability)	Sales Income
1. Handwound Coil	$ 3.000	x	_____ %	$ _____
2. General Dymo	1.500	x	_____	_____
3. Superior Electric	4.000	x	_____	_____
4. Herman Transformer	1.000	x	_____	_____
5. Alpha Transformer	2.000	x	_____	_____
6. Circle D. Centrals	3.000	x	_____	_____
7. Easton Motors	1.500	x	_____	_____
8. Fractional Motors	3.000	x	_____	_____
9. Acme Motors	2.500	x	_____	_____
10. Bartlett Transformer	1.000	x	_____	_____
11. Zip Electric	3.000	x	_____	_____
12. Taft Electric	500	x	_____	_____
13. Macro Electric	500	x	_____	_____
14. Roth Motors	1.000	x	_____	_____
15. ABC Transformer	3.000	x	_____	_____
16. Ace Motors	1.500	x	_____	_____
17. Air Conditioning Corp	5.000	x	_____	_____
18. Amp Motors	3.500	x	_____	_____
19. Eastern Windings	1.500	x	_____	_____
20. Holmes Electric	3.000	x	_____	_____
21. Manual Electric	1.800	x	_____	_____
22. Micro Electric	2.500	x	_____	_____
23. Twister Coil	3.000	x	_____	_____
24. U S Lyndon	15.000	x	_____	_____
			Total Sales Volume Generated	$ _____

FOR EXAMPLE ONLY   TERRITORY PLANNING FORM   Week ending _____

DAY	MONDAY			TUESDAY			WEDNESDAY			THURSDAY			FRIDAY		
Hours	Account No	People To See	%	Account No	People To See	%	Account No	People To See	%	Account No	People To See	%	Account No	People To See	%
8 30 – 9 00	2A	WAIT	–												
9 00 – 9 30		DE	5												
9 30 – 10 00		DE	4												
10 00 – 10 30		DE	3												
10 30 – 11 00		WAIT	–												
11 00 – 11 30		PA	4												
11 30 – 12 00		PA	3												
12 00 – 12 30	LUNCH	PA	3												
12 30 – 1 00	"	"	–												
1 00 – 1 30	TEL-DA APPTS		–												
1 30 – 2 00		TRAVEL	–												
2 00 – 2 30		WAIT	–												
2 30 – 3 00	21	PA	5												
3 00 – 3 30		TRAVEL	–												
3 30 – 4 00		"	–												
4 00 – 4 30	6	PA	10												
4 30 – 5 00		PA	7												
Subtotals	22% FOR #24 5% FOR #21 17% FOR #6														

TERRITORY PLANNING FORM

Note: To play this game. it will be necessary for you to make *eight* copies of the Territory Planning Form below. One set of four is for practice. the other set of four for record.

Week ending _____

DAY		MONDAY			TUESDAY			WEDNESDAY			THURSDAY			FRIDAY		
Hours		Account No.	People To See	%	Account No.	People To See	%	Account No.	People To See	%	Account No.	People To See	%	Account No.	People To See	%
8:30–9:00																
9:00–9:30																
9:30–10:00																
10:00–10:30																
10:30–11:00																
11:00–11:30																
11:30–12:00																
12:00–12:30																
12:30–1:00																
1:00–1:30																
1:30–2:00																
2:00–2:30																
2:30–3:00																
3:00–3:30																
3:30–4:00																
4:00–4:30																
4:30–5:00																
Subtotals																

Now That You've Played (And, We Hope, Won) Salesmanship: The Time-Is-Money Game, You'll Want Your Salesmen To Play It, Too.

For the game to pay off for you and your salesmen, you'll need a prize for the winner, and your salesmen will need time to play—two or three hours is usually required. They'll also need an opportunity to discuss their results with other salesmen.

Here's a procedure to follow for getting the most out of the game:

1. **Three or four weeks in advance** of your next sales meeting, distribute copies of the game to your sales force, along with an announcement of the prize, and instructions to mail scoring sheets and territory planning forms to you one week before the meeting.

2. **Arrange to have contest entries checked** to make sure the rules have been followed and applied correctly. Usually it is sufficient to check just the 10 highest scorers. From that group select a winner and two runners-up. The winner will be the salesperson who chalks up the greatest sales income for the company. In case of a tie, duplicate prizes will be awarded.

3. **At the sales meeting,** present the prize to the winner. Allow an hour and a half for the winner and the runners-up to describe the methods and procedures they used to achieve their high scores, and how those methods and procedures can apply to their own territories.

Complete sets of this game are available for use by your field salesmen. Order by writing to Sales Management's Sales Builders Div., 633 Third Ave., New York, N.Y. 10017, specifying that you require sets of *Salesmanship: The Time-Is-Money Game* (Game No. 5). Phone 212/986-4800.

© Copyright 1976, Porter Henry & Co., Inc., New York, N.Y.

This game was devised by Stewart A. Washburn, vice president and director of special projects, Porter Henry & Co. Washburn, who is a chemical engineer, graduated from the Massachusetts Institute of Technology. For 10 years, he headed his own firm of market development and sales training consultants. In 1963, he joined Porter Henry & Co., where he has directed the reorganization and retraining of sales forces for such clients as Allied Chemical, American Motors, Diamond Alkali, and Holland American Cruises. His special areas are small business management, market planning, computer utilization, performance evaluation, and incentive compensation.

Appendix D

Case of the Suspect Salesman

Jim Lee graduated from college in June of 1975 with a major in business administration. He was hired by the Casco Drug Company in September as a sales representative trainee and assigned to Sal Lucci's district.

Sal was the Exeter district sales manager for the Casco Drug Company (see Exhibit 1). His 11 sales representatives covered New Jersey, parts of Delaware, and Pennsylvania as far west as Lancaster. The district was considered an important revenue producer for the company.

Like the other 300 Casco sales reps, Jim Lee sold a wide line of prescription and over-the-counter drugs to doctors, hospitals, drug retailers, wholesalers, and chains. Sales reps called on doctors to introduce new products and to remind them of old items with the objective of having the doctor prescribe Casco brands. With retailers, wholesalers, and chains, the reps checked inventory, introduced new products, and sold items being specially promoted.

The performance of the reps was evaluated primarily on the basis of sales in their territories. However, consideration was given also to the number of calls per day, number of products presented per call, the supervisor's assessment of their work, and their success in following the current sales promotion plan.

As a sales rep, Jim could improve his sales primarily in two ways:

Source: Reprinted by permission of *Harvard Business Review*. "Case of The Suspect Salesman" by Albert H. Dunn (November–December 1979). Copyright © 1979 by the President and Fellows of Harvard College; all rights reserved.

Exhibit 1
Casco Drug Company

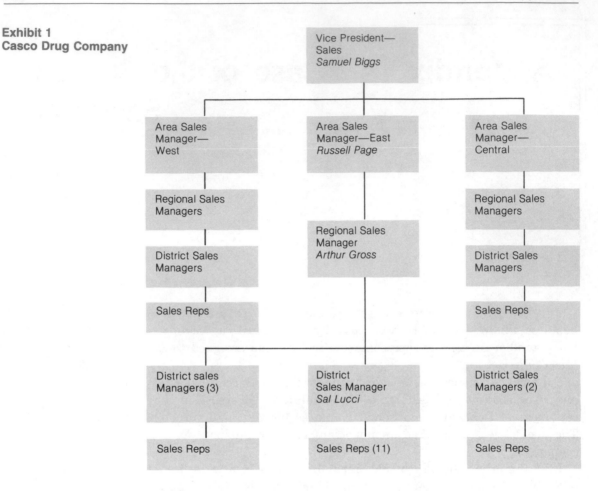

by increasing the number of calls he made in a week and by improving the quality of his relationships with doctors and middlemen. For example, he might make additional calls on some doctors who were in their offices on Saturday morning, he might schedule presentations to hospitals for Saturdays and holidays, or he might take extra time to advise wholesalers and retailers on inventory and promotion.

Like all Casco sales recruits, Jim Lee first worked his way through the sales orientation schedule (see Exhibit 2). For those reps who showed outstanding management potential, after some time in the field there was a sales management development program.

Each year three to five of the most promising reps joined the headquarters sales staff in Chicago. Here they were exposed to a variety of management problems, indoctrinated in the corporation's promo-

Week	Activities
1	District assignment; beginning company orientation and territory indoctrination.
2–5	Full time at Sales Training Institute (Chicago): product information, sales policies and procedures, work in selling skills and techniques.
6–17	Work-assigned territory, traveling one week each with two training coaches* and district manager; biweekly correspondence instruction; regular quizzes and evaluations from the institute.
18–21	Full time at the institute: advanced instruction in product specifications, use, and performance; sales techniques.
22–27	Work the territory; biweekly correspondence instruction, regular quizzes, and quiz scores from the institute for the last six weeks.

**Exhibit 2
Sales orientation
schedule**

*Senior salespeople from the trainee's district.

tion strategies, and given the opportunity to assist headquarters staff in decision making.

After about two years, those who were successful in this program returned to the field as assistant managers in large districts or as managers of smaller districts.

The problem unfolds

As part of his sales orientation training, Jim was sent in October 1975 to the Casco Sales Training Institute in Chicago for an intensive one-month indoctrination in the company's products, sales procedures, and selling techniques. In the regular summary report to Jim's district manager, the director commented on the young man's month in Chicago:

> Jim's bright, very bright, learns quickly, and retains well. But he certainly has his own ideas about how we should run things! Some of his ideas are good; in fact, we've implemented several of them here, but the others are a waste of everybody's time. This is probably just a function of his inexperience. He'll learn fast and be a winner!

When he read this comment, Sal recalled some recent experiences with other young salespeople and noted in the margin, "Another young revolutionary???"

In November, Jim was assigned to his territory and worked it for three months, traveling a week each with two training coaches and Sal. During this period he prepared the regular correspondence assignments from the institute and took examinations on the material. He went back in February for another month at the institute and in

March returned to his territory and completed his training with six weeks of correspondence instruction from the institute.

Jim throws a party.   In the late fall of 1976, Jim stopped by Sal's office to invite him to a party the following Sunday. "There are a bunch of us who hang around together, watch TV, play golf—you know," Jim said. "We're going to watch the Jets and the Giants on Sunday, and we'd like you and Mrs. Lucci to join us at our house around 1:30."

This invitation was a new one for Sal. He couldn't remember one time when he and his wife Betty had been asked to an informal party by one of his junior people. Sal didn't like pro football, and he preferred to read the paper on Sundays. Also he didn't like having to shave and put on a tie over the weekend. But he thought it would be impolite not to accept Jim's invitation.

When Sal and Betty drove to the Lee's home, they noted that the house, though small, was located in the most desirable and expensive neighborhood of the city. Several of the cars parked in front of the house were sports models. "Damn well not company cars," Sal muttered.

In addition to Jim and Carol Lee, there were five other couples. Among them were two of Sal's reps, a lawyer, a physical therapist, and an assistant professor at the university. The Cutlers were the only other couple from Sal's generation—Tom Cutler was Sal's office manager.

The party centered around a large color TV, where the game was in progress. The volume was set high, but nobody seemed to listen except the professor who sat as close as possible to the set. Everyone talked loudly over the noise. The conversation was liberally laced with obscenities. All the young people were casually dressed; only Sal and Tom Cutler wore ties. The lawyer and the professor had full beards.

The guests drifted between the living room and the kitchen for drinks; someone had started a pyramid of empty beer cans in a corner. The guests kidded with each other in easy familiarity. The lawyer was "Judge," the professor "Specs," and the salesmen "Huckster."

Carol Lee took Betty Lucci on a tour of the house, and during the halftime intermission the Lees set up a cold buffet. The Luccis and the Cutlers left midway through the fourth quarter. On the drive home, Betty said, "I don't know what Jim Lee makes and I don't care. But I know what we're making and how we can afford to live. That house! Wall-to-wall carpet, expensive furniture, microwave oven,

Sal was annoyed. The meetings were not a life-or-death matter, but for Jim to be absent without an explanation struck Sal as a breach of discipline. Also, the success of the Friday meetings depended on full participation. Asked later about this absence, Jim said he had had an emergency problem with an important customer. This turned out to have been the case, but Sal was still not satisfied with how Jim had handled the matter.

In the summer of 1978, Sal was traveling with veteran salesman Howard Cohen. At lunch Cohen related a recent experience. Three weeks before on a Saturday afternoon, he and Lee had teamed up to make a presentation to a group of specialists in a large hospital on the border of their territories. Cohen thought the presentation had gone excellently and told Jim so. But Jim persisted in asking for criticism and feedback on his part of the presentation and on his preparation for it. The older salesman went on:

"Hell, he should worry! Number two in the district and number five in the country. I should be asking him for tips! But he's all over me for suggestions—won't let go. Doesn't seem right. Why does he do that, do you think?"

Sal replied, "I get the same reading, Howard, when I'm out with him. Always wants criticism—I just don't know. Frankly it's really beginning to bug me."

A question about Jim's honesty.   In February 1979, while Sal was traveling with Jim, they called on the purchasing agent of a large drug chain. Jim went to the warehouse to check stock, leaving Sal with the buyer. The buyer was enthusiastic about Jim's work for them, citing several innovations Jim had suggested in buying and inventory procedures. The suggestions had saved the chain considerable money.

Several months later Sal received a letter from Samuel Biggs, the sales vice president, commending him "on the fine job you are doing in developing Jim Lee." Attached was a carbon of Biggs's letter to Jim congratulating him on "being number one in your district and number two in the whole country."

In June, Sal was invited by an important customer to golf at his club on Tuesday afternoon. When he was on the 14th tee, Sal saw Jim in the distance with three other men. They were obviously enjoying themselves, more interested in jokes and horseplay than in serious golf.

Sal was furious that one of his reps would play golf on a workday afternoon. The question of what he should do about it occupied

color TV, stereo to all the rooms—and in the best section of town! I'd
say they've got a rich uncle somewhere."

Sal replied, "From what I know about Jim's finances, it's more
likely they've got a lot of mortgages, IOUs, time payments, and no
insurance."

Sal gets irritated By May 1977, Jim's sales performance was
clearly superior, and Sal wrote him a personal note congratulating
him on his "outstanding selling record." A few months later Jim's
expense account included an item of $83.60 for "dinner and entertain-
ment for Doctor and Mrs. Link and self at Pine Grove Inn." Professor
Charles Link was perhaps the leading scholar-researcher in the world
in the field of targeted delivery of encapsulated agents and was on
the faculty of a local prestigious university.

Tom Cutler disallowed this expense item on the ground that Dr.
Link had no direct influence on Casco sales in Jim Lee's territory and
that contact with academic researchers was the sole responsibility of
the corporation's new product group, not of the territory reps. Jim
challenged this decision in a memo to Sal:

> Dr. Link is tops in the world in targeted delivery. We're into it too.
> Who knows what his work will produce next month or next year? We
> might want to know about it or have a shot at it. It's a pleasure to talk
> to him about his research. And what in hell does an office manager
> know about selling anyway? Sal, I protest in the strongest terms. Ex-
> plain to Cutler how it is!"

Sal agreed with Cutler and was angry at being caught between his
office manager and one of his best sales reps. Over the weekend he
called Jim to discuss the matter and found him still upset. Sal explained that Cutler was only applying corporate expense policies as
he was required to do. After some further discussion, Sal said he considered it a one-time incident from which Jim had learned something
important about Casco's expense account policies. He asked Cutler to
allow the expense.

Casco's national sales report for the quarter ending March 31, 1978
showed Jim Lee to be second in the Exeter district and fifth nation-
ally.

Every other Friday afternoon Sal's people met to discuss mutual
problems and to receive new information and instructions. Without
advance notice to Sal, Jim was absent from one of these meetings in
May. Sal inquired if he was ill. An assistant in Sal's office said she
had coffee with him that morning and he was fine.

Sal's mind more than his golf game for the rest of the round.

That evening, Sal called Lee, saying he had seen him on the course that afternoon. "What gives?" Sal asked.

"Those are some pretty important people," Jim replied.

"You mean important to us?"

"Could be. You never know."

"Are they customers?"

"No. Not right now, but they could be someday."

Sal decided Jim was not telling the truth, but he thought he had gotten the message over to him, and for now this was enough. Sal said, "Okay, just wanted to be sure there wasn't anything fishy going on. Thanks."

Sal blows a fuse.   Wednesday, August 22, 1979 was a scorcher. By the time Sal got to his office he was soaked. The air conditioner did not help either his perspiration or his temper. For Sal, Wednesday was "crap day" because he was chairbound all day to sign letters and do the other paperwork he so thoroughly despised.

Late in the morning there was a noisy greeting in Sal's outer office, and in came Arthur Gross, the regional sales manager (see Exhibit 1). Sal was not expecting him. They chatted for a while about Gross's golf game, then discussed some business problems. Finally, Gross explained his unannounced visit:

"Had some business up the line and since I'm here, I came in to talk to Jim Lee. Sam Diggs let Russ Page [area sales manager—East] know he's very interested in Lee for this year's management development program. Thought I'd talk to Lee about this because I'll have to make the recommendation to Russ. Can you get us together? I've got a 6:40 flight out of LaGuardia."

Sal asked his secretary if Jim had called in, as all reps did each day before noon. It was 11:45; he had not called in.

As he left for lunch, Gross said he'd call about 1:30 to see about the meeting with Jim in the afternoon.

Sal tried not to show how furious he was. Where was that young jerk? At noon Sal left for his appointment—still no word from Jim. He told his secretary, "Find Jim before 1:15. Check his weekly call program and call customers if you have to! I don't give a damn if you have to call out the Marines—find Jim Lee!"

An hour later Sal was back. His secretary's note read:

> Got Jim's wife. He's a Big Brother—you know that social service stuff. He's taken his "little brother" to a ball game. Gone all afternoon. She

said he does this sometimes so the kid won't think he's just a weekend Big Brother. I've gone to lunch. Jenny.

Sal balled the note up and threw it against the wall. He stared out the window. He was mad. How would he look to Gross when he couldn't find one of his men? "Jim's a great salesman and a great pain in the behind!" he thought.

Gross's call came all too soon. Was the meeting with Jim Lee set up? Sal debated whether to lie or tell it like it is. He decided to cover for Jim. No, the meeting wasn't set up, Sal told the regional sales boss. Jim was home with the flu, but he was interested in being considered for the management development program. Maybe when Jim got back on his feet, he could come out and see Gross. Gross said that was a possibility. He would think about it. After a few pleasantries, he hung up.

Sal was beside himself. "That damn kid can't get me in this mess! He knows better! Taking company time for golf or Big Brother or whatever else he damn well wants to—covering up. Thinks he knows how to run the company—making his own rules. This has got to stop!"

He told Jenny:

"Tell Jim to be here at 8:30 tomorrow morning. I don't want any crap from him. Get that bastard in. I want to see him tomorrow, *here!*"

Questions

1. Why is Jim behaving as he is?
2. Why is Sal behaving as he is?
3. Do you find yourself sympathetic to Jim? To Sal? Why?
4. What do you expect Sal will do in his meeting with Jim?
5. Do you think Sal's probable action is the right action for him to take? Why do you think so?
6. Ideally, what do you think Sal should do?

Glossary

Notes

Name Index

Subject Index

Glossary

Chapter 1

Bagmen were textile industry sales personnel during the Industrial Revolution.

Buyer's market refers to a situation in which products are plentiful.

Caveat emptor means "let the buyer beware."

Commercial traveler was the term applied to field sales personnel toward the end of the 19th century. The term is still used today in some industries.

Drummers were 19th-century sales representatives.

Marketing concept suggests that all parts of an organization are oriented toward solving consumer problems and meeting the needs of the marketplace.

Peddlers were self-employed salespeople during colonial times.

Personal selling can be defined as an interpersonal persuasive process designed to influence some person's decision.

Seller's market refers to a relative scarcity of goods.

Traders were the earliest sales personnel to operate in ancient societies.

Chapter 2

Creative selling is persuasive selling that attempts to get new business away from competitors and to create demand for a new product.

Detailing is a missionary sales activity. A good example of detailing is the sales forces in the pharmaceutical industry.

Field sales personnel perform their primary function at the customer's place of business or residence.

Inside sales personnel are the customer's contacts within their suppliers' organizations.

Maintenance salespeople are charged with getting sales volume from existing customers.

Missionary selling involves contacting indirect customers in an effort to pull the product through the marketing channels.

New-business selling is concerned with the actual conversion of prospects into customers.

Order receivers are salespeople who routinely process customers' orders.

Sales development is concerned with the creation of new customers.

Service selling is low-keyed and oriented toward assisting the customer with the completion of a sale.

Technical selling refers to increasing sales to present customers through the provision of technical advice and assistance.

Trade selling involves selling to middlemen.

Chapter 3

Backdoor selling is a technique for selling industrial products through contacting engineering and production personnel in addition to purchasing agents.

Cognitive dissonance refers to the mental state of an individual who feels that his or her attitudes and behavior are inconsistent.

Culture represents the ideas, customs, skills, and arts of a given people in a given period.

Demographics are written descriptions of people indicating characteristics such as marital status, age, height, weight, sex, residence, and education. Demographics that relate to buying behavior are useful in professional selling.

Dictionary approach is a method of alternative-purchase selection in which the buyer makes the selection only on the basis of the most important decision factor. Other decision factors are used only if there is a tie between two or more alternatives on the most important factor.

"Good-enough-on-all-factors" approach is a method of alternative-purchase selection in which the buyer selects the first alternative that exceeds a minimum level of acceptance on each decision factor.

"Good-enough-on-at-least-one-factor" approach is a method of alternative-purchase selection in which the buyer selects the first alternative that exceeds a minimum level of acceptance on one or more—but not all—decision factors.

Multiple-source purchasing is the practice of purchasing critical components or supplies from more than one supplier.

Needs are perceived wants that motivate human behavior. Human needs can be categorized in several ways, but Maslow's needs hierarchy is probably the most widely accepted categorization.

Offsetting approach is a method of alternative-purchase selection in which the buyer ranks the alternatives on all relevant decision factors. Rank values are then summed for all factors for each alternative, and the alternative with the best score is chosen.

Predispositions are the tendencies of individuals to behave in certain ways in certain situations and to make human behavior consistent. An individual's predispositions are a function of individual characteristics, group influences, and cultural influences.

Postpurchase evaluation occurs after a purchase. Buyers gather information to determine if their decision was a wise one. The process may be informal, as in the case of ultimate consumers, or it may involve an extensive purchase review, as in the case of industrial buyers.

Sealed bids is a purchasing practice that requires each supplier competing for an order to prepare a price quotation in accordance with detailed specifications and to submit it to the buyer in a sealed envelope by a certain date.

Sole-source purchasing is the practice of purchasing components or supplies from only one supplier.

Chapter 4

Customer sales plan is another name for sales plan.

Customer target is a group of customers that is to receive a major share of marketing attention because the firm feels it is in the best position to serve it and wants to do so.

Goal is a desired future state for a business. Sometimes called an objective.

Gross profit is the difference between the selling price of a product and the cost to produce it.

Key-account strategy is a sales plan in which marketing and sales efforts are concentrated on the firm's major accounts.

Marginal customer is a customer judged to be barely profitable or unprofitable to a firm.

Market share is the percentage or portion of the total sales in a market going to a particular company.

Marketing communication is the transmission of information to the customer, usually about the company or its products. It is generally thought of as a process with five elements: source, sender, message, receiver, and feedback.

Marketing mix is the makeup or distribution of marketing efforts divided into four broad categories: product, price, promotion, and distribution.

Marketing profit is the gross profit less marketing expenses.

Promotion mix is the makeup of promotional strategy or the distribution of promotional efforts among the major elements of personal selling, advertising, and sales promotion.

Sales promotion involves the use of other promotion efforts to supplement and strengthen sales and advertising. Examples include point-of-purchase displays, samples, and sales aids.

Selectivity is the process of screening out communication efforts. There is selectivity of exposure, selectivity in perception, and selectivity in retention.

Chapter 5

Chain of prospects is when a salesperson tries to get one or more additional prospects from each one interviewed.

Cold canvassing is securing prospects through unsolicited contacts by the sales force.

Inquiry involves a close examination of some matter in search of information.

Key influence method of prospecting utilizes people who command respect within their social, work, or professional groups.

Lead is some person or business that might need the salesperson's product or service.

List brokers are firms that sell mailing (or prospect) lists.

Prospect is a sales lead that the salesperson has identified as needing or desiring the product or services.

Qualifying means assessing a prospect's ability and authority to buy a product.

Referral is a prospecting method in which the customer is asked to introduce and recommend the salesperson to prospects.

Spotters are people who make specialized surveys or canvasses to assess the needs of prospects.

Chapter 6

Approach consists of both getting the sales interview with the right person and opening the sale.

Buying procedure is the process by which a customer undertakes the job of buying. Usually thought of in terms of a series of steps.

Cold call is a sales call made without any prior contact with the customer.

Degree of product interest is a classification technique that indicates the amount of interest a customer has in a product.

Hard sell is a very aggressive, high-pressure selling technique on a specific customer.

Preapproach is the salesperson's preparation for a forthcoming sales call.

Preparation is consideration of the *what, who,* and *how* of a forthcoming sales call.

Product benefit is a possible satisfaction of a customer's needs or wants from purchase and use of the product. It is used as a sales point.

Product feature refers to a characteristic of a product that may make it attractive or important to a customer or group of customers.

Purchasing involvement is a classification of customers based on their primary role in the purchasing process.

Repurchase refers to the maintenance of purchases at their present level or an increase in purchase volume from existing customers.

Selling technique is concerned with the amount of aggressiveness used by the salesperson.

Soft sell is low-keyed selling aimed at developing a satisfactory relationship with a customer.

Chapter 7

AIDA formula is a standardized learning approach involving four selling steps—awareness, interest, desire, and action.

Balanced selling is an approach to the sales presentation that mixes, through interaction, equal parts of customer orientation and salesperson control.

Canned sales presentation is a highly structured sales presentation involving a memorized format for the salesperson.

Credibility is evidence of the seller's product knowledge and shared interests with the customer, which build customer trust.

Empathy is the ability to understand the other person's point of view.

Group selling is a selling situation in which the salesperson makes a sales presentation to more than one customer.

Indirect question is an unstructured question to which there may be a wide range of answers.

Interaction is the match of the customer and the seller in terms of personalities, taking into account the effect of one party's personality on the other.

Need satisfaction is a sales presentation approach built around three parts: determination of customer needs, agreement with the customer over his or her needs, and showing how the product will fulfill these needs.

Participation is active involvement of the customer in the sales presentation.

Sales presentation is the message delivered by the salesperson to the customer.

Stimulus-response is an approach to the sales presentation based on the idea that the seller's actions trigger appropriate responses from the customer.

Team selling uses more than one salesperson in calling on a customer. As a member of the sales team, a salesperson may or may not have an active part in the formal sales presentation.

Variable sales presentation is an unstructured sales presentation that the salesperson adjusts to fit a particular customer.

Chapter 8

Audiovisual sales aid is any device that permits customers to see and hear about products and their benefits at the same time.

Demonstration is the showing of product benefits to the customer. It may appeal to the senses of smell, touch, and taste as well as sight and hearing.

Illustrator is a visual sales aid dealing with only a part of the sales presentation.

Mobile demonstrator is a sales aid that can be moved to the site of the sales presentation.

Organizer is a sales aid that tells the complete sales story or sales presentation.

Plant visit is a demonstration at the company plant to show the customer how the product is made and to demonstrate company capabilities.

Chapter 9

Counterquestion is asking "Why?" in response to an objection.

Flexible price policy allows the sales representative to negotiate a specific price with the buyer.

One-price policy sets a specific figure and does not allow the sales representative to negotiate price.

Positive conversion transforms an objection into a reason for buying.

Rebuttal is an immediate response to answer a direct objection.

Restating the objection is a method of handling an objection that shifts the emphasis to a more favorable posture.

Sales resistance refers to anything the prospect does or says to prevent or delay the salesperson from successfully closing a sales interview.

Warranties and guarantees are assurances that a product will perform satisfactorily.

"Yes, but . . ." approach is a technique whereby the seller notes agreement with a prospect's objection but then counters it with additional information.

Chapter 10

Alternative decisions is a closing technique in which the prospect is asked to make a choice between alternatives equally favorable to the seller.

Assumptive close assumes that the person has decided to purchase the item.

Balance sheet close presents the negative factors as well as the benefits related to the product.

Closing is that point in the sales presentation at which the salesperson secures the desired agreement from the prospect.

Closing cues are verbal statements and physical actions (or signals) that suggest a buyer may be ready to purchase the product.

Critical feature close concentrates on a single feature that the seller believes is of primary importance to the prospect.

Direct approach is a method of closing in which the prospect is simply asked for the order.

Emotional close seeks to motivate the person to buy through appeal to such factors as fear, pride, romance, or the need for peer group acceptance.

Extra inducement close uses a *clincher,* a selling point that is held in reserve until the actual closing attempt.

Silent close or **silent trial close** is a closing technique in which the salesperson stops talking and looks at the buyer.

SRO method (standing room only) is a closing technique in which the prospect is told that the purchase should be concluded now, since the merchandise will probably not be available later.

Summary and affirmative agreement is a closing technique whereby the salesperson summarizes the major features, benefits, and advantages of the product, pauses at each point, and seeks agreement from the prospect.

Trial closes are closing attempts used to determine the prospect's disposition to the product and the sales presentation.

Chapter 11

Activity reports are sales reports containing the name and location of each customer or prospect contacted, the type of call, and a brief description of the result of the call.

Call reports are sales reports recording the purpose and result of sales calls.

Callback schedule lists a sales representative's planned visits to customers.

Clue management is a salesperson's technique of picking up ideas of how a product can satisfy the needs of potential customers through careful examination of the clues provided by present customers.

Expense reports are sales reports listing all business expenses incurred over a set period of time.

Reworking is a practice whereby sales personnel call on existing customers to either protect or increase the current level of sales.

Sole source refers to a vendor that is a firm's only provider of a particular product.

Tickler file is a file that assists the salesperson to plan calls on new and established customers on a regular, recurring basis.

Chapter 12

Account classification involves sorting customers into categories according to their relative profitability to the seller.

Call reports are sales reports recording the purpose and result of sales calls.

Productive selling activities consist of those tasks directly related to increasing sales effectiveness.

Routing plans refer to how a salesperson intends to go from sales call to sales call in covering an assigned territory.

Self-management consists of the preapproach and time management.

Time management refers to the process of optimizing the amount of time a salesperson spends in front of a customer.

Unproductive selling activities consist of tasks that are necessary in selling but do not contribute directly to the sales effort. Driving and wasting time are typical illustrations of unproductive selling activities.

Chapter 13

Bonuses are achievement rewards not directly related to sales.

Career path is a series of steps employees go through in preparation for advancement.

Combination plan is a compensation plan that has a set salary as well as a commission component.

Commission plans link salespeople's compensation directly to their sales productivity.

Competitive wage refers to a compensation plan that is about standard for the industry.

Drawing accounts are advances against commissions earned by the salesperson.

Expense accounts are payments to cover the legitimate costs of fulfilling the job requirements of selling.

Fringe benefits are financial rewards that are not directly tied to a firm's compensation plan.

Guaranteed draw is a compensation plan whereby the salesperson is not liable for repayment if the draw is more than the commissions earned in a given time period.

Point systems award points or credits for achievement in a certain area. The net point total is then converted to a compensation payment on a periodic basis.

Sales contests are special promotions that are intended to motivate sales personnel to aggressively market a particular item or product line.

Smorgasbord plan allows the employee to select the mix of salary, commissions, bonuses, and fringe benefits that best suits his or her needs.

Straight-salary plans pay sales personnel a given amount at specified times.

Chapter 14

Continuous sales training involves refreshing, improving, and updating the selling skills or marketing knowledge of experienced personnel.

Initial sales training deals with the preparation and orientation of new sales personnel.

Job rotation is a training procedure that has the trainee spend fixed amounts of time in various departments of the company or with different types of customers.

Programmed instruction is a self-study technique that divides the material into short sections of discussion and review items.

Refresher training deals with practical problems such as classifying prospects, handling objections, and closing.

Role playing is a sales training method in which a sales setting is stated and trainees assume the role of salesperson, prospect, and others involved in the case.

Self-management refers to the way in which a salesperson covers a territory and serves a group of customers.

Chapter 15

Acceptance testing is a quality control procedure for determining whether an incoming shipment is acceptable.

Detailing is a missionary sales activity. A good example of detailing is the sales forces in the pharmaceutical industry.

In-store retail selling involves the sale of goods and services to consumers in retail stores.

Retail selling is the sale of goods and services to consumers.

Service selling is a field of sales in which salespeople spend most of their time maintaining sound relations with their regular customers and calling on these customers on a recurring basis.

Standard of living refers to the quantity and quality of goods and services the average consumer can purchase with his or her financial resources.

Substitute selling is a sales technique for encouraging customers to purchase merchandise different from what they had requested.

Suggestion selling is a sales technique for encouraging customers to buy additional items or to buy larger quantities of an item.

Total product cost is a concept used by industrial buyers to determine the total cost of using a supplier's product in a firm's operation.

Trading up is a sales technique for encouraging the customer to buy more expensive merchandise or more merchandise than originally intended.

Chapter 16

CLU (Chartered Life Underwriters) is the professional designation in the life and health insurance fields. It is granted by The American College.

Listing is an agreement between a seller and a real estate firm concerning the sale of a property.

Market analysis refers to a step in real estate selling that includes competitive advantages of the property, drawbacks to the property, general and area market conditions, reasons for selling, and requirements of the seller.

National realty networks are organizations, often franchise agreements, that link real estate sellers in various geographic areas.

Open house is a sales technique used in the real estate marketplace. A property is made available for inspection at a designated time.

Showing refers to a potential buyer's visit to a property. The real estate sales agent is typically present during a showing.

Chapter 17

Close rate is the salesperson's record of closed sales divided by sales calls.

Consultative selling helps the buyer select the necessary items to accomplish a task.

Marketing information systems are designed to produce relevant information and probable competitive reactions helpful in making marketing decisions.

Megaselling is modern terminology for "big ticket" or "big order" selling.

National account selling refers to the assignment of one salesperson to deal with all aspects of an important customer's purchasing program. National account selling provides a coordinated approach to key accounts.

Product selling is concerned with obtaining a particular sale with a given customer.

Specialist selling is a sales method in which the sales force is organized according to the customer groups to be served.

Systems selling is a sales method in which the firm markets a complete service or product line rather than individual items.

Notes

Part 1

*Glenn Frank, in George W. Crane, "Salesmen Are the Sparkplugs of Civilization," *Sales and Marketing Management*, February 4, 1980, p. 37.

Chapter 1

1. Adapted from pp. 135–54 in *Ten Greatest Salespersons* by Robert L. Shook, Copyright © 1978 by Robert L. Shook. Reprinted by permission of Harper & Row, Publishers, Inc.

2. William J. Tobin, "Drama and Daring: Bag the Big Ones." From the January/February 1974 issue of *Marketing Times*, the official publication for Sales and Marketing Executives International.

3. Ralph S. Alexander and the Committee on Definitions of the American Marketing Association, *Marketing Definitions*, published by the American Marketing Association, © 1960, p. 21.

4. A. L. Kirkpatrick, "Selling As A Career? A Challenge," *The Marketing Mix* (Georgia State University), October 1973, p. 2.

5. Donald Robinson, *The Salesman: Ambassador of Progress* (New York: Sales and Marketing Executives, International, 1967), p. 4.

6. Murray Campbell and Harrison Hatton, *Herbert H. Dow: Pioneer in Creative Chemistry* (New York: Appleton-Century-Crofts, 1951), p. 30.

7. This section is based largely on David L. Kurtz, "The Historical Development of Professional Selling," *Business and Economic Dimensions*, August 1970, pp. 12–18.

8. See Richard T. Hise, "Have Manufacturing Firms Adopted the Marketing Concept?" *Journal of Marketing*, July 1965, pp. 9–12.

9. "NCR's Radical Shift in Marketing Tactics," *Business Week*, December 8, 1973, p. 102.

10. Bureau of Labor Statistics, *Occupational Outlook Handbook, 1980–1981 Edition* (Bulletin 2075), p. 188.

Chapter 2

1. See Martin Everett, "Dana's Clutch Hitters," *Sales & Marketing Management*, April 7, 1980, pp. 31–34. Copyright 1980. The list of sales categories is reprinted from p. 34.

2. Stephen X. Doyle and Benson P. Shapiro, "What Counts Most in Motivating Your Sales Force?" *Harvard Business Review*, May–June, 1980, pp. 133–40.

3. Herbert M. Greenberg and Jeanne Greenberg, "Job Matching for Better Sales Performance," *Harvard Business Review*, September–October, 1980, pp. 128–33.

4. This list is suggested by H. Robert Dodge, *Field Sales Management* (Plano, Texas: Business Publications, © 1973 by Business Publications, Inc. 1973), p. 165.

5. Creative and service selling are discussed in: Theodore N. Beckman, William R. Davidson, and W. Wayne Talarzyk, *Marketing*, 9th ed. (New York: Ronald Press, 1973), p. 451.

6. See George N. Kahn and Abraham Shuchman, "Specialize Your Salesmen!" in *Salesmanship and Sales Force Management*, ed. Bursk and Hutchison, pp. 26–34.

7. This section is based on Robert J. Boewalt, "The Inside Salesman's Revolt," *Sales Management, The Marketing Magazine*, February 1, 1971, pp. 19–20. Copyright 1971.

8. This discussion follows Dodge, *Field Sales Management,* pp. 169–71.

9. See Louis J. Haugh, "Detailmen—Salesmen Who Don't Sell," *Advertising Age,* February 13, 1978, pp. 67–68, 70.

10. Ibid., p. 68.

11. Ibid., p. 70.

Part 2
*Quoted in *The Detroit News,* January 22, 1978, p. 5-B

Chapter 3

1. Robert L. Shook, *Ten Greatest Salespersons* (New York: Harper & Row, 1978), p. 34.

2. "Truth, Marketing Concept Are Answer to Consumerism," *Marketing News,* November 15, 1973, p. 5.

3. Many other differences between ultimate consumers and industrial buyers can be found in: Industrial Marketing Committee Review Board, "Fundamental Differences between Industrial and Consumer Marketing," *Journal of Marketing* 19 (October 1954) 152–58.

4. "Defense Industry Profit Study," a report to the Congress by the Comptroller General of the United States, B-159896, Washington, D.C., March 17, 1971, p. 3.

5. George W. Aljian, ed., *Purchasing Handbook* (New York: McGraw-Hill, 1958).

6. Robert E. Weigand, "Why Studying the Purchasing Agent Is Not Enough," *Journal of Marketing* 32 (January 1968): 41–45.

7. Abraham H. Maslow, *Motivation and Personality* (New York: Harper & Row, 1954).

8. Editors of *The Wall Street Journal, How They Sell* (New York: Dow Jones Books, 1965).

9. Robert F. Gwinner, "Base Theory in the Formulation of Sales Strategy," *MSU Business Topics* 16 (Autumn 1968): 37–44.

10. David M. Stander, "Testing New Product Ideas in an 'Archie Bunker' World," *Marketing News,* November 15, 1973, p. 4–5. Reprinted from *Marketing News,* published by the American Marketing Association.

11. Mack Hanan, "Selling the Biggest Benefit of All: Profits," *Sales Management,* November 1, 1971, p. 46. Reprinted with permission from *Sales Management, The Marketing Magazine,* copyright 1971.

12. Leon Festinger, *A Theory of Cognitive Dissonance* (New York: Harper & Row, 1957).

13. This is the classification scheme devised by the Survey Research Center at the University of Michigan.

14. "Singles and Mingles. . . A Meaningful Marketing Explosion," *Grey Matter* 45 (January 1974).

15. "Consider Cultural Factors When Analyzing International Markets," *Marketing News,* October 15, 1973, pp.3–4.

Chapter 4

1. Robert L. Shook, *Ten Greatest Salespersons* (New York: Harper & Row, 1978), p. 161.

2. Jon R. Katzenbach and R. R. Champion, "Linking Top-Level Planning to Salesman Performance," *Business Horizons,* Fall 1966, p. 91. Copyright 1966 by the Foundation for the School of Business at Indiana University. Reprinted by permission.

3. Adapted from Ernest C. Miller, *Objectives and Standards of Performance: In Marketing Management,* AMA Research Study #85 (New York: American Management Association, Inc., 1967).

4. William F. Christopher, "Marketing Planning That Gets Things Done," *Harvard Business Review,* September–October 1970, p. 61.

5. From *Sales Management, The Marketing Magazine.* © 1971.

6. Adapted from Alfred R. Oxenfeldt, *Executive Action in Marketing* (Belmont, Calif.: Wadsworth, 1966), pp. 48–49.

7. Richard V. Dempster, "Black & Decker Cuts through Marketing Myths," *Industrial Marketing,* June 1968. © 1968, by Advertising Publications Inc., Chicago, Illinois.

8. Roger A. Strang, "Sales Promotion—Fast Growth, Faulty Management," *Harvard Business Review* 54 (July–August 1976): 116–17.

9. Suggested in part by Harold C. Cash and W. J. E. Crissy, "The Salesman's Role in Marketing," *The Psychology of Selling* 12 (1965):26, 62–68. Personnel Development Associates, P.O. Box 3005, Roosevelt Field Station, Garden City, NY, 11530.

10. Ibid., p. 68.

11. Theodore Levitt, *Industrial Purchasing Behavior: A Study of Communications Effects* (Boston: Harvard University, Graduate School of Business Administration, 1965), p. 25.

12. Ibid, p. 29.

13. Ibid., pp. 32–33.

14. Ibid., pp. 35–37.

15. Adapted from Donald F. Cox and Stuart U. Rich, "Perceived Risk and Consumer Decision-Making—The Case of Telephone Shopping," *Journal of Marketing Research* 1 (November 1964):33–34, published by the American Marketing Association.

16. Ibid., p. 34.

17. Ibid.

Part 3

*Edison quote from B.C. Forbes, *Men Who Made America Great* (originally published in 1917. Reprinted by The Hamilton Press, Box 583, Brookfield, Wisconsin) p. 93.

Chapter 5

1. "The Battle to Boost Sales Productivity," *Business Week,* February 12, 1972, pp. 68–69.

2. "Now: The Ersatz Salesman," *SME Forum,* September 1973, pp. 3–4. Also see *The Wall Street Journal,* March 22, 1973, p. 1.

3. "Now: The Ersatz Salesman," p. 4.

4. *Managing for Growth in a Changing Market* (Dearborn, Mich.: Ford Marketing Institute, 1973), p. 25.

5. New York Life Insurance Co., *The Prospecting Guide,* p. 3. Quoted in Carlton A. Pederson and Milburn D. Wright, *Salesmanship: Principles and Methods,* 5th ed. (Homewood, Ill.: Richard D. Irwin, Inc., 1971), pp. 293–94.

6. "Battle to Boost Sales Productivity," p. 69.

7. Ibid.

8. Adapted from Pederson and Wright, *Salesmanship,* pp. 305–6.

9. "The New Supersalesman: Wired for Success," *Business Week,* January 6, 1973, p. 48.

10. See Don Korn, "Tales of Hoffmann–La Roche," *Sales Management,* March 19, 1973, pp. 27–31.

11. "The New Supersalesman," p. 45.

12. Murray Harding, "Who Really Makes the Purchasing Decision," *Industrial Marketing* 51 (September 1966):76–81.

13. Pederson and Wright, *Salesmanship,* p. 343.

14. "Getting to Know the Grocer at Big G," *Sales Management,* April 10, 1970, p. 30.

15. Reprinted with permission from *Sales Management, The Marketing Magazine,* © 1970.

16. "Salesmen Speak, Syntex Listens," *Sales Management,* May 14, 1973, p. 8.

17. J. N. Bauman, "Rebirth of the Salesman," *Dun's Review,* March 1968, p. 99.

Chapter 6

1. James O'Hanlon, "The Rich Rewards of the Salesman's Life," *Forbes,* October 16, 1978, p. 157.

2. Ron Lovell, "Salesmen's Problems: New Way to Solve Them," *Industrial Distribution,* June 1965, p. 53.

3. From *Sales Management, The Marketing Magazine.* © 1972.

4. This section is based in part on material reprinted by permission of *Sales Management, The Marketing Magazine.* © 1973.

5. Robert Papierowicz, "Two Keys to Productive Sales Calls," *The American Salesman.* © January 1964, p. 39.

6. Ibid.

7. James E. Skinner, "The Gates Approach to Learjet Sales," *American Aviation,* September 30, 1968, p. 42.

8. Reprinted with permission from *Sales Management, The Marketing Magazine.* © 1973.

9. Skinner, "Gates Approach to Learjet Sales," p. 42.

10. Reprinted with permission from *Sales Management, The Marketing Magazine.* © 1971.

11. Barry J. Hersker, "The Ecology of Personal Selling," *Southern Journal of Business* 5 (July 1970):44.

12. From *Sales Management, The Marketing Magazine.* © 1972.

13. Results reprinted with permission of *Sales Management, The Marketing Magazine.* © 1972.

14. From *Sales Management, The Marketing Magazine.* © 1972.

15. Reprinted with permission from *Sales Management, The Marketing Magazine.* © 1972.

16. Ibid.

17. Ibid.

18. *The Visible Salesman,* Research Institute of America, New York, 1971.

Part 4

*Bosworth quote from Studs Terkel, *Working* (New York: Pantheon Books, 1974), p. 224.

Chapter 7

1. Tish Myers, "Real Estate Tour Finds Various Sales Pitches," *The Detroit News,* May 18, 1980, p. 5–L.

2. From *Sales Management, The Marketing Magazine.* © 1973.

3. David Mayer and Herbert M. Greenberg, "What Makes a Good Salesman," *Harvard Business Review,* July–August 1964, p. 120.

4. Frederick E. Webster, Jr., "Interpersonal Communication and Salesman Effectiveness," *Journal of Marketing* (July 1968):7, published by the American Marketing Association.

5. From *Sales Management, The Marketing Magazine.* © 1973.

6. The discussion follows Harold C. Cash and W. J. E. Crissy, "A Point of View for Salesmen" *The Psychology of Selling* 1 (1965). Personnel Development Associates, P.O. Box 3005 Roosevelt Field Station, Garden City, NY, 11530.

7. Webster, "Interpersonal Communication and Salesman Effectiveness," p. 8.

8. From *Sales Management, The Marketing Magazine.* © 1973.

9. Reprinted by permission from *Sales Management, The Marketing Magazine.* © 1973.

10. Marvin A. Jolson, "Should the Sales Presentation Be 'Fresh' or 'Canned'?" *Business Horizons,* October 1973, p. 85. Copyright 1973 by the Foundation for the School of Business at Indiana University.

11. Ibid.

12. See Harold C. Cash and W. J. E. Crissy, "Tactics for Conducting the Sales Call," *The Psychology of Selling* 5 (1965). Personnel Development Associates, P.O. Box 3005 Roosevelt Field Station, Garden City, NY, 11530.

13. Ibid., pp. 29–30.

14. Carl I. Hovland, Irving L. Janis, and Harold H. Kelley, *Communication and Persuasion* (New Haven, Conn.: Yale University Press, 1953), p. 21.

15. From *Sales Management, The Marketing Magazine.* © 1973.

16. Ibid.

17. Ibid.

18. Ibid.

19. Hovland, Janis, and Kelly, *Communication and Persuasion,* pp. 100–102.

20. From *Sales Management, The Marketing Magazine.* © 1973.

Chapter 8

1. *Entree,* Fairchild Publications.

2. From *Sales Management, The Marketing Magazine.* © 1965.

3. D. C. Carter, "Showmanship and the Salesman," *The American Salesman,* p. 23 © February 1970.

4. Edward J. Hegarty, *Making Your Sales Presentation Sell More* (New York: McGraw-Hill, 1957), p. 143.

5. Example based in part on Carter, "Showmanship and the Salesman," p. 24.

6. Dean M. Wood, "Back to Basics Has Garlock O.E.M. Salesmen Flipping over Flip Chart," *Industrial Marketing,* January 1974. © 1974 by Crain Communications Inc., Chicago, Illinois.

7. James E. Skinner, "The Gates Approach to Learjet Sales," *American Aviation,* September 30, 1968, p. 42.

8. "Mobile Demonstrator Sells Doubtful Buyers," *Industrial Marketing,* January 1965. © 1965, Advertising Publications, Inc. Chicago, Illinois.

9. Jenness Keane, "Prove Your Performance on the Spot," *Industrial Distribution,* February 1962, pp. 78–79.

10. Skinner, "Gates Approach to Learjet Sales," p. 42.

11. Based in part on material from *Sales Management, The Marketing Magazine.* © 1973.

12. "Tools of Selling," *Industrial Distribution,* November 1964, pp. 49–50.

13. Example from *Sales Management, The Marketing Magazine.* © 1965.

14. Based in part on material from *Sales Management, The Marketing Magazine.* © 1965.

15. Based in part on Edward Y. Breese, "Demonstration," *The American Salesman,* pp. 29–30 © May 1970.

Part 5

*Folkoff quote from "Maryland Company Sells Customer Benefits," *Sales & Marketing Management,* January 1979, p. 26.

Chapter 9

1. Tedd A. Cohen, "Red McCombs: Making Money's Fun," *Forbes,* September 15, 1980, p. 124.

2. An interesting discussion appears in Dan Weadock, "Your Troops Can Keep Control—and Close the Sale by Anticipating Objections," *Sales & Marketing Management,* March 17, 1980, pp. 102, 104, 106.

3. Carlton A. Pederson and Milburn D. Wright, *Salesmanship: Principles and Methods,* 5th ed. (Homewood, Ill.: Richard D. Irwin, 1971), p. 401. © 1971 by Richard D. Irwin, Inc.

4. Gary M. Grikscheit, "An Investigation of the Ability of Salesmen to Monitor Feedback," Paper presented at the 1972 annual meeting of the Southwestern Social Science Association, Marketing Section.

5. A similar list is suggested in Pederson and Wright, *Salesmanship,* pp. 402–4.

6. "Why Some Salesmen Don't Like Howard Valentine," *Sales Management, The Marketing Magazine,* May 28, 1973, © 1973.

7. A similar list is suggested in Pederson and Wright, *Salesmanship,* pp. 404–6.

8. This film is discussed in "How NCR Uses Training Films," *Sales/Marketing Today,* May 1966, p. 13.

9. See Ed Reavey, "Better Service: Society's Pressing Need," *Marketing Times,* May–June 1973, p. 30.

10. Jay Beecraft, "Set Goals with—Not for—Men," *SM/Sales Meetings,* March 15, 1968, p. 228.

11. Herb True, "How to Sell Quality." Reprinted from the January/February 1973 issue of *Marketing Times,* the official publication for Sales & Marketing Executives International.

12. True, "How to Sell Quality," pp. 29–30.

13. Techniques 1–3 are outlined in *Seven Steps in Selling Retail Photographic Salesmen* (Jackson, Mich.: Photo Marketing Association-International, 1970), p. 7.

14. The need for such a plan is suggested in Pederson and Wright, *Salesmanship,* pp. 424–25.

Chapter 10

1. Fred Kirsch, "There Never Was a Salesman Like Girard—Says Girard," *The Detroit News,* February 17, 1980, pp. 1–D, 11–D. Copyright, 1980. The Evening News Association, The Detroit News.

2. "Supersalesman Eagle Talks Selling," *Business Week,* January 6, 1973, p. 47.

3. Marvin A. Jolson, "Direct Selling: Consumer vs. Salesman," *Business Horizons* 15 (October 1972):87–95. Copyright 1972 by the Foundation for the School of Business at Indiana University.

4. William J. Tobin "One-Call Sales—Very Profitable," *Specialty Salesman,* September 1973, p. 50.

5. Joseph W. Thompson, *Selling: A Managerial and Behavioral Science Analysis,* 2d ed. (New York: McGraw-Hill, 1973), p. 522.

6. Edward W. Wheatley, "Glimpses of Tomorrow," *Sales Management,* May 1, 1970, p. 41.

7. The exception to this generalization occurs when the prospect is presold before entering the sales interview. In this case, the salesperson tries to close during or immediately after the approach segment of the normal selling sequence.

8. Several of these techniques are discussed in Robert Connolly, "Courage and Audacity: Keys to Closing Sales," *Marketing Times,* March/April 1973, pp. 24–26. Also see David Yoho, "13 Steps in Closing Sales," *Marketing Times,* September–October 1973, pp. 21–23.

9. "The New Supersalesman: Wired for Success," *Business Week,* January 6, 1973, p. 49.

10. From *Sales Management, The Marketing Magazine,* February 19, 1973, p. 4

11. Sales summaries are examined in George Anderson, "Tell Him What You Told Him," *Marketing Times,* January–February 1972, pp. 11–14.

12. See Robert E. Karp, "Creative Advertising Strategies: The Two-Sided Approach," *Business and Society* 12 (Fall 1971):18–25.

13. Walter Gross, "Rational and Nonrational Appeals in Selling to Businessmen," *Georgia Business,* February 1970, pp. 2–3.

14. See John R. Stutevelle, "The Buyer as a Salesman," *Journal of Marketing* 32 (July 1968):14–18.

Chapter 11

1. "Milton Bradley: Simon Says its a Winner," *Sales & Marketing Management,* January 14, 1980, pp. 18–19. Copyright 1980.

2. Mack Hanan, "Learn Something New about Selling? Don't Let it Happen Too Often," *Sales Management,* December 10, 1973, p. 40.

Reprinted with permission from *Sales Management, The Marketing Magazine,* © 1973.

3. John Douglas and Kenneth Poorman, "Why Customers Come Back to Buy Again," *Nation's Business,* November 1973, pp. 74–75.

4. Ibid.

5. From a presentation by Frank Lawrence of GO, Incorporated, of Birmingham, Alabama, to the International Harvester Truck Division's Baltimore Sales Clinic, March 5, 1974.

6. William M. Hutchinson, Jr., and John F. Stolle, "How to Manage Customer Service," *Harvard Business Review,* November–December 1968, pp. 85–96.

7. Editors of *The Wall Street Journal, How They Sell* (New York: Dow Jones Books, 1965).

8. Robert R. Blake and Jane S. Mouton, *The Grid for Sales Excellence* (New York: McGraw-Hill, 1970), p. 39.

9. J. J. Arntz, "Is the Split between Production and Sales Necessary?" *Industry Week,* May 21, 1973, pp. 48–49.

10. Ibid.

11. Gerard Carney, "Finding New Sales and Profits with Your Present Customers," *Sales Management,* April 1, 1971, pp. 17–20.

12. Lawrence, *International Harvester* presentation.

13. Michael J. Maki, "Is Something Sneaking up on You?" *Sales Management,* November 12, 1973, p. 71.

Chapter 12

1. Raymond Dreyfack, "A Guide to Profitable Salesmanship," *Sales & Marketing Management,* April 7, 1980, pp. 36–37.

2. E. Patrick McGuire, *Salesmen's Call Reports* (New York: The Conference Board, Inc., 1972), pp. 18–21.

Part 6

*Miller quote from John Bartlett, *Familiar Quotations* (Burton: Little, Brown, 1968), p. 1071.

Chapter 13

1. "Syntex Helps Them Choose," *Sales & Marketing Management,* October 6, 1980, pp. 11–12. Copyright 1980.

2. An interesting discussion appears in A. Benton Cocanougher and John M. Ivancevich "'Bars' Performance Rating for Sales Force Personnel," *Journal of Marketing,* July 1978, pp. 87–95.

3. This data is reported in William B. Mead, "The Life of a Salesman," *Money,* October 1980, p. 118.

4. "Oakite Changes Its Chemistry," *Sales & Marketing Management,* July 9, 1979, pp. 8–9.

5. "A Better Way," *Sales & Marketing*

Management, April 4, 1979, p. 19. Copyright 1979.

6. An interesting discussion appears in Jacob Gonik, "Tie Salesmen's Bonuses to Their Forecasts," *Harvard Business Review,* May–June 1978, pp. 116–23.

7. See Nathan B. Winstanley, Jr., and Michael J. Reynolds, "Paying Off In Challenges," *Sales and Marketing Management,* April 10, 1970, pp. 26–28, 94.

8. John I. Leahy, "Total Motivation = Top Performance," *Sales Management,* April 30, 1973, p. 13.

9. These plans are discussed in numerous other sources, although the plans' names may vary from source to source. See for example William J. Stanton and Richard M. Buskirk, *Management of The Sales Force,* 5th ed. (Homewood, Ill. Richard D. Irwin, 1978), pp. 309–13. The same expense policies can also be applied to nonselling exployees. For instance, a limited allowance plan is common among government employees at both state and federal levels. The reporting requirements of an unlimited expense account are essentially those of the Internal Revenue Service.

10. Mead, "Life of a Salesman," p. 118.

11. Herbert H. Greenberg, "Art of Working with People," *Automotive News,* January 21, 1974, p. 26.

12. D. W. Mahmer, "Salesman to Superstar: Challenge Is the Key," *Sales Management,* April 30, 1973, p. 28.

13. Robert F. Vizza, *Training and Developing the Field Manager* (New York: Sales Executives Club of New York, 1965).

14. H. Robert Dodge, *Field Sales Management* (Plano, Texas: Business Publications, 1973), p. 33.

15. Herbert Mossien and Eugene H. Fram, "Segmentation for Sales Forces Motivation," *Akron Business and Economic Bulletin* 4 (Winter 1973):5–12.

Chapter 14

1. The Corgard story is told in Sally Scanlon, "Squibb Takes Training to Heart," *Sales and Marketing Management,* March 7, 1980, pp. 33–35. Copyright 1980.

2. The discussion follows H. Robert Dodge, *Field Sales Management* (Plano, Texas: Business Publications, 1973), pp. 222–50.

3. *Managing for Growth in a Changing Market* (Dearborn, Mich: Ford Marketing Institute, 1973).

4. "Make Sales Training Come Alive," *Sales/Marketing Today,* May 1968, p. 18.

5. Max Fuller, "Training Retail Salesmen: A Pilot Program," *Sales/Marketing Today,* April 1969, pp. 12–15.

6. Dodge, *Field Sales Management,* p. 223.

7. *See Sales and Marketing Management,* February 21, 1977, p. 90.

8. This issue is examined in David Kurtz "High Salesmen Turnover: A Function of Lengthy Training Programs?" *Carroll Business Bulletin* 11 (Winter 1972). Also see David L. Kurtz, "Relationship between Training and Turnover," *Review of Business* 9 (March–April 1972).

9. Some of the following material is based on Albert H. Dunn, Eugene M. Johnson, and David L. Kurtz, *Sales Management: Concepts, Practices, and Cases* (Morristown, N.J.: General Learning Press, 1974).

10. "The Rush to Slides," *Sales & Marketing Management,* July 7, 1980, p. 9.

11. See Robert Whyte, "Cure for the Ailing Presentation: Salesmen Behold Thyself," *Sales Management, The Marketing Magazine,* October 1, 1973, pp. 11–12, 15.

12. "Making Salespeople Behave," *Sales & Marketing Management,* July 9, 1979, pp. 16–17.

13. William H. Knauer, "Championship Selling," *Sales/Marketing Today,* June 1969, p. 24.

14. Morgan B. MacDonald, Jr., and Earl L. Bailey, *Training Company Salesmen,* Experiment No. 15 (New York: National Industrial Conference Board, Inc., 1967), p. 12.

15. See Leon G. Schiffman, "Programmed Instruction: Its Use in Sales Training," *Industrial Marketing,* February 1965, pp. 82–86.

16. See J. Porter Henry, Jr., "Can Machines Teach Salesmen to Sell?" *Sales Management,* July 20, 1962, pp. 38–39, 95–96, 98, 100, 102–103; "Programmed Instruction Pays Sales Knowledge Dividends," *Industrial Marketing,* March 1967, pp. 62–65.

17. Adapted from Dodge, *Field Sales Management,* p. 234.

18. Ibid., pp. 238–50.

19. Ibid., p. 238.

20. "Show and Sell at Mattel," *Sales Management,* March 19, 1973, p. 10.

21. Richard Cavalier, "Selling Is Still a People Business," *Sales Management,* February 19, 1973, pp. 42, 45–46.

22. From *Sales Management,* November 10, 1970, p. 33.

Part 7

*Olsen quote from "DEC: The Minicomputer Model," *Duns Review,* December, 1979, p. 48.

Chapter 15

1. Somerby Dowst, "Go-getters Capture the Buyer's Vote," *Purchasing,* August 21, 1980, pp. 46–56.

2. Peter F. Drucker, "Marketing and Economic Development," *Journal of Marketing,* (January 1958):252–59, published by the American Marketing Association.

3. Laurence W. Jacobs, *Advertising and Promotion for Retailing: Text and Cases* (Glenview, Ill.: Scott, Foresman & Co., 1972), p. 7.

4. V. Parker Lessig, "Consumer Store Images and Store Loyalties," *Journal of Marketing* 73 (October 1973):72–74, published by the American Marketing Association.

5. Pierre Martineau, "The Personality of the Retail Store," *Harvard Business Review* 36 (January–February 1958):52–53.

6. John O'Shaughnessy, "Selling as an Interpersonal Influence Process," *Journal of Retailing* 47 (Winter 1971–1972):33.

7. Arnold R. Swinnerton, "A Sound of Different Drummers," *Dun's,* June 1972, p. 101.

8. Murray Kreiger, "Smaller Store: Stress Customer Communication," *Stores,* April 1972, p. 9.

9. William H. Bolen, "Customer Contact: Those First Important Words," *Department Store Management,* April 1970, pp. 25–26.

10. Ibid.

11. E. B. Weiss, *Merchandising for Tomorrow* (New York: McGraw-Hill, 1961), pp. 47–50.

12. James C. Cotham, III, "The Case for Personal Selling: Some Retailing Myths Exploded," *Business Horizons* 11 (April 1968):76.

13. Swinnerton, "Sound of Different Drummers," p. 101.

14. John A. Martilla, "Word-of-Mouth Communication in the Industrial Adoption Process," *Journal of Marketing Research* 8 (May 1971):173–78, published by the American Marketing Association.

15. Bert H. Schlain, *The Professional Approach to Modern Salesmanship* (New York: McGraw-Hill, 1966), p. 164.

Chapter 16

1. John F. Cyr, *Training and Supervising Real Estate Salesmen* (Englewood Clifffs, N.J.: Prentice-Hall, 1973), p. 118.

2. Ibid., pp. 118–20.

3. Ibid., pp. 180–81.

4. The Ohio Association of Realtors.

5. Don Korn, "You Deserve a Broker Today," *Sales & Marketing Management,* May 16, 1977, p. 32.

6. Ibid., p. 33.

7. The following based in part on Warren J. Wittreich, "How to Buy/Sell Professional Services," *Harvard Business Review,* March–April 1966, pp. 128–30. Copyright © 1966 by the

President and Fellows of Harvard College; All rights reserved.

8. Ibid., p. 128.

9. Ibid., pp. 128–29.

10. Ibid., p. 129.

11. Based on information supplied by The American College, Bryn Mawr, Pennsylvania.

12. Based on information supplied by American Institute for Property and Liability Underwriters, Malvern, Pennsylvania.

13. Eleanore Carruth, "New Aims for an Army of Insurance Agents," *Fortune,* April 1977, p. 132.

14. Ibid., p. 133.

15. Ibid.

16. *The NML Career Agent in Focus,* Northwestern Life Insurance Company, 1978, p. 14.

17. Ibid., p. 15.

18. *A Career That Counts . . . with a Company Where You're Not Just a Number* (New York: The Equitable Life Assurance Society of the United States, 1977).

Chapter 17

1. Richard H. Duskirk, "Industrial Sales: Where All The Money Is," *The Seattle Times,* October 12, 1980, p. H 1. © 1980 Suburban Features Inc.

2. "Birth Of A Salesman," *Nation's Business,* August 1970, p. 32.

3. Leo G. Wilsman, "What a Salesman Should Be," *Sales/Marketing Today,* December 1969, p. 15.

4. Guyod is quoted in William B. Mead, "The Life of a Salesman," *Money,* October 1980, p. 118.

5. "Birth Of A Salesman," *Nation's Business,* August 1970, p. 32.

6. Ibid.

7. This section is based on "Specialist Selling Makes New Converts," *Business Week,* July 28, 1973, pp. 44–45.

8. Louis E. Boone and David L. Kurtz, "Marketing Information Systems: Current Status in American Industry," in *Combined Proceedings, American Marketing Association, 1971,* ed. Fred C. Allvine (Chicago, 1971), pp. 163–67.

9. An interesting discussion appears in Alan J. Dubinsky, Eric N. Berkowitz, and William Rudeluis, "Ethical Problems of Field Sales Personnel," *MSU Business Topics,* Summer 1980, pp. 11–16.

10. See Thomas Reuschling, "Black and White in Personal Selling," *Akron Business and Economic Review* 4 (Fall 1973):9–13.

11. Reported in "Marketing Newsletter," *Sales & Marketing Management,* September 15, 1980, p. 29. Copyright 1980.

12. Many of these trends have been suggested numerous times in other sources. See for example, Albert H. Dunn, Eugene M. Johnson, and David L. Kurtz, *Sales Management: Concepts, Practices, and Cases* (Morristown, N.J.: General Learning Press, 1974), pp. 469–71.

Name index

Subject index

*This book has been set Linotron 202, in 10
and 9 point Century Schoolbook, leaded 3
points. Part numbers are 28 point Helvetica
Bold and part titles are 30 point Helvetica
Bold. Chapter numbers are 28 point Helvetica
Bold and chapter titles are 30 Helvetica Bold.
The size of the type page is 36 by 47½ picas.*